DEC 0 8 2014

D1575353

JACK BE NIMBLE

JACK BE NIMBLE

THE ACCIDENTAL EDUCATION OF AN UNINTENTIONAL DIRECTOR

JACK O'BRIEN

FARRAR, STRAUS AND GIROUX   NEW YORK

Farrar, Straus and Giroux
18 West 18th Street, New York 10011

Grateful acknowledgment is made to Anne Kaufman Schneider for permission to
quote from *You Can't Take It with You.*

Library of Congress Cataloging-in-Publication Data
O'Brien, Jack, 1939–
    Jack be nimble : the accidental education of an unintentional director /
Jack O'Brien. — First edition.
        pages   cm
    Includes index.
    ISBN 978-0-86547-898-5 (hardback)
    1. O'Brien, Jack, 1939–   2. Theatrical producers and directors—United
States—Biography.   3. Television producers and directors—United States—
Biography.   I. Title.

PN2287.O185 A3 2013
792.02'33'092—dc23
[B]
                                                                    2012048077

Designed by Jonathan D. Lippincott

www.fsgbooks.com
www.twitter.com/fsgbooks • www.facebook.com/fsgbooks

10   9   8   7   6   5   4   3   2   1

For Richard Easton . . . who kept insisting . . .

For Trish Conolly and Nicholas Martin . . . who were kind to listen . . .

For Donald Moffat, Jennifer Harmon, Clayton Corzatte, Frances Sternhagen, Christina Pickles, Brian Bedford, Pamela Payton-Wright, Ralph Williams, Gordon Gould, Page Johnson, Bob Moss, George Darveris, and all other existing alums who lived and survived it . . .

And finally, for Rosemary Harris . . . "for remembrance"!

CONTENTS

JACK BE NIMBLE

PROLOGUE

There are forces that govern our lives, just as they govern nature. We are taught them, and if we pay close attention, they turn up over and over, reasserting their values. We sometimes like to file all this under the heading "Fun with Education," don't we? For example: What are the laws of physics? Anyone remember? Hands? (We all look sheepishly around at each other.) Like most of us, I must have learned them at one time; probably in high school, but other than that there were three of them . . . or four of them? . . . I'm damned if I can remember. What I do recall is the following:

1. A body at rest tends to remain at rest.
2. A body in motion tends to remain in motion.
3. To every action there is an equal and opposite reaction.
4. Don't wear white after Labor Day.

So who speaks? I am a camera? A seagull? No, in truth, I am a director. Still, when you come right down to it, I believe I am actually a pinball!

Let me explain: I am, as I say, a professional director. Plays, mainly, and musicals, although yes, I've done opera, and some television, and even a couple of French people once, who stopped me walking on the rue de la Paix from their car in Paris while looking for Les Halles. (I actually helped them!) Because, of course, a director directs, and I've been telling people where to go, and more or less what to do once they get there, for quite some time now.

I took two degrees from the University of Michigan, but neither of them was in directing, or even theater. So I find myself curious about what turned me into a person of this profession. I look around me, at my friends, at others working in theater, and find myself amazed at where I've landed. Who starts out to become a director? Well, of course, these days the universities and colleges are bursting with young men and women feverishly pursuing careers as directors of theater. And to be honest, it baffles me.

Oh, I don't mean to insult higher institutions across the land making an honest buck out of these various curricula, nor to impugn their viable processes. It's quite possible that this is a generational issue, like tattoos and tweeting. But, speaking for myself, I've always assumed you had to become lot of other things first before you decided to be, or determined you were to be, a director. From my perspective, you have to be there, don't you? Wherever "there" might be. I've always thought it imperative to BE there physically, next to someone in the trenches who is taking aim, firing, actually doing it, missing, swearing, trying again. You need to witness their pain, their inchoate angst, their lack of articulation, to finally be able to provide help, probably. You have to see what they do, observe them, and if you are lucky—even better—fail!

But study it? In a classroom? Even in a lab? I've got to be honest . . . I don't think I get it. I've always believed if you wished to be a goldsmith in the Renaissance, you had to sit next to Cellini very quietly, watching over and over again how he transcribed a small rod of metal into the miracle of a single gold leaf. And then you might come to understand how a Cellini leaf was better than a Manno di Sburri leaf, because I bet it was! Reading a "How To" book just wouldn't cut it. Or equally disappointing, sitting in the back of a Florentine classroom, watching Maestro di Sburri mumbling up front, probably wouldn't serve either. Of course, the major problem here would be how you might get an introduction to Cellini in the first place so you could sit that close. But that, obviously, is pretty much the subject at hand.

I said, remember, that I was a pinball. And try as I might to refute this airy idea, I don't think I can. Because, as a youth, I was what was referred to in those days as a "dreamer." I sat for hours on end on a sofa or against a tree, lying in a hammock or on a gritty towel facing the Saginaw Bay, sometimes (sorry!) even on the toilet . . . dreaming. "Jack!" came the inevitable voice—from the kitchen, from those waiting in a car, from the porch, from another floor, another room— "What are you doing? No, *really*! What on earth are you *doing*?"

"Nothing," was the reply. "You're *dreaming*!" they said, and so branded me. And I was. But of what?

I'm not sure it mattered. I don't recall any specific dreams, any persistent clouds of theatrical fantasy that played themselves over and over in my mind. That isn't the point. What is the point is what finally got me moving, and in what direction: and that, I contend, has to do with the laws of physics. It just never occurred to me that they might lead to the world of theater.

And so . . . we had better seriously review those four laws.

PART ONE

A BODY AT REST
TENDS TO REMAIN AT REST

1

Consider the lowly pinball; yes, it's a ball bearing, no question. It's round and it's shiny. That's basically it. Well, not to put too fine a point on it, the same thing might be said of me. I've always exhibited something of "roundness," and no matter what my shape or weight, I almost inevitably get the same comment from friends I've not seen in some time: "You've lost weight, right?" No. No, I haven't. In all probability, as the decades accumulate and like most other men, I gain. But I might well be one of those people you remember as having been, well, larger, rounder than I am. And shiny, also, no argument. Because I understand it has been recently discovered there are people born with a genetic disposition toward optimism, and here I stand—hardwired for happiness, as it were: round and shiny. And if it takes something to get the ball started rolling in one direction or another, it didn't seem altogether likely to occur in the land of my birth.

I was born in Saginaw, Michigan, the evening of the eighteenth of June in 1939. My mother was in labor in St. Mary's Hospital, and my father was down in the car in the parking lot, listening to Jack Benny on the radio. World War II was revving up, which would eventually reverse the damages of the Great Depression, the scars of which marked almost all the adults that comprised my family and my family's circle of friends. But this was not a sad time. My father, J. George O'Brien, was a complex, spirited guy, a small businessman who was basically a salesman. He had served in the Navy at the conclusion of World War I, enough to get some advanced education in Annapolis, but just how much or what kind was never shared with me. For a while he worked for Reid Paper Company in Saginaw, until he and another junior executive left to go out on their own, and before his death in 1957 at the age of sixty-three from cancer, he had become something called O'Brien Enterprises, which entailed leasing a fleet of cars to busy businessmen, doing some packaging designing, and primarily representing a new process called Cry-O-Vac, the plastic second skin affixed first to turkeys and hams that was about to proliferate all over the country, for which he was to represent exclusive sales over seven Eastern states.

During his tenure at Reid Paper Company, he caught the eye of a young secretary, Evelyn MacArthur, the daughter of a Saginaw executive of the Automobile Club of America, who was himself a Scot born in Glasgow, and the proud, patrician father of three other lovely young daughters—Marion, Bernice, and Aldine. Evelyn, easily the prettiest of the four daughters, was then engaged to a young man named Carl "Cullie" Berger, a fledgling in the automobile business, and whether a date had been fixed for their nuptials is lost in the mists of time, but even so it was not enough to dissuade my father, who proposed to Evelyn, and, by God, eloped with her to New York on the spur of the moment, leaving Cullie and the consequences to fade into an oft-repeated comic anecdote. My father was thirteen years older than my mother, and their rail journey to their honeymoon in New York—where they tied up with his close friend, the songwriter Gerald Marks ("All of Me") and his sophisticated, towering wife, Edna, a troubleshooter for the Newspaper Guild at the time—was marked by Mother's weeping throughout the entire journey and once, in Manhattan, covering up her lack of social and language skills by pointing to an item in French on a menu and bravely ordering poached eggs rather than the substantial wedding meal she was hoping to have. Naturally, she never let on that it had been a mistake.

In the library of Imaginary Farms, my home in Connecticut, hangs an oil portrait of my mother, dated 1933, painted by my father's cousin, H. Cranston "Bud" Dolan, an amateur painter, but a good one. It portrays a rather serious, lovely young woman in a white summer dress with a becoming neckline scalloped in red and blue, her hair enclosed in a matching white cloche, who seems at best to be politely enduring the process. Had she been fortunate enough to sit

My father, J. George O'Brien. As the pose might suggest, no lack of self-confidence here: quite a guy! (Collection of the author)

for someone like Whistler, for example, she might have been encouraged to relax more obliquely, but she wasn't, and so the results never made it aboveground or out of any basement we as a family ever occupied until I was settled in Manhattan and asked to have it sent to me. It may well have secretly pleased my mother to be rid of it, for she exhibited nothing but derision for it throughout my childhood. There is a decidedly melancholy air to her expression, but the melancholia at this time was yet to be substantiated.

In 1935, Evelyn and "O'Bie," for such was his universal and affectionate name, had their first child, Robert, born dead, and devastatingly delivered by their close friend, Stuart Yntema, a young ex–army physician who had become our family doctor, and who never again touched my mother in so much as a physical examination. I recall, around the time I was ten or so, sobbing on my bed on Park Street over a disappointment for something I had expected to achieve at school. In a rare glimpse behind the parental divide that always existed between my sister and me and our parents, my mother confessed that in her entire early life she had never known a single moment of unhappiness or disappointment until, she said, "Bobby was born dead." She paused for the effect to stifle my sobs before going on. "I think being handed something like that as one's first defeat is a fate I wouldn't wish on anyone. This is nothing by comparison, it's just what happens. You'll be fine." And she patted me reassuringly and left the room. We rarely, if ever, referred to my dead brother again, and although there were ritual and frequent trips to Forest Lawn Cemetery, where my father's parents were buried and where grew a collection of MacArthurs and O'Briens as the years piled up, we would inevitably stop silently for a moment at the small grave marker under a spreading fir tree, marked only with "Robert H. O'Brien 1935." My brother Bobby remained outside the screen door circle of our allowed awareness, something reverent, sad, and ultimately apart. I longed for him. For the idea of him, as well. I still do.

Janet, my only sibling, was born the following year, on December 12. In those days, of course, women were kept confined to the hospital for fully ten days before being released to go home. When my mother finally arrived at Park Street with her beautiful daughter, it was December 22, and in her bedroom, which eventually became our bedroom, was a tiny white Christmas tree, a sweet nightlight that was subsequently pulled out of storage each year thereafter as its own celebration and the harbinger of the Christmas to come. I can only imagine the mixed feelings that little white tree must have triggered in my parents as they thought back on a heartbreaking earlier Christmas.

The joke, of course . . . because there was always a joke . . . was that on the twenty-eighth of that June of 1939, when Mother brought me home from the hospital, it was hot, it was summer, and Nursie Devitt was clearly itching to get her hands on me. So Mother and Dad packed Janet into the car, and off they went to our grandparents' cottage on the Saginaw Bay for the Fourth of July holiday ahead. I was healthy, I was obviously in the right hands, and they wanted to give Janet some attention. As it happens, the exterior of the house was also being painted over this period, and when they returned home on the fifth of July, they were amazed to learn the painters had stuffed cotton batting in their ears, so intense, so interminable, so powerful was the wailing of Baby Jack. This story was repeated endlessly over the years with everyone roaring with laughter at the implication that this kid was loud then, and would always be loud. I was in my mid- to late thirties when the wife of a close associate in San Francisco, with two or three children of her own, exclaimed with horror how everyone knows that one of the cardinal rules is never to separate an infant from actual physical contact with at least one of its parents for something like the first six months. Mother and Dad didn't know this then; they believed I was getting the best care in the world. And I didn't know it until I was an adult, but issues of abandonment that have haunted me all my life must have begun right about there.

But Michigan in the forties! Oh, my God! How, without the benefit of a Norman Rockwell, can one represent the dappled sunlight, the innocence, the inherent freshness of that time? In my baby book, meticulously kept by my proud father in his florid and nearly baroque handwriting, is a snapshot of the house on Park Street, neatly named Twin Elms. It had two of them on the corner lot of Park and Mott, two giant trees so huge, so powerful, they might serve as templates for characters in a Tolkien story. The one nearest the front

Twin Elms, 1021 South Park, Saginaw, Michigan, in 1939. My father's home when my sister, Janet, and I were born. (Collection of the
author)

steps, spreading above the generous porch upon which a squeaky
glider in its period striped fabric swung, was squat, thick, and masculine, a kind of judicial or professorial elm, massive with branches,
lacy with leaves. And the one on the side of the property, I was always reminded, went "up the furtherest without a single branch than
any other tree in Saginaw." I have no idea if this is remotely true; like
so many of my family stories, it had more the ring of authority than
of actual truth.

Among my first real memories is one of me seated on my tricycle
at about five years of age, gazing upon the lawn brilliantly studded
with blooming dandelions, a field of lavish, glowing gold surrounding the house. I felt unmistakably rich; I recall clearly thinking myself
the most fortunate and clever of lads, secure and, in the only word
that I can somehow associate with that feeling . . . "inevitable."

Another scene alternately flashes into view: My sister and her friend are secreted in our bedroom having a play session, with bath towels wrapped like huge turbans around their heads, chattering like proverbial magpies. I am seated just outside the closed door of that bedroom, banished from their society, with, of course, an identical terry towel turban wrapped around my head. I am not invited in, nor even allowed communication, although I continually shout eager suggestions through the closed door. And I'm both stumped and furious. I was obviously such fun, and clearly able to adapt to any creative situation with as many, if not more, resources than they! I didn't understand it then, and I don't now. But I think one kind of handwriting was already emerging on that wall, outside where the two little girls played. A choice was being expressed, if not already made: I preferred to sit sullenly in the hallway in a terry cloth turban, courting a muse neither athletic nor, quite honestly, "appropriate," as my mother might have expressed it.

We were good kids—that much is true. The axis that seems to separate this century from the last stands out to me as significant. It represents the moment before children began to grow up so quickly, as they do today. No television, of course. No Internet. No "parental controls" were necessary because we could so easily be excluded from whatever influences were deemed inappropriate. "Dad, could I please stay up tonight to listen to . . ." "No, you cannot!" Case closed. I think back on my high school graduating class, in which there was one group of boys who might well have lost their virginity by graduation day—two or three at the most. Then there was our group: we were, so far as I can ascertain, all virgins prior to going to college. And proud of it, too!

Well, in my case, I would say I was relieved. I did not abstain from any moral obligation. To be honest, I was "otherwise engaged." I have loved and adored women all my life, from childhood on, but was never, I confess, truly sexually attracted to them. When I hear people debating what makes a child one thing or another . . . "nature or nurture," genes, whatever . . . I think back on my childhood fantasies, and although I never wished to be female, I felt a closeness, a sense of identification with my female side, if that isn't being too coy, far stronger than with any similar male influences. I was, we remember, a "dreamer," sitting for hours with a magazine or a book, or staring

Left to right: Me; my mother, Evelyn MacArthur O'Brien; and my sister, Janet, 1944. I vividly recall my determination to raise my left eyebrow. Camera-ready at five years old! (Collection of the author)

off into space to the consternation of my parents. I had no affinity for throwing or, God knows, catching a ball; any spheroid going any-where near me caused an immediate sense of panic and a serious im-pulse to scream as loud as possible. I would sit on my bicycle, urged by my mother to "find some kids to play with, for crying out loud," hanging on the metal mesh of whatever neighborhood chain-link fence was closest, hoping, praying, dreading that the indifferent scramble of boys playing whatever game would look up, see me, and say something like, "Hey, O'Brien! Just what we need! Get your ass in here and help us, will you?"

No one ever said that. So I drifted through the high school years with the growing awareness that I might be funny, like my dad, or clever, like both my parents, or even manipulative, like my mother; and so in that context I began to cobble together the scraps of a personality that could gloss over the problem areas with a light touch, take advantage of the gifts modestly, without seeming to be too pushy, and finally, well, "pass." So off I went to college, with an arm-load of prizes skillfully garnered over those early years, smart as a whip, newly appreciated for my musical and lyric gifts as someone useful to include, and best of all, as the single, significant 1950s epi-thet would have it—popular! You just couldn't do better than that.

2

You can move a ball bearing from one place to another if you're care-ful, you know, without disturbing it. The same can rarely be said of an actual pinball, because the whole point of being a pinball is to bang into something, compelling it in another direction, where it bangs into something else, lighting up various bumpers along the way, or ringing bells, or popping in and out of holes . . . you get the idea. But without an initial push you don't have much activity. Look-ing back on my life's journey from this perspective, one can readily see that considerable movement has characterized my lifestyle as well as my professional work. People keep saying they are astonished by how much energy I have, but I neither pay much attention to that nor take any real credit for it: these energy issues, these tendencies are most probably genetic, like my optimism, so I really cannot take pride in the fact. Dad was a fireball; my mother played near-championship golf for years; my sister practically ran the largest department of one of Michigan's major universities for decades . . . we're active people.

Not so much in the fall of 1957, mind you. This shiny pinball, gently transported to the variegated, leaf-stained sidewalks of the University of Michigan in Ann Arbor, was promising, and yes, "pop-ular," but anything but emotionally secure or even aware. The world itself immediately became enlarged a thousandfold, and as one emerged from the passive green grotto of Saginaw simplicity, the campus of the university roared with unimaginable sophistication and limitless challenges. I moved as in a dream, only partially regis-tering the intensity of classroom procedure and occasionally raising that Midwestern voice with a naïveté that surpasseth understanding. No real movement yet, but plenty of potential.

ME (raising my hand in a freshman English course in which the cynical instructor is skewering Wordsworth for his overly romantic imagery in "I Wandered Lonely as a Cloud"): I'm sorry, but why can't we be allowed to appreciate this for what it is? Why shouldn't Wordsworth express his enthusiasm, his love for springtime and nature, if he wants to? What's wrong with that? I know what that feels like! I've grown up loving visions like this one—beautiful flowers against the sky, gorgeous blossoms on a hill, the whole exciting thing! I know just how that feels. Why can't we just take him at his word without making fun of him? I'm certainly willing to!

THE PROFESSOR (drily, after a significant pause): Mr. O'Brien . . . I'm so happy for you.

It was thrilling, this vital environment into which I had been plunged. I was more an observer than anything else, moving lemminglike with the rest of my crowd along a prescribed avenue of expectation, asking no real questions, just happy to be on the ride. What was going to happen, did I think? I had no real idea. I went to the university because that's what all the rest of the bright, well-prepared, upper-middle-class kids from polished white Midwestern neighborhoods like mine did. Pick a curriculum? Sure. Prelaw. How about that? As a patrol boy in my elementary school days, I had stood guarding the dangerous crossing of Genessee Avenue under the baleful glance of a dour retired police officer named Mr. Palm while holding my arms horizontally to keep other classmates from the traffic and staring over my shoulder at a white clapboard house nearby, complete with its neat little office addition. It had a charming white door surrounded by sparkling windows upon which the sign ATTORNEY AT LAW hung in the morning sun like something out of the opening shot of an RKO film starring Rosalind Russell and Ralph Bellamy. Surely I could do that. Be a lawyer. Anyway, it would be four more years of college life before I had to get serious about any of it. Meanwhile, almost mindlessly I rushed the fraternity scene like every other lemming, with no real hope of being selected. After all, why should this be different from other confrontations with my male peers, all of which had found me wanting in some essential way? I aimed low, praying that one or two of the smaller houses might find me acceptable, only to be crestfallen and embarrassed as one after another passed me by. And on the final night, trudging up the hill to the glossy, glamorous Delt House with no remote hope of inclusion, I was stunned to be offered an opportunity to join. Yes, I was later to understand that one of the brothers, a high school upperclassman from Saginaw, had demanded I be pledged, but primarily because I played piano by ear and might prove a valuable asset for various campus activities. No matter . . . I floated back down to my dorm that night fully three feet off the ground, buoyed by the miracle that was allowing me sudden access to perhaps the largest collection of narcissistic prealcoholic youths on the campus. I couldn't believe my luck!

So far, no real movement, no actual push, no compulsion to do more than be the same dreamer but in another, somewhat tonier environment. I was a good student, and with some degree of application I found I could maintain the same grade point average I had sustained in high school, A-/B+ material without raising so much as a sweat. And then, with all this mapped out before me, leering enthusiastically and even convincingly as I was expected to do at the pretty Dee Gee and Kappa pledges around me . . . a tremor occurs. And the pinball begins to shudder . . .

Early in the jubilant autumn of my freshman year I received a phone call from my mother to tell me that my father, not feeling well, was coming down to Ann Arbor to U Hospital for a few tests. Something called a prostate was mentioned—I believe the first time I had ever heard the term. And down he came, defiantly driving himself, with my mother dancing attendance. Three short weeks later, during an evening pledge function, I was summoned to the hospital. My father, it appeared, was dying. For the first ten days or so they could find nothing substantial; then, eventually, they discovered that there was a small leak of cancer cells being released from a lung into the bloodstream randomly, rather than metastasizing into something substantial they could identify. My father had been a mild smoker, Chesterfields, as I recall, but casual. He loved to say that he never smoked until after lunch, and if lunch wasn't served until mid- or late afternoon, he could easily not light up until then. I remember watching him while riding in the front seat of the car alongside him; the smoke on the end of his cigarette was a beautiful blue; but when he inhaled and exhaled, naturally, it came out a grimy gray. I couldn't imagine that that was necessarily good, and I was never able to become a smoker myself, although, during college, I made several brave attempts—it was such a grown-up and, well, masculine thing to do. But Dad had stopped smoking almost ten years before this, so it was hard to connect cigarettes with his condition. They had begun cobalt treatments, and the night he died, his attending physician explained to my mother that they had decided to suspend treatments, since they were obviously doing no good, and he had probably six to eight months left to live. Shockingly, he was dead by the time the doctor got to the room. The oncologist couldn't believe it and ordered an autopsy. There was no reason for him to have died that suddenly. I've always believed, since he was a vigorous, vital man, that on some curiously Irish level he intuited his condition, and believing semi-invalidism to be intolerable, "found the exit." Honestly. That's what I think. At any rate, by the time I arrived from the Delt House, I entered the hospital to see his closest friend, Bill Mason, speaking on the telephone to someone in Saginaw, stricken and unable to meet my eyes. But I didn't have to be told. My mother, my sister Janet, a senior at the university at that time, and I all met outside his room in the corridor, dumbly, drily embracing each other, too stunned to make sense. Privately, I stole away to enter his room where the body lay, a member of the staff making notes. A tag was already tied around his right big toe. She smiled up at me. "It's my father. Is there anything I can do to help?" I asked stupidly. She shook her head and thanked me, and I left the room, feeling not only stupid but incomplete. Surely something should have occurred between us, something mythic, some final father-son confrontation that would help me, help me resolve something. And I had even managed to miss that.

I don't feel I knew him very well. Being thirteen years older than my mother, he always seemed to remain at something of an emotional distance. Was this my imagination, or was it true? Many years later, a spiritualist I visited, who knew virtually nothing of my family history, deftly identified the existence of my dead older brother, and suggested this loss had so devastated my father that "letting go" to a second son was almost more than he could bear to risk until he was certain this one would survive. She claimed he had had to reserve some private part of his heart in such a way as never to be hurt like that again. I never took it seriously until I lost my last lover some years ago, even more suddenly, an accidental death that rocked me, and I know to what degree I find it nearly impossible to let myself feel that vulnerable ever again. I do not mean to suggest that my father didn't love me, didn't relate to me. He was always supportive, even if he was, as befits the period, a bit stern. True, he had little patience with my "dreaminess," but yet he was so thrilled with my early songwriting efforts that he went to the trouble and expense of having demos made of me playing and singing my eleven-year-old compositions, sending them off to Gerald Marks in New York as well as various other business contacts who must have been somewhat astonished to receive them. Did he intuit that I might be gay? He did his level best to steer me over to his end of the playing field. He silently endured my failing miserably at his most cherished sport—dry fly-fishing—at which he was of professional caliber himself. I stood, sweating profusely, for hours on end, practicing casting a dry fly into a teacup across the yard of his fishing lodge in the north of Michigan without demonstrating a modicum of enthusiasm or talent. He took me into spiky, frosted cornfields along with his English setters while we trained them to point and fetch using patience and a clothesline, even allowing me the honor of giving one the name Jeep, which happened to be my favorite word in all the world at that point. (Not as ridiculous as it might seem—one needs a single-syllable name for a dog in the field— "Here, Aloysius!" won't cut it.) And even though I was an excellent shot, guns didn't interest me in the least. I discovered I had the ability to ape the cawing of crows, and the one moment of sporting pride I recall was when he planted me in a thicket and had me call crows over to where he and his hunting buddies were hidden in blinds, waiting to shoot the destructive pests for which the state paid a bounty.

He was a superb raconteur, so hilarious that he could keep an entire room of friends and relatives roaring with laughter at "stories" he told, endless strings of politically questionable jokes involving Germans, Russians, Jews, the Irish, all laced in the most unbelievably outrageous accents imaginable, stories that had not so much punch lines as mounting little chapters of hilarity building to a tear-streaming conclusion—he was that funny! After his death, as I was going through his personal items, I came upon a small black leather ringed notebook. Upon each page was neatly typed the opening paragraph of each one of these fabulous stories—with no punch lines included, of course. If he could remember how to get in, he'd know how to get out. So, in that sense, he "took it with him." And to this day, I cannot remember a joke for more than for twenty-four hours. I can be funny, God knows, I inherited that much from him. But jokes? Never. He was, among his other professional interests, celebrated as the unofficial "Toastmaster" of Michigan, and was repeatedly engaged to open various functions, luncheons, conventions, all of which he did with panache and guaranteed laughter. At home he allowed himself to be more the fall guy, the brunt of our . . . well, okay, basically *my* . . . good-natured ribbing, like a scratching post serving a kitten. If he'd survived, I do not doubt we'd have become great friends. But he didn't, and the almost mystical disappearance he made, three short weeks vanishing into oblivion, was as unreal as it was curiously disaffecting. I cried and I worried a bit, but to be fair, I felt in some degree enlarged by his death. I had survived the inconceivable loss of my father, I was still functioning, and without my realizing it, the last barrier to my pursuing a career in the theater had been lifted. The actress Carrie Nye, a wise and witty woman and the late wife of Dick Cavett, once observed that you never really become an adult until your parents die. And in this case, there was quite suddenly no one blocking the door in front of me, no one to whom I had to explain or defend my course of action. I might feel bereaved, but I was also set free. Free, did I say? Movement at last! But where? And more important, to what?

3

Almost too quickly the brief cloud that was my father's death dissolved in the consuming excitement and activity of the University of Michigan, a climate peppered and enriched by the presence of an element completely foreign to me—the newly emerging Beat culture of the early sixties. Beatniks were everywhere in their black turtlenecks, eyes lined with kohl, slouching around the campus with green bookbags and hangovers. They sat in the Michigan Union drinking cups of coffee and smoking endless cigarettes, watching everyone through narrowed eyelids with a universal disdain that was simply thrilling. Principal among them were David Newman and his eventual wife, Leslie England, Jewish kids from New York who, having failed to gain acceptance to any of their first-choice top Eastern schools, like many other undergraduates, took the next best thing, and the next best thing was Michigan. He wrote for the campus newspaper, *The Michigan Daily*, and took special interest in extracurricular theatrical activities, like the campus musical theater troupe, MUSKET (Michigan Union Shows, Ko-Eds, Too), intellectually slumming on the periphery of showbiz, as it were. Newman eventually strode out of the university and into film history via *Esquire* magazine, and along with his partner Robert Benton wrote *Bonnie and Clyde*, among other scripts. He was that singular icon, exotic beyond belief to me, a genuine university "star," and to orbit anywhere near his circle, breathing the same air, was to participate in an obliterating glamour that to a great degree helped to dispel both my grief and the emotional uncertainty I felt about my future.

The major difference between the playgrounds of Saginaw, onto which I was never invited, and the evolving world of amateur theatrics at the university was that in the latter case, the one thing most essential to smart upperclassmen was the presence of an eager, adoring audience. And there I sat! I daresay my life moved fatally into its new direction the night the young faculty director of campus musicals invited me along with Newman, his fiancée, and a handful of other upperclassmen to Detroit for Chinese food! Wow! This was, no question about it, the Big Time: Jews and Chinese food, all in the same evening! You just don't recover from something like that. You go with it, or you are condemned forever to a limbo of ordinariness— Not Wanted on the Voyage.

Defining moments, wouldn't you say? A little moo shu pork, a few laughs, and the next thing you know you've gravitated a quarter inch from where you were to where you are headed without even suspecting. For so many people in the arts, these tiny moments collect until the magnetic pull is finally felt and identified. It can be as mundane as a first cigarette, an innocent cocktail, a toke on a nearby joint for the unknowing addict. Less sinister even than that. It can be simply the pure static sound of applause. I'm fairly certain that that's what tripped me up. One moment you are sitting in an aisle seat at a high school assembly, your stomach a veritable biology lab of suicidal insects; the next moment, "it"—whatever "it" happened to be . . . a poem, a recitation, a brief song—is over, and you stand for a moment stark naked in the tangible sound of the room's approval, and nothing has happened but that you have chosen your life's work—you just didn't realize it. But somebody, or something, gets your attention, arrests you, and slowly your neutrality turns into color. My generation was hardly the first to discover this. Although I most assuredly got splashed by standing too close to the generation just ahead of me. Let me explain.

Ours has been an active theatrical climate here in America over the past few hundred years. If we don't have that much global history behind us, we have very vivid antecedents. Edwin Forrest and Edwin Booth raised their early American banners for others to follow, and there were those who heeded that siren song like Eva Le Gallienne, in the twenties and thirties, who worshipped her European contemporary Eleonora Duse and wished to emulate her. She also fell under the spell of, and in love with, a Russian actress, Alla Nazimova, which caused the combustion that became her remarkable Civic Repertory, the last time for decades that New York would experience a company playing genuine repertory.

For a country suffering through the Depression, theater became a way to lift up the spirit, to challenge authority, to defy the gods, to express anger. John Houseman took this kind of rage and crafted *One Third of a Nation* for Hallie Flanagan and the Federal Theatre Project out of it; his closest collaborator, Orson Welles, infused a Fascist *Macbeth* with similar audacity, and the Mercury Theatre was born, one of the most important expressions of America's emerging contribution to world culture. These were not artsy types, but powerful men and women with voices lifted in support of the society in which they found themselves. "LeG," as Le Gallienne was known, managed to blend her passion for a Russian lover with a passion for classical theater. Houseman, who later defined his personal ethic with the sound bite "We make money the old-fashioned way . . . we *earrrrrn* it!" had once cornered the international grain market before entering film and theater, and was tough on others, tougher on himself. The arts were not merely decorative to these movers and shakers; they were a way to make a difference. In my case, it was Sir Tyrone Guthrie who flung down the particular gauntlet that was to galvanize a generation of young professionals after the Second World War, and managed to pull me along in their wake.

Exhibit A: *A Life in the Theatre*, Guthrie's great personal memoir. Coming over in 1952 from England and Ireland, where he had made his reputation, Sir Tony took on nothing short of creating a Canadian National Theatre at Stratford, Ontario, lifting existing theatrical standards as high as his own six-foot-five-inch frame. He loved challenges that were equally daunting, and in defining this new degree of excellence for North America he summed up his general opinions with typical ringing Irish rhetoric: the United States, he claimed, would never have great actors until they had a great theater; and a great theater was achievable only with the existence of vigorous repertory companies, as opposed to the occasional commercial enterprise. Only by experiencing acting in a repertory environment could American actors systematically climb the ladders of the world's great theatrical literature and achieve world-class status.

It wasn't as if the United States was theatrically deficient at the time. The nascent regional movement we currently enjoy was only beginning to poke its collective head up across the country. The efforts of pioneers like Nina Vance and Margo Jones in Texas, the Fichandlers at the Arena Stage in Washington, D.C., or Angus Bowmer out in Oregon had not yet achieved the status they would eventually enjoy, not as receptacles of recycled Broadway fare, but rather as the seedbeds from which so many distinguished careers and plays would begin traveling the opposite direction to New York and subsequent commercial success. But by the midcentury mark, Le Gallienne had left Nazimova as well as her rep days behind her, and Welles had become too big—both physically and emotionally—to be contained on a stage. Houseman, swinging between his careers as a movie producer on the West Coast and a theater producer in the East, had invested some of his protean efforts in Stratford, Connecticut, in the attempt to rival Guthrie's brilliant start-up in Canada. And elsewhere, John Lithgow's father, Arthur, a fascinating theatrical mountebank and sometime educator, was mounting a Shakespeare festival in Yellow Springs, Ohio, of all godforsaken places, while the likes of T. Edward Hambleton and Norris Houghton were sitting off-Broadway with their Phoenix Theatre, fanning the fires with revivals and occasional verse plays. Hambleton, whose fortune came from his family's ownership of the Baltimore and Ohio Railroad, had at that time something like $100,000 per year that he could afford to lose any way he chose, and he chose to support off-Broadway theatrical events. In the 1950s, $100,000 was a healthy amount to invest.

Still, Guthrie's edict about American acting amounted to "fightin' words" for a large percentage of impressionable young men and women who at that time seemed to have graduated from one notable source—Carnegie Tech in Pittsburgh, as Carnegie Mellon University was then called. Some recent periods have seen Yale, or Brandeis, or the North Carolina School of the Arts, or usually the Juilliard School producing a bumper crop of promising talent, but in the mid-fifties, Carnegie Tech was the one spewing out such gifted young people as costume designer Ann Roth, or actress Sada Thompson, or lighting designer Jules Fisher. And, newly minted and eager to show off and polish their new skills, many of these grads showed up at Arthur Lithgow's Antioch Shakespeare Festival in Yellow Springs, committing themselves to insane summer seasons of everything from *Richard II* through *Richard III* in rotating repertory in a matter of weeks, ingesting enormous chunks of verse with no time to think, let alone rehearse, and yelling to each other in the dressing rooms as they were pulling on their tights, "Which one is it tonight?" They often went running into a battle scene or a transition with hilarious results, shouting the wrong cue or breathlessly showing up as the wrong character. But many of today's most celebrated actors cut their creative teeth in such out-of-the way and bucolic marathons, among them two Carnegie Tech graduates in particular—Ellis Rabb and William Ball.

And how to do either of them—let alone both—justice when each is worth a volume of his own? It may not be reductive to say that at the midpoint of the twentieth century, Bill Ball and Ellis Rabb both responded to Guthrie's challenge by individually shouldering a commitment to American classical theater that may well have shaped most of what exists today, although sadly neither of these names seems to ring much of a bell in current theatrical circles.

Ellis was the first to bite: at the time Guthrie's book was making the rounds, he was appearing in Houseman's summer Shakespearean season in Stratford, Connecticut, and as a leading player in the company, he had been given Katharine Hepburn's small cottage by the Housatonic for his residence. He used to recall that he lay reading the Guthrie volume in the living room on Hepburn's own chaise, and when he got to the offensive passage dismissing the potential of American actors, he hurled the volume through the nearest window directly into the Housatonic River. Now, experience teaches me that Ellis's aim in most things was usually less consistent than that, but it makes a wonderful opening shot for a movie, should any of us wish to film it.

Be that as it may, he was to marry the English actress Rosemary Harris about this time, and along with his good friend, the Canadian actor Richard Easton, and several others, they decided to send postcards to everyone they knew with classical experience in and around Manhattan. The network quickly spread to include most of the young and upcoming actors of their generation—most of whom promised to meet once a week at the Sullivan Street Playhouse. Ellis demanded, regardless of their previous qualifications, that they all choose partners and perform scenes for each other as a beginning exercise. Actors came and went, as they usually do whenever these kinds of activities get stirred up, but the group began to identify themselves as APA, the Association of Producing Artists. The idea, of course, was that they would not passively wait to be hired, but would choose to be responsible for their own destinies; and before long the fledgling company had found its first engagement in Bermuda, mounting a three-play repertory of Shaw's *Man and Superman*, Chekhov's *The Seagull*, and a musical adaptation of *The Loves of Anatol*, based on the Schnitzler play, featuring Rabb, Miss Harris, Easton, Dorothy "Dee" Victor, Eve Roberts, and others. One cannot say they lacked ambition. This summer engagement was followed by another, in Princeton, New Jersey, and the ball was decidedly set in motion.

A few years later, in 1965, a full-page announcement appeared in *The New York Times* proclaiming another new company called ACT (the American Conservatory Theatre), this one headed by William Ball, and initially centered in Pittsburgh, where many of the company, including Sada Thompson, Michael O'Sullivan, René Auberjonois, and others were located. And as Rabb's company peripatetically explored various places on the eastern seaboard, Bill's company eventually settled in San Francisco, encouraged by McNeil Lowry of the National Endowment for the Arts and substantially underwritten by the San Francisco clothing magnate Cyril Magnin.

Bill was the older by a few years—short, stocky, round-faced, and powerfully voiced, a fearless actor with a healthy ego; Ellis, a Southerner, was tall and attenuated, with a head of curls, ice blue eyes, and an almost lethal charm whenever he chose to employ it. Each was on fire with theatrical ambition, impatient, brave, and reckless, and by the late fifties, each had had enough significant success—Ellis as the star of an off-Broadway production of Molière's *The Misanthrope* and Bill as a director of a very flashy production of Pirandello's *Six Characters in Search of an Author*—to command attention as talent deserving of being followed. The two classmates, who once celebrated their first postgraduate trip to Paris by standing atop the Eiffel Tower ignoring the view and arguing whether "To be or not to be" in *Hamlet* should precede or follow the nunnery scene, were off on their separate, occasionally collaborative life journeys. And the landscape was shifted just that much—a challenge by a towering figure of impeccable British classical pedigree, and suddenly two new companies are born, conceived by two rival young American firebrands not content to serve a regional market but ambitious for a national profile.

The year is 1961, two years after Ellis Rabb has mailed his postcards and four years before Bill Ball was to take out his ad in *The New York Times*. Tyrone Guthrie has yet another role to play, stepping up to this new American pinball table and pulling back the spring-loaded plunger, his fingers delicately on the flippers on each side. And I, shiny with confidence, am at rest for perhaps the last time ever, in the Delt House of the University of Michigan.

4

"Georgiaaaaaa . . . Georgia . . . the whole night through . . ." sings a familiar voice in our musical interlude.

In the generous if threadbare living room of the Delta chapter of Delta Tau Delta, out Geddes Avenue on the University of Michigan campus, one may yet find a somewhat scarred and drink-stained baby grand piano. On any given Saturday night of the school term from, say, the autumn of 1958 through 1961, at about 10:30 or so, whatever the theme of that particular party—be it Halloween, a pledge formal, or the classic toga party—one might observe various fraternity brothers and their dates begin to smile in my direction and either put their drinks down, or, more likely, refill them one last time, moving en masse into the living room to group themselves expectantly around that same piano. Because eleven o'clock was when my "set" inevitably began. My Saginaw high school chum Tom Princing, who had so generously put me up for inclusion in this group of upper-middle-class "face men," as attractive fraternity boys were called, wasn't wrong about me: I could indeed play the piano well enough by ear, and I could indeed come up with material suitable to divert a university audience. But perhaps the real capper was that, best of all, I didn't cost anything. Each social Delt event was structured to conclude with the one activity for which the brothers were justly celebrated. We were known to be singers, and each year we acquitted ourselves with distinction at the fraternity/sorority singing contest. But to be honest, this particular weekly event meant something more to me. In my imagination, it was practically a nightclub act! On the very first night I was "bid" into the fraternity, the brothers, knowing something of

my alleged musical prowess and having fortified me with several
shots of neat Scotch whiskey, managed to get me swiftly to the keyboard, as if they were trying out a new bicycle. Someone was playing,
or more probably "messing around," only to be shoved aside for my
debut. Glowing with excitement up at the phalanx of handsome faces
around me, I asked for suggestions, smiled obligingly, and so entered
into the annals of the fraternity as their own personal jukebox.

I loved pleasing them, and whenever they called out the title of a
song, I could usually manage to play some version of it for them to
sing along. True, I had limited options. I had endured piano lessons
for about five years, from approximately the age of five to ten, but my
skill at reading music fell sadly behind my natural instinct to pick out
melodies by ear. And since laboring over printed sheet music bored
me to death, a slick, superficial improvisation took over with the alacrity of a rampant bed of kudzu, corralling me into one of three
keys—C, G, or F. That's pretty much it. The brothers would call out
the titles of popular songs—"Wake Up, Little Susie," or "Dream" by
the Everly Brothers, or, if snow was falling beyond the windows,
"Winter Wonderland," or "Baby, It's Cold Outside," and off I would
go in one of my three negotiable keys, the boys either straining gamely
for ungenerously high notes, or growling painfully for the lows, depending, but thrilled by my seemingly inexhaustible store of musical
material. They would grin approvingly down at their dates, as if I
were some kind of performing house pet, which, indeed, I managed
happily to resemble. Finally when the usual requests had been exhausted and it was time to close up shop, I would launch into my own
"set"—beginning with the Devil's solo, "The Good Ol' Days," from
Damn Yankees, which had become a kind of signature, then straying
effortlessly into the Noël Coward song book—"Nina," "Uncle Harry,"
"Mad Dogs and Englishmen"—all in a fairly accurate replication of
Coward's celebrated clipped speech, and inevitably ending with the
Master's priceless send-up of Cole Porter's "Let's Do It." This last bit
never failed to bring the house down, to such a degree that I began to
expand on its possibilities, beginning with Porter's original lyric,
then segueing to the Coward adaptation, and finally creating my own
"university" version of complicated and Porter-perfect interlocking
rhyme schemes with which I thrilled onlookers by including them in

a salty celebration of "Delt" humor and thus laying them somewhere very near the aisles, if not the exit. It was thrilling; and the nearly overwhelming gratitude these sexy young bucks felt at being able to treat their dates to a "special finish" to any given evening spilled over into their mounting affection for me. I bathed in this misplaced adoration, blatantly flirting, begging for more, while all the time leaving my abandoned date to sip her solitary cocktail in some corner while the boys crowded around me as if I were some aphrodisiac talisman for getting laid. They didn't think all much about their feelings for me. I did.

I wasn't all that bad, mind you. What I had, beyond the ability to pick up pseudo cocktail piano by ear, was a strong, on-pitch singing voice, and an obvious talent for mimicry that stretched back into my childhood. As a lad, I was so enamored by the films of Judy Garland that I recall willing my jaw into an unbecoming overbite just to be as "like her" as I could, thus condemning my parents to years of expensive orthodontics. At seven or eight I could get down on my knees and do Jolson; I could whip around the living room like Fred Astaire, or even better, Gene Kelly, whose rugged athleticism was more to my liking. No social engagement of my parents' was safe from a command performance of singing or dancing or usually both. I might have to be egged into the spotlight, but once there, I would run the gamut of my catalog without so much as breaking a sweat. My sister and I fell so in love with the cast album of *Kismet* that we committed the entire score to memory, caterwauling in the backseat of the car while our parents stared stoically out the windshield, suffering through "And This Is My Beloved" for the umpteenth time. As I grew somewhat older, I found I could mimic Alfred Drake's phrasing in *Kismet*, his timing, even a syrupy approximation of his "semi-class" baritone. Not content with banging out all the Hit Parade selections to my mother's delight on the family piano after dinner, I began writing my own tunes and lyrics, rather charming distant echoes of existing pop songs, but passionate with conviction I bravely treated friends and relatives to my little original repertoire of "Rockin' Revival" or "My Blues Are Baby Blue," the very compositions my father was destined to preserve in demos that arrived unexpectedly and unbidden on the desks of his business associates.

It had to have been a source of enormous pain to my sister, Janet, who would slave over the sheet music to that most irritating of all melodies, "The Third Man Theme" with its endless zither motif, only to rise from keyboard and find "Smarty-Pants" slipping directly in behind, tearing it all off flawlessly by ear without so much as a thought. Unpardonable behavior! I'm amazed she didn't murder me. It all came a bit too easily, to be honest, these musical gifts, having had their genesis in the fringe vaudeville and barbershop quartet enthusiasms of my father. I was, then as now, basically a show-off, loving the limelight and perfectly happy to occupy it until something else, or someone else, came along to claim it. Want me to sing? I'll sing. Want me to play? I'll play as long as you want. I learned to move quickly, to leap from thought to thought, subject to subject, impression to impression with the alacrity of a mountain goat. It wasn't serious. It was just fun!

But the pinball was clearly on the table now, and dangerously out of what we call the "comfort zone," and so destined to collide with all manner of interesting things. The fall of 1958, the campus extracurricular musical organization, MUSKET, was doing *Carousel*, and one of my fraternity brothers, an enormous, burly lad who was the former center on the university football team, had been cast as Mr. Snow. In spite of his gigantic size, he possessed a comically tiny and tender tenor voice, and so was a charming idea for the role. But as a first-year law student, he was overwhelmed with classwork, and very early in the rehearsal period he had to pull out. With the briefest of backward glances, as he departed he told the director and conductor that he was sending them the perfect substitute who would be ideal for the part. Yes . . . surprise! It was me!

Bump. Slowly I began rolling toward the magnetic pull of something far beyond my control. I walked into a room in the Michigan Union, sang "When the Children Are Asleep," and, pushing a bit that high A natural, sealed my destiny. A fraction the size, experience, and image of my massive fraternity brother, I reached for inspiration to the readiest image—Jacques Tati, whom I had just seen in *Mr. Hulot's Holiday*, and, staggering awkwardly out of rhythm toward Carrie Pipperidge, once more mimicked my way into a characterization.

That Carrie Pipperidge was being played by a classmate named Judy Heric at the moment seemed entirely incidental. We had tangentially met the previous year, playing two minor roles in a production of *Anything Goes*. She registered with me immediately as a sparkplug of energy—petite, dark-haired and dark-eyed, quicksilver and effortlessly hilarious. She was, as were many young women of the time, almost aggressively sexy, but utterly without guile. The margins of sixties *Playboy* magazines were festooned at the time with tiny dark-haired gamines clad basically only in black stockings, with enormous breasts, giddy and playful. That was the essential characterization she chose, masking a will of steel, a gleaming soprano voice, and cagey, feline intelligence. We adored each other on sight, and for the better part of that year and the next, I fully expected that this relationship would finally help turn the heavy sexual page under which I seemed destined to remain secretly inert. That it didn't eventually ignite might just be a matter of timing, or of cowardice, or even, perhaps, the unexpected pressure from one other significant player. And "player" was the operative word.

I stood by the piano during a late rehearsal for *Carousel*. The director, with the aid of the choreographer, was putting together the iconic Carousel Waltz, the ravishing piece of music with which the classic musical begins. He turned to the piano and said, "Okay, can we just try this? Bob, are you ready?"

The pianist to my right looked up. He was sitting cross-legged at the keyboard, his glasses sliding down on his nose, staring uninterestedly at the scene before him. "The overture," he said to no one in particular, "oh, yeah . . . okay, I guess," and, flipping the pages back in his score, arrived at the beginning of the book. He looked closely at the key signatures, raised his eyes to mine with a shrug, and dug in. It was immediately clear that he had never seen the music before nor given it so much as a passing thought. But he tore into it without hesitation, and riveted, I stood next to him, my eyes scanning the furious blur of notes on the page just ahead of where he was playing, reaching over to turn the pages so he wouldn't have to break stride. To say I was amazed is a considerable understatement. My own sight-reading abilities, limited to a painstaking scouring of, say, the treble tenor line, crumbled before this technical onslaught. In the background, the dancers lumbered through their paces, but my eyes were glued to the page and to the hands flying near me. The waltz finished with a flourish, and everyone in the room turned instinctively to the keyboard, giving the player an impromptu round of applause. He was sheepishly pleased, ducking his head somewhat. "Wow," I said ineffectually, and then pushed on. "You sort of weren't ready for that, were you?" "Naw," came the laconic response. "But hell . . . if it's written, I can play it!"

And so began my initial awareness of Bob James, who was to play such a key role in my life, and Judy Heric's as well. She and I were all bogus showbiz glamour, or what we assumed would pass for such luster. He was blunt as a meat-ax, disengaged, faintly contemptuous of the air above his head where we both professed to skip and dance. What he was, at the time, was tolerant of me, and obviously attracted to her. So finally, at the cast party for our successful opening performance, at which she and I had stolen focus, the reviews, and a lion's share of the attention with our confident performances, he turned to me and said directly, "Are you . . . um . . . you know, doing anything with Judy?" "Doing anything?" I said guardedly, feeling the mask as well as the ground beneath me slip slightly. He went relentlessly on. "Because if you aren't, I'd like to ask her out." Was my reply swallowed, or expansively magnanimous? I can't be sure. I recall being both impressed that he was asking permission, and at the same time embarrassed that it must be so apparent that I was not taking proper advantage of a dazzler obviously deserving of the rapt attention of any red-blooded college student. And just that quickly was the subsequent judgment made and received. Whatever game I might think I was sustaining was blown away. Bob had watched, waited, respected the timing that would bring a reciprocal sexual relationship to a boil, and, not getting a clear signal, was not remotely interested in wasting more time. I, on the other hand, felt something curiously like relief: I had been "found out," in one sense, but was not being tainted nor contaminated by my rival in the process. Are you in or out? was the issue. The rest didn't seem to matter to Bob at all.

Soon we were almost always and inevitably three. Sometimes two, but for only brief periods. For Judy and me, *Carousel* was only the beginning. We were tireless, we were aggressive, and we were loud.

Loud counted. Microphones in theater were just about to surface in 1961 when the fragile soprano of Anna Maria Alberghetti first floated over Broadway's Imperial Theatre in *Carnival*. But such expensive equipment was not yet available to universities across the country. In the tradition of Jolson, of Merman, of Mary Martin, the intrinsically key element in all musical performance at the time was not athletic prowess, or a standard of beauty, or even a deft acting talent, but rather the ability to be heard over twenty or twenty-five pieces in the orchestra pit. Judy and I had that talent in spades—if subtlety and dimension were not our calling cards, volume was. We followed our success on the dramatic periphery of *Carousel* the following year by climbing the Everest of *Kismet*. Judy, surely one of the smallest La-lumes on record, distinguished herself by teasing her hair into a helmet above her head and spraying it stiffly gold. She looked like a tiny industry award, and on opening night she accidentally snapped the waistband of her harem trousers and, in the time-honored show business tradition, pretty much dropped her pants onstage to thunderous approval. And I, as we know, self-trained practically from the pediatric ward in the role of Hajj, managed to throw my mimicry across the footlights, convincing the audiences that I was forty, a father, a baritone, and straight. More or less. Whenever possible, we two found the opportunity to play opposite each other, on student television projects, in classroom exercises, and even, from time to time, by deigning to appear in the arid and austere sobriety of theater department productions. We must have been insufferable!

Bob and I were destined for our own duo experience as well, for meanwhile, flushed with my fraternity-club-act celebrity, and while powering through a list of seemingly limitless and improbable acting roles, I had continued to write music and lyrics, ditties vaguely reminiscent of other established works, but just sassy enough to pass. Better lyrics than melodies. I decided to write my own musical theater piece, digging through research in the university archives for my subject, Christopher Columbus, of all characters, and his 1492 voyage to America. (This being a musical and this being me, the gimmick, of course, would be the smuggling of women on board, and the inevitable fact that they were the sole reason America was discovered!) The thing about all early success is what a natural amphetamine it proves to be, how it feeds on itself, how easily the dish runs away with the spoon. And the other universal truth is the utter lack of fear one has whenever staring at that metaphorical high dive for the very first time. "I loved your early stuff" is a cliché funny as well as heartbreaking, because the early work is so often effortlessly spontaneous. One doesn't perceive the abyss ahead, the incipient danger. We love discovering people and happily proclaiming their success; we just don't like them to make a habit of it. And so once one has delivered the first effort, the second or the tenth or hopefully the resulting canon may well be better for the experience, but certainly more difficult if not painful because of knowledge gained. In my enthusiasm I felt compelled to do everything—do the research, write the book, compose the lyrics as well as the music, all with an eye to playing the central role of Columbus myself. Knowing nothing of music theory, of course, all I could possibly offer was the single melodic line composed in . . . yes! . . . one of three basic keys, and even more hilariously, all crafted in my current affectation—green ink! Big, fat jolly notes bounced across my staff-lined score like children's wrapping paper, and I deftly recall an afternoon in the underlit apartment in which our *Carousel* musical director, dabbling in extracurricular sadomasochism, lived, when I sat down to the keyboard in the presence of probably twenty or twenty-five classmates to "audition" this material. I was determined that MUSKET would produce it, and was eager to enlist everyone I could think of in my campaign. Bob James attended that session, or at least part of it; he was the squarer of the roommates living in the flat, and if memory serves, I was careening somewhere through part of the second act when he and Judy quietly got up and disappeared. She had no choice, obviously. He remained, at best, respectfully uninterested.

But the rest of the crowd were dazzled, and undiminished and undaunted I solicited one emotional backer after another until even the university staff director became convinced that this project might fly. There was one obvious obstacle: orchestrations. The idea of doing an original musical was daunting enough for a campus organization that had only the barest and most primitive financial backing and had annually ridden the safe formula of replicating Broadway hits. The faculty advisers, intrigued, to give them credit, were still sober enough to realize that my one-man band wasn't also going to include orchestration, copying the parts, and conducting, no matter how enthusiastic I might appear to be. The edict came down: this project cannot be considered unless the entire piece is fully orchestrated before rehearsals begin. And not only before the first rehearsal—by the end of the current spring term!

I was making my way down the charming Nichols Arcade, a series of quaint shops connecting West University and the street immediately behind, upon which the music school was located, when just outside the Betsy Ross Coffee Shop, where the university musical cognoscenti traditionally collected, who should be coming my way but Bob James! I had just received the body blow about orchestrations, and rather than sinking into a morass of self-pity, I just looked confidently ahead of me; and ahead of me stood a slender, slightly round-shouldered, polite young Missourian jazz pianist with a thin face distinguished primarily by enormous eyeglasses, and who, quite separate from our mutual theatrical endeavors and his successful courtship of my best friend, had been making quite a name for himself as a versatile musical force to be reckoned with.

"Hi! Hey, Bob!" I said, standing directly in his way. "You know that musical I was playing over at yours and Ed's the other day?" "Yes," came the wary reply. And I launched into my improvised pitch: It was a practically a "sure thing" for production the following fall but for the little problem of orchestrations. I knew he was skilled and one of the indisputable stars of the music school—would such an assignment ever appeal to him? It was also clear to me that with Judy Heric securely in my back pocket, for him to turn me down outright might not sit so comfortably with the Lynn Fontanne side to her musical Alfred Lunt. Bob suggested we adjourn to one of the practice rooms in the basement of the music school and have a look. And we did. Without much comment, he looked over the dazzling green, black, and white array of lead sheets, making small pencil notes of chord changes in the margins above my fat Technicolor efforts. Usually I had taken a rather sweet musical phrase and simply repeated it a second time; he suggested, most diplomatically, a change here or there that might refresh the melody without destroying my . . . what? . . . Grandma Moses approach. And finally, at one point, he provided a vaudevillian flourish to end one of the numbers that sent us both into paroxysms of laughter. I was thrilled and amazed—here was a legitimate theatrical complement to my work, something I never would have imagined. He, on the other hand, was grateful for my delight. We kept playing the phrase over and over, and, as we have done so over the intervening fifty or so years, continued to laugh, that glorious roar of emotional white water that leaves one helpless. As well as creating friendship! There is simply not enough to be said for a sense of humor. All my best relationships have depended on it.

I'm wondering . . . do we not tend to remember the failures more than the successes? They teach us more, that is certain; and one clearly remembers the bad reviews far, far more vividly than any praise. But there are milestones, no question, that remain upright in the landscape we move past . . . and *Land Ho!* is one of them. I have had genuine success in the theater during my lifetime, but it may well be that this moment was the defining one. I vividly recall five scheduled performances, all sold out, all accorded what was at the time the unimaginable response of a standing ovation. During the final performance, waiting in the stage left wings and listening to Bob conducting his kick-ass overture with university and faculty players in the pit, I silently dedicated the performance to the memory of my father, because I knew to what degree this would have thrilled him. It certainly thrilled me. The entire event was astonishing, and I can point back with pride to the achievement of having won the BMI Award in 1961 for the "Best Collegiate Musical" in the country as proof this isn't mere hyperbole. We weren't prepared for such success, to put it mildly. Judy had repaired to Taylor Township nearby to do her two-year stint of student teaching and hadn't been allowed to share this particular triumph with us, but it sealed Bob's and my contract, as friends and as creative collaborators. We were sharing a tacky little house on Division Street, the provenance of one Marie Kilborn and her son who had rented it to us, thus giving rise to the epithet "Kilborn Place—a Heck of a Place, a Speck of a Place," a quote from the radio comics Bob and Ray, particular favorites of our respective fathers as well as ours. I had a bedroom off the hallway to the bathroom on the second floor; Bob occupied the room down at the end. One steamy night as we prepared for sleep, he walked from the bathroom past my open bedroom door. "So," he began carefully, pausing and leaning against the jamb, with the hall light silhouetting him from behind, "we probably should take this seriously, don't you think?" "Seriously?" "Yeah. I mean, it's staring us straight in the face, isn't it? I mean, do you want to do this?" The direct tone of the question was familiar: Are you in or out? I had heard it before, and that subject matter had turned out to be just as weighty and consequential as this one was going to be. "You mean, like, as a career?" "Yeah," came the immediate response. I felt flush, a torrent of emotion I couldn't express and prayed I wasn't being betrayed by my usual tearing up. "Yeah! Wow! Yeah! I think I do."

"G'night," was the pleased response, and he padded down the hall to his room. We had no air-conditioning, and our respective rotating fans were the only discernible sounds as I lay in the dark. *Wow!* I repeated to myself. Lerner meets Loewe, huh? Just that quickly. Why not? After all, it's what I'd assumed I'd end up doing.

5

I believe I left Sir Tyrone Guthrie standing at a pinball table. Not such a ridiculous image as it might seem. Because if there is one thing that truly distinguishes a life in the theater, in particular, and careers in the arts in general from what one might consider the workaday world, then "play" is most assuredly a major component. It may be a cliché to say the way to avoid the drudgery of work is by pursuing a career in something you truly love, but it is still true. And although theater offers more than a generous measure of guaranteed failure, particularly if one is doing it properly . . . that is, passionately, full throttle, without the proverbial safety net or an eye to critics' approval . . . when it is all going in the right direction it provides a high unlike anything else. Some time ago, after I had assumed artistic directorship of the Old Globe Theatre in San Diego, we had the opportunity to create a production of Thornton Wilder's *The Skin of Our Teeth* not only for the stage, but simultaneously for American Playhouse as a television presentation as well. It was decided that we would do a live taping before an audience directly to network feed of a special performance of the play, thus using both television and the concept of an actual theatrical production as the very Wilder-appropriate background for the broadcast. This approach was the brainchild of my close friend, Lindsay Law, then head of American Playhouse, who seemed never to acknowledge the word "fear." But live to network feed? That is such an act of pure folly it is almost never done, because one is virtually without control, without any recovery mode from gaffes that might occur and that could otherwise be edited between the initial taping and the airdate. In this case, because the theater was in San Diego and the telecast was originating from New York, by the time I finished the actual taping, which had begun live on the West Coast before an invited audience at the hour of five, and I had joined the audience at a postperformance reception in our scene shop, American Playhouse had already broadcast the production to East Coast viewers and here it was, three hours later, being witnessed by the celebrators on monitors installed around the shop. The assignment had been a near conceptual impossibility. There were hundreds and hundreds of shots to be called without so much as a break in the action; everything had to be perfectly executed, not taking into consideration routine occurrences that affect any normal stage production during performance. For example, at one point in the taping of the action of the third act, a cameraman holding a portable Steadicam was meant to be physically attacked by one of the actors as part of the prescribed business, carefully rehearsed in the initial camera blocking. During the broadcast, however, the actor in question became so adrenalized that he literally knocked the cameraman over, and we instantly lost use of the equipment. You could hear the stifled reactions in the truck as all observers tried not to alarm me or interrupt my concentration. What could we do? As it happened, the camera swam back into focus just as the crucial shot it had been written to serve was being called, and the exhalation of air from ten or twelve sets of lungs was palpable. When I finally emerged from the finished taping to join the audience watching the monitors with glasses of wine in their hands, I realized that the show had gone off without a mistake, and knowing how high the stakes had been, I experienced a kind of euphoria I had never known before or since. Athletes refer to this as being "in the zone," and it is truly indescribable, and there is no practical way to reproduce it without accomplishing an equal effort. A bank teller's job rarely provides such an unlooked-for perk, barring, of course, the odd encounter with the likes of Bonnie and Clyde.

Guthrie must have enjoyed some aspect of this feeling at Stratford, Ontario, when he first lured major talent like Alec Guinness and Irene Worth into a tent to inaugurate his audacious theatrical experiment there; but having done so, he was now looking for a similar challenge, something that might possibly give him yet another feeling of being "in the zone." He found it by offering his professional services to several areas in the Midwestern United States, places that had never been synonymous with a classical theatrical standard; and in winnowing the choices down to Minneapolis, Minnesota, Ann Arbor, Michigan, and Indianapolis, Indiana, he zeroed in on three places most likely to welcome such an experiment. Minneapolis won the contract as well as Guthrie's genius, but shortly thereafter, in the early sixties, the University of Michigan announced the launching of its own professional theater program. To those of us toiling in what had seemed a fairly standard theatrical program there, this was Big News indeed. And perhaps it was just coincidence that Minneapolis and Ann Arbor would find themselves making news cheek by jowl, twin sparks of theatrical excitement in what had been pretty much considered the backwater of American culture. Then again, perhaps not.

Because here, suddenly, two paths seem to diverge ahead of us, as in a Frost poem. One path is what officially "happened," and the other? Well, the other will be revealed after we reflect a bit on one of my earliest lessons—the curious thing about truth. Early in the twentieth century, the great Nobel laureate playwright Luigi Pirandello, one of my literary heroes, began experimenting with his perception of truth. *Così È (Se Vi Pare)*, is the title of one of his early plays—*Right You Are (If You Think You Are)*—and everyone, from Italian audiences of the time up to possibly O. J. Simpson in recent memory, has had cause to nod and more or less fall into line. There are many kinds of truth, and bafflingly, like particles in quantum physics, they seem to appear to exist simultaneously, contradictory, yes, but there you are! Tyrone Guthrie's timely appearance in Minneapolis and the concomitant creation of the Professional Theatre Program at Ann Arbor may well have been mere accidents of fate, but there is another version of all this, and it's probably too soon to shine a light into that dark, forbidding cave. We need to introduce one more principal player before we can do so. Let me build a temporary metaphoric theatrical set first, into which I can wander back later to do some serious damage . . .

The year is 1962. Guthrie is already ensconced in Minneapolis when onto the campus of the University of Michigan stride Robert

C. Schnitzer and his wife, Marcella Cisney. These married professionals have been retained by the regents of the university expressly to guide into existence the newest jewel in the university's crown—the PTP, as the Professional Theatre Company became known—an ambitious graduate program in theater arts through which one could earn a master's degree in performance, something the university had never before offered. Schnitzer is tall and mustachioed, with the easy gait and overly familiar grin of a floorwalker; she is short, blunt, and black-haired, a dyed-in-the-wool New Yorker with a no-nonsense attitude and a passing resemblance to Tenniel's Red Queen, with lipstick and pearls for added softness. We'll return to a closer examination of all this once the rest of the cast has signed in, but this is as good a place as any to pick up our evolving narrative.

"Mr. O'Brien!" Marcella trumpeted enthusiastically, rising from behind a small mahogany desk in an equally small office cubicle tucked away in the Women's League. "I'm so happy you could make it." Dressed in a severe black suit and a silk blouse with a jabot that nearly obliterated her short neck, she negotiated the small space between the desk and the wall like a ballroom dancer, her hand extended, all her teeth on generous display. She had a flat, rather nasal delivery, and considerable attack. "We've been watching you—will you take a seat?" There was barely room for even another chair in the office, which had frosted windows on two sides, and taking her strong grip, I was steered and plopped into it. We seemed too large for the room, too bulky, too loud, like figures clumsily clinging to a wall in a Giotto fresco. Marcella heaved one ample hip onto the corner of the desk and loomed over me protectively. "You've got yourself quite the reputation around here, you know," she began. I felt unaccountably nervous—flattered, yes, but at the same time uneasy. I wasn't clear why I had been summoned to her office. With the announcement of their new position, the annual appearance of a resident acting company on campus, and a fall season that promised no fewer than four exciting productions had come the equally exciting news that six acting fellowships were going to be offered to qualified graduate students to play small parts, cover other roles, and more important, to bear witness to the exciting rehearsal process, something that was mysteriously being denied all other aspiring mortals on campus.

"I understand that I managed to miss your little musical"—she smiled apologetically—"what with our jumping in here with both feet, trying to get all this going at the same time, you know, both Bob and I have had our noses right down to the . . . you know . . . down to the . . . to the whatever. I had no idea you were that talented!" She spread her hands wide before me, like Harry Houdini, or maybe Ben Vereen. "*Land Ahead*, wasn't it? "*Ho!*" I managed. "*Land Ho!* About Columbus. We did a recording, would you like one?" "Sure! You bet," came the reply, "but did that have to mean you weren't going to audition for one of the fellowships? I can't tell you how disappointed I was. I kept expecting to see your name on one of the applications—you're all anyone talks about around here." I knew that wasn't true, but the protest stuck in my throat. She was grinning like she'd just won me in a lottery, and I rather liked it. "Now don't tell me we don't get access to you at all this fall. I won't hear of it!" "Well, what would I do?" I asked innocently. "Well, dammit now, that's more like it!" Marcella said, turning on her heel and making her way back behind the desk to face me.

As the recently appointed heads of the fledgling program, the Schnitzers had their work cut out for them. They had been expected to join the faculty of the ultraconservative Speech and Theatre Department, to help institute the architecture for a new program that would interface with graduate studies on campus as well as to produce first-class theatrical events of such stature as would not only enrich the campus profile but also attract top-level students to the university, rivaling the excitement currently mounting in Minneapolis and elsewhere across the country. The frenzy of publicity surrounding Guthrie's astonishing selection of Minnesota as his newest cultural target had rung like a veritable tocsin—"Step up or get out of our way!" was the message. The Schnitzers had recently been employed by the State Department, guiding a tour of Wilder's *The Skin of Our Teeth* to Scandinavia—as it turns out, a very different production from the televised one I was to create some twenty years later. As a matter of fact, this production had originated in New York as part of a network television series, and it had come replete with a starry cast that included the great American director George Abbott in a rare acting performance as Mr. Antrobus, with Helen Hayes as

Mrs. Antrobus and Mary Martin in the pivotal part of Sabina. That Schnitzer was general manager for this tour, and his wife listed as director, was all that was actually known about the two of them, but it seemed legitimate enough and certainly trumped anything Ann Arbor might have to offer. All too swiftly, references to both Mary Martin and Mr. Abbott vanished, while it seemed that Marcella was incapable of uttering a single sentence without including Miss Hayes's name somewhere in it. They had been, one was led to believe, bosom buddies, practically a vaudeville team, and Marcella had even gone so far as to name a small bedroom in the house she and Schnitzer were renting "the Helen Hayes Suite," although the idea of that great American icon slipping into one of the twin beds it contained on any given night stretched the imagination a bit far. All this theatrical camaraderie might be stimulating, but although the Schnitzers were aggressive in shouldering their new responsibilities, they had as yet no real connection with the student body. From the superfluity of posters and brochures evident everywhere on campus, it was clear they had managed to hire a young group of touring actors called the APA Repertory Company as the centerpiece of their activities. This troupe had been performing in Milwaukee the previous year in a made-to-order repertory of plays that included one or two being offered for the Ann Arbor season, but selling unknown actors to an indifferent student body was going to take more than advertising.

Marcella now leaned back in her chair and crossed her legs at the knee. If she'd had a cigar, she would have lit it as she smiled, warming to her task. "I have the feeling we are destined for each other—you and me," she said. "See, what we're looking for, what we *really* need is our own front man around here—someone who walks the walk and talks the talk, and know what? If you are serious about wanting to lend a hand—that's where you could come in, Buster!" I wasn't certain for a moment if she thought my name was actually Buster, or if she was simply leaping pell-mell into a kind of intimacy I found thrilling, but I could feel what was coming next, and I shrank back into the chair. Again, she was ahead of me: "No no no no no," she said, rising in place and leaning over the desk toward me, "don't get nervous, my God! I realize you are practically a household word around this place, and I wouldn't *dream* of taking advantage of you in any

way—you've got more on your plate than . . . than . . ." and not able
to identify who had more on his plate than me, she charged ahead,
now sure of her goal. "But my God! Why didn't I think of this before? What's wrong with me?" She smacked her forehead with the
heel of her hand, and I was sure they could hear the blow as far away
as the football stadium. "You're heaven-sent, aren't you! Come on!
Tell me the truth! You're my guy!"

What can I say?—I liked her. Yes, it was hard sell, and yes, she
was—what was the word I was about to learn for the first time?—
"hondeling" me . . . but I hadn't experienced a rush like that before,
and her combination of direct address and showbiz savvy was exhilarating. She proposed that all I had to do was appear at mealtimes at
various sorority and fraternity houses armed with her precious brochures and talk up the new company. I could be my own boss, I
didn't have to actually sign up subscribers, and although I might already have missed the first opportunity to sit in on director Ellis
Rabb's rehearsal process, I was far and away the front-runner for
anything that might follow. Mr. Rabb already seemed an implicit fly
in Marcella's ointment, and although I tried my best to find out what
lay behind his determination to keep everyone out of his rehearsal
process, she grew dark and taciturn whenever the subject was raised.

"Eccentric," Marcella muttered with a shrug. "Those guys always
are." Her eyes clouded a little, and a muscle in her jaw kept time with
her flicking foot. But the puzzle remained unsolved. Something felt
wrong. The value of having a professional acting company on campus
would obviously be for students to be able to sit and observe, listen,
see what it was this man did that might engender a frisson of excitement about his arrival in Ann Arbor, even though no one had yet seen
his work. He must have been a student himself at one time—what
would provoke him to operate in such isolation? I was eventually to
learn, but not from Marcella.

She became my coach, and I was eager to please her. I trotted
around all that spring, toting a cardboard sign with glamorous photographs inexplicably featuring Helen Hayes framed in Marcella's trade-
mark hastily smeared glitter. I have no idea how many subscriptions
my personal appearances were good for, but both Schnitzers grinned
with pride whenever they saw me. And spring melted into summer,

and summer produced more activity than I could imagine, first the furor of Bob's and my second musical, *Bartholomew Fair*, and then the much-heralded appearance of APA's first season on campus. It may be significant that other than these two milestones, I cannot remember one single thing of an educational nature that would bear witness to the fact that I was even enrolled as a graduate student at Michigan. Other than the fact that the adviser of my graduate thesis, which was meant to be on Jacobean drama, was a gentle blind professor by the name of Mueschke, whom I persuaded to allow me the latitude of substituting for a written thesis the adaptation of the musical Bob James and I were presenting. *Bartholomew Fair* might have been suggested by Jonson's bawdy play, but I'm afraid it owed more to the spirit of Lerner and Loewe's recent Broadway effort *Camelot* than revelatory scholarship pertinent to Jacobean drama. To be honest, I retained the names of the major characters, but I pretty much threw out a script that I felt was musty and obscure; and if Professor Mueschke noticed this, he seemed content to leave it to my discretion. MUSKET was taking another chance on us, and this time there didn't seem to be a suitable role for me, so I cast a young graduate student I was futilely hoping to woo as the lead and took over the reins as director as well as choreographer instead. No, that's right! It even says so in the program. "Entire production Directed and Choreographed by . . ." Apparently, my devotion to mimicry extended to the world of dance, appropriating Jerome Robbins's exalted billing as well, but it seemed finally less about creating "steps" than about herding a lot of college kids around in spirited ensembles. By this time Bob had become sole composer, as befits a distinguished composition graduate, while retaining his roles as orchestrator and conductor, and I, having taken a more modest view of my compositional gifts, was contented with writing lyrics and the book. And my choreography, of course. An entire busload of my mother's friends came down from Saginaw for the final performance, and although they seemed thrilled with the event, Mother took me aside at one point to confess her disappointment that I didn't appear onstage. It was difficult for her and her friends to understand exactly what it was I did if they couldn't see me romping around in some period getup. With typical candor, she rarely let any opportunity go by to express her preference for *Land Ho!*

Thus I narrowly escaped being the original target of the remark—"I prefer your early work!"

APA arrived for their inaugural season just a month or so later into the very same Lydia Mendelssohn Theatre we had just vacated, hard upon this second premiere, successful if somewhat less flashily received than *Land Ho!* The opening production was to be Sheridan's *The School for Scandal*, followed in swift succession through the late fall by productions of George M. Cohan's farce *The Tavern*, Ibsen's *Ghosts*, directed by and starring Eva Le Gallienne, and *A Penny for a Song*, a little English comedy by John Whiting. Although I was not to find myself in the acting company of that inaugural appearance, I did find myself with my date front and center at the gala performance as reviewer for the campus newspaper, *The Michigan Daily*.

Although one could imagine Marcella squealing with delight at the news that I was to be the evening's reviewer, it could not be laid to her Machiavellian hand. As if my forays into the fields of cabaret entertainment, acting, musical comedy headlining, lyric writing, occasional composing, directing, and now fledgling choreography weren't proof enough of a dervish spinning giddily out of control, I had also been reviewing occasional movies and theater events staged off campus for a while. One of my classmates in playwriting was Edmund White, later to gain celebrity as a writer of protean style and one of the key chroniclers of the emerging gay culture of the twentieth century. On one of our evenings in Ann Arbor as graduate students, I had accompanied Ed to review a minor Tony Curtis movie, and we enjoyed it so much in spite of our expectations that we shared credit for the rave. It was after that review appeared that the paper would occasionally reach out to me whenever Ed or another regular was not available. I can't believe I didn't intentionally toss my hat into some appropriate ring to gain the plum assignment of evaluating APA's premiere of *The School for Scandal*, but whatever else, it would indicate where my best intentions were. They were about to swerve dramatically.

Push the flipper button on your right side! Connect with the ball bearing . . . And . . . !

6

. . . It is now fifty years later. Paint clings stubbornly to canvas; gesso adheres to a wall. But in the blurry, inexact distance, memory shifts. Is there anything more fleeting than performance? Anything that depends more on individual perception, a point of view, a fresh receptor? The house lights dim. Is the curtain up or down? Hard to recall. So the first thing one remembers is sound: a fusillade of Scarlatti as the house is dimming, a clattering of silvery harpsichord sticks falling from a glittering height, and out of the darkness . . .

We must establish that university theater—mid-twentieth-century university theater—was anything but experimental. There was a space; the space was the stage house, usually hung with fabric we call "blacks" but that simply separated "onstage" from "offstage." And whenever you put actors onto the stage, they were pretty much distributed left to right, to fill up that space. Sometime later in the century a brilliant Englishman named Peter Brook would define that as "The Empty Space," but not yet. Nothing so fancy here in Ann Arbor. Nothing too imaginative on the stage of the Lydia Mendelssohn Theatre. Tell the story. Put the actors where they can be seen. "Don't bump into the furniture."

From out of the darkness a woman is walking downstage, partially clothed: she is in a powdered gray and black wig, her corset visible, wearing pumps, an open negligee, lace draped around her shoulders, crinolines and stockings below, and she is accompanied by servants of the period in mobcaps and aprons, in breeches and buckles, carrying things—a small table, a mirror, stools and chairs, jars of makeup and pots of crimson rouge. They stop and face us;

they are standing on a platform—it appears to be a large pentagon, raked downstage to upstage with a step up at the top. Across the front of this step one can pull a series of curtains painted to represent various interiors—Sir Peter Teazle's library, Joseph Surface's drawing room, Charles Surface's home, a pub. The curtains are on rings, and the rings hang on invisible wires that stretch across the stage.

There are servants, as I say: these are my classmates—Barbara Sittig, Rod Bladel, and others, graduate students of the university's Professional Theatre Program—who have been awarded the hotly contested fellowships. They are, for the most part, the ones carrying tables, mirrors, and such, and from time to time, behind a scrim contained within the parameters of the pentagon upon which the play is enacted, they pause, kneel on the chairs, gossip into each other's ears, giggle, and depart—and when they have departed, a curtain has been pulled, chairs have been rearranged, gossip has been exchanged, and a new location and a new scene has effortlessly appeared.

I had never seen anything like it in my life.

But now, as the servants stand attentively looking at us, the woman speaks: she is Lady Sneerwell, and in this case, she is being played by an actress I have never seen before—Cavada Humphrey.

"A School for Scandal!" she begins by addressing us in the audience in mezzo richness, "Tell me, I beseech you / Need you a school, this modish art to teach you?" And out it poured, sexy, vibrant, comfortable, immediate, a kind of period piece I had never imagined, neither artificial nor stilted but fresh, direct, packing a terrific wallop balanced in both comprehension and comedy. Sir Peter was Will Geer, who later attained television immortality as Grandpa Walton, and Mrs. Candour, pouty, plush, and giddily distracted, was Enid Markey, who had been the very first Jane in the early Tarzan movies. Page Johnson as Snake, Clayton Corzatte as Charles, David Hicks as Sir Oliver, Keene Curtis as Backbite, all in the early stages of careers that would find their way to Broadway, to the regional markets, to film and television. Principal among them were Rosemary Harris as Lady Teazle, and Ellis Rabb, artistic director of the APA Repertory and director of this particular production, as Joseph Surface.

Ellis made his entrance into the first scene stalking directly across the farthest downstage path possible, taking two steps for every word as he approached Lady Sneerwell: "My . . . dear . . . Lady . . . Sneer . . . well, . . . how . . . d'you do . . . today?" His mouth was curled in a sour little smile, his hand already outstretched for hers, and if a university audience had been disposed to applaud the entrance, unfamiliar with the actor and unused to such a gesture, this entrance would not afford the opportunity. He was tall, lithe, graceful, with the hint of dim pomposity that set him up as someone ripe for a fall. He was utterly comfortable in this artificial society, with a voice rich and plummy, a born comedian. I liked him immediately, but his wasn't quite the explosion Miss Harris achieved in the following scene.

More Scarlatti, more servants, a beautifully choreographed transition of people exiting, furniture swiftly being rearranged, and as the actors cleared, she swept through a center door following a parade of servants carrying beautifully wrapped packages. Her hair was raspberry, a wig obviously, but Midwestern university budgets had limited access to such outrageous colors: I was convinced that Rosemary Harris had strawberry-red hair and that the designers had surrendered to the fact and designed the entire production around it rather than compromise her beauty. Behind her stumped Will Geer, exasperated, wheezing out his opening lines: "Lady Teazle, Lady Teazle, I'll not bear it!" She plucked a small hatbox from the hands of the nearest servant and plopped down on a bench, small red satin slippers peeping out from under her skirts, with laughter fairly bubbling out of her throat: "Sir Peter, Sir Peter, you may bear it or not, as you please; but I ought to have my own way in everything, and, what's more, I will, too." There was a country lilt to her speech, brashness in her r's, and she wrinkled her nose irresistibly. She had it all— beauty, poise, the assurance, the attack, the trick of broken laughter captured somewhere within her voice . . . this was glamour, pure and simple.

They played with a dizzying swiftness, sure of their gestures, their intentions, the decorated language, and we were brought smack up against Restoration playing as it should be played, laughing long and hard as the play tore by. Finally came the great screen scene, one of the true comic gems in all dramatic literature. There was nothing fancy, nothing posh about Will Geer, that most American of actors. That he identified with the spirit, taste, and relish of Walt Whitman was evident in every aspect of his personality, onstage or off, an actor who had come through the punishing experience of being blacklisted by the House Un-American Activities Committee in the fifties for his leftist leanings during the Depression, then pulled from complete obscurity by John Houseman for his Stratford, Connecticut, seasons. Will had managed to survive that devastating time by working as a gardener. Houseman himself had employed him, a yard laborer when he could not find work as an actor, and now, like some aging Johnny Appleseed, wherever and whenever he found his next employment, he spent his spare time digging around the perimeters of theaters, putting into the soil all the plants and flowers named in the Shakespeare canon. Here onstage he was gruff, he was raw, he panted and huffed his way through text, but he was irresistible, and a roaring delight as he teased about the existence of a "little French milliner" secreted behind Joseph Surface's screen. Tension built to an incendiary pitch until Will managed to pull down the screen at the very moment Ellis reentered to confront them and to find the humiliated, scarlet-faced Miss Harris exposed. The laughter and applause from the audience at this phenomenal moment was deafening. The actors froze in place as the ovation built, and through the sustained laughter one could hear Clayton Corzatte braying Charles's line, "Lady Teazle, by all that's wonderful!" More laughter. And as it subsided, Will Geer topped it with "Lady Teazle, by all that's *damnable!*" Another roar.

Charles Surface has a delicious paragraph in which he invites one after another of the participants to comment upon the action and justify themselves, which, naturally, none of them can do, and after wrapping it all up before departing, Corzatte's Charles left the three stranded actors to their consequences.

Ellis swallowed and softly began: "Sir Peter . . ."—huge laugh . . . —"notwithstanding—I confess—that appearances are against me . . ."— another, even longer laugh, after which he staggered, stumbled, hurled himself through a pathetic and disastrous explanation ending with "and this, you may depend on it, is the whole truth of the matter."

It wasn't, of course, and Miss Harris stepped elegantly forward, her eyes lowered, to clear everything away with simple candor, humility, and honest shame. The scene, immaculately done by everyone, proved conclusively how fresh and direct great literature can be when it is simply and truly honored. But the best was still to come.

At the conclusion of the play is an epilogue written not by Sheridan himself but by a "Mr. Coleman," one of the famed actor-managers of the day. In it Lady Teazle graciously allows her fellow actors to withdraw into the wings, then steps down to address us, as, indeed, Lady Sneerwell had done with the prologue at the beginning of the evening. Rosemary Harris, holding a large straw hat in her hand, rose to the occasion in every sense of the word. Smiling up into the waiting house, she began:

> I, who was late so volatile and gay,
> Like a trade-wind must now blow all one way,
> Bend all my cares, my studies, and my vows,
> To one . . . dull . . . rusty weathercock—my spouse!
> So wills our virtuous bard— . . .

I have always believed that along with the seminal experiences of living—childbirth, the death of a parent or a loved one, falling in love or the first experience of a sexual nature—the confrontation with a great performer ranks as indelibly as circular rings that mark a tree's growth. We each remember specific historic moments in our lives that stand out from our parade of days—where we were when we learned of Kennedy's death, or where we sat when we watched the unimaginable horror of 9/11. But there are simpler moments that register just as vividly as the surprise of a butterfly alighting briefly on one's finger, or blurting out a defense of Wordsworth; with performances, it can be the shock of Callas or Merman or even Jolson at their searing height. Whatever guise in which it comes, one is changed for all time, and there is no turning back. Four-thirty in the afternoon at Carnegie Hall, listening to Horowitz? You don't recover. For me, Rosemary Harris reciting the epilogue to *Scandal* is one such moment. She swooped, she soared, she caressed the words, built them impossibly high, brought them down to earth like music. I cannot do this myself, but all these years later, I can, in reflection, hear and even approximate those phrases as she laid them before us. There was laughter and, for me, tears pouring down my face. I couldn't believe

the joy I felt as she came to the conclusion, speaking directly to each
of us:

"Blessed were the fair like you; her faults who stopped
And closed her follies when the curtain dropped!
No more . . . in vice OR error to engage, . . .
Or play the fool . . . at large . . ."

. . . and here she raises her arms to the balcony, beaming on the
entire audience, drawing the words out almost impossibly long . . .
"on life's . . . [she lifts her voice rising on tiptoe for the next word] . . .
great . . . [the word is pushed to the top of her register as her arms
widen, and then, as she sinks to the floor in a curtsy lowering her
face nearly to the floor, she sighs the very last word] . . . stage."

The resulting applause was a thunderclap, and she reached immediately left and right for the company to join her in a swirling curtain
call with actors sweeping up and down the stage in fours and fives,
the next group coming down between the departing players as they
moved away. We were dumbfounded. This was beyond all expectation. We, at the University of Michigan in Ann Arbor, theatrically
speaking, had arrived!

There was a lesson here, if any of us had been able to unscramble
it in the flood of elation and excitement that followed, a lesson Guthrie himself would have known and appreciated, a lesson even Ellis
Rabb would have had to acknowledge. Rosemary Harris, born in In-
dia and raised in England, had trained at RADA, the Royal Academy
of Dramatic Art, as a student, and her great teacher there was a stern,
idiosyncratic woman named Mary Duff, who, when I finally had the
opportunity to meet her, wore a jet black National Health wig and
was as flinty and exacting as a military drill instructor. This very epilogue that had so devastated me was the result of Mary Duff's specific orchestration. Every gesture, every word, every inflection had
been drummed into Rosemary's ear and mind by a veritable martinet
that knew precisely the value of the spoken voice, the power of the
operative word, the architecture of written speech. This was no accident of performing, no burst of improvisatory creative genius alone,
although few actors in my experience have commanded the technique

and clarity of Miss Harris: this was a perfect illustration of what it meant to be born into, trained within, and instructed in the apotheosis of craft—an actor, liberated. We were looking at the living example of Guthrie's edict: without the power, experience, and familiarity with the world's greatest works, an actor remains grounded, unable to scale the heights.

We swam into the reception in one of the larger rooms of the Women's League, the members of the faculty and the Speech and Theatre Department, the "insiders," as it were, the invited, after the rest had left the Mendelssohn. I remained in a state of suspension. What on earth could I possibly write in a review that wouldn't seem as if I had been idiotically brainwashed by what I had seen. I spotted my beloved acting teacher, Claribel Baird, and her husband, William Halstead, the chairman of the department. Claribel stood as usual, a cigarette in her expressive fingers, a woman in her late sixties at the time for whom the epithet "handsome" was invented. She had a prominent aquiline nose and wore her hair, steel gray, swept into two white waves that moved back from her brow, accentuating that nose. She was inspiration personified, someone for whom one longed to be good enough and yet who never for a moment allowed her standards to shift. She was a great teacher—of the likes of James Earl Jones and on down the line. If I was no great shakes as an actor in her classes, at least I wore her down over the years to become something better— her friend.

She now greeted me and my date with customary warmth, raising her arms to me as she did. "Marvelous, didn't you think? Oh, my, we thought it was thrilling." She waved her cigarette in the direction of Halstead, who, as usual, was looking over everyone's head as if searching for some better place to land. "Bill and I saw them a year ago in Milwaukee, aren't they splendid?" I pulled her aside, leaving my date and the professor staring at each other, as if across a body of water. "I'm the reviewer, Claribel," I began breathlessly. "I'm doing the review for the *Daily!*" "Oh, *good!*" came the reply. "What fun you'll have!" "Yes, I said, "but I can't just write a string of superlatives, can I?" Then, producing my little notepad, I brought up the only negative thought I could find. "I didn't care for Corzatte all that much," I began. "That accent! Is it Texas? I mean, he's so—" but she cut me off.

"Oh, Bill and I think he's amazing!" she countered. "The attack, the clarity, the precision! Oh, no, he's first-rate, no question about that." She looked over at her husband, realizing she would be wise to rescue him, and began to move away. Ellis and Rosemary were just entering the room at the far end, and all eyes were turning to them. "Was there anything you didn't like?" I asked pathetically. And as she moved off, she said over her shoulder, "No, not really, although it was odd to see the Sneerwell withdrawing in the second half—so self-conscious, didn't you think?"

My review ran the next day, a complete rave with the single exception of my mentioning that "it was curious to see Lady Sneerwell seem to withdraw in the second act . . ." Of Rabb and Harris, I had indeed to reach for enough superlatives. In one of the early scenes, Ellis had worn a floor-length dressing gown of green brocade, and I mentioned that he had stalked the stage "like an eighteenth-century cucumber." It was the sort of thing university reviews often thought clever reporting, and Ellis never let me forget it.

But the fat was in the fire now, and I began seriously to long for some inside glimpse of this work process, these actors, this director. Although I didn't review the rest of the season, it continued to be extremely impressive. *The Tavern*, a classic farce by George M. Cohan, was the exact opposite of the *Scandal* experience. Flimsy canvas scenery, rendered by the designer Lloyd Burlingame in the fond, period style of early Americana, a single room, all highly melodramatic and near camp. This exaggerated farce-playing reached its apogee when Miss Harris, lisping around the stage outrageously as Miss Virginia, fluttered too close to the painted fire and furiously had to beat out the imaginary flames at her hemline. Ellis Rabb was the Vagabond, played originally by George Grizzard when APA had presented an off-Broadway season at the tiny Folksbiene Playhouse in New York (now the National Yiddish Theatre). But Grizzard, ironically, was absent from APA at the time, having been invited by Guthrie to open his inaugural season in Minneapolis playing Hamlet, and Henry V. Rabb was virtuosic in his affectionate portrait of a period leading man, all passion and romance. Anne Meacham, who had scored recent success off-Broadway in a flashy revival of *Hedda Gabler*, was Violet, the demented mystery woman, and Joanna Roos, who Marcella insisted was the "next Helen Hayes," was the wife of the governor, with the rest of the company comfortable and secure on American soil. Then came a sotto voce production of Ibsen's *Ghosts*, directed and led by Le Gallienne herself, who offered an historic link by reprising one of her own Civic Repertory roles, Mrs. Alving, in her own translation. She spoke in the most remarkably still and effortless voice imaginable, just barely audible, so that one had the feeling of leaning forward all evening to hear a performance of intelligence and delicacy that demanded one pay attention. The final effort, *A Penny for a Song*, was a bit of disappointing period whimsy done to showcase the charm of Will Geer in which Miss Meacham was utterly miscast as the dewy ingénue Dorcas, exhibiting all the warmth of a trained cobra. One was altogether able to understand the strengths and the limitations of repertory casting—often an exceptional actor in one production could come up short in another role, whereas a more limited talent might be able to slip in and out of a variety of roles most convincingly, without appearing remotely artificial.

The season was an unqualified success—and the enthusiasm for the company led by Miss Harris and Mr. Rabb was the talk of the campus. The Schnitzers were mightily relieved, and plans were immediately laid for the winter repertory after the first of the year, during which the company would present three Shakespeares—the *Midsummer Night's Dream* that had first drawn the Schnitzers' initial interest in Milwaukee, then a new production of *Richard II* followed by a modern dress production of *The Merchant of Venice*. What was of more significance to me, the company's ranks would have to swell considerably to offer these larger-cast efforts, so more local actors were to be screened.

I had been primarily distracted all fall by the assurance that Bob James and I were destined for a major career writing for the musical theater on Broadway. The consecutive creation of two successful musical projects—*Land Ho!* and *Bartholomew Fair*—just one year apart had not only garnered a BMI Award for Best Collegiate Musical for the former, but had brought us to the attention of an actual New York agent, Theron Raines, and a music publisher, Edwin H. Morris & Co., who had on their roster the likes of Jerry Herman, among others. *Bartholomew Fair* saw the return of Bob's and my essential third,

Judy Heric, who had been student teaching and now was taking on the leading role of Grace Wellborn in *Bartholomew Fair*, and taking on Bob as well, since they had become engaged. They were to be married the following year with me as best man, after which Bob was enrolling in the six-month program of active duty to fulfill his obligation to the draft. I kept putting off having to face such a looming confrontation myself by teaching at the university, which removed me, for the time being, from the draft. But sooner or later . . . I knew proclaiming myself to be homosexual would take care of that problem once and for all, but with family connections to the Saginaw draft board, I couldn't face that defining reality—and my mother— yet. I wasn't ready, and I wasn't that confident. In addition, Bob's professional commitment to pursue our writing as a team, as opposed to following his natural bent as an emerging young jazz artist, was something I had to take with a sense of responsibility. He had won top honors at the Collegiate Jazz Festival with his own trio the previous year, bringing him to the attention of Quincy Jones, but here he was, still insisting we identify the perfect material for our Broadway debut. All he had to do was fulfill his obligation to military service. I, on the other hand, had bade farewell to my cabaret status at the Delt House, but what of the siren call of this acting company?

Was I to be a writer, or should I submit to the lure of this company? The university's prestigious Avery Hopwood Awards for Fiction and Drama had recently been announced, with my comedy, *A Matter of Style*, getting second dramatic honors. I had written the play as an arrogant response to a member of Ed White's and my playwriting class, Milan Stitt, who years later had a commercial success with *The Runner Stumbles*. Milan had written a play that contained both an actress and an enormous staircase without taking proper advantage, I thought, of either one. I felt it my obligation to set the record straight. The resulting farce, suggested by the career of actress Irene Dunne, who left show business to join the United Nations, had its principal parts written with Claribel Baird and Marcella Cisney shamelessly in mind. The two women did me the honor of reading the script and, duly flattered, felt no further obligation. The Speech Department, however, had already announced a production of this play for the following spring, so with the authorship of two musicals as well, my writing career was certainly looking up. I kept telling everyone that I was "the most produced student writer since Arthur Miller" with no idea whether that was true. It certainly *felt* true! Be that as it may, the Schnitzers insisted on sending me up for yet another audition for the coming Shakespeare season, with the implication that it was just a matter of my showing up.

"Are you nuts?" Marcella said to me as she ushered me down the main corridor of the Women's League to her tiny office. She had her enameled fingernails securely into my left shoulder and was steering me like a gondola. "Seriously! This is the opportunity of a lifetime. How many of these positions do you think are going to come up for grabs? Look what you've done for these people! For the program alone!! They *owe* you a goddamn position—I told Bob you shouldn't even have to read!" "Really?" I said, impressed despite my resolve to pass. "What did Mr. Rabb say?" We swung around the corner nearest her office. "What does he ever say?" she sniffed impatiently. "We don't talk all that much these days. I'm too busy." She muttered something else under her breath that I missed as she shoved me ahead of her. "You get over there, Buster!" she said over her shoulder, turning into the door where a phone was ringing. "It's yours for the taking, I'm telling you it is!"

In one way, I didn't have much of a leg to stand on, socially speaking, since I hadn't had more than an oblique introduction to Ellis by this time. There was an occasion when the "cream," let's call it, of the department had been huddled together for an initial presentation, like clumsy calves at a State Fair judging. But Ellis's lofty acknowledgment might have been lifted from the Royal Family itself: "Howjado" was the universal passing remark. And whenever I went to the call-board outside of Professor Halstead's office, my name somehow never appeared. So the fellowship wasn't exactly "for the taking," and the amazing thing is the degree to which I didn't get it. Well, you know, chemistry, right? Instant attraction. Love at first sight. Or the opposite. Ellis Rabb, it appeared, found me quite resistible. Repeatedly. And yet it didn't penetrate. I'm trying to recall just how many times I stood up before him and did my audition. But I can really remember only one in particular.

7

Emerging from the Seventh Avenue subway at Sheridan Square, the uninitiated might become confused, as the oblique path the avenue makes rushing south intersects not only Sheridan Square, but several other streets going off at odd angles. Christopher Street is the most famous one, having been immortalized not only in a song in Leonard Bernstein's musical *Wonderful Town*, but also as the crossroads of emerging gay culture in New York during the sixties. Today Number 77 Christopher Street looks pretty much as it did—a chipped enameled door tucked near the eastern end of the block—as when I presented myself for one more audition for Ellis Rabb. Bundled up against the raw January cold, I peered at the list of names over the buzzer. "Rabb/Harris" was in the middle, and I pushed the button and waited for an answer. Did I think this encounter might be different? Well, at least it was New York this time, not Ann Arbor. And there was to be no one else present but me.

The buzzer before me engaged, and I pushed open the door. "Come on, Speed," came a coaxing voice from above. "You can do it, love—come on!" and down the staircase before me came Rosemary Harris, dressed in a navy pea jacket with a magenta knitted angora hat and matching gloves. Just behind her, bumping his way down the four steep flights, thumped an elderly dachshund named Speed, the first of a procession of Ellis's dogs I was to know over the years. As she swept Speed up in her arms, she smiled and waved vaguely at the staircase behind her, saying, "Ellis is up there waiting. Good luck!" whereupon the door closed behind her and she and Speed vanished.

"Keep climbing, it's on the fourth!" came the impressive voice from above. I looked up to see a sleeve disappear from view as a phone rang somewhere in the distance, and I trudged up the steep flights. The door stood open, and from the depths I heard a one-sided conversation going on. I walked into the vestibule hung with coats, scarves, and hats on pegs and hooks along both sides of the bathroom. To my right ran a short hallway into a dark bedroom from which I could hear the voice, and to my left was a wide archway opening into a lovely high-ceilinged room with tall windows facing the street below. There was a fireplace with a delicate white carved mantelpiece, a white couch with comfortable chairs scattered about, and nearest the windows, a round marble table with the remnants of breakfast still upon it, coffee cups, crumbs, and an overflowing ashtray. The small kitchen was out of sight to the left, and as I moved into the living room for a better look, the same voice came from behind me. "I am so sorry," it said, "that fucking telephone never stops . . ." Ellis extended his hand to me as if we'd never met. "Howdjado," he offered in his patented Southern style, "it's so good of you to do this— your Christmas break and everything." I murmured something idiotic, as if midwinter trips to New York were an everyday occurrence, and as I slipped off my coat, he plunged straight ahead. No social amenities, it seemed. "What were you going to do?" He meant my audition, and this time, believe me, I was ready. "Benedick in the orchard," I replied, and, with a grim little nod he lit a cigarette and sank down into the nearest white armchair, folding his legs beneath him. In spite of the fact that it was the dead of winter, he was barefoot, wearing cotton drawstring pants that might have served as pajamas and a knitted boatneck sweater with ragged sleeves that he continually pushed up. He fixed me with narrowed eyes, pulling at the cigarette and studying me like a specimen in a lab, pursing his lips, folding his arms, and fluffing up his head of frizzy hair at the back. There was evidence of dandruff about his shoulders, but I averted my gaze, and since there were apparently to be no more formalities to be enjoyed, I stood back and let it fly.

"Ha! Ha! Ha! Ha!" I began, hearing myself bray out a mindless laugh, as inexperienced actors tend to do when pretending to relax. "I do much wonder how one man, seeing how much another man is a fool when he dedicates his behaviors to love . . ." This endless sentence is not half over: the need for a lungful of breath at this point had proven to be my undoing in acting classes, and determined to conquer it, I had adopted it as my classical piece once I mastered the breathing. ". . . will become the argument of his own scorn by falling in love!" Somewhere in the apartment the phone rang once again. Ellis unfolded without a thought, rose, and, trailing a cloud of cigarette smoke, walked directly out of the room and into the bedroom beyond without so much as a backward glance. "And such a man is Claudio," I found myself continuing. What else was I to do? He had not put up a hand to stop me, nor interrupted me, nor signaled me in any way. Was I to proceed? What was the appropriate response? Blindly I lurched ahead, only slightly louder, in case he couldn't hear me from the depths: "I have known where there was no music in him . . ." The ringing had stopped, and a voice I had to identify as Ellis's was again speaking quietly to someone at the other end. Still, my eyes wandering around the room in a kind of blind panic, I went insanely on: ". . . but the drum and the fife, and now would he rather hear the tabor and the pipe." Maybe this was a test! I found myself thinking. What would any bona fide professional do, should his audience simply get up and walk out? Quit? No way! He would be unshaken, unyielding, right? He would serve the goddamn play above all—even if a fire were raging! *That's* the kind of actor Ellis Rabb was looking for! My mind pursued this pathetic rabbit of a thought while my tongue charged on, and I lifted my voice for emphasis so quite honestly, anyone in the apartment building might easily hear. "I have known when he would walk ten mile afoot to see a good armor . . ."

I nailed it! I knew I did. I sold it! The room fairly reverberated to my vigorous recitation, the couch and the chairs stunned into mute appreciation. There was no stopping this kid. I was, whatever else you might say, professional down to my very toes. And anyway, there was no turning back now. I might be auditioning for an empty room, all right, but goddammit, I gave that room my best shot! I squinted in the direction of the darkened bedroom. "Ha. The Prince and Monsieur Love," I concluded confidently, "I will hide me in the arbor," and as if on cue, Ellis walked back into the room and plopped down in his chair. He turned without so much as the blink of an eye, snuffed out his cigarette in the nearest ashtray, and said sweetly, "And what else did you bring?"

What are the specific tumblers that must fall into sequence for one person to relate to another? Do we ever recognize them? This little comic scene had a predecessor years earlier, as I was later to be told, for when applicants auditioned for Carnegie Tech in those years, they, too, had to trot out their wares for the assembled faculty to be reviewed, and, as is usual, there was a three-minute limit on whatever piece was chosen. When Ellis Rabb, at eighteen years of age, presented his credentials to the professors, having chosen the opening soliloquy from the final act of *Richard II* as his audition, the bell went off not once, not twice, but three times before that Southern accent could be effectively silenced. "Mr. Rabb! . . . Mr. Rabb! . . . please, Mr. Rabb! . . . we've heard *quite* enough, I assure you! . . ."

Ellis didn't share that fact with me in his living room on Christopher Street on that occasion. Some years later, I sat at another dining table of his, on Riverside Drive, among four or five close friends, when he chose to tell the anecdote himself, sparing neither the details nor his nasal, whining, hilarious Tennessee accent, a mini-performance that made us howl. I looked down the table wondering whether he might realize the similarity to my own experience and invite me to join in. But the look he gave was familiar, Ellis reveling in his own legend. Privately I was coming to realize that we might have more in common than we were ready to acknowledge.

8

"Darling! Over here!" I was crossing through the corridor of the Frieze Building, where I had just taught one of my acting seminars in the late fall. It was the policy of the department to help various gradu-ates' financial positions by offering occasional sections of acting courses to supplement their incomes. It wasn't much, but it was some-thing, and at the very least it was keeping me at arm's length from the oppressive threat of the draft. Claribel Baird stood just outside her classroom, sneaking a cigarette before her Greek Oral Interp class, furtively signaling me. One was allowed to smoke in those days any-where in public buildings or even in a corridor, but not inside the actual classroom. Claribel's hands, emaciated with their tracery of blue veins, betrayed the actual age her vibrant spirit and her Roman profile didn't, and whenever she stuck a cigarette between two bony fingers and tipped her head back briefly to inhale and exhale smoke in a less offensive direction, she looked like an exotic bird of prey, with half-lidded eyes, distracted but alert.

"We're all going to help out," she began cryptically. "All of us in the department—even me! I'm the Prince of Aragon's mother, can you stand it? In a *wheelchair!*" She turned and laughed, bending slightly from the waist to discreetly flick her ash into a corner. I had no idea what she was talking about and asked for clarification. "They can't find enough actors for *Merchant,*" she went on, stubbing out the cigarette on the stone floor before her. "Well, how could they?" She straight-ened up with sudden military precision and stuffed the butt into her Kleenex. "Students can't be expected to compete on that level. So I volunteered. I'm awfully sorry it isn't Robb directing"—for about the

Left to right: Professor William Halstead; his wife, Professor Claribel Baird; and me. Ann Arbor, 1973. (Collection of the author)

first two years of the company's residency, Claribel elegantly mispro-nounced Ellis's last name—"but we simply must give them support. So I volunteered you, too!" She gave a little laugh and waved me off, turning to reenter the classroom. "But, Claribel," I protested, "I'm pretty sure he doesn't want—" She cut me off: "Thursday at two. The director is Baldridge, I think his name is. See you there. It'll be such fun!" and she was gone, closing the door behind her.

The initial furor of APA's impact had subsided to some degree, and although I had enjoyed their autumn season, I had not seriously thought much about the upcoming festival. Once again, Ellis had passed on my most recent audition, and I had buried any disappoint-ment in a flurry of other activities. "Jack," my parents, my teachers, my endless advisers had always beseeched. "Can't you do just one thing at a time? Finish what you've started, for crying out loud . . . *then* go on to something else!" I was never good at this, it didn't make sense, frankly. Why would anyone confine himself to a single activity when multitasking was so much more interesting? And since I've always believed myself to be good at juggling activities—I find it re-freshing—I don't believe I've ever felt bored in my life. That might have something to do with it.

But as requested, I showed up the following Thursday afternoon for the interview. Richard Baldridge, an intelligent, haunted individual who leaped to his death from a window in the Wellington Hotel some four or five years later, served APA in its earliest phase as basically a dramaturge, although the term was not in use in the sixties. No one did research for a director but the director—it was part of the job description. If the play was set in an unfamiliar period or place, one went to the library and read up on it before rehearsals began. A director was expected to know. Baldridge was not a professional director, but someone with the unique talent for discovering lost plays and unusual authors, an "ideas man," being himself multitalented. *The Tavern*, for example, was a play he insisted Ellis consider, trapping him one summer afternoon in a field and forcing him to hear it read aloud; now, here in Ann Arbor, where budgets were increasingly an issue, he helped create period costumes for the production of *Richard II* out of inexpensive felt, hot-gluing gold designs on them. The clothes were rigid, stiff, and hot, to be sure, but they were also beautiful. With Ellis distracted with directing *Dream* and trying to learn the role of Richard II, he needed time to himself. Baldridge also further eased the strain on the budget by conceiving a modern dress production of *The Merchant of Venice*, inspired by Fellini's *La Dolce Vita*. Period productions are costly; modern dress ones can be more easily budgeted. Over the years, many attempts at modernizing *Merchant* have been tried by many directors and designers, but to my knowledge, this was the first to cross-reference the mores of Fellini's Italy. The point, of course, was that Christians and Jews were both reprehensible, which is textually valid. The play is, among other things, about the corruption of love by money, and in Baldridge's version, Shylock, portrayed by Paul Sparer, was nothing less than a Rothschild, rich, elegant, more refined than anyone else onstage, elevated in status above all but Antonio. It was an original approach, and one that Ellis himself was to attempt at least twice over the following years—once for Bill Ball's ACT company in San Francisco, with Michael Learned as Portia, Ken Ruta as Antonio, and Peter Donat as Shylock, and finally at Lincoln Center with Rosemary Harris as Portia, Sydney Walker as Shylock, Phil Bosco as Antonio, and Christopher Walken as Bassanio.

I had left my interview with Baldridge as confused as I began it. Looking me over briefly, he asked if I knew any French. I responded that I could manage; I had taken French in high school, and one semester at the university, but counted among my closest friends a fraternity brother who had majored in French, whose constant confidante was a Belgian diamond heiress; they spent hours speaking French over coffee and insisted I do the same. Baldridge smiled grimly. "Don't worry about it," he said, "we'll just play it by ear." I racked my brain—I couldn't recall any French passages in *Merchant*, and what on earth did "playing it by ear" mean? He offered me the role of Monsieur LeBeau, thrusting a paperback copy of the play into my hand, and told me to show up at one o'clock on Tuesday afternoon. Before I could inquire further, I found myself out the door, frantically thumbing through the script. I couldn't for the life of me remember a character named LeBeau. Who was French in *Merchant of Venice*, anyway? Weren't they all Italians? I searched the dramatis personae in vain, and only later, going line by line, did I locate the following passage:

NERISSA: What think you of the French Count, Monsieur LeBeau?
PORTIA: Well, God made him for a man, so let him pass for one . . .

Oh, dear. This was ominous. Not only did Monsieur LeBeau have no lines in the scene, but the inference was impossible to ignore. I stared into the mirror. What had Mr. Baldridge seen?

I presented myself in the small arena theater below Trueblood Auditorium in the Frieze Building at one o'clock the following Tuesday. APA was using the space to rehearse, and members of the company stood around in small groups, chatting, drinking coffee, sharing cigarettes, with the ease of familiar colleagues. Those of us from the department, knowing no one else, collected on the other side of the room. I looked around. Claribel was nowhere to be seen. I wasn't certain what that indicated, but since her character was to be confined to a wheelchair, and there was no trace of "the mother of the

Prince of Aragon" listed anywhere in the dramatis personae either, perhaps the smallness of the part measured against her teaching load had earned her a special dispensation.

General introductions were made—Baldridge thanked us for showing up and asked us to identify ourselves, but after we did so, to a smattering of polite applause, no one of the acting company responded in kind. It was some time before I could identify all the unknown faces—Sydney Walker as Antonio, Paul Sparer as Shylock, Laurinda Barrett as Nerissa, Will Geer as Old Gobbo, his daughter, Ellen Geer, as Jessica, her husband, Ed Flanders, as Launcelot Gobbo, Keene Curtis as Salario, and so on, including, of course, Rosemary Harris as Portia. She sat away from the company wearing a cotton smock with a turtleneck beneath, the sleeves pushed up, and her hair, prematurely graying, pulled back and fastened with a rubber band. She was hunkered down on a stool, staring into her script. On her knee was a floppy straw hat which at one point she moved to her head, tucking the grim little ponytail up underneath. She seemed altogether ordinary, no trace of the glamorous, raspberry-tressed Lady Teazle anywhere; she might easily have been another teaching associate.

There was some initial business to do before we were to begin blocking, and Baldridge assigned a few lines to some of us, which justified our presence. I was pleased to be given a small exchange with Miss Harris, which I dutifully committed to memory on the spot. Then Baldridge began to explain the scene and his concept of the play. We were all swept up by the brave modernity of his ideas. He wanted Portia's suitors to have been hanging around Belmont for ages, waiting for a judgment while sponging off her generosity. He stood in the middle of the rehearsal space, a pencil in one hand, his script in the other, as the extras were sorted through and briefly described— the German needed to be boorish and clumsy, dressed in morning clothes to signify his wealth; the Englishman, as suggested by the text, drunk; and Monsieur LeBeau, of course, the last to be described, was going to be, well, flashy.

"Mr. O'Brien, you will wear, I think, something like white clam-diggers, barefoot, of course, maybe one of those happi coats, I believe they are called." He pointed to a large carton where various props and rehearsal clothes had already been collected. I could see the sleeve of an orange linen garment draped over one edge of the box. "When Miss Barrett mentions you, be standing with the others at the top of this staircase, and then chatter in French—oh, anything, you know, just make it up!—and run down the stairs to Miss Harris, grab that hat she's wearing, do a little dance and finish about here at the drinks cart where you can pour yourself a Scotch. Oh, yes, and then just pout."

There was utter silence from everyone in the room. "Would you mind?" he said, peering down at his clipboard. I swallowed. "You mean now? Right now?" I said in a small voice. "If you would," he replied, moving away. "Laurinda, cue him, will you? and we can see how it goes."

My face stung. Every eye in the room was glued to me, and the silence was absolute. Baldridge sat down in a metal chair with a sigh, tossed his script on the floor, and rocked back on the chair legs to watch me, his hands clasped behind his head. I didn't know what to do, where to look, how to even follow the slender thread of consciousness I clung to. I could distinguish nothing but the thumping of my own heart as I put my head down and walked over the taped surface to where the others were clustered, as if on a raised balcony. They moved a bit away from me, as if I might be a carrying a rare disease.

I dimly heard Laurinda Barrett's cue. "What think you of Monsieur LeBeau?" she offered timidly, and I took a brief breath and plunged off, skittering down the taped indication of a staircase, "Mais, qu'est-ce que tu penses, qu'est-ce que tu fais, ma chouchou à la crème," I began shrilly, "et dites donc! pourquoi un chapeau comme ça? Ç'est tout à fait affreux!" I plucked the hat off the head of the open-mouthed Rosemary, turned my back with a little kick, and, as had been suggested, tangoed over to the drink cart for a Scotch before snapping an icy moue over one shoulder.

There was an intake of breath from the crowd, as if they'd just witnessed the Hindenburg bursting into flames; then the room broke into applause, laughs, and cheers. Through this came the clarion voice of Miss Harris: "God made him for a man, so let him pass for one," she sighed, and again, laughter rocked the room.

Talk about your trial by fire! Keene Curtis told me years later they loved me on sight. No one could believe that Baldridge would be so insensitive, to say nothing of cruel, to toss a such a piece of

Ellis and Speed, the first great theater dog I was to encounter, in a list that would eventually include Eva Le Gallienne's Yorkie, Nana; the Housemans' Royal Standard Poodle, Sam; and eventually my own Norwiches, Pumpkin, Trudge, and Winston. (Robert Alan Gold)

business to a teaching fellow in full view of the entire professional company. But he did. And it appears that I tossed it right back.

The next few days of rehearsal went by in a blur. Baldridge, pleased that he had discovered a ready interpreter for whatever outrageous bits he could devise, began to feature Monsieur LeBeau in as many moments as possible, until Ellis, who had been away in New York on company business, returned to see a run-through. I don't recall much of what took place, but I have a distinct memory of Ellis's glasses reflected in the darkened house as we waited onstage after running the scene twice for him. The two directors whispered together for two or three minutes while we all stood silently; then Ellis disappeared up the aisle without a word. My bits, virtually every one of them, were cut that afternoon. Naturally, I was disappointed, but the amazing thing was, although many members of the company, including Rosemary, were kind enough to find an excuse to come up to me at some point and offer their sympathy that Monsieur LeBeau had been hacked to smithereens, I could only feel the warmth of feeling inside, not outside this company. I might even belong.

I learned one other vital lesson within that first afternoon, and it had to do with Rosemary. There are actors who, by dint of their individual brilliance, can make other actors better just by being onstage with them. Rosemary Harris was such a talent. Whenever she was in residence, the company rose to meet her, and no other actor had quite the same effect as she. At the end of that rehearsal day, we ran the suitors' scene together with others to see what we had, and it was finally time for me to face Miss Harris with our single exchange. Her back was turned from me as the moment approached, and I moved over to her, as directed. She turned, and I nearly lost consciousness. I cannot describe what it was to face the impact of her concentration, the willfulness behind the words. She spoke and I went blank. "Up," it's called in the theater. Others might suggest "buck fever." Whatever it was, it meant we had to go back and repeat the scene, and the next time I was ready for her and somehow managed to spit out my one line. I had begun this enterprise with a sigh of disappointment that I wasn't being offered something worthier. Now I saw just how far I had to go. My university triumphs were nowhere in evidence. The only appropriate word seemed to be "amateur."

9

Merchant caused something of a sensation. It often does; but the louche modernity of this languid, bitchy interpretation, which brought the difficult fifth act into special relief, created particular excitement within the community. After the drama of the trial scene, the badinage about rings and their value to the respective lovers can seem like small potatoes. But here, where personal loyalty and integrity came smack up against the selfish prejudices of a haughty, spoiled society, the last scene of broken promises sustained the dramatic arc in a way I had never imagined. "So shines a good deed in a naughty world," breathed Miss Harris ruefully, arriving back at Belmont from the trial scene, and the acrid hint of bitterness to come was ominous. You would think everyone involved with the production would have been proud—this was, after all, hardly "safe," polite theater, but a healthy testing of a great text in the midst of the intellectual climate best suited to understand it.

The Schnitzers, however, were reportedly furious. And conspicuously missing in action. From the moment I became immersed in *Merchant* rehearsals, and with no further need for hawking subscriptions in midseason, I had drifted off Marcella's radar. Even though I had not been allowed to sit in on the Ellis Rabb rehearsal process, I had managed to infiltrate the company socially, and if I thought about it at all, I simply assumed that Marcella had felt she'd made good on her promise to get me involved and had moved on to other things. Nevertheless, rumors flew. Something unhealthy was afoot, and around the campus I began to hear that the Schnitzers had taken umbrage at what they perceived as flagrant anti-Semitism in the production; they were personally shocked and offended, and it seemed within the realm of possibility that the company might finish the winter's residency and simply disappear. Negative impressions of Ellis Rabb and his future plans circulated, rife even among the regents, that powerful board so removed from direct contact with university personnel as to seem practically mythic. How could this be? My regular appearances as Monsieur LeBeau, albeit in a decidedly muted performance, were catnip to me. There I was, actually onstage with them—if briefly—and the proximity to genial Sydney Walker, hilarious Keene Curtis, collegial Paul Sparer, and the others ramped up my awareness of a professional standard that had heretofore been just theory to me. In addition, the risk factor of this particular production was clearly less about anti-Semitism than the revelations a contemporary take on a classical text can provide. Audiences might be shaken up, true, but they were also thrilled. Tickets were impossible to get. The idea of all this being swept away from us aspiring professionals seemed anathema to me. I didn't understand what could possibly cause such bad blood between APA and the Schnitzers, but it was obvious to me that an apolitical voice cried out to be heard. As one of the representatives on campus for whom these benefits were meant, I even felt responsible.

What, I wondered, should I do? To whom might I appeal? I had had as yet no direct contact with Ellis Rabb other than a string of colorless auditions that landed me nowhere, plus the feeling that my judiciously edited Monsieur LeBeau was his handiwork. I shuddered to think what he might have made of my Hajj the Beggar in *Kismet*, but that was obviously now so much mascara under the bridge.

One thing I have to give myself: I was fearless. As the self-appointed campus leader of All Things Remotely Theatrical, I was passionate about this, but the remarkable thing about having had no contact with anyone—the Schnitzers in particular—meant that I was completely innocent of any ulterior motive. I decided to go right to the top, and to me, the top meant the vice president for academic affairs, Roger Heyns. Dean Heyns was a stern, avuncular figure on campus, and although I cannot recall if I'd ever had occasion to meet him or serve him in any capacity, I certainly had no qualms about calling his office and making an appointment. Shortly after this

period, Heyns went out to UC Berkeley, where he became a celebrated and distinguished chancellor in 1965, serving through some of
the most turbulent days of student protest in the 1960s and building
upon his reputation for being tough and uncompromising.

It happened that my appointment with Dean Heyns fell on a
Thursday morning, and Ellis Rabb had earlier scheduled a meeting
for the graduate teaching faculty on Wednesday afternoon toward
the end of the day in order to answer questions and to mitigate his
seeming lack of interest in the department. I made certain to enter
the classroom early, and took a seat at the back of the room.

At precisely four o'clock, Ellis walked into a gathering where
twenty or so graduate students and teaching fellows were quietly
chatting. Claribel, as his host, was meant to accompany him to effect
whatever introductions were necessary, after which she was to leave
him alone with us. Ellis was dressed in tan corduroy slacks tucked
into very high boots, laced to the knee. He wore a silk shirt over
which he'd pulled on another of soft wool. The neckline was open
enough to reveal a considerable amount of chest hair; and he had
elaborately wrapped his long neck in an ecru silk scarf tied in the
front in a tiny bow. Above all this rose an interested, angular face
featuring prominent cheekbones, a strong chin with a permanent
steel blue trace of stubble, and ice blue eyes topped by an unruly co-
rona of wiry salt-and-pepper hair. He looked every inch the director,
and had he had a riding crop in his left hand, I wouldn't have been at
all surprised. The assembly quieted down to a hush as Claribel made
her charming introduction and, giving him a peck on the cheek,
waved goodbye.

Ellis was Southern, almost professionally so. He had enormous
charm, which he could turn on in the blink of an eye and use to his
advantage when nothing else seemed effective. I cannot pretend this
audience hadn't been skillfully thought out—he knew well the rancor
surrounding his ironclad rule of exclusion and how much that had
disappointed the group before him. But as I saw him do repeatedly in
the years that followed, he rose effortlessly to the challenge and not
only put everyone at ease, but placed them within a circle of intimacy
that was impossible to resist. When the full force of that considerable, if self-conscious, energy targeted anyone, grievances would

disappear and resistances melt. He was funny and relaxed. He explained the need to keep rehearsals private and inviolable. He illustrated the difficulty of allowing actors to "make mistakes" rather than "perform," and that he would go to his grave to assure that no actor under his guidance would ever be exposed before they had the material and the process completely within their own control. He mocked the insecurity he immediately felt whenever an "outsider," even a designer, first penetrated the sacred circle of protected concentration he tried so hard to maintain. He couldn't have scripted a more instructive, more generous scene, and every trace of irritation that had been wheeling around the department corridors over the past months vanished like so many startled crows. At the conclusion, with no more questions to be asked, he was given a warm, spontaneous hand, and stood patiently while a plethora of admirers crowded around for their single moment of acknowledgment. I remained far back in the room, waiting for my chance. Finally, when a trio of giggling department secretaries had taken their leave and he was picking up a small leather shoulder bag with scripts in it, I approached.

"Mr. Rabb?" I said quietly. "Yes, hello there," he said a bit less absently than he had greeted the others. "I'm not sure how much you might benefit from a gathering like this." I ignored the oblique apology, the half-open door this might indicate. "I have just one question for you." I stood as close as was comfortable in order to keep my voice from carrying. "I have an appointment with Dean Heyns tomorrow morning. I just wondered if there was anything you wished me to say to him."

Ellis's blue eyes widened in astonishment and he stood staring at me, silent for a count of at least ten. Then, with considerable force, he grabbed my arm and steered me out the door. "Come with me," he said under his breath, and within minutes I found myself seated in the rented car the university had given him, on the way to the house the program had provided for his comfort. He hadn't asked if I was busy; he hadn't given me so much as a chance to explain or elaborate; he hurried with me like someone hostilely pursued into the parking garage, out of the driving rain and into the car, offering a string of half-realized statements, explanations, protests as we went. There was virtually no prologue to this conversation, nothing even social in tone—he spoke to me like a peer, like a friend, and I was immediately undone. We drove out Geddes Avenue, past the Delt House, which I watched go by on the right like a relic from a former life. The house the Schnitzers had found for Ellis and Rosemary was not far from the house they had secured for themselves with its "Helen Hayes Suite," but decidedly more modest. It was a gray clapboard house, decently furnished, but that evening, all I saw of it was the front room, which had a small dining room directly behind it, and one tiny bathroom off the central hall. Rosemary was nowhere in evidence, having gone back to New York during the beginning of rehearsals for *Richard*, since, as the Duchess of York, she had only one major scene at the top of the play and would be able to handle that blindfolded. Ellis left me standing in the parlor as he disappeared into the kitchen, talking all the time, and, slamming the door of an unseen refrigerator, reappeared bearing a half gallon of ubiquitous Almaden Chablis and two jelly glasses. He plunked himself down on the carpeted floor, and I followed suit. As he poured the wine, he looked at me and said directly, "How much do you know?" "Know?" I repeated blandly. "Gosh, I guess nothing. That's why I wanted to find out if Dean Heyns should—" I gasped for breath. I wasn't expressing myself correctly. "See, I keep hearing these awful things about what the Schnitzers think of *Merchant*, and I can't believe that—"

He thrust a glass into my hand, held his up for silence, took a swig from his, and said, with a pursed smile, "I hope you've got some time. It's quite a story, I promise you." I leaned back against the front of a prickly sofa, instantly relaxed for the first time since I had contacted the dean's office. "I've got all the time in the world," I said. And how true that proved to be!

We're all of us pretty much suckers for a good story, aren't we? I don't necessarily mean this one, but I mean stories by which we find ourselves grabbed by the scruff of the neck, helpless, unable to avert our gaze, even against our will. Ghost stories can certainly do that, and although the story I am about to share has no "ghost come from the grave" that I know of, still, on that particular rainy night in Ann Arbor, Michigan, Ellis Rabb spun out the following tale of subterfuge involving the State Department, a cover-up by the university itself, and the bizarre path by which he and his actors had found themselves in Ann Arbor. Is it true? There is, finally, no way to know: almost all the key players are dead now, which makes this both delicious and, yes, more than a little unfair. I include it here because, as in the best magic acts, I was watching the left hand exclusively while the right one was slowly tightening its grip around my life. Herewith, as best I can recall it, is Ellis's own horror story.

It begins, as any decent Hitchcock homage would, with a hero, one we've already met—Tyrone Guthrie. In Ellis's version of how this all unfolded, Guthrie had indeed gone public with his invitation to Minneapolis, Indianapolis, and Ann Arbor, hoping to identify from one of them the essential funding support he would require. As we know, Guthrie chose Minneapolis, with its powerful business community represented by Beatrice Foods, General Mills, and other rich sources of funding, and Ann Arbor, once the news became public, was immediately exposed as red-faced with shame and embarrassment for dropping so significant a ball. That no invitation had been officially extended by the University of Michigan, according to Ellis, amounted to an unpardonable gaffe. A group of enlightened educators and professors, not officially representing the university per se, but adventurous enough to sponsor a yearly event called the ONCE Festival promoting avant-garde music forms, scrambled belatedly to invite the great man to at least meet with them before making his final decision; and he did indeed come, but he was invited neither to the house of Harlan Hatcher, the university president, nor to any official reception by the regents, and so with no evidence of substantial support from the university, Guthrie thanked his hosts and returned to Minneapolis.

This was a scandal, pure and simple, and an outcry went up from the faculty of the university, fed by the humiliating embarrassment of their ONCE Festival colleagues. A great public relations opportunity had been fumbled, and something had to be done about it. The university hastily announced a plan to form its own Professional Theatre Program to rival Guthrie's. But who should head it up?

Now if we remember our facts, touring Europe at that time was the aforementioned Wilder production of *The Skin of Our Teeth*, featuring Helen Hayes, Mary Martin, and George Abbott, of which Marcella had been so proud. Its company manager had been Robert C. Schnitzer, and Marcella Cisney, who had been listed on the tour as production stage manager, was now its titular tour director. And although I have only Ellis Rabb's word for what follows, and even if every single detail is not certifiable these many decades later, it still has the ring of truth about it.

Something had gone very wrong with that State Department tour. Accounting on the financial end wasn't tallying. Word was circulating that the books for the European tour indicated a strong possibility of misappropriated funds. And since the missing money was State Department money, if it proved necessary to call an investigation, Congress would have to be notified and the current administration could end up embarrassingly compromised. The Schnitzers found themselves in an increasingly uncomfortable light with a clock ticking loudly in the background and a public accounting imminent. How could disaster possibly be avoided?

Then, out of the blue, comes a phone call from the University of Michigan to the State Department: Would they happen to know any qualified professionals who might be available and interested in heading up their nascent new Professional Theatre Program? *Would* they!

Ellis stopped the breathless rush of narrative, poured us more wine, taking his time, and looked ironically at me, quoting Tennessee Williams with his ripest Southern inflection: "Sometimes there is God so quickly!" The Schnitzers were summarily hurried out of Sweden and bundled off to Ann Arbor into the welcoming arms of the University of Michigan, the tour came quietly home, and the State Department was off the hook—and good riddance, too. Before you could say Jack Robinson, everything was falling neatly into place for all concerned.

Ellis was warming to his task, and I was goggle-eyed. He lit another cigarette, rising to shake the overfilled ashtray into the grate of what was obviously an electric fire, and moved over to the couch. I remained on the floor, holding my breath. What, indeed, did the Schnitzers have to offer the university, when you came right down to it? The State Department tour was their highest-profile job ever. Whatever had occurred when Marcella took over the direction of a show that had its genesis on American television, only Miss Hayes could be thought of as remaining anything like an actual friend; her good nature would make it impossible for her to turn anything but a deaf ear to gossip no matter how self-evident. What the Schnitzers quite obviously didn't have was much of a plan for the new program, so with virtually just months left to deliver, they were getting desperate. Hearing that APA was performing a successful rep season at the Fred Miller Theatre in Milwaukee, they hopped immediately over to Wisconsin to see what they could find.

"And what they found, of course," Ellis smiled wickedly, "was *us*—a spanking fresh touring company of actors conveniently without a home." APA was playing in repertory not only Sheridan's surefire *School for Scandal*, but a sweet, lyrical production of Shakespeare's *A Midsummer Night's Dream* as well as a treasure from the lost American canon, George M. Cohan's farce *The Tavern*. The Schnitzers couldn't believe their luck: this company, which came with its own sets, its own costumes, an undisputed leading lady, as well as her brilliant director husband, was the answer to all their prayers. They offered APA two separate seasons—one in the fall of three existing productions, plus a Shakespeare festival over the following winter during which APA could add a new show to its own rep. Contracts were drawn up and signed. APA had two guaranteed years of residency with a mutual option for renewal, plus the financing to mount into their rep other productions of common interest, and the Schnitzers could take the credit. There was just one unresolved issue.

Ellis crossed and recrossed his legs in an attempt to get more comfortable, then finally bent over, unlacing the tall boots; within minutes he was barefoot, running his fingers through his hair and flexing his strong feet. "You see," he began, "it all sounded innocent enough: on the contract it was spelled out in black and white, 'Robert C. Schnitzer, Producer, and Marcella Cisney, Director.' On our side," he continued, "was my name as artistic director and Bob Gold's as managing director. But then," he said, rising and towering over me, "when I looked closer, it didn't say 'Marcella Cisney, Director,' it said 'Marcella Cisney, Artistic Director!'" He paused for dramatic effect, and I swallowed more of the tepid sweet wine, not knowing what point he was about to make.

"I smelled a rat," he said, snatching up the nearly empty bottle. "I didn't exactly fall off a turnip truck, you know. Marcella had seen an opening, and she was going for the jugular. It was just a matter of moments before she would propose that she be invited to direct one of the inaugural productions. So I went into action: the company would honor their commitment to the university, but no one . . . *no one* not previously employed by APA was to be added to the company roster or admitted into rehearsals at any time—not university students or faculty, not Robert C. Schnitzer himself, and most certainly *not* 'artistic director' Marcella Cisney."

"Wow," I offered, thinking carefully back on Marcella's formidable ego and beginning to make sense of her cooling attitude as the season had evolved. And Marcella wasn't alone in her reaction. A public howl of protest had indeed gone up. How could he! How *dare* he!! This was humiliating enough for the Schnitzers, who clearly would not be seeing Marcella installed as creator of any of the new productions, but a severe blow to the university as well. "I got around all this in two ways," he concluded proudly, bringing me up-to-date. "I promised to offer professional scholarship positions to six of the Theatre Department's most qualified students to carry spears, observe, if they promised to remain completely quiet, and"— he raised his brows comically—"I said I would hold occasional seminars and lectures for graduate students . . . and didn't *that* prove to be my lucky day!" He raised a glass to me, and I responded. "That was the deal, take it or leave it!"

So the Schnitzers, fuming, and the university, stung, took it. And everyone went about the business of selling season tickets to a company no one had ever heard of and that rang no bells with the student body. "Which is where you fortunately came in," Ellis said as he drained his glass. "But now the handwriting is on the wall: they want us gone, pure and simple. We've become too popular, and she hasn't got a professional leg to stand on—they hadn't bargained for that." He rose and stretched lazily. "I assume you have more than enough for your interview in the morning."

I rose stiffly, aware of my newfound proximity with the brilliant director before me and convinced that I had found, if not the gist of my complaint to Dean Heyns, certainly something worth fighting for.

I reached for my jacket, and Ellis grabbed his keys, slipping his feet into sandals. "My God! It's three! How time flies when you're having fun!" He smiled at me, holding the front door open, and we walked out together into the wet night to his car.

Together! I couldn't believe my luck. My head was spinning, and it had little to do with the excessive wine we'd consumed. Had it been only a matter of hours since I waited at the back of a classroom? And where was I now? What did this mean? I climbed into the front seat while his voice droned on, and we were off. *Off!* I smiled to myself. No question about it . . . we were rolling!

PART TWO

A BODY IN MOTION
TENDS TO REMAIN IN MOTION

10

So those are the mechanics—the flipper knocks a ball bearing, and what was once passive is active, no longer a still silver orb, but voilà! a bona fide pinball, pure energy, and when properly played, capable of lighting up a few bells and whistles. Did I feel remotely torn? Disloyal to Marcella and Schnitzer by listening to all these unsubstantiated allegations? It would be reassuring to confess a few sleepless nights, or even a curiosity as to if and how such a plan might possibly have evolved, to say nothing of wondering if Marcella herself might be being unfairly judged and dismissed. But I was in love. Not sexually, and not even emotionally, but the next best thing—engaged and committed for the first time in my life. There before me stood someone exciting, magical, powerful, to whom I now had unrestricted access, and the fact that Ellis Rabb had kept himself isolated from everyone else in the mix and now seemed to need my help added to the hypnotic pull. I had already witnessed something of his vision and gone into print about it, with no expectation that this might affect my own life; and now, in moments, he had revealed to me his cause, and was making it *my* cause; he had been challenged on artistic means, and had risen to that challenge like a Hapsburg defending his tiny principality.

As a matter of fact, I still liked the Schnitzers very much, and on some level I believed my feelings for them were separate from their political actions. Making enemies—political or otherwise—was not in the cards for me at that point, nor, in truth, in the decades that have followed. It may be the WASP thing. Looking back on my family, I realize that conflict rarely came into it. My mother was virtuosic at the art of evading the uncomfortable. She wanted everyone to like her, first and foremost, and no matter how strong her opinion, it was couched in the most gracious and diplomatic terms. She could suffocate with charm. Her concrete and nearly immutable assumptions must have been hell on my sister, who was as fundamentally unlike her as I was, in other ways, unlike my father: not just superficially, but deep in the bone. As far as the Schnitzers are concerned, I'm amazed at the naïveté that let me believe I could get away with such a double standard of loyalty, which I continued to do. Over the next year, and even after I had joined the company as a professional, the Schnitzers remained cordial and polite with me. We were never again close—Marcella must have seen me as having "gone over"—but with all her aggressive, restless energy, her grim determination to cling to the cliff face no matter what, she earned my respect. Over the next several years she was even able to carve out one or two productions of her own under the aegis of the program, particularly a play called *Wedding Band* that she produced and directed starring Ruby Dee, which went beyond the confines of the university circuit.

Pathetic apology: Writing about the arts is no picnic unless the art is tangible. When one is writing about an author, it's an easy matter to pick up a volume of the work and judge for oneself whether a biographer's assessment is valid. If it's a painter, the proof, should it survive, hangs on a wall for all to see. But the performing arts are evanescent, which accounts, perversely, for a large part of their allure. In a society in which the detritus of landfill threatens to overwhelm us in plastic water bottles, something as fragile as a recalled performance is to be cherished, if not ever replicated.

In theater, personality often powers performance as surely as sex has done with history. We may not altogether understand it, but when someone as individual as a Rosemary Harris walks onto a stage, something indefinable happens. It is reported that when Dame Peggy Ashcroft was a student at RADA, Mrs. Patrick Campbell, ancient and doddering but still compos mentis, was invited to see the graduating classes perform their final exercises. True to form, Mrs. Pat was placed in a straight-backed chair front and center, and as often is the case with the elderly, went promptly to sleep. But when young Peggy Ashcroft began her piece, the great old actress suddenly sat bolt upright in her chair, her eyes blazing, and said in her stentorian contralto, "There's someone in the room!"

And so there was. APA and all it achieved now resonates so far down the corridors of time as to be nearly indistinguishable from any other good and worthy theater company similarly vanished. Still, to reflect on its history and not make some attempt to revive a bit of its magic on the page is, I think, pointless. One may not entirely succeed, but one needs in some way to attest to lightning in a bottle.

John Houseman writes in his wonderful autobiographies that Ellis was the only authentic genius he encountered, other than Orson Welles. High praise indeed. The sheer effort of powering a company through a decade of continual production alone should assure Rabb of a niche in some theatrical pantheon or other, had he never set foot on the stage; but he did, and how he loved doing so.

He was always arresting, and often better than that, but not in everything. Tall, aristocratic in demeanor, he wanted mostly to appear on the stage as "veddy, veddy beautiful," as he comically put it in his plummiest tones, be it Prospero in *The Tempest*, Tanner in *Man and Superman*, or the Baron in *The Lower Depths*. He had confidence onstage and a strong, rich voice, so with his innate energy, he did extremely well in Shaw as well as Sheridan. He was a romantic by nature, and when it worked, as in his delightful turn as the Vagabond in *The Tavern*, or perhaps his most memorable performance, as the eponymous hero in *Pantagleize*, he was wonderful. Though he was better suited to comedy than to darker roles, I nevertheless saw him give one really stunning classical performance, shortly after my initiation into his ever-expanding circle of admirers in Ann Arbor. It was in the role of Richard II during that first Ann Arbor winter, and Ellis was later to confess to me that he felt it all going downhill as an actor after that, as the egocentric concerns of a serious actor had to be subordinated to the ever-increasing responsibilities of directing, fund-raising, and producing as the business of the company began to take over. I watched him, over the years, assimilating these exhausting responsibilities without a clue that I would need these lessons a few decades on, when I took over my own company in San Diego. I also, as the comic side of fate would have it, happened to witness that performance.

As the American composer Ned Rorem puts it in one of his diaries, "History is never fantastic while it's being lived." If there is one comic thread that binds us all together, it is the familiar lament "If I had only known then what I know now!" But we don't. In the early sixties, Ellis Rabb was meteoric, possessed of galvanizing energy and consumed by a passion for whatever he believed in—be it his company, the intrinsic rightness of a move onstage, a romantic interlude, or the preparation of a meal. It was impossible to be around him and not get sucked into the vortex of whatever preoccupied him. But that behind all this fury of excitement lay certain realities, even of a chemical nature, never occurred to us, least of all to him, until much later.

Ellis was the only child of C. W. "Happy" Rabb, an insurance executive with Treadwell & Harry in Memphis, and Mary Carolyn Ellis Rabb, his high-strung mother, born in Helena, Arkansas, and worth a small volume of her own, no doubt. She was vivid, ambitious, bright, and, unfortunately, also bipolar, although in the early part of the last century not much was known or acknowledged about this devastating condition. She was, in addition, alcoholic, and there were inevitable periods when she was mysteriously "unavailable," lost in a saturated spell familiar to some Southern women, lying in her bedroom with the draperies drawn against the afternoon sun while her faithful housekeeper, Louise, stood guard and attended her until it all passed. This was the genetic disposition that Ellis inherited, and early on, whenever the power of his brilliance coincided with his euphoric highs, he could electrify a dinner table or a rehearsal without question; he was sensational. But even by now, in the early sixties, the emotional output could occasionally fray, and the particular acting performance I witnessed, I believe, offers an indication of a pattern we were to see more and more throughout the decade. It was Ellis's intention to direct and play *Richard II* with Baldridge working part time as art director and part time as his editor, but the effort of the workload of previous months was beginning to take its toll. It was clear that most of us volunteers for *Merchant* would not be needed for *Richard*, since the company could easily fill the roster by doubling and tripling their assignments, but with Ellis unusually nervous about a big new part, raw and edgy as he was, it was thought advisable to supply an understudy for him.

There are three servants in *Richard*, listed as Bushy, Bagot, and Green, who figure tangentially in his downfall. They have little to do and are inevitably doubled with other, longer roles, and over the years the parts have sometimes become referred to, archly, as "Pussy, Faggot, and Queen." In order to accommodate Ellis in the title role, actors were taking on more than one or two assignments, but in all the shifting around, there was no one available to cover Bushy.

"Jack," the stage manager, said to me one afternoon, "can you dig us out of a hole? I need a cover for Bushy in *Richard II*, and no one is available. Can you do it?"

Dilemma. I was flattered, naturally, to be sought out for an additional assignment, but I had already committed too much time to the recent *Merchant*, and my other responsibilities were suffering because of it. Also, the fact that whenever one covers a part, one is required to be at the theater every night of performance until the curtain goes up was a problem: I had an important social conflict looming. Both of my roommates, Bob James and Tom Jennings, were about to depart for their voluntary six months' military duty, and I had planned a huge farewell party on the night of one of the early performances, so I couldn't guarantee them my exclusive presence.

The stage manager seemed not to care. "Naturally, you'd finally be admitted to all the rehearsals," he said, taking a dramatic pause to underscore the importance of what followed, "and, you know, you've never seen Ellis directing . . ." I got the point; I had already gained more proximity than anyone outside the Equity company, but this unexpected assignment would put me in the actual room while he was creating. A fleeting image of a smoldering Marcella flitted by. What a coup! Nevertheless, I had just been cast in a department production that was going to be rehearsing simultaneously, so any practical observation of Ellis was going to be out of the question. "No problem," the stage manager said airily moving off. "You're a pro. You'll nail it."

I'm not altogether certain that Ned Rorem, in his observation of history, shouldn't have added, "Be careful what you wish for," but he didn't. I had sought proximity, and now proximity was seeking me. I looked down at the script in my hands, shrugged, and turned back to my other duties. Look, there weren't that many Bushy speeches to learn; I would get to them. What had he just said? I was a pro.

It was a tough Michigan winter that year, masses of wet snow, winds blowing full blast, an identical pairing of Januarys and Februarys meant to test the resolve of even the most intrepid native. And the bad weather seemed to duplicate itself politically as well, with the conflict between Ellis and Marcella growing, if anything, ever more glacial. On one particularly stormy Friday night, Le Gallienne herself had returned to Ann Arbor to see the *Richard* and to confer with Ellis about her future assignments. On that same evening, Ellis's great friend Craig Noel, artistic director of the Old Globe Theatre, arrived from San Diego as well, eager for his meeting with Ellis about directing something at the Globe the following summer. There were, I promise, witnesses other than me for what occurred. It was the end of an exhausting week, and the arrival of two friends whom Ellis was eager to impress unfortunately coincided with a particularly hostile session that had occupied most of Friday afternoon between Ellis, his business manager, Bob Gold, and the increasingly icy Schnitzers. Lines had been drawn, tempers had flared, harsh words had been spoken. The meeting had gone badly, and as a result Ellis was going to be denied even a glimpse of his guests before curtain time. Enraged, threatened, desperate for a rest and backed up against a wall—a position he could never tolerate—he stormed out of the Schnitzers' office, shouting that he would not appear at the evening's performance. If his contribution as an actor was so fucking unimportant to them, they could fucking well get on with the fucking evening's performance without it—he was shattered, betrayed, and now too ill to play. Craig Noel, calling that afternoon at the box office to pick up his ticket, found the theater's minty attendant mopping his brow and whining, "Oh, we've had such alarums and excursions!"

As this little drama was unfolding, I was blocks away at the house I shared with Bob and Tom, preparing to entertain about forty of their friends at a party. It was after five-thirty in the afternoon when the telephone in our downstairs hallway rang. I picked up.

"You'd better get over here," came the strained voice of the stage manager. "Ellis is out, and the understudies are going on. You're Bushy. Get a move on!" Before I could open my mouth, he hung up. He had a few other calls to make.

Jesus! Two problems. One was that in about two hours, friends were going to arrive expecting a party, and the host would be absent. But that was hardly the worst of it. I had not learned a line of Bushy. Not intentionally. I had kept the script next to my bed, but I've never been much good at reading anything at the end of a day. Once I climb between fresh sheets, I go to sleep. The fact has been substantiated by a series of irritated lovers over the years, but I always thought it was a good thing. The idiocy of leaving the script lying about was a crucial oversight. I honestly meant to learn the speeches—I was even vaguely familiar with the scenes—but no, not one word had been committed to memory.

I bolted from the house barking apologies to the two astonished honorees and promising that I would be back just as soon as possible. If Ellis decided to play at the last minute, of course, I would be back before eight. If not . . . I left Bob and Tom openmouthed in the hall-way, each holding an unopened bottle of wine.

The dressing area beneath Trueblood Auditorium in the Frieze Building was a hive of activity. Dressers were scurrying everywhere, trying to adjust costumes from understudy to understudy, while the actors were shifting mental gears that would bring other assignments into focus. The stage manager moved through the melee with a grim expression and a clipboard upon which his to-do list had been scrib-bled. Ellis's understudy, Jonathan Farwell, married at the time to Will Geer's youngest daughter, Kate, stood to one side of the hallway, scanning the script and raising his eyes to the ceiling while his lips moved silently. An undergraduate dresser rushed over, hurling a large felt costume over me and thrusting a worn leather belt into my hands. "Here," she said, "that's yours! They say you don't have to change out of it, just keep it on no matter what—continuity, at least—right?" she threw over her shoulder as she moved off to someone more impor-tant. I found myself enveloped in thick, faintly sour-smelling felt from which only a portion of my face emerged. Without having much of a neck myself, I was a frightened tortoise peering out of the stiff collar at the mounting chaos around me. "Um . . . but what about the blocking?" I wondered out loud to no one. "This way," someone commanded, as several of us were herded up to the stage.

For about ten minutes, I was pushed around in various patterns while the other two, reviewing their parts of Bagot and Green, went over their moves. Those actors obviously had had their rehearsal, and they reviewed the exercise without paying much attention to me. Instructions were succinct to the point of code. "Kneel when Jonathan says 'this impious . . .'" the next word obliterated as the stage manager, pushed for time, turned from me. All sounds were muffled by the overheated felt carapace I struggled beneath. "Back up, back up, back up to right here," he barked, his fingers digging deep into my shoulder while he pushed me back across the raked platform, "and keep your eyes on the floor until Keene says . . ." and came another incomprehensible phrase as I searched my pages in vain for a clue as to what he'd just said.

It was now past seven o'clock, and the frenetic tempo of the previous hour dropped like the temperature outside while everyone silently reviewed their assignments. I had two speeches under my belt by this time. Well, okay, one. Nearly. But there was more to cram and I was beginning to panic. Trying to stay out of everyone's way, I retreated to the upstage area above the set, where a little room made of white muslin fabric had been created as a solitary dressing area for Ellis alone, where he could enjoy a degree of concentration away from distractions. Hanging outside it on two wooden pegs were the cylindricals he needed to fill out his tights. Having excellent calves but thin thighs, he had to don half-trousers of concentric rings of closely sewn cotton strips under his tights to give proper proportion to his legs. They looked rather like the body of a dead sheep hanging in the half-light and I felt suddenly embarrassed, like a voyeur staring at something private and personal. I retreated to the greenroom in growing despair, wondering if Bushy might possibly carry some piece of parchment of deep personal importance along with him at which he might casually glance from time to time. Like, let's say, during two entire scenes.

The greenroom was uncharacteristically empty twenty minutes before curtain, as everyone was scattered backstage mumbling their speeches in an indistinguishable drone. I had the place to myself. I lumbered nervously back and forth with difficulty, since the heavy felt I was wearing had been safety-pinned up at the ankles, while I drummed over the lines for my last appearance. As I moved toward the door connecting the greenroom with the auditorium beyond, it suddenly swung open, and I was face-to-face with Ellis himself. He looked insane. His eyes blazed sightlessly as he looked through me, and his hair stood up on his head as if electrified. "Hold the goddamn curtain!" he shouted into my face. "I'm fucking playing!"

The next ten minutes have evaporated from memory, stamped out, no doubt, by a combination of relief at not having to produce text I never mastered and the sheer energy it took everyone else to shift back into their regular roles, to say nothing of getting Ellis into his cylindricals, tights, wig, doublet, and fourteenth-century yellow coat with tippet sleeves that fell to the floor.

With joy I tore down to the dressing room, struggling to get out of my damp felt gown. "Where the hell do you think you're going?" said the stage manager as I ran past him on the stairwell. "I'm throwing a party," I crowed. "Ellis is back. You don't need me!"

"That's what you think," he replied, snagging me by the nape of my heavy garment. "He's a total mess! Didn't you see him? He may not last through the first scene! You're staying until intermission, just in case." And he disappeared stage right, where he was preparing to begin the show. I shed my costume, slipped back into my party clothes, and looked for some perch from which I could watch the proceedings. The production, which had opened to respectable reviews, was sold out, and on this wet Friday night there wasn't a seat to be had.

Ellis loved to act. He fairly luxuriated in it, as he did with cigarettes and wine. He was theatrical by nature. His first words spoken onstage as a child were in a play, scripted by a beloved early teacher with the improbable name of Fairfax Proudfoot Walkup, entitled *The Jade Bracelet*. In performance, at something like nine years of age, he stood up and addressed the audience directly, saying "My name is Mei Ling, and I am the most important personage in this play."

How true. No matter what he undertook, from preparing an elaborate dinner for friends in improvised living quarters to staging the battle of Borodino for the Piscator *War and Peace*, he remained without question the most important personage on view. Even now, years after his premature death, it is impossible for friends who knew him to gather without the conversation inevitably coming around to

Ellis. This personal magnetism could give even his mannered performances gravitas, and if Oscar Wilde had lavished his genius on his
life, as reported, Ellis's gift for theatricality was equally ubiquitous
whether he was traveling in a car, or sitting over a candlelit meal, or
curled up on a sofa as light faded into twilight. He spun his own
enchantment, smoking and toying with his unruly cap of hair. He
was tremendous fun.

Knowing something of the architecture of Trueblood Auditorium, I made my way up to the lighting grid high over the auditorium,
where I could see the stage below without being observed, and settled
myself on my stomach to watch as the lights dimmed.

The title role in *Richard II* is daunting. It demands an aptitude for
making verse sound effortless and undecorated. The role is of an arrogant elitist who feels, by God's grace, so far above the reproach of
his challengers that when he is finally faced by his cousin Bolingbroke, who has a legitimate claim to the throne, he misjudges his in-
fallibility and is shockingly deposed, then murdered. Bolingbroke
goes on to become the first of the Tudor kings, Henry IV. When the
play premiered, it was considered pretty hot stuff, since the very no-
tion of usurpation of the divine right of kings, especially with Queen
Elizabeth, the last of that Tudor line and unmarried, sitting on the
throne without an heir, resulted in prosecutions for sedition. It must
have taken some degree of delicacy to say nothing of courage for its
author to risk it onstage. Richard's text is poetic and convoluted, and
since he is obsessed with the subject of betrayal, any actor with a ten-
dency to self-pity can easily fall into the trap of sentimentality, trying
the patience of an exhausted audience.

This test was proving to be pretty thin ice for Ellis. With license,
at last, to appear both romantic and heroic, he had asked his old
friend the designer Robert Fletcher to create his costumes. Fletcher,
who was destined to enjoy success as principal designer for the early
Star Trek television series, among other things, was as florid in his
taste as Ellis was in his. He produced, as a gift, all of the designs for
the king's clothes in this production. But the fairly modest budget
could ill afford comparable designs for anyone else. And that is where
the enterprising Baldridge stepped in with his yards of felt and his
hot glue gun. If the fabrics weren't all going to match, at least the sil-
houettes would.

Now dressed in the cylindricals that filled out his legs to perfection, and sweeping around the stage in literally yards of material (perhaps no actor or director of his generation moved fabric better than Ellis Rabb), he reveled in playing a poor put-upon monarch whom no one seemed to understand. As the poor put-upon artistic director of a struggling troupe continually under fire by an unsympathetic management, he leaned somewhat heavily on the subtext, and the performance, beautifully spoken and flashy to look at, was, for the most part, anchored in limpid-eyed emotion.

But not tonight! From his first entrance, Ellis was clearly livid—furious, in fact. How dare they! How dare the Schnitzers, and, indeed, the world at large, try to wrest from him the one thing he cherished above all, the one activity that justified all peripheral effort—acting! The scene he'd thrown in front of Bob Gold and the Schnitzers at the League during the afternoon had inflamed his adrenaline, requiring an outlet in action, not just sulking in his tent like Achilles. After all, where was the pleasure in stirring up a tempest if you couldn't enjoy the results?

He stormed out onto the stage wearing a canary yellow doublet, a rakish green hat on his head. He flung himself on the throne sideways, his perfectly proportioned legs dangling over its arms, the picture of arrogance and contempt, insultingly defiant. You couldn't take your eyes off him.

Richard, like most abusers of power, doesn't get it. He knows his choices may not please many—they are not meant to. They please him. He also knows he has been placed upon the throne of England by the hand of God Almighty, and only God Almighty can take him off it. In the most reductive terms, the actor playing Richard has one major transition—in the prison scene at the end of the play he realizes, suddenly, that but for God's, all power is temporal, and he wakes up to acknowledge his transgressions just before he is murdered. Ordinarily, at the very first suspicion of his subjects' disapproval, Ellis's Richard would play the sympathy card. But tonight, fueled by mutinous anger, he made a genuine discovery. Rather than extend a lament for the better part of three hours, he was in blazing denial. No matter how much evidence began piling up that he was doomed, he countered everything with glittering irony. He sneered. He posed, the pure manifestation of someone dangerous blind to all but his version of the universe. It was something to see, and two moments remain indelible to me.

The first is the familiar soliloquy when Richard returns from Ireland to hear of the mounting insurrection in England, which begins "For God's sake, let us sit upon the ground and tell sad stories of the death of kings." Dressed in a huge cape (naturally) lined with what appeared to be wolf fur (naturally), Ellis would typically put his hands out for support, sinking gracefully to the ground, eyes brimming with tears, while he worked his way through that great verse. Tonight, infuriated with the possibility that anyone challenged his authority, he plunked himself unceremoniously down—bang! The supporting players, expecting neither Ellis nor the king to react so quickly, scrambled to get down as well—"no head higher than mine" being the applicable rule—and the effect was not merely awkward, but shocking. The speech became a bitter comment, anything but sentimental. It made tremendous sense. Later, in the deposition scene, Ellis was to give himself an amazing exit—a move perhaps no other actor of his generation would dare, let alone be able to execute. Now dressed in gray velvet lined with silver for this final confrontation with Bolingbroke, the collar drawn tightly around his neck, and with a train that had to be eight feet long, he was pretty impressive even without speaking a word. Bolingbroke, more fighter than monarch, was in military garb, but whatever the politics, only one man was king.

What was a given, and what was Ellis? It was hard to tell, which gave his performance an improvisatory effect that was remarkable. He tore through the play as if he wanted it over and done with, but this impetuous pace blended perfectly with the trajectory of an arrogant monarch condescending to teach the underlings about real power and privilege. At last he stood before Jonathan Farwell's Bolingbroke upstage at the throne. His carefully rehearsed movements were played so swiftly they felt accidental. He lifted the crown from his own head, picked up Bolingbroke's hand in his, and after holding the crown between them for a moment in a mock tug-of-war, he abruptly lowered it onto his rival's head and, faster than thought, kissed Bolingbroke on both cheeks and plunged to the floor before him, his forehead nearly touching the stage. Once again the court—the actors—could barely keep pace. Some, now slow to comply, seemed to be struggling with their conscience as to whether to kneel

in support of the king or stand in defiance. It was social pandemo-
nium.

Then this remarkable exit. He began backing away from Bolingbroke without breaking his gaze, moving somehow over the eight-
foot train and exiting inexorably away from the astonished Henry
diagonally, trailing the inverted train like a sea creature streaming
weeds. Trains are deadly enemies of actors. Actresses, who have the
most opportunity to employ them, inevitably beg the costumer to
cut them down because they are so treacherous. To back down a
raked stage without being able to see where one is going is one thing.
But to do it while moving over eight feet of heavy material is impossible. He moved deliberately, slowly, while the audience held their
breath. It must have taken three minutes of utter silence. The effect
was everything it was meant to be. Royalty was withdrawing from
the stage, pulling all the oxygen from the room with it. No one who
witnessed that exit would ever forget it.

Many people are talented, and a few are even gifted. But to be
considered great is a pinnacle only a handful in any generation
achieve. I have no idea if, had he not had to split focus between running a company and performing, Ellis could have delivered more performances like this one. But the great roles need something beyond
facility and charm. So who can tell? But that exit! Who but Ellis
would have conceived such a thing? Whatever his gifts as an actor,
flashes very near genius appeared over and over in his directing. I
couldn't take it all in at the time, lying on my stomach in the grid
above the stage, but somehow I intuited that there were finally two
indisputable things that drew people into a theater: a personality of
truly magnetic appeal and the mark of an original imagination. One
lives to hear "You've got to see this performance to believe it!" Or
equally compelling, "If you see just one this season, it's got to be this
one!" It's what constitutes "box office." This young company, with a
star like Rosemary Harris and a director gifted with true imagination
like Ellis Rabb, was hitting two for two.

It was well past midnight when I walked, dazed, back into my house
on Wilmot Street. The party was long over, and Tom Jennings had gone
to bed. Empty bottles were stacked everywhere, and the tablecloth in

the dining room bore the stains of wine and food that signal a great evening, even with no host present. Bob James was nowhere to be seen, which meant that he and Judy were prolonging their goodbyes somewhere privately. The house was still, and the only light in the living room came through dusty plate glass windows from the streetlamp on the nearby corner. I sat on the couch, lost in thought. I had found myself unable to move throughout the entire performance, unable to leave my perch at intermission even for a moment. I had not wanted to interrupt the spell of the performance to ascertain if I might be free to go back to my own life. That life paled beside what I had just witnessed on the stage. I obviously had a great deal to learn. Now just one thought remained fixed before me: How in hell was I ever going to be able to learn it?

11

The circus left town. APA, once the Shakespeare festival was concluded, pulled up stakes and returned to New York to face their future, and the campus settled back into the perspective I knew only too well. I had the spring production of A *Matter of Style* still ahead, classwork to complete, and an unusual dilemma to face. One of the tenured professors in the Speech and Theatre Department had suddenly died, and there was no one to teach the graduate acting section. Over the summer, my loyal patron, Claribel Baird, supported by her husband, Professor Halstead, suggested that I fill the void. The only problem, of course, was that you cannot be *attending* graduate school while *teaching* in graduate school. The handwriting was on the wall, and I withdrew from graduate studies, abandoning my plans for a Ph.D., and so destroyed my last defense against the draft. I was still pained to have to declare myself openly homosexual, which would have done the trick in a jiffy, because even though I was "out," I had had such appallingly little practical experience. As I was usually the youngest sympathetic listener in my crowd, I became the confidant of every other emerging gay friend, all of whom regaled me with chapter and verse of what they had done, with whom they had done it, how it felt, the sometimes complex mechanics involved, what happened afterward, and, of course, the endless applications of activity these discoveries led to. I knew everything. I had done nothing. I was frozen in the headlights of the early sexually active sixties, when being gay was just one degree worse than being a card-carrying Communist, and far less glamorous. I had a learner's permit in my pocket, but I was humiliated to be seen laboring over "Teaching Little Fingers to Play" when I knew how to hum the Concerto Grosso.

In most ways life was quieter and a little empty. I went through the motions of what was available without much enthusiasm, taking a stab at a relationship with a classmate I was meant to be thrilled to bag, winding up staring at a stranger in the bed beside me and wondering why we didn't ignite. Basically, my subsequent academic and emotional life lacked the frisson of excitement the connection with Ellis and the company had supplied, and if I tried to reach out for some contact, Ellis was anything but a willing correspondent. He never could spell, and didn't enjoy reading. One of the witty remarks the director Stephen Porter was often to repeat was "The only plays Ellis knows are the ones Jack reads to him." It was of course an exaggeration, but since Ellis had inherited from his near-blind father a genetic disposition toward detached retinas, Stephen wasn't all that far off the mark. I solved the correspondence problem by inventing a humorous letter in which I posed a series of probing or personal questions to which I had supplied at least four or five possible answers, labeled (a) to (e), that he could simply check off and send back. The letter, I assumed, was impossible to ignore, but he surprised me by sending it back, having scratched out most of my bons mots and substituting a wittier word, or, better, happily circumventing the entire subject by some other means. I never had the remotest attraction for Ellis, nor he for me, which was unquestionably the saving grace of our long, checkered association, but I must confess a thrill at seeing his handwriting on the return envelope, almost as if I were hearing from a lover; and that should have been a clue as to the degree of the inexorable pull Ellis and APA were exerting on my pledge to play Alan Jay Lerner to Bob James's Fritz Loewe.

I made a beeline to New York over spring vacation for the ostensible purpose of interviewing for teaching jobs there, but in truth more to renew contact with Ellis and the others, such as Keene Curtis and Richard Woods, who had been so friendly toward me. While there, of course, I submitted to a half-earnest series of interviews with a few universities. I simply cannot believe my chutzpah. Who would expect to waltz into Manhattan in April and grab a hotly contested teaching job for the fall? I would. I set up interviews with Hunter, Pace, nd Columbia, among others, showing up in some instances when I s almost certain they had filled their faculty quotas for the following year but still hoping against hope that my charm might prevail. I returned to Ann Arbor a week or so later empty-handed, having managed to spend remarkably little time on either my academic pursuits or with the distracted members of Ellis's company.

Then, in the warmth of the late spring, the pinball, seemingly stuck in a neglected corner, whams alive. The telephone in my kitchen rings, and picking it up I recognize the voice of Ota T. Reynolds, then chairman of the department of Speech and Theatre at Hunter College, who had been kind if sternly resolute with me during our interview. I had nevertheless left my credentials behind with the distinct feeling that at the very least, I made her laugh. "Mr. O'Brien," she began, "I know I told you when we interviewed a month or so ago that we were full up, but something seems to have changed, depending . . . Would you, by any means, know phonetics?" Interesting question. Because no, naturally, I never studied, nor had even come anywhere near phonetics. And yes, of course, without batting an eyelash I answered, "Do I ever!" She thereupon offered me two sections of public speaking, beginning in the fall, as well as two of voice and diction involving a mastery of phonetics, both of which were required beginning courses for all Hunter students. And thus was I employed. Unprepared and unqualified, but employed.

The migration of a close-knit circle of graduates, it seems, can often seem like that of birds: we all take off east together in the bright assumption that something like a living version of *My Sister Eileen* or *Wonderful Town* is about to enfold us. My intimates in dribs and drabs graduated from Michigan not only to New York, but into the period-perfect, dappled sidewalks of Brooklyn Heights. That previous year, Erik Hendriks and Jerry Lawrence had preceded us, setting up their digs in the Heights along with a siren call that we were expected to join them as soon as possible. Erik, a more life-experienced fraternity brother, had been my mentor, a kind of Virgil for my new gay life. His lover, rechristened Jeff, an alum of the *Carousel* that had happily tossed Judy Heric and me onto the campus stage, had had the original intention of bedding me, his innocent Mr. Snow, and during the run of that production had invited me to Detroit to see a first-run, hard-ticket film. I was so nervous as well as excited at the prospect that I insisted Erik come along as well, as a kind of gay duenna, I suppose.

Jeff was appalled, and duly discouraged. But it wasn't more than a week later that I watched the pair of them skip off together into a romantic sunset. I recall equal portions of rue and relief. But they remained key figures in my life over many hilarious and wonderful years, and I followed their precepts religiously. Especially Erik, a gifted amateur painter of considerable skill, who changed his name with a finger snap from Jerry Coon to Erik Hendriks. He guided my social education through parallel enthusiasms for Northern European Renaissance painting, the music of Samuel Barber, the works of Beckett, the rudiments of conversational French, Constant Comment tea, all of Callas, a considerable amount of Björling, and Julia Child's volumes, and he tossed in for good measure a handy reference map for every conceivable position of gay sexual congress possible. For me, this was like learning addition by attending seminars in advanced calculus. As a couple, Erik and Jeff had laid out the rules our set would be wise to follow, which began with living in Brooklyn Heights, and all but Bob and Judy complied. As soon as Bob had dispensed with his six-month service obligation, they married that same autumn, with me as their best man, and chose instead the West Seventies in Manhattan, where Bob could more easily access the active music scene, and Judy, her elfin beauty disguised beneath a babushka and dark glasses, might more safely ride the subway up to Spanish Harlem to her teaching job, which she maintained to support them.

My initial delight with living in the civilized Promenade area of Brooklyn Heights sobered when I realized I had overlooked one detail: Hunter, in those days, had two campuses—the famous one on the East Side of Manhattan, and another up in the Bronx. I wasn't meant to join the Manhattan faculty. I was, instead, bivouacked at the very end of the IRT subway line that I caught each morning at Borough Hall and from which I descended an hour later at the Jerome/Woodlawn terminal far from Manhattan. My classes for the next year and a half were all in the Bronx, so during the two solid hours of commuting each day, I managed to augment lapses in my education by staying one lesson ahead of the classes in phonetics and by reading the classics I had ignored as an undergraduate on the journey.

I threw myself into teaching, something I loved doing and still find exhilarating. At that time it was required of all Hunter students to have one section of public speaking and, worse for them, one in voice and diction. A New York accent was considered by the college to be a blight on its graduates, who were meant to use standard American speech. To an individual, they all resented the implication and hated the class. After all, their parents "tawk'd loik dat," so how could they put on airs at home and keep peace, or infer that their folks were somehow deficient? Staying literally one lesson ahead of the classes during that first semester, I turned up the wattage of my patented need to please as many people as possible: I performed, I mocked, I invented, I demonstrated, and I was funny. I justified this behavior as my personal teaching technique, but all I did was to dip back into my Delt House persona and let fly. The word was out: if you gotta take the damn thing anyway, get O'Brien. Professor Reynolds glowed with pride when she learned of my prowess with the required burden, but I felt my fellow teaching mates edging away from me in suspicion.

It was on the occasion of the APA Christmas party of 1963 that pinballs and Christmas ornaments were to collide. At the end of the year, while persuading the Bronx at large that a more universal vowel sound might better serve their lives, I received an invitation to the party given at the West Side apartment shared by manager Bob Gold and composer Harvey Schmidt of *The Fantasticks* fame. Tiny Bob Gold, looking like an extra in a Marx Brothers movie with his shiny bald head and very round black-rimmed glasses, served, or rather endured, Ellis's imperious lack of interest in business details by becoming the numbers guy. To describe him as five foot four would be generous, which made for a rather comic pairing as he bopped earnestly behind Ellis, stalking myopically ahead, wreathed in cigarette smoke with his coat draped over his shoulders and some aspect of silk floating behind. Gold must have had family money, as APA couldn't pay more than a pittance, and Harvey Schmidt, of course, had already made a killing with the Little Musical That Could . . . and Did . . . and Did. Schmidt was as bearlike and sloppy as the miniature Gold was impeccable and tidy, and they opened their home to the company, friends, and acquaintances for a Christmas celebration one crisp, windy evening.

I arrived around eight, which I believed to be fashionably late, only to realize that a great deal of the party had already begun to disperse. Or, in some cases, collapse. Actors past and present had arrived nearer six with the enthusiasm theater folk have for free food and free liquor, all hell-bent on recapturing their essential if intermittent camaraderie. The more ebullient of the group—led by Keene Curtis, Dick Woods, and the hilarious Page Johnson, who belied his darkly glamorous looks with one of the sharpest and wittiest tongues of the set—were still in full hue and cry. Clayton Corzatte, like me, had just arrived with his wife, Susan, dressed for the party in a bright red corduroy sheath adorned with rows and rows of black ball fringe. Page turned around and said, "Good God, Susan! You look like you shot your sofa!" She drifted toward the drinks table as if she'd been beaned with a two-by-four. Ellis and Rosemary were still there, as well as Dee Victor, her nose redder than usual with holiday cheer, the two Geer sisters, Sydney Walker, Eve Roberts, and others. In one of the larger rooms wandered the small, bespectacled wife of one of the young actors of the company, who, too many sheets to the holiday wind, decided to correct her lack of admirers by occasionally raising her skirt over her head as she drifted around. She had taped a red bow to the front of her panty girdle, and from the depths of the raised skirt you could often hear the muted cry "D'you like me?" Nobody seemed to mind.

I never really cared for parties. Especially large ones. And this one was no exception, because there were so many close associates in the room who knew one another well, with no idea who the student teacher might be. I much prefer six to eight people, no matter who they are, to large social gatherings, so at about ten o'clock I put on my hat and coat, and after puzzling over to whom I should offer my thanks, opened the front door to see two gentlemen in overcoats, scarves, and gloves facing me. As I stepped back to allow them to pass, I felt someone grab my coat from behind. It was Ellis. "No, you don't," he growled into my ear. "That's T. Edward Hambleton of the Phoenix Theatre. We'd given up hope he was coming. Sit down and play that goddamn piano . . . he expects a party, and I don't want to embarrass him!"

How many were left by this time? Twenty? Fourteen? Only a sparse few of them, including the panty-girdle flasher, were sprinkled around the piano where I sat playing over and over "Have Yourself a Merry Little Christmas," and that old Delt favorite, "Baby, It's Cold Outside." Other than the inverted skirt, the rest of us kept silently staring down at the far end of the room where, behind closed glass-paneled doors, Ellis and Bob Gold were huddled with T. Edward Hambleton and Norman Kean, his general manager. They sat on four dining room chairs, their knees nearly touching, their heads bent conspiratorially together. Finally they rose and opened the door, and all heads at the piano, save for the singing skirt, snapped back to me and my concert. In less than ten minutes the party had emptied out into West End Avenue, me as well, no more in possession of what had happened within those closed doors than before.

Well, what *had* happened? T. Edward had a theater, the East 74th Street, under the protective wing of the Phoenix as well as a property he was hawking, the Edwin Piscator adaptation of *War and Peace*. He was in need of a director and actors. Ellis, on the other hand, had actors, a repertory of plays, and nowhere to play them. It seemed, on the surface, a marriage made in theatrical heaven, but T., as he was universally known, wasn't necessarily interested in APA's rep, only its brilliant director, so that evening he said his polite no and took himself off into January. But January produced no better idea, and certainly no more auspicious director, and there on the distant horizon was the glimmering possibility of Rosemary Harris as Natasha. So before long a deal was struck: the Phoenix would present, that spring, a season of APA's repertory of plays—Pirandello's *Right You Are*, *The Tavern*, and Molière's *Impromptu at Versailles*, with *Scapin*, and for this gesture, Ellis Rabb would open his following season with *War and Peace*. Once I learned of this, I assumed that it was my version of "Have Yourself a Merry Little Christmas" that must have sealed the deal.

Come early spring, I myself threw a party one weekend for some of the APA actors down in Brooklyn Heights during which a very different kind of deal was struck. We were all sitting around the narrow living room of the apartment on the corner of Remsen and Henry Streets, with Keene, Ellis, and Sydney Walker seated on the couch as if waiting for a train. I was, I blush to confess, at Ellis's feet, and although it was unintentional, it seemed utterly appropriate. Ellis was discussing the remounting of *The Tavern*, which he was again to direct as well as play the flashy role of the Vagabond. Richard Baldridge, who had originally served as something of an objective eye for Ellis during the Ann Arbor season, had recently left the nest with no new assignments to his liking. The group of actors began to take affectionate jibes at their leader's proclivity for what they suggested was overacting. Ellis looked archly at his empty glass, tolerated the sarcasm for a while, giving as good as he was getting, and finally rose wearily to his feet, saying, "I don't need any more of this abuse; all I need is more wine and a good cover." "Lover?" someone snorted. Everyone laughed. Ellis chose to ignore the remark. And then, to me, as I poured Chablis into his glass, he went on, "What these philistines never understand is that one needs help at a time like this, not sarcasm." For emphasis, he put a hand to his brow, sinking comically back into the sofa with one of his favorite Kaufman/Hart quotes: "Is there anyone who suffers as I do from the gross inadequacies of the human race?" "What's a cover?" I asked in earnest. Keene piped up: "Someone who stands in for Ellis, saying his lines, but isn't as good as Ellis or he gets fired." Everyone laughed again. Sydney Walker added, "It's often helpful if the person covering can do it in a bathing suit, so we don't lose our concentration." "Or mistake him for Ellis," added Dick Woods. Applause. "No, I'm serious," Ellis went on, "Rosemary says that Olivier . . ." and the rest was drowned out by affectionate groans of derision. Ellis was forever quoting Rosemary about Olivier, and the company liked to pretend to suffer the indulgence. Over this, Ellis proclaimed, "Well, it's true! Olivier has the best cover imaginable!" Rosemary Harris was over at the Chichester Festival in England, where Laurence Olivier was directing his revival of Chekhov's *Uncle Vanya* in the illustrious company of his peers—Michael Redgrave, Joan Plowright, Dame Sybil Thorndike, and her aged husband, Sir Lewis Casson. Olivier had contacted Rosemary and invited her to play Ophelia opposite the young Peter O'Toole to open the new National Theatre in *Hamlet*. He knew she was involved with her new American company, but the commitment would only be for eleven weeks, dictated by the complicated film restrictions on O'Toole at the time. Ellis and Rosemary were both thrilled about this, and it seemed quite possible, until Olivier further decided to suggest that Rosemary replace Joan Greenwood, famous for her idiosyncratic voice and drawling speech, in the key role of Elenya in his *Vanya*. He had decided to bring this brilliant Chichester production into London to join the National season. Ms. Greenwood was pregnant, meaning she couldn't accompany them in the move, but for Rosemary this would now represent a commitment of an entire year, not the original eleven weeks. Although this couldn't help but be an ill-timed blow for Ellis and APA, it was obviously an opportunity Rosemary could not afford to pass up, although it would mark an extensive physical separation between husband and wife in their relatively young marriage. Rosemary went with Ellis's blessing, and the full knowledge that this separation couldn't help but have consequences. So over she went, in truth bringing a degree of reflected glory on this young company in America. And all the while, scraps of anecdotal information kept coming back to the company from her rehearsals in England like glorious inside gossip. Whatever APA was, whatever it might become, there above and beyond always stood the theatrical royalty of Great Britain with their National Theatre, something America might never achieve, and everyone was fascinated to know how it all worked, practically speaking. "Rosemary says" was a phrase that echoed continually, not only because she had already achieved a pre-star reputation inside and outside APA, but also because what she said and thought mattered so deeply to Ellis. The company often fondly referred to her as "the Truth Matron," even to her face, but Ellis took her opinions as divine law and expected everyone else to follow suit. Now, in my apartment in Brooklyn Heights, Ellis went on: "Rosemary says that whenever Bob Lang is on as Sir's cover, and she has her back to Astrov in the scene, she literally cannot tell if it's Olivier speaking or Bob." The room fell silent. Wow. So that was British professionalism. What did we know?

There was a pause. "I'll do it!" I heard myself saying suddenly. "I'll be your cover!" Ellis looked down at me. "Will you?" he asked, narrowing his eyes. "Will you really? There's no pay, we can't give you anything, you understand." I nodded. "And it wouldn't be easy. You'd have to copy my every inflection, learn every crook of the finger, every pause I took, so that there would be no possible adjustment for the company when I'm directing out front. You'd literally have to do what Bob Lang does!"

I was overwhelmed with what was being said, while still smarting a bit over Ellis's rejection of me as an actor. "Will you watch me when I'm playing for you?" I inquired in all innocence. Ellis took one of his patented pauses, while the others held their breath for the payoff. Then, the sepulchral reply: "I won't be able to take my eyes off you!" Everyone in the room laughed long and loud, but I honestly didn't get the joke.

In Cohan's farce *The Tavern*, an affectionate spoof of the quintessential American melodrama, the Vagabond comes on talking and continues to talk in melodramatic paragraphs throughout the play, either the ravings of a madman or the hyperbole of a poet. If Ellis needed proof of my loyalty, this would be it it. I would learn the part cold on my subway rides and turn up on the first day of rehearsal words perfect so I could give my full concentration to Ellis's every move and blink of an eye. Just as he'd directed.

Conveniently situated directly behind what was once the East 74th Street Theatre was a building called the Bavarian National Hall, and it was there that APA, thanks to Hambleton's patronage, secured rehearsal space, and there, one warm early spring day, that the cast of *The Tavern* gathered for its initial rehearsal. Most of the company had played in previous engagements. Clayton Corzatte was repeating his role of the hillbilly son, Zach; Richard Woods and Joanna Roos were back in their roles of Governor and Mrs. Lamson, which I had witnessed in Ann Arbor. Page Johnson's nearly definitive "crazy man," Willum, who had the play's most famous line—"What's all the shootin' fer?"—had now been passed to another actor, and for this new off-Broadway engagement, Keene Curtis would debut in the relatively small role of the Sheriff. Johnson, never one to brood or play spoilsport at not being cast, masked his disappointment by sending a note to the company which ended with "and if Keene Curtis is playing the Sheriff, I'm putting all my money into lipstick stock."

But it was in the two major women's roles that the production would differ significantly from what I had seen. In Ann Arbor, Rosemary Harris played Miss Virginia, one of the most outrageous bits of farce acting I can recall. In that production, Ann Meacham was Violet, a schizophrenic drama queen if ever one were written. Miss Meacham had previously made a name for herself in the late fifties in a series of off-Broadway revivals of Ibsen, and when Ellis first went to interview her, this actress of cobralike intensity entertained him wearing a white lace peignoir and, with her hair tumbling down around her shoulders, led him to the sunlit balcony of her apartment, where she served him a breakfast of fresh strawberries. Ellis, enchanted, believed that beneath the serpentine exterior of this ice princess beat the heart of a lost ingénue, so he cast her in all the wrong parts for that first Ann Arbor season—Maria in *The School for Scandal*, Violet in *The Tavern*, and Dorcas, the dewy romantic lead in John Whiting's fragile little farce *A Penny for a Song*. Her morning moment of ingénue innocence was the only one she ever achieved, and with no semblance of a sense of humor, she managed to cancel out even the comedic powerhouse of Will Geer in the Whiting play. Miss Meacham was clearly not for APA, but the coup this time around was Nancy Marchand returning to nail Violet perfectly, among her other roles. Nancy and Ellis had been inseparable classmates at Carnegie Tech, and although she was a year or two ahead of him, hers had been the talent Ellis most admired before he met Rosemary. She was his Arkadina in *The Seagull* at the Folksbiene, with Rosemary as Nina and Clayton Corzatte as Constantin, and although the two actresses were always respectful and polite to each other, one sensed a frisson of tension whenever they were brought together. But Rosemary was now in England for this engagement, and Ellis was free to openly revel in every acting choice Nancy made. As she began to apply her comic invention to the feverish line readings of this demented character, he stood to one side, hugging the elbow that supported his cigarette and chuckling. She could do no wrong.

Neither, I was to discover, could the new Miss Virginia. When Ellis had announced his intention to revive *The Tavern* for the 74th Street Phoenix season, along with the news that Miss Harris would not be returning from London in time to join the company, I couldn't imagine what would possess him to attempt the play without her as its comic linchpin. "Christine Pickles is going to play it, and she'll be hilarious," he said in the car as we drove together down Seventh Avenue toward the garage on Sheridan Square where he kept his small green convertible. I was dismissive. What kind of name was "Pickles" for an actress, anyway, I joked lamely. "Her uncle is Wilfred

Pickles, a famous music hall star of the London stage. I adore her, she is divine, and you clearly don't know a goddamn thing about it!" he snapped, impatient at my ignorance. I held my tongue.

Christina Pickles, who was without that final *a* in her name at this time, born British, was briefly married before meeting Victor Lobl, her second husband, who became the father of her children, Rebecca and Oliver. As Miss Virginia, instead of the bone-china idiocy that was Rosemary's hallmark, she clumped about like a gawky English schoolgirl fresh from the lacrosse fields, all elbows and immense blue eyes, the exact opposite of Rosemary's creation. Sydney Walker, who stood always as if braced against an imaginary wind, was the landowner Freeman, and Jane MacArthur completed the major players as Sally, the love of Zach's life.

Since the majority of the company had played the production before, there was no need to sit down for a table read. In the interest of expediency, Ellis announced, they would just get up on their feet and basically review their old blocking. "And, oh yes, this is Mr. O'Brien, who has graciously consented to serve as my rehearsal cover," he said dismissively, and everyone smiled encouragingly at me, with no idea of what was in store for them.

The Tavern is a perfect send-up of the kind of nineteenth-century melodrama that was a staple of the American theater for nearly a century, and Ellis's production was a tribute to every bit of it. As I've said, the three flat, painted scenic walls were two-dimensionally rendered with a painted fireplace downstage right including a painted stone mantel, over which was featured an immense painted moose's head. In an inspired moment of lunacy, Nancy Marchand glimpsed it over her shoulder and shrieked as if she were about to be attacked. The most memorable gag of the production, however, was up center. Each time the flimsy canvas door was opened, an offstage stagehand tossed handfuls of leaves into a nearby fan, thus obliterating the person entering in autumnal fury, while, backstage, other unseen hands shook an old-fashioned thunder sheet violently and beat on a timpanum. These were charming, melodramatic special effects, and the capper, of course, came at the end of the play when the Vagabond opened the door to leave, free and unrestrained, and instead of the expected autumnal blast, apple blossoms cascaded around his head.

But first there were the initial scenes to block, which Ellis did with a patient consideration of actors' concerns. Finally it was time for him to make his first entrance. He walked up to the taped markings on the floor which signified the door, script in hand, and, throwing his right arm out, entered braying "What a night! What a glorious night! What a damned fool any man is to be *indoors* on a night like this!"

The Vagabond is nothing if not bravura, and Ellis strode down center, cigarette ash spraying left and right while he gestured with one hand holding a pencil, his script in the other, his glasses pulled down on his nose so he could see his lines, very few of which he seemed to remember from the previous season. He moved left, turned upstage, whirled about, moved down right to peer into someone's face, did a small jig, and, while streaming the text, ended his opening tirade near the stairwell, where Nancy Marchand stood on the landing, waiting for her next cue. I stared at him as if my entire life depended upon it. I watched every detail, his arms, his carriage. I registered exactly where he turned, when he turned, making a mental note of which inflection swooped up, which cascaded down to the bottom of his considerable vocal range. I was going to will myself into a veritable copying machine, National Theatre of Great Britain and Robert Lang be damned! Further business and moves were sorted out as Ellis continued to block, and eventually he walked off the set, saying "Now, let's see what we've got, shall we? Jack, will you do the honors, please?"

They began again at the top of the play, moving not much faster nor more impressively through what they had just done, only occasionally looking up from their scripts in the direction of whomever they were addressing. Clayton pranced gingerly as Zach, and Nancy Marchand made her entrance, distraught and exhausted, collapsing into a chair. Water was sought, and she was seen to—"Take this woman to a room without a window!" Things seemed to be plodding along fairly well when Ellis's entrance came up. I stepped up to the center space, and when the cue was given, whirled through the door like an insane thing, arms flung out in the exact pattern I had seen Ellis execute, but, of course, the difference being that I was not carrying a script nor a pencil. I was giving a performance. I had committed the entire part to memory on the IRT, and by God! out it came, written in boldface type.

"What a night," I roared, echoing as closely in my tinny Michigan tenor as I could every inflection I remembered. "What a glorious night! What a damned fool any man is to be indoors on a night like this!" I strode down to the footlights, whirled to my left, staggered over to peer into someone's astonished face, did a jig identical to the one Ellis had executed, and managed to do it all pretty much on a single breath. At the conclusion of this display there was stunned silence. Nancy Marchand slowly withdrew the cigarette from her lips, and in that unmistakably nasal tone, peered out into the room. "Um . . . El? Is he gonna do that?"

One thing about life's lessons: one may feel stung when they hit, but something important manages to get through. Rehearsal is by definition a private process. What one does not need in the room is the distraction of a "performance," at least not before everyone else has some idea of what they might be doing themselves. This was a lesson I was going to have to learn over and over, but once I had turned down the volume and the need to "be seen," I managed to do my job properly. I was becoming less an actor and more an observer, but the exercise of putting myself thorough Ellis's acting choices, disciplining myself to figure out why he moved at any certain moment, was to prove invaluable to me in my determination to turn myself into a perfect amanuensis.

Even under the spell of the National Theatre, Ellis kept his nose to the local grindstone with one eye trained across the pond to what Rosie might be experiencing at the National. Into our midst on a visit came playwright Peter Shaffer, urbane, witty, at the height of his popularity, and Ellis was captivated by the way Peter tossed effortless bons mots left and right like so much confetti. Beyond the obvious social pleasures, the concept of an artistic director having a living playwright at his beck and call haunted Ellis. I sat in the waning light of the Christopher Street apartment one afternoon while Peter talked about how he worked with Olivier, and how Sir Laurence would give him his instructions. Ellis was riveted. This was something he had yet to consider—a playwright in residence, responding to his executive creative needs. John Osborne's play A Bond Honored, which we were discussing and which had been scheduled, was fairly short. Sir Laurence felt something else should be coupled with it to make a full evening's entertainment, but what would that be? Olivier turned to Shaffer to solve the problem and supply something light, a farce to refresh the palate after the drama, as the Greeks used to do. Maggie Smith and Robert Stephens were starring in the Osborne and would have to be cast in the second, but "don't make Maggie's part too big," said Sir Laurence to Peter, "she's already got a lot on her plate. But she'd better be funny!" The result, of course, was Shaffer's inspired *Black Comedy*, which has long outlived Osborne's Spanish adaptation in memory and pedigree. Ellis loved this idea. Why shouldn't APA do the same? As wineglasses were refilled, he toyed with having a play written for APA, and once more sensing there might be a void to be filled, I began thrusting idea after idea before him in the weeks that followed, with little response: a one-act farce I dashed off was followed by an ambitious melodrama about a wealthy family arguing over a philanthropic foundation to be created from their ill-gotten fortune. This concept, at least, managed to distract him. Over dinner one night, he fantasized about how he thought the play should work. He pulled at a cigarette and stared thoughtfully up into the light. "I think my character should never speak in the first act at all, but when I do come on, at the very end, let's say, the entire chemistry must change without my speaking a single word." He launched a circle in the air of cigarette smoke. "And I want to look," and I joined the next phrase in perfect tandem—"veddy, veddy beautiful!" We both laughed, but I went instantly to work, writing what I thought to be sophisticated parts for Nancy Marchand and her husband, Paul Sparer, for Sydney Walker, and a few others, including a small, bitchy part for Rosemary in case she might return and feel left out. At the end of the first act, when Ellis's character had already been discussed ad nauseam by the rest of the characters, I wrote that he drifted through the room and up a vast staircase trailed by his young lover and exited into their bedroom wordlessly, and then Nancy's character "turned front, and exhaled an expansive cloud of smoke." Curtain! "Point, match, and Pulitzer," I thought.

Or maybe not. It all may sound a bit more promising than what I produced, but whatever else, my daily presence in Ellis's life put us in a continual dialogue. What did he think of this? Why wouldn't that idea work just as well? "Let me in!" was my unspoken refrain, and through it all we were becoming better and better friends, laughing more than anything else. And laughter inevitably prevails.

Sitting together in the living room at Christopher Street one winter afternoon, we were ruminating over all of this as my determination to do something, anything—write a play, throw a party, learn a part, contribute somehow—reached its zenith. He was in one of his early "up" periods, and he was now giving me complete consideration, neither joking nor patronizing. He said, putting aside my latest rewrites, that the problem was not that I was one kind of writer as opposed to another kind, but simply that I wasn't a writer at all. I was, to be perfectly blunt, a teaching fellow at Hunter College dabbling in the arts. "You're standing outside the chain-link fence, watching the game," he said dispassionately. "It's no good. You can't play safe and have it both ways. You'll never really make any kind of contribution unless you commit yourself. Period. Unless your whole life depends on what you do, you can't ever expect to be taken seriously."

The chain-link fence! It hit me fully in the face. I was back in Saginaw again, on that bicycle, holding on to the cold steel of the playground fence, watching, while others actually did something. Was that going to be my life? Was I going to stay on the fence, creatively, sexually as well, in every aspect of my life, the "perfect third," the acquiescent observer, or was I going to finally get into the game? I took a deep breath, and out came the pinball's fatal line: "What should I do?"

He stood up decisively. "I think you obviously have to join the company!" he said, and exited into the tiny kitchen out of my sight. I couldn't believe my ears! Here was the lifeline I had been praying for. I followed him where he was fussing with the coffeepot. "What do you mean? What as?"

He looked back at me, startled. I had the immediate feeling that he hadn't thought beyond this, hadn't judged the seriousness of our conversation. He began to improvise. "You'll be my assistant. I need someone to help me, I can't possibly be expected to handle all this without some support." He lit the stove under the carafe, warming to his subject. "You will do everything, the correspondence, the telephone calls, balance my checkbook," and then with a vague wave in the direction of the bedroom, "organize Rosemary . . . You'll take my notes, you'll take dictation, you'll . . . you'll . . ." He ran out of specifics. "It'll be wonderful. But the point is, you'll finally be on the inside. I think you should take it or leave it—a leap of faith. What the fuck difference does it matter what you do? At last you'll be in the theater. Not outside."

Inside. That struck a chord. At this moment, Bob James and I were actively pursuing a couple of possible writing projects over at Edwin H. Morris music publishers, compliments of Sylvia Herscher, but they were still far from reality. She had introduced us to the British librettist Hugh Wheeler, who would write *Sweeney Todd* in the late seventies and who was working on a libretto called *Dieu le Veut* ("God wills it"—a battle cry of the medieval period, in which the comedy was set), and with the continuing patronage of Stuart Ostrow, who had also surfaced back when *Land Ho!* won its award, we were working on a sketch for a college campus musical: "write what you know," right? We had written a few good songs, we were spending as much time collaborating as we could afford, but Bob was moonlighting now accompanying the great Sarah Vaughan on tour as her music director; he was legit, at least, and where was I? Teaching public speaking at Hunter College. Big difference. Bob was in music; I was in school. My father's old pal Gerald Marks arranged an interview for us over at Chappell Music Company to meet Dr. Albert Sirmay, a portly little Viennese of seventy years or so, dressed always in a white lab coat, who had cared for the likes of Cole Porter and his peers over the decades. Dr. Sirmay fixed me with a suspicious eye. "Are you rrrich, Mr. O'Brrrrien," he burred in his middle-European accent. "No, sir, not really. Why?" "Vell, how do you expect to surwive? Cole vas rrrich! He could afford to wrrrite his lyrics. How can you dewote the time necessary to be rrrreally gut? Vat vill you do?"

Vat, indeed? I existed in no-man's-land. Not within the industry, nor even working for a producer. Here, at last, was someone inviting me over to the right side of the room. It wasn't an offer to do lyrics for a Broadway score, but it wasn't Voice and Diction, either.

I think there are words one says, one hears, that do in fact change everything. Words have power, and the expression of them, heard by another person, can move the mountain more swiftly, more assuredly than all of Mohammed's prayers. We all may understand the fatality of the five words "I don't love you anymore." One cannot retract them no matter how hard one tries. Conversely, this invitation of Ellis's, this challenge of mine, had been answered definitively, and I knew that the offer would never come again.

"When?" I said quietly. "As soon as possible," came Ellis's answer. He flashed one of his pursed-mouth smiles, both intimate and ironic, and, pouring acid coffee into a dirty mug, walked out of the room and into his bedroom. The subject was closed. The next move was mine.

He offered, through the Phoenix, a salary of exactly half what I was making at Hunter. My teaching was netting me $250 a week. Ellis offered $125. I called my mother and tried to explain. I sat with Professor Reynolds and said, in spite of the fact that she was already dangling before me the possibility of tenure at Hunter, even without a Ph.D., that I thought I must go.

Both women solemnly agreed, both of them sitting securely on the far side, where logic and reason live. My mother told me she loved me and believed in me. Professor Reynolds said she always knew I wasn't really serious about an academic life but she had sought me out just the same, she liked having me around, and she graciously wished me well and shook my hand.

I would finish out that winter term at Hunter, then make the leap of faith that had been sketched out for me. And on that first morning, when I emerged from the subway at Christopher Street and Seventh Avenue, I presented myself like a shining schoolboy at Ellis's apartment. As I took off my coat and looked around, I heard Ellis from the recesses of his bedroom in a towering rage about funding, or budgets, or availabilities, or all of them, calling out to me: "Jack? Is that you? Take a letter! I'm quitting! I'm disbanding APA! I've had it. I'm going to destroy this fucking organization before it destroys me!" He strode through the room, half dressed, a hairbrush in his hand, torturing his hair as he went, dandruff flying, not even looking at me. "Send a letter to Bette Davis, to Marlon Brando, to"—he marched back out into the bedroom in search of cigarettes, howling back the names of one impossible film and stage star after another—"Chris Plummer, to Geraldine Page, to Hal Holbrook . . ." And as I sank down on the edge of the sofa, I thought, *Can I still call Hunter, or is it too late?*

12

On January 22, 1965, Ellis had the following message typed and put on the company call-board, complete with four black "warning" arrows surrounding the word ATTENTION! written in black capital letters:

LADIES AND GENTLEMEN OF APA

I am happy to announce I have engaged a full-time assistant who will, I think, make me a more efficient person, better able to serve myself, the cause, and all. Some of you are familiar with his shining, happy face—Mr. Jack O'Brien, of all trades, master of each. His phone number is JA 2-1556. Use it.

Love,
Ellis

P.S. I leave you all for one week of rest. I shall do my best not to think of you. Try and find me! Be kind, one to the other.

E

Lovely. And even better—when I now regard that forgotten piece of paper, recently restored into my hands by Miss Harris herself, it is clear that not only did I type that on my own IBM Selectric typewriter myself, but it was I who applied the arrows. No job too small!

Like a shuffled low-value playing card, I was absorbed into the company by following Ellis around like a puppy until I became established. As the message indicates, he hired me and left town—for a brief sojourn in the Caribbean accompanied by Victor Lobl, Christina Pickles's husband, as his companion, and I watched performances of that Phoenix season from a wary distance. Before Ellis left on that brief holiday, I asked him to make some kind of announcement to the company. "What kind?" was his response. "Well, don't you think they should know that I'll be taking notes? That I will be coming around after the performance with, you know, observations and things?" He didn't take even a moment to phrase his response: "When it is time for you to give the company notes, both you and they will know it." And he was gone.

The judgment didn't sound to me altogether like Ellis, but it had a ring of truth about it. Of course this couldn't just be a baton passed from one to another on goodwill alone. It would have to be earned.

And so to the earning. My first assignment was Rosemary. She had only recently returned from her booking with Olivier and the Brits, and now she was being left home while Ellis once more slipped away. He understood how important it was that I not seem to be simply "his," but rather "theirs." Rosemary wasn't always enthusiastic about the cadre of men, primarily gay men, who surrounded Ellis. When they were wed, for example, he had no fewer than nine grooms-men for the wedding party—not all gay, of course—while she was completely alone. Neither of her two sisters was available to make the trip over from England for the ceremony. When queried by the min-ister as to the advisability of this—who would she pass her bouquet to, and what if she were to faint?—she responded candidly, "It's far likelier that Ellis will faint than I will!" But as much fun as he and I were having—two Geminis jumping over each other like porpoises eager for the next distraction—he knew that our association must ex-ist on an altogether professional basis, and that basis included attend-ing to Rosemary as well. To my obvious disappointment at being left behind, he said, "You'll get the next trip, I promise. Much better . . ." He meant the idea, not necessarily the trip.

But how was this to be effected, practically speaking? I had been hired by Ellis to attend him—my management skills yet untried and unknown—primarily because we were kindred spirits. I had been privy to the social ambivalence that was an open secret—he was a married man with a decidedly gay past, and although Rosemary cer-tainly understood much of that past, the present had yet to be actu-ally tested so far as their marriage was concerned. And, in the honored

Gemini tradition, I was to be placed precisely between them, a buffer of service to them both, obviously, but variously, with the tacit understanding that some things could and would be shared among us, others best not. No other instructions were ever spoken. Ellis obviously trusted me. Rosemary was meant to trust me as well, but only so far as a part of the scenario went. That this might be patently unfair ultimately both to Rosemary and to me was never acknowledged.

The morning he and Victor Lobl left for the Caribbean, I presented myself at 77 Christopher Street, ready for duty. Rosie was standing in the middle of the living room waiting for me. She was barefoot, dressed in a full-length nylon peignoir of pale pink flowers, her ample breasts free within, and her prematurely gray hair secured at the nape of the neck by the ubiquitous rubber band. She stood in the midst of a sea of papers, letters, contracts, scraps, as if walking on white water, turning in circles and looking bemused. We dug in— this pile was correspondence, and this one was out-of-pocket receipts to be filed . . . this pile went to the accountant for tax purposes, and . . . "give me your checkbook, and let me see if I can't do a little reconciling." We ended up on the floor until four o'clock in the afternoon, basically making piles, and laughing a good deal. She was, in the relief of getting it done, like a child at play, and chaos was slowly beginning to disappear. Over the next few days we continued to work together. I wrote checks, I mailed overdue papers, I scheduled appointments, and we went out to two different terrific evenings. That first night we attended *Sweet Charity*, which was the first time I ever saw Gwen Verdon live, and the first time I understood what "triple threat" meant. She could sing, God knows she could dance, but she was also an incandescent actress, and I found myself in tears during "If They Could See Me Now!" experiencing the melting of all resistance that occurs in the presence of a star. Like a sleepwalker jolted awake, I sat in the theater suddenly reminded of my original calling. That woman up there, was she so very different from the woman sitting beside me? Was I drifting off my prescribed course? And if so, should I not be following Cy Coleman rather than Ellis Rabb? Perhaps it was all the same thing. "Inside," at last . . . We left exhilarated, but it was a night or so later, when we took in the film of *Mary Poppins*, that Rosemary was reduced to childlike delight and pulled me along with

her. I became immediately identified as her private nanny, and "Spit
spot!" was the command I could use to get her moving. I was "Nanny
Jack" to her then, and I have remained so over the past fifty-plus
years. Few others "in service," I believe, have lasted quite so long.

The lights dim to half, and somewhere from behind and above the
audience comes a bloodcurdling scream: *"Juuuuuuddddiiiiiiittttthhhh!"*

I stood in the very back of the small balcony of the East 74th
Street Theatre, howling my lungs out, while from backstage other
voices joined mine. The house had just gone to black, and from my
perch above the orchestra, I could barely make out the shapes of
actors scurrying into their positions at the top of the play before
the lights were to come up. The play was Giraudoux's *Judith,* a
post–World War II French take on the Jewish princess who be-
headed Holofernes and became a legend of independence and brav-
ery. It had enjoyed moderate success in London, where it was
primarily known as the vehicle in which that great Scot Sean Con-
nery played the role of Holofernes clad only in a gold lamé jock-
strap. This version, however, would become a landmark for the
performance of its leading lady, who was returning to APA after her
triumph in London. And to get *Judith* as well as Miss Harris onto
the East 74th Street stage was going to take considerably more
screaming than mine.

The repertory for the spring of 1965 was *Man and Superman,*
again directed by Stephen Porter, with the inclusion of the famous
"Don Juan in Hell" scene. Ellis was Tanner, Nancy Marchand was
Ann Whitefield, and Rosemary was Violet, playing the second female
lead from which she would once again scoop up a majority of the reviews. *War and Peace,* having had its out-of-town birth in Ann Arbor
during the University of Michigan fall season, was the season's centerpiece. Rosemary was the improbable childlike Natasha—"At the
beginning of the play, I am thirteen years old and don't come into the
story, but Mama says that a girl of eighteen who is unmarried is a
dis*grace!*" she chirped in the tableau vivant that began the evening.
Nevertheless, the event itself proved to be a company display of terrific ensemble acting rather than a showcase for anyone other than

Ellis as director. The season's centerpiece was meant to be *Judith*, and as Rosemary professed to admire the play and longed to do it, the assignment figured strongly in the mix of magic and loyalty designed to lure her home.

But the earth had turned slightly in her absence, as it inevitably does. Old habits being difficult to break, and separation and loneliness having taken their toll, Ellis had fallen inadvertently under the spell of a University of Michigan graduate, a young actor named John Allan Macunovich, tall, classically good-looking, with an ebullient spirit and a voice and laugh to match. The university world at that point was very much his oyster. Ellis had attended a university performance of *The Importance of Being Earnest* in which John Allan played Worthing, and since the director was Claribel Baird, whom Ellis found as irresistible as did everyone else, it was only a matter of time before Claribel was pleased to introduce Ellis to her awestruck cast. And it wasn't much longer before John Allan was getting advice from Ellis about acting . . . which led to dinners . . . which led to . . .

John Allan was a golden youth, an unwieldy colt, golden with health, his hair golden, his voice, alas, not so much golden as loud. He possessed what Shaw would call the "life force," and that kind of energy always held a fatal attraction for Ellis. And if no one took any of this seriously at the beginning, we were soon to find it our preoccupation. John Allan was sort of around, and then he was continually around, and then with the sound of a braying laugh that could shatter cement, he was in the company. He was engaged to be in *War and Peace*, understudy Hector Malone in the Shaw, and play one of the hangers-on in the court of Holofernes in *Judith*.

As Rosemary returned to begin rehearsing, two immense issues were waiting at the door. One was the role of Judith itself. At this point in her career, she had dazzled as Ophelia, as Desdemona, as Lady Teazle, as Violet in *Man in Superman*, in virtually every part but a title role. Her ability to shoot from the side, to walk onstage and capture everyone's affection, was indisputable. But what she had yet to do was to carry a show. To play the title role is to assume responsibility for the evening, to load other careers, other expectations on one's shoulders and prepare to honor them as well as deliver. Although there are other roles in *Judith*, and the long second-act scene with Holofernes, when he seduces her, offers a duet for two matched players, the play was not called *Judith and Holofernes*, it was called *Judith*. It was time for Rosemary to take the next step in her career, and that meant playing the title role and proving that she had the range, the stamina, and the chops to land the event. She knew this, and so did Ellis, and this vehicle, not yet seen in an American production, was designed to showcase her beauty, her charm, her seductive wiles, and her considerable emotional range. Tall order. Daunting, one might say. These are inevitably private compartments, and one can only speculate what transpires behind closed doors. But finally, who cares? Only the people involved—but I have always subscribed to the theory that "one knows." The certainties in life are death and taxes, no question. Also, I insist, knowing whether someone else in the room is bedding your significant other. Don't kid yourself, you know. You might not want to know, and you might persist in turning a blind eye, but dammit, you know! The standard response is rarely "I had no idea!" It is all too often "I thought so!" Or, more to the point, "I knew it!" We are, after all, as much animal as anything else, much as we prefer to elevate ourselves. Rosemary did not seem especially happy at that time, and if you chose the reason as one from column A rather than column B, you wouldn't be faulted. Life, rehearsals, and relationships were not stopping for any of this, they were all moving inexorably ahead, and there came the morning when I sat against the wall with my notepad in Ellis and Rosemary's bedroom while she stood upright in the bedclothes in that negligee, her hair wild about her head, her fingers plunged within it, her face splotchy with red and crying, howling with rage and pain "I can't! I can't! I just can't!" until, inexplicably, two words registered, offered nearly subliminally by Ellis: red wig! "Oh!" she shuddered, sinking to her knees in relief in the rumpled sheets. "A *red* wig? Well, of *course* I can play her if she's a redhead!"

And the subtext? In a play in which murder is the ultimate act onstage, was there possibly another impulse to murder in which the leading actress might find a source of inspiration? John Allan remained seemingly oblivious to everything, bobbing like a blond cork on the surface of stormy seas, while Ellis contrived to see him in secret and yet with equal determination tried to keep his marriage in balance. The audiences built for the rep, and with them the company's impact on the theater community at large. One night, while signing in for *Judith*, Rosie, having noticed several limos parked out front, remarked cheerily, "Ooooh! We've go' the carriage trade, we 'ave!" in a comic Cockney accent. And so we had. *War and Peace*, an endless cavalcade of inventive staging by Ellis against an all-black surround, featuring elements like a crystal chandelier glowing overhead to represent a ballroom, or toy figures of soldiers and cannon, and a river of silk ribbon placed on a raked platform to locate the battle of Borodino, demonstrated just how much invention he had; it flowed over everything, it encased the production in music cues pulled from Prokofiev and Shostakovitch, while his curtain call, a parade of humanity amid whirling red flags ripping in and out of the ensemble as they marched to the mounting strains of the Red Army Chorus, stands as one of the most powerful theatrical images I've ever seen onstage. I have robbed every conceivable image from it over the intervening years with relish and gratitude.

The rep continued to sell out, and Ellis, high on a cocktail of success and the stimulating danger provided by two compelling and very different lovers, found himself with an appetite for more. He and T. Edward Hambleton decided to combine the resources of the Phoenix Theatre and APA into APA-Phoenix and to apply for a substantial grant from the Ford Foundation to enable them to approach the throne of the Shubert empire and move operations to Broadway, right in the thick of the commercial enterprise. They proposed to take up residence at the classic Lyceum Theatre, east of Broadway on Forty-Fifth Street. This expanded appetite of his was as ambitious for the company's growth as for his own success.

Ellis had a long-held belief that roles in the rep should be shared by various actors in the company, thereby offering a badly needed vocal rest to senior members while allowing the emerging talent to grow and be nurtured in the true classical tradition. Great roles are not meant to be played eight times a week, any more than great opera roles should be sung by the same voice over consecutive performances. Creating a production around experienced actors necessitates that the junior members learn to reproduce the same performance exactly, perfecting their craft from observation. Ellis once despaired that there wasn't a class for the art of mimicking so young actors could replicate and then come to understand how results were achieved. It's hardly an original concept; the Berliner Ensemble, the Moscow Art Theatre, the Comédie-Française have all practiced this for generations, and in spite of occasional spats of jealousy, or the inevitable case of favoritism, which is always bound to happen, it still remains a vital and important practice. Whenever such issues arose within APA, Ellis was quick to charm everyone with the night out of town in Leeds or Bath, when Olivier's production of *The Master Builder* was already in half hour and both Joan Plowright, who was ill, and Maggie Smith, who had heeded the call and journeyed down from London, were in their respective dressing rooms, both dressed in their leather aprons, both making up to play Hilde Wangel, knowing full well the other was present. Although each was grimly determined to go on, Joan played that night, as I recall. She was, after all, Lady Olivier. Ellis shared the role of Tanner in *Man and Superman* with Donald Moffat, while Nancy Marchand shared Ann Whitefield with Rosemary; and since Rosemary was already playing Violet, she shared that role with Christina Pickles, while Donald, whenever appearing at performances opposite Ellis's Tanner, played Tavvy, which he shared with Richard Jordan, and on and on it was encouraged to go.

There was the inevitable afternoon in another season when Ellis called "Places" for a rehearsal of *The School for Scandal* and Donald Moffat, Marco St. John, and Ellis collided down right, each of them ready to begin the scene. Ellis, need I add, ended up playing!

The I Ching attempts to counsel us that whenever life presents itself at its fullest, that is the precise moment when one must be most on guard, most attentive, most cautious. "Attempts to counsel us" is probably appropriate, because I'm never sure I fully absorb that lesson. And the wheel was about to begin its descent, if not spin dangerously off its axis.

In the early spring of 1965 the company was at its fullest component of acting strength in years with Rosemary back, Nancy Marchand and Paul Sparer on board, Donald Moffat, Sydney Walker, Christine Pickles all involved, plus the young married couple Richard Jordan and Kathleen Widdoes rounding out a flourishing ensemble, all enjoying full houses and the rising tide of approval. Ellis, acting less and leading more, had put his shoulder to the wheel of pursuing funding for his and Hambleton's dream of moving the enterprise to

Broadway. The coming season looked auspicious, with a revival of the Kaufman and Hart classic *You Can't Take It with You* scheduled, along with a Stephen Porter production of Ibsen's *The Wild Duck* and a world premiere of a short play written by Archibald MacLeish, *Herakles*, to be directed by none other than Alan Schneider, fresh from *Who's Afraid of Virginia Woolf?* and one of the highest-profile directors Ellis had ever invited into the company. It seemed the perfect opportunity for Ellis to take one last respite before plunging into the season ahead. In *Sports Illustrated* that spring, a glorious photo spread caught my eye, and I rushed into Ellis's apartment with it. "Look, El," I said, thrusting the magazine into his hand. "Have you ever seen anything so beautiful?" There were pictures of the glittering Mediterranean coastline with elegant hotels featuring rows of balcony windows framed in gauzy curtains, everything pristine white and cerulean blue—this was before the horrific collapse of the Mideast that was some years ahead. "It's Beirut, who knew! Have you ever?" "Book it!" came his giddy response, tossing the magazine back at me. "You mean it?" I said, hardly believing my ears. "I promised you a trip, and this is it!" was his response. "I think we should sail, don't you?" he went on, sorting absently through some kerchiefs to knot around his neck. "There must be something crossing this spring worth four or five days of our time." I suddenly felt uncomfortable. Ellis was generous and impulsive, and picking up a check for dinner might be one thing, but a trip abroad was another. I was hardly flush at this point in my life, but some vital instinct lead me to the next thought: "I'd expect to pay my way, you know," I said with an earnestness that surprised even me. "At least so far as hotel rooms go, the transportation, that kind of thing." He smiled charmingly, pulling on his leather jacket. "Are you insane? You can't possibly afford my standard of luxury," he teased. "Well, okay," I said. "Then let me pay what I *can* pay. I mean, what I *would* pay if I were going anyway . . . considering I that wasn't born in Memphis, Tennessee, to indulgent, extravagant parents . . . and you can just make up whatever difference applies. I mean, if some night you prefer to eat in some expensive restaurant and want me along with you . . ." Ellis cut me off with a laugh, grabbing his leather satchel of scripts and his cigarettes and heading for the door. "Right! Terriff-i-york!" he said, using one of his favorite original expressions. "So that should take care of one meal during the whole trip, don't you think?" He opened the door and then, as he disappeared down the staircase, "Bring that magazine with you, will you?" he added. "I'll get the car. But you'd better start planning to-day." And then, as I watched his head disappear down the staircase, "Oh, and don't forget. There'll be three of us. You, me—and John Allan."

I believe my response was something in the nature of "Jesus wept!"

13

For many Americans, a major rite of passage is putting that initial foot onto European soil. Travel can be life-changing, and at the very least broadening; and although I had skipped around the Continent with college chums prior to my senior year—an inveterate outsider and tourist—I was now to be invited, by comparison, "inside." The *France* had one final transatlantic voyage scheduled before being permanently retired that spring, and the direction was New York to Le Havre. The morning of the sailing, a tiny cadre of friends came down to the pier to see us off: Ellis and me . . . and John Allan. It goes without saying that Rosemary was not present in gloves and a lovely straw hat to wave goodbye. I remember little of the pre-sailing celebration, except for the fact that the night before, John Allan and Ellis occupied my bedroom in Brooklyn Heights, and "Nanny Jack" was displaced to the living room couch. Our plans, the itinerary, the bookings, the plotting, the machinations, the half-veiled truths, the baroque explanations, all blur before me like something fast-forwarded.

Voot! Voot! sounded the massive steam whistle, and in two languages, visitors were invited to leave the ship. We three were left behind, in a second-class stateroom with bunk beds and a single twin added, so to say we were cramped is an understatement. In retrospect I wonder how often the *France* was called upon to accommodate three adults in one room where the third occupant wasn't under the age of, say, six. I was assigned the top bunk, which is to say I was placed up on a shelf as if blindfolded, gagged, and heavily sedated and not paying any attention to whatever the other two roommates might do during their sleeping hours. Considering how much we all were drinking at the time, this didn't turn out to be difficult. But I'm getting ahead of myself. No, I'm *rushing* ahead of myself, because the atmosphere was getting tense, and when things are tense, one finds oneself wishing to look ahead to the end of the story to see who might still be left alive. Some tension is always to be expected whenever one is embarking on a trip, but in this case, the amount of diplomatic work it took to get these three occupants into this particular stateroom was anything but easy. Well-wishers eventually left, however, handkerchiefs were waved at the shore, Statues of Liberty were respectfully gazed upon, bags were hastily shoved under beds, and as we chugged resolutely out of sight of Manhattan, we three sat down to our first luncheon in the dining room.

Ellis's mouth was set in a grim line. What had seemed a lark, a private respite from all other entangling alliances, had proven not only a strain but emotionally draining. He was never comfortable being deliberately deceptive, and even this "treat," without Rosemary's full compliance, was going sour. John Allan was ebullient, carefree, interested in everything on board with the exception of Ellis. And I found myself nervously speaking French to the help in an odd attempt to prove once and for all just how helpful I could be. An attractive waiter bobbed in and out to our respective rights, taking orders, and with a manic intensity, I insisted upon translating everything he said from French to English and back again, although his skills in both languages could obviously leave me in the conversational dust. Ellis kept glancing at me darkly as if to remind me I was responsible for the whole unfortunate mess. It wasn't until the dessert course was being announced that the tension finally broke. The waiter said quietly to me "Do you wish dessert, sir?" right in the middle of one of my most spirited and desperate monologues, to which I swiftly turned and in an impeccable French accent, answered him in English: "No, nussing for me, sank you!" There was a count of about four as we all glanced at each other, and then all three of us burst into gales of laughter. You simply cannot get phonier than speaking English with a French accent to a French waiter.

The crossing dissolved into a series of gray, blowy days. John Allan was like a child let out of school, running about the ship, taking advantage of the gym, the pool, the sights and shops aboard, trumpeting his enthusiasm in all directions like a vocal garden spray. Ellis was quiet and tolerant for the most part, but primarily spent time with me in deck chairs while wrapped in blankets against the early spring chill, sipping consommé brought to us by a series of ship's attendants I nicknamed "cookie boys." Our nightly drink of choice at the time being vodka stingers, by evening's end I found myself close to passing out. There was one horrifying night when the stabilizers on the ship broke, and as the waves hurled themselves at the starboard side, Ellis and I, wildly drunk, ended up dancing alone on the afterdeck, howling songs into the oncoming wind. Everyone else had been confined to their cabins. It was meant to be a kind of victory dance, I believe, the final expiation of "all things John Allan," but I recall turning over in my narrow bunk the following morning, blind with a hangover, to see Ellis and John Allan on the adjacent bed, staring up at me and laughing at the groan of agony the sight of their reconciliation produced. The truth was that I could never tolerate liquor to the extent that Ellis could, and my resulting hangovers would last until at least four o'clock the following afternoon. By that time my cabinmates had been up for hours, out playing table tennis, eating, and thoroughly enjoying themselves. Struggling to sit upright at an evening meal, and having missed some critical transition, I would hiss frantically to Ellis "What happened?" only to receive a dismissive wave and a "Later!" as recompense.

But any reconciliation was short-lived, and as we approached the harbor of Southampton, where the British passengers were to disembark, Ellis breathed out one of his unmistakable alarms: "Hmmm!" he said, staring out the porthole grimly. Our private joke was that whenever I heard that sound, I was to drop whatever I was doing and pack. And this would prove no exception. The final two days of sailing had seen John Allan drifting further and further from our society with Ellis growing more and more impatient, until he turned to me and snapped, "We're leaving! Get everything together." In the blink of an eye, we were dumped on British soil at Southampton, and just as swiftly aboard a train for London on our way to visit Ellis's best friend, Richard Easton. At least, that was was said aloud. But privately, to me, Ellis made it clear: we were to spend a day or so with Richard while I arranged to "disinvite" John Allan from the remainder of the trip, as best I could. Within the current climate of confusion and pressure, John Allan could do nothing right, and, oblivious to Ellis's growing irritation, he was making matters worse. It would be my job to invent some reason that John Allan might better enjoy Europe alone than with Ellis and me. His return would be paid for, but the departure and the details would be left to his own discretion. The straw that broke Ellis's emotional back was when he made one last attempt to be forgiving only to see, as they were strolling together through Westminster Abbey, his young swain, ignoring his lecture about Henry V, a role he had recently played as an undergraduate, hyp-notized instead by the image of his own shadow on the wall combing all that blond hair. John Allan had to go!

Diplomats are not born, but made, I presume, from just this kind of assignment. How do you explain to a young man who had every reason to expect three wonderful weeks of vacation with his experi-enced paramour that he would be much happier somewhere else alone? I blush to remember what I did to put this across, but John Allan was neither stupid nor frightened. Life for him was for the liv-ing, with us or without us. He was capable of bouncing back, which he continued to do over the next decades in unexpected ways, at one point even managing all the catering on American Airlines. And late in Ellis's life, it was John Allan who came to his rescue out in Los An-geles, helped him, aided him, proved beyond a shadow of a doubt that he was made of finer stuff than this *jeune premier* crossover could possibly indicate. At this point, however, the only role model that rose before him seemed to be Jean Seberg in *Breathless*. Rather than returning directly to New York, he decided to experience Paris first, where, as it turned out, he supported himself for a while as she had, selling the *Herald Tribune* on the Parisian streets. But if my French was compromised, his was nonexistent, and the last words we spoke to each other in London, where I had spent the better part of two days convincing him of the wisdom of this new plan while Ellis re-treated to the safety of Richard Easton's Earl's Court Terrace flat, was a cheery "Toodle-oo!"

"Toodle-oo," I managed, with an equally big smile on my face. Disappointed, he repeated patiently, "No, toodle-oo! Toodle-oo!" before looking down in confusion at his French phrase book. I peered over his shoulder. He had his thumb on "Tout à l'heure," the French slang for "See you later!" *Oh, Jesus,* I thought, *what have I done?*

But before all this, Richard had met us waving enthusiastically at Waterloo Station, a riveting, expansive, and charming presence. He was playing Nick in the West End production of *Who's Afraid of Virginia Woolf?* at the time, and since I only knew his reputation through Ellis, I was eager for the chance to see for myself precisely who it was that Ellis Rabb thought highly enough of to create a production of *Hamlet* for him. I presented myself at the theater the very next night to see for myself. Sexy, commanding, and effortlessly energetic, Richard had come up through the cream of the Canadian theater ranks in Montreal, transferring into Guthrie's company in Stratford while still in his late teens and finally settling in London, where he was enjoying a career in the West End. It was when appearing as Charles Surface in the exalted company of Sirs Gielgud and Richardson for the famous West End revival of *Scandal* that his remarkable energy caused the flustered Gielgud to remark, "Oh, for God's sake, Richard, why must you be so big? Why can't you be graceful, like me?" Ellis loved to repeat this story, usually in his own rehearsals.

But he and I took instant measure of each other on sight, knowing full well what was required to be a familiar of Ellis's without getting, as it were, in the way. We had no illusions about any of it, and Richard helped me over subsequent years to put Ellis's strengths and weaknesses into perspective without sacrificing either loyalty or compassion. He was an enthusiastic and enchanting host in London, or in fact anywhere, and Ellis quickly recovered his sense of humor in Richard's company as if he'd taken a tonic. I found this power of recovery a relief, wondering all the while how Ellis could sweep so completely under his personal rug a relationship with someone like John Allan, one he had spent such effort in constructing.

But on we went, we happy two: first arriving in the brick-red dawn of an Egyptian sunrise in Cairo only to find our lodging at a Hilton Hotel with strangely greasy stains on the carpets and walls. Hungry from our overnight flight from London, we dropped our bags and instantly ordered for our breakfast club sandwiches from room service; and shortly thereafter up came a tray with Cokes and two attempts at the traditional club sandwich with the most peculiar chicken I've ever seen folded into it. "What's that?" I said, peeling back the toast to reveal a gray, anonymous meat tucked under the lettuce. "That's Egyptian chicken," came Ellis's dismissive reply. At that very moment, off the balcony of our room, an immense bird flapped by, peering hungrily into the window at us. "My God, what's *that?*" Ellis cried. *"That's* Egyptian chicken," came my sullen answer. Flies the size of one's fist came dive-bombing down on Ellis as he attempted a swim in the hotel pool later that day, so after one brief trip out to the Pyramids, during which the camel driver repeatedly snaked his hand up my pantleg as I clung to the sleepy camel he commanded, we beat it out of Cairo without even so much as a backward glance at the legendary museum nearby. Ellis, it must be said, was never one for museums. I realized that I would have to find my own time to sneak away to enjoy such events, if sneaking away ever were to prove possible. We moved immediately on to Beirut and into the luxe arms of the classic St. George Hotel, now a distant memory in that bomb-scarred city. As Ellis was unpacking his bags in the room, he turned to me, his face blank. "Where, exactly, do you suppose we are?" he said. "What do you mean?" I replied. He looked sheepish. "Well, you pretend to know everything—where in the world *is* Beirut, do you actually know?" To be honest, I had no idea, and went immediately to the hotel literature for a map. "El!" I trumpeted in complete astonishment. "We're in Asia fucking *Minor!*" We might as well have booked the moon—we couldn't have been more delighted with ourselves, rather than embarrassed by our parochial ignorance.

Beirut in the mid-sixties was lush and sophisticated and probably more European than any Middle Eastern city could have dreamed of being, and we quickly settled into routines of sleeping late, sunning, reading, and doing as little sightseeing as possible. No word from America. No communiqués about box office, or performance reports, or even personal messages from anyone. We floated through days of rest and sunshine and gourmet meals, sending off postcards like intermittent paper airplanes, and I began to think that all might finally be well again. That thought usually presages something very different.

In the fifties, when Ellis had been an undergraduate, he had traveled one summer by himself to Greece, where he was befriended by a

Greek cabdriver. Ellis, like all theatrical people (present company excepted, of course!), tended to embroider, and, as we eventually discovered, whatever didn't come under the skill of his embroidery might be leavened somewhat by his fantasy life, which could be guaranteed to make the story sexier, with him, need I add, in the star part. In this case, he recalled a Greek god of a cabdriver named Alecco, whose wife was confined at the time having a baby and who followed Ellis about in his cab like a lovesick dog until he was at last permitted to show Ellis all of Athens, as well as, we were informed, quite a bit more of Alecco. Over the decades, Alecco and his wife, Nafsika, maintained a tradition of annual Christmas cards, so when we found ourselves in Beirut and realized we were next due for a stopover in Greece, Ellis contacted Alecco and arranged for him to drive us around Athens and down into the Peloponnesus. We arrived in Athens by prior arrangement to meet the composer Conrad Susa, who had been involved with APA since its inception and who was yet another Carnegie Tech graduate as well as a close personal friend. Conrad was to make up the new third of our party, and together we gathered our bags in the steaming Greek sunlight and stood at the curb waiting for our legendary guide to arrive. Like something out of an MGM movie, a VW convertible appeared, covered in dust, and screeched to a stop before us, its horn beeping frantically. "Elios! Elios!" came the Greek accent behind the wheel. "Elios, I am here!" And then, as if we hadn't understood it in English, he reproduced his own version of the horn. "*Beep-Beep!* Eh? Eh? *Beep-Beep!*" Out from behind the wheel came an immense, hirsute, utterly adorable man, well over six feet tall and nearly as wide. His face was split in a grin revealing a missing tooth or two, a grizzled stubble of black and gray hair covering his cheeks. He didn't seem like the Zorba the Greek of Ellis's story. He seemed, rather, more like three Zorbas the Greek! "Look," he gestured at the open backseat behind him, "just like you say!—'Alecco—convertible!' you say, 'We need Greek sun!' So, you see? we have convertible! You get Greek sun, aaaaand . . . you get Alecco!" Laughing, he embraced each one of us in turn, crushing our ribs like potato chips, then hurled our bags in a tumble into the back, where, so far as I could see, Conrad and I were meant to ride. I tried to catch Ellis's eye. Was this really happening? Is it what he remotely

Jack on the veranda of the St. George Hotel, Beirut, Lebanon, 1965. A mere season before the necessity and appearance of "Harriet Piece," my one and only toupee. (Collection of the author)

expected, not having seen this romantic figure from his past for so long? Smiling enigmatically, he slipped obediently into the passenger seat, skillfully managing to avoid my gaze.

In a matter of moments we were in our hotel, but not for long. Alecco had planned everything down to the second, lunches, dinners, evenings drinking ouzo and smashing plates with Nafsika, their children, and their friends, realizing we had only a matter of days in which to do it all and determined to whip us through Greece as if it was a diorama—from the monuments of Athens to Mount Olympus, from Delphi to Corinth. At every stop, at every hillock, Alecco would point to any sheep or goat in sight and, rising in his seat, bray or baa at the poor animal, whichever was appropriate, making enough noise to stampede the flocks. Needless to say, the first eight or ten times this happened, we clapped our hands like appreciative children, while attempting to catch the endless fruit he picked and tossed over his shoulder into our overflowing car. But after three or four days, these animal sounds began to grate a bit: there is not much variety a Greek cabdriver can give to the bleat of a sheep, and I found myself staring murderously at the back of Alecco's thickset neck, the gray-black curls falling over his collar, wondering what had become of the Greek god of "Elios's" youth and suspicious that this movie star of memory had been garroted by a Greek quadruped mimic who would just as soon hurl us, bleating, off Mount Olympus.

It was but a fleeting thought, and there also came the golden afternoon we sat down outside a taverna on the way back from Corinth for lunch where the owner, another friend of Alecco's, produced a towering platter of fresh grilled shrimp and bowls of feta cheese, basil, and cut tomatoes along with several bottles of crisp Greek white wine and a loaf of crusty bread meant to be soaked in jade-green olive oil. Ellis was regaling us with another memory of his and Alecco's first excursion, now tamped down from the purple history of earlier versions, when in the distance we heard a sound at first indistinguishable, separating into something that resembled words—"Rahhb! Meeester Raaaab! Telefonoooo!" over and over again, growing ever closer. Surely we were mistaken; no one in this sunlit, dusty village of Naphlion could possibly . . . But there in the distance, padding ever closer on bare feet, came a youth of eighteen or so, howling into the noon sun "Telefonoooo! Meeester Raaab!"

The Greek convertible, replete with a trunk's worth of native fruit, with Alecco in the front seat and Ellis and Conrad Susa in the back. (Collection of the author)

Ellis Rabb, Conrad Susa, and me: Athens. (Collection of the author)

"El, that's you!" I offered. Ellis put down his glass of wine and stared at me for a moment. "You don't really think that there is anyone in this village that knows my name . . . ?" and simultaneously came the refrain from the youth, now standing directly in front of our table: "Meester Rabb! Come! Come! Telefono! America!"

What are the chances? Alecco guided Ellis to the nearest telephone with the help of the young man while Conrad and I worked feverishly on the shrimp before us, believing a transatlantic call that tracked us to the Peloponnesus could be either very good or very bad, but whichever, we were not going to see a lunch like this again for some time.

Ellis returned ashen. He slumped into his chair and raised a full glass of wine, downing it before he could speak. "Disaster!" he said, glowering at the two of us. "The Ford Foundation grant has collapsed. We didn't get it!" We pushed our chairs back, dropping our forks. "That was T.," he went on. "He doesn't know what this means. No Broadway, that's for sure. But the future? If there *is* a future?" He drifted off, staring beyond us at the oblivious Greek life stirring up dust in the streets beyond. We could see Alecco, unlocking the convertible across the street and watching us warily, already smelling a sea change. Ellis narrowed his eyes. "Hmmm!" he said—his universal signal. I turned to Conrad. "Well, I better start packing, I know that much," I said under my breath. Ellis stood up and threw a handful of Greek banknotes onto the table. "Right!" he said loudly. "We're going to Paris. Tonight!" and he strode off. Alecco had already started the car. "What's in Paris?" I asked as Conrad and I caught up. The answer was short and decisive: "Houseman!" was all he said.

14

Rainy Parisian boulevards appear to dissolve when viewed from a taxi in the French twilight, becoming a solid mass of blue-gray as their identifying features fade. The French call the twilight by two different names: *l'heure bleue* is the earlier, beautiful blue hour, while *entre chien et loup* is a bit later on—between dog and wolf! It was drizzling gently as our cab made its way from Orly Airport to the north of Paris and the rue de Prony—very *entre chien et loup*. I peered at the façades of tall windows rushing past, curtained against the quotidian traffic. Ellis and I had spoken little on the flight from Greece, our thanks having been expressed to Alecco and his family, our hasty goodbyes made to Conrad, who was continuing on his own, everything shoved to one side to make room for the larger, more prevalent anxiety of the moment: the future, or lack of it. I read and nodded off on the plane, glancing occasionally over at Ellis, who was quietly smoking by the window—one could still smoke on planes in those days—staring blankly at the indifferent horizon ahead. Strain, as usual, was beginning to irritate his personal Achilles' heel—the floaters in his right eye and the threat of a detached retina. Still holding his cigarette, he repeatedly brushed up his right eyelash with his fourth finger, as if a blot of dried theatrical mascara were the problem and not genes. I thought of the empty space in my mind presently labeled "Houseman," and I was nervous. I knew basically only what most people knew, that John Houseman had once been the celebrated partner of Orson Welles and a creative force in Hallie Flanagan's famous WPA theater movement during the Depression. I had heard something of *The Cradle Will Rock* and knew he was still a film producer of note. As one of the original producers of the American Shakespeare

Festival at Stratford, Connecticut, he had over the years employed nearly everyone on both sides of the APA-Phoenix aisle. He had directed Ellis more than once and was a close personal friend of Hambleton's, so it made complete sense that Ellis and T. would reach out to him as a knowledgeable consultant while contemplating what lay ahead. No one in the business had more overview and experience than Houseman. Even as the cab approached his Parisian apartment, Houseman was in the process of reinventing himself for the umpteenth time. Stratford was over and he was out, causing him a period of decidedly uncharacteristic depression. At this eleventh hour came the offer from New York to cofound the Drama Division for the Juilliard School with Michel St. Denis, and a third act of Houseman's life was about to unfold, with an Oscar for acting, new-minted celebrity, and a fortune as an advertising spokesman all lying ahead of him. At present he was still living in Paris with his wife, Joan, and their tiny Yorkshire terrier, Mousey-Cat, in an apartment in the elegant building our cab now pulled up before—no. 109 on the rue de Prony in *"le bon 17ième arrondissement."*

In the imaginary unfilmed MGM version of life, produced by Houseman himself, there would naturally be an elegant tracking shot past the grim-lipped concierge, up the steps and into the vestibule of the apartment; an establishing shot of the room, perhaps, silver-framed photos on draped tables, pools of subtle, warm lighting, an obscure painting or two glowing in the distance . . . But in the selective vaults of my own memory, very little of that opening sequence registers. A soft-voiced, elegant gentleman, easily Ellis's height, must have greeted us first, his handshake brief and firm, a customary little bow from the waist, perhaps, as he acknowledged me, and then he must have swept Ellis away into the depths of the interior, talking already in that cultivated, polished tone that betrayed nothing of his Romanian birth, everything of an English public school education. I don't in truth remember much of that. Mostly I remember Joan.

She was dressed in a long brocade skirt, a cream peau de soie blouse with a jabot, and little flat slippers. She had a cigarette parked in the corner of her mouth, seeming a bit distracted, even nervous. She was shy. From midair, it appeared, she produced glasses of champagne for everyone, then looked around for more to offer.

On the cusp of fifty she was still a stunning beauty. Born in Paris to a Russian mother and an American father, Jack Courtney, who soon left his small family behind, she had been raised in and around the intellectual salon her mother managed to keep on a restricted income. Joan's mother, whom I never met, was the confidante of many a celebrated French painter and writer. Through that weekly salon, Joan, when just a child, encountered Picasso, among others, and she became, in her teens, a model for the house of Dior. Tall and willowy, with pale ash-blond hair and a beautiful face, she married a dashing French count, Guy de Foucauld, when they were teenagers, but when he decided to pursue a career as a soldier of fortune and resolved to go to Spain to fight in the war, Joan accompanied him as far as the Pyrenees, where she kissed him goodbye. He marched down to Spain to fight, and she returned to Paris alone.

About this time, John Houseman, swinging alternately between his careers in theater and film, became involved with the actress Joan Fontaine. Houseman had, all his life, an affinity for cool, aristocratic blondes, and Miss Fontaine, no exception, was expected to be his second wife. He had been married briefly much earlier to another movie actress, Zita Johan. I was told that when Houseman brought Joan Fontaine out to the fortress he had designed for himself on South Mountain Road in Rockland County, in upstate New York, he expected her to be suitably impressed and maybe even a little awed. Instead, Ms. Fontaine took one look at the isolated stone edifice in which he had intended to place her, took a taxi straight to New York, and boarded the very next flight back to Hollywood.

If John was devastated, he didn't stay that way long. Joan Courtney, having separated from but never actually divorced her French count, crossed the Atlantic to New York and stepped off the ship wearing the first example of Dior's New Look to be seen in America. Although her English was limited, it didn't take her long, with her spectacular looks and exotic French appeal, to get a job as a receptionist at the Museum of Modern Art, and it was in this context that she first met Houseman, on the rebound from the icily unforgiving Miss Fontaine. Photographs of the two women at that time reveal an astonishing resemblance, and perhaps it was this quality that initially attracted John, but soon her originality became evident and irresistible, and they married. They had two sons, Michael and Sebastian. But curiously enough, as Joan laconically explained it all to me, she never bothered to secure a French divorce from the count, who seemed not to mind, and, traveling restlessly throughout his life as he did, never had occasion to remarry.

I recall once arriving at Ellis's apartment on Christopher Street to find several pieces of beautifully scarred luggage stationed in the foyer, marked with a gold coronet and the initials GdeF. Guy occasionally stayed at Ellis's when the apartment was available, while crossing through New York with the blessing of John and Joan. When he predeceased her, dying sometime in the seventies, his French title by law was transferred to the eldest son of his still official wife. Michael Houseman, who resides in Paris with his brilliant anthropologist wife, Marika, is the accidental recipient of this rather comic bit of arcane French law. At least that's the way I understood it from Joan.

Houseman moved through their life together with the demeanor of a ship of state, while Joan, always a step or two behind, coped, supported, and did her best to make his life comfortable as well as beautiful. The night we arrived, Houseman had arranged for a transatlantic conference call with T. Edward Hambleton and his associates, and he and Ellis immediately disappeared together to another room; Joan graciously turned her attention to me, left behind with the baggage. That I was "left behind" in more ways than one must have been obvious to her. This was Paris. I was Michigan, top to toe, and out of my depth. Making effortless conversation, she guided me into their bedroom and plunked me down on the satin duvet near a French telephone fitted with an extra earpiece, designed for listening in, not for speaking. I was more grateful for her reassuring presence as she hovered from room to room pouring champagne than for the refill she provided, and found myself paying more attention to her than to the mingled grunts of the men on their transatlantic call.

But what now? The enterprise for the following season was only partially in place as things stood, with just the contract with the University of Michigan to sustain us. The Ann Arbor season, *You Can't Take It with You*, *The Wild Duck*, and the premiere of MacLeish's *Herakles*, were meant to form a basis for a subsequent Broadway engagement that would require major support by the Ford Foundation. Without the grant, the move was impossible.

Ellis and I flew back to New York in virtual silence. The best and most experienced minds available to us were helpless to do more than suggest regrouping while hoping a better solution might appear. What had imperceptibly changed was the clout of Houseman, now moving from onlooker to a player about to step full-time into the arena. And what was changing for the pinball himself was the expectation of Houseman and Joan being very different flippers indeed. All I really knew for certain was that I was headed back to Ann Arbor. Period.

As I have indicated earlier, I'm fascinated by Pirandello. So it's convenient that Pirandello occupied such a prominent place in the early work of APA. *Right You Are (If You Think You Are)*, or *Così È (Se Vi Pare)*, as it's known in Italian, was originally directed for the company by Stephen Porter and eventually returned to the repertory as the perfect vehicle for none other than the First Lady of the American Theatre, Helen Hayes, in her company debut in Los Angeles. But that doesn't completely account for my affection for this playwright. Because, upon Ellis's and my return to the New York, two different truths, two different narratives were unfolding in a way Pirandello would have both recognized and approved of, destined not only to alter the future of the company, but to draw a line in the sand involving wives, sweethearts, and old friends. The exact nature of what took place, however, depends greatly upon which version of the story you choose to follow. Myself, I wonder how Pirandello himself might have coped . . .

Judith was coming out of the rep, leaving *Man and Superman* and *War and Peace* to close out the last season of APA at the Phoenix off-Broadway. The final weeks of performance were especially tense. For one thing, Ellis and I had been absent on our excursion. For another, the simmering conflict running just beneath the surface of the relationship between Rosemary Harris and Nancy Marchand was always there. It was basically chemical, as such things often are—nobody's fault. But Nancy had been one of Ellis's closest and most valued allies since their Carnegie Tech days. And then Rosemary, trumping "best friend" as "wife," made it a bit crowded at the top of the bill on the rare occasions they were together on the roster. Although Nancy had played Arkadina to Rosemary's Nina in the original Folksbiene *Seagull*, Rosie was in London when Nancy and Paul returned to the fold. And there, suddenly, was *Judith*, and Ellis's dream of once more seeing his two favorite actresses on the same stage, but this time with Nancy clearly playing support. Talk about "walking on eggs"! And so to Pirandello:

On the day the women are meant to rehearse, for whatever reason, Ellis decides to leave them alone in the room so that they can explore the crucial scene between them unobserved. Ellis and I arrive after a prolonged lunch at Vasata, a Hungarian restaurant nearby, to find to our relief it has all gone swimmingly! "It was just like what happened between Joanie and me," Rosemary chortles, remembering her *Vanya* rehearsals in London with Joan Plowright as Sonia with her as Elenya. "We were like sisters! We had the best time!" Nancy smiles, saying very little, but either way, Pirandello doesn't much care. He is only interested in putting forth two utterly disparate scenarios, his favorite sport. And O. J. Simpson, I believe, would approve.

In the first fantasy scenario our Italian playwright has sketched for the company, Ellis's absence has caused considerable friction backstage, with the usual grumbling about the company being repeatedly "leaderless." So Nancy and Paul suggest a company meeting one night after a performance of *Judith*. Rosemary is reluctant, and prefers not to have anything to do with it, but nevertheless the meeting is scheduled after the curtain comes down while various members of the cast are wiping off their makeup and getting out of their costumes, peripherally involved, trying to ignore the rising tension backstage. Emphatically, Nancy insists that "something must be done," and she proposes that Paul, as a senior member, should take a more active position, sharing the leadership and spreading the authority wider within the ranks. Rosemary takes umbrage and, saying something to the effect of "I don't want to listen to this," she gets up and starts out of the dressing room. Nancy goes after her: "No you don't!" she reputedly says loudly, "you come right back here!" and with that she grabs Rosemary's famous red wig and pulls her back into the dressing room. Some blur of a swift, clumsy catfight ensues, the women are separated, and the next thing everyone realizes, Ellis has materialized almost overnight like a deus ex machina and has summarily fired Nancy and Paul on the spot—they are gone from the roster as well as the theater by the very next evening's performance. Christina Pickles smoothly assumes the role of Violet, and Rosemary, Nancy's understudy as Ann Whitefield, moves into the lead in *Man and Superman*, since she had played it before. Christina also substitutes for Nancy in *War and Peace*, and the show goes on. "At this performance, the role of Ann Whitefield, usually played by Nancy Marchand, will be played by Rosemary Harris." Thunderous applause.

And . . . curtain! (Perhaps a faint "Bravo!" is heard from the depths of the house. Possibly a woman's voice?)

Alternative Pirandellian sketch: During the performance of *Judith* comes a moment when the character of Judith has been directed to embrace the whore Susannah. Rosemary has been blocked behind and above Nancy Marchand, who is playing Susannah, and she holds Nancy's head in her hands. But over the warp and woof of performance, Nancy has found Rosemary's grip increasingly uncomfortable, and to signal this, she tends to wriggle a bit. This both distracts Miss Harris and, to be honest, irritates her, so she tightens her grip on Nancy's jaw and neck and completes the scene with Miss Marchand virtually immobile. When they come offstage at the end of the scene, a confrontation inevitably boils over. Sean Gillespie, the stage manager calling the show that night, still on headset, flips his switch to alert the production stage manager, Bob Moss, down in the office with the following message: "Come quick! Nancy has just slugged Rosemary!" With typical editorial freedom, Sean had gotten it wrong: Rosemary had turned to walk away from Nancy, and Nancy, smarting, reached out and literally pulled Rosie's wig off. To some, this quickly became known as "the Wig Pull Heard 'Round the World." But by the morning, as reported, Paul and Nancy are indeed gone from view, and the show, with the identical juggling of roles indicated, goes steadily on. Blackout! Quick curtain. More applause.

(Two quiet boos may be heard in the house this time—possibly a man and a woman?)

You pays your money and you takes your chance, so says the barker in the carnival. Is either of these stories true? Are both? Ellis, in the privacy of his and Rosemary's boudoir, clearly insists on the first. The existing members of the stage management, their luster undimmed but retaining considerable patina over time, are equally insistent on the second. Pirandello laughs. "Così, è (se vi pare)" is his comment. And, as usual, he's right.

15

We circled each other in the mass confusion of the Christopher Street bedroom. Suitcases were on the floor, on the unmade bed, and clothes were piled everywhere. Rosemary was packing, Ellis was packing, and I was scurrying between their loads of clothes trying to help, trying to edit as best I could, basically trying to keep up. We were planning to drive to Ann Arbor so Ellis would have the use of his car, but there was no way everything strewn about the room could possibly fit into the small Chevrolet convertible he owned, to say nothing of leaving room for Rosemary's world. Would we have to take two cars? Would we be coming straight back? Would we go somewhere else? Would we just stop and disband?

"Why-oh whyyyyyy-oh why-O!" "Why did I ever leave Ohiooooooo?"

Two voices are crooning on the Pennsylvania Turnpike in a rented car, filled primarily with things Rosemary and Ellis couldn't stuff into their small convertible, which is practically everything. They are somewhere on the road ahead of us in that convertible. And Patricia Conolly and I are blending our voices in the lovely duet from *Wonderful Town*. We're pleased with our performance, and sorry that others on the highway can't share the effect. Trish, a tiny, spirited, eccentric Australian actress, had dropped into our lives and, like a country bur, seemed to be sticking to us. A friend of Rosemary's from Chichester, Trish found herself in Manhattan under heartbreaking circumstances. Her father, in his early sixties, had died suddenly of a heart attack aboard a transcontinental flight on his way to visit her in London, and Trish was now stopping by New York after having accompanied the body as well as her grieving mother back to Australia. She had seen to all the arrangements, fended off another of her consistent suitors' hands, and was now returning to an uncertain future in England. On this stopover, she called Rosemary just to say hello, and Rosie immediately invited her to stay and visit for a day or so.

Things for the rest of us were in a whirl with much to be done before rehearsals began. Among the distractions was a first read-through of the scheduled premiere of MacLeish's *Herakles*. Rosemary suggested that while Miss Conolly was in town she could pinch-hit for one of the roles yet to be cast. A creature of impulse, Trish was attracted by the excitement always whirling around Ellis as well as being reunited with her friend. Rosie was close to few Americans outside the company, and Trish's arrival was fortuitous. The recovery from the painful incident involving Paul and Nancy had been swift, with Rosemary made understandably uncomfortable by a situation Ellis could only ascribe to his own guilty pleasures. Now, with no other emotional distraction in sight, he rallied immediately to her side—her champion once more—and they bounced back into one of the happiest and most productive periods of their marriage.

Trish was dazzled by all the bustling intrigue, while Rosie, a fellow Virgo, substantiated her credentials. She had had the good fortune as well as difficulty of following another exceptional Australian actress, Zoe Caldwell, on the professional circuit from Australia through London to New York. Caldwell, who had made her sensational debut at Stratford-upon-Avon as, believe it or not, the First Fairy in the Peter Hall production of *A Midsummer Night's Dream*, was replaced by Trish in the same role for a different RSC production. Having found her way into the Chichester company, she became the understudy to Joan Greenwood, whom Rosemary later replaced as Elenya in the celebrated *Vanya*. The production at Chichester was *The Broken Heart*, a rarely performed Jacobean monstrosity by John Ford in which the leading character dies at the play's end, literally of a broken heart. At one matinee when Ms. Greenwood was indisposed, Trish Conolly stepped from the shadows. She had always had, among her resources, a direct connection with her audiences, and this day it proved no less. After her simple, moving death, the next word in the script was to be spoken by the character portrayed by the play's director, Olivier himself. He had blocked himself downstage with his back to the audience. Normally, he turned and spoke the play's final lines, and the curtain fell, but on this afternoon, director Olivier made an alteration. He slowly approached the bier upon which Trish lay, knelt, and, kissing the hem of her gown, paid a tribute that could only be appreciated by the rest of the players. Then he rose, spoke his line, and ended the performance. I, for one, had never heard of anything like it before or since.

Now here was Trish beside me, chattering away, making me laugh and keeping me awake in a bonding ritual familiar on most highways, a happy consequence of the claustrophobia of a car. We left Manhattan as acquaintances. We arrived in Ann Arbor as life friends, and never looked back. Having made the journey to Ann Arbor, of course, she found little to do, but we were all having such a great adventure that she consented to play the small part in *Herakles* as well as tossing off the alcoholic tart Gay Wellington in *You Can't Take It with You*, with about three lines and a dirty lyric to sing, but with that goofy crossover she became an integral part of the company and our lives.

Rosemary had decided she wanted to play the role of the ingénue, Alice, in the Kaufman and Hart. This was another one of the decisions I witnessed as the three of us sat upon the unmade bed at Christopher Street one Sunday morning. Like the dutiful assistant, I had read and reread the comedy, and I was eager to see how Ellis would cast it. Penny Sycamore, obviously the leading lady's role, seemed to me to be the part Rosie would prefer. I knew she loved the rare opportunity to do comedy, and this seemed a perfect fit; but I confess amazement when it was not Penny, but the seemingly colorless part of Alice that she chose. Ellis concurred immediately. But Rosemary was nearing forty at this point, and as radiant as she was onstage, how on earth did she think she could pass for someone in her early twenties? Were they deluded? My early enthusiasm for the project began to dim a bit. Whatever interesting direction Ellis might have in mind, it seemed unlikely that miscasting Rosemary Harris was much of a key.

Other original casting, unfortunately, had Nancy Marchand as Mrs. Kirby, with Paul Sparer as the Russian ballet instructor, Kolenkov. To make matters worse, Nancy's big acting plum of the new

Patricia Conolly, by way of Australia and Chichester, England, 1967. (Robert Alan Gold)

season was meant to be Gina in *The Wild Duck*, the major reason for choosing such a difficult play. Now the Sparers were gone and the cards needed to be reshuffled, and quickly. Ellis was not one of those directors comfortable reaching for new faces. His template was set at Carnegie Tech through Stratford, Connecticut; from then on, he mined that roster until it became clear his circle of acquaintances was beginning to ripen dangerously on the vine while he conveniently overlooked newer possibilities. True, he occasionally made attempts to reach beyond the familiar—Carrie Nye, Christopher Plummer, or others that never materialized—but usually if the leading lady's part wasn't ideal for Rosemary or Nancy, he was stymied or even uninterested. Now, friends in the company suggested Betty Miller as an exciting substitute for Nancy's roles. A great favorite of the Panamanian director José Quintero, Betty stepped into the void with her husband, James Greene, who picked up a series of minor roles as well. When Betty first appeared at the Ann Arbor tech in *You Can't Take It with You*, as the stiff, rigid Mrs. Kirby, she wore a fox stole with her black wig parted in elegant wings of silver gray. One wondered for a moment if Vivien Leigh hadn't been cast. She was perfection.

Turning a blind eye to our present funding crisis, we were dancing on the edge of the abyss, but having a wonderful time doing it. Trish Conolly and I found apartments near Ellis and Rosemary in what was basically married student housing at the university, and many mornings we crowded around their small kitchen table while Rosie, padding about in bare feet in that ubiquitous nylon peignoir, rolled up her sleeves to fry bread in bacon fat accompanied by glorious eggs for our breakfasts. Off campus, Stephen Porter was rehearsing *The Wild Duck* in an abandoned factory with huge floor-to-ceiling windows opening onto dusty autumn trees. Since rehearsal rooms are usually windowless affairs, we felt liberated. Betty Miller as Gina, Donald Moffat as Hjalmar, Christina Pickles, Clayton Corzatte, Sydney Walker, and the others slogged through the text while young Jennifer Harmon ascended happily to her first major role as the young Hedwig. Back in Beirut during Ellis's and my vacation, I had read the Ibsen to him during some of our afternoons, and my breathless version of Hedwig's panicky plea "the wild duck, Father!"—sounding like a demented Margaret O'Brien—inevitably made him collapse into paroxysms of laughter. Whenever things were tense over some administrative gaffe, I could mimic Hedwig's whine to bring him back into good humor. Stage business in this production necessitated that actual food be served—sandwiches made, fresh bread cut, cheeses sliced, potato salad doled out—and we grew cozy and plump nibbling the leftovers from endless Porter run-throughs.

Herakles provided a very different climate. As the lone assistant on the company payroll, I soon began taking notes not only for Ellis, but also for Stephen Porter's Ibsen, so it was inevitable that I would find myself attached to Alan Schneider for the MacLeish. Alan, arriving intermittently from some other production in some other city, looked around on the first day and said, "Who's my assistant?" Stuck for an extended staff, Ellis immediately volunteered my services. He, too, was flying in and out in pursuit of funding. The differences among the three directors were stark. Porter was hands-off in the extreme. He displayed an enormous grasp of the world of the play on his first day, then as quickly as possible blocked and ran and ran and ran the results. That was pretty much the extent of his direction. No extensive notes sessions, nothing to be adjusted further except to hear him say at any point during the day, "I think . . . with profit . . . we might run that again!" Glances were exchanged, smiles suppressed, and everyone got up to do it all over. With good actors and a good script, one could see how the problems gently sorted themselves out as the shape, faithful always to the author's intentions, emerged. Performances always shone; Stephen's hand, not so much. But his original gloss was so accurate, so fine, and his homework so complete, that grateful actors could proceed with confidence. Alan, on the other hand, whose seminal *Who's Afraid of Virginia Woolf?* had made him the most sought-after director in the commercial theater, fell decidedly on the opposite end of the spectrum. All the avuncular professorial energy displayed by Stephen Porter was winnowed down in the other rehearsal to an axis that had two poles of interest: Alan and Rosemary. No one but her existed for him, and no one else was needed. I'm struck by the thought that she was, frankly, the sole reason he came at all. He wanted to know about her, how she ticked, what made her work. Period. He kept a strong hand on rehearsals, his manner as brusque and terse as Stephen's was nonexistent. And

he wasn't altogether happy with the rest of it. The title role of Herakles proved more than a stretch for the stoic, almost paternal Sydney
Walker, but Rosemary could do no wrong. Whenever they disagreed
over a line, a move, an interpretation, Alan was at his most skillful,
his most patient, his most diplomatic. Rosemary, red-faced at one
point from trying to make sense out of the dry, poetic text, stood on
the edge of the stage complaining into the auditorium where Alan and
I sat about some business Alan had suggested. "She wouldn't *do* that!"
she said. "I'm sorry, Alan, but it's nonsense, just nonsense. She's not
going to stop at this point for a move like that, she just isn't! She
wouldn't do it! I know that! I promise you! She wouldn't!" Silence.
And then slyly from next to me in the darkened distance came Alan's
quiet reply: "She might!" Another silence, then Rosie began to laugh.
"You're right," she conceded. "She *might!*" A point for him: and one
for her, as well. They were a murmuring duet of admiration. Not so
the others, most particularly Jennifer Harmon. If she was being gently supported in her *Wild Duck* rehearsals, she became a withering
target for Alan. I was shocked. Ellis treated every member of his company with respect and patience. He cajoled. He confirmed. And here
was our most famous guest director hurling sarcastic abuse at a de-
fenseless actress in her twenties. I could barely contain my outrage
that Ellis's guest would behave so rudely toward his company. I began
to take this abuse personally, compensating with a kind of manic activity that left all my previous efforts in the dust. Alan would conclude his rehearsal, and before he could summon the company for
notes, being momentarily distracted by the normal issues, I would be
standing at his elbow with a freshly typed set of immaculate notes.
"What are these, yesterday's?" he said, confused. "No," I responded
tersely. "Today's!" He couldn't believe it. Sitting next to me in the
back row one afternoon, he offered the oddest compliment I'd ever
received. At least I thought at the time it was a compliment. "Do you
act?" he said to me. "Me?" I answered. "No, not anymore." A beat.
"Why?" Alan, who preferred to have a beautiful young girl at his side
as an assistant, squinted into the distance and answered, "Because
someone should do a production of *The Importance of Being Earnest*
for you to play Algernon, that's why." And that was all there was to
it. Was that meant to be a good thing?

Over the ensuing years we ran into each other often. While I was serving as artistic director for the Globe in San Diego, he was on the faculty of UCSD in La Jolla until his death. He frequently attended our openings and was always an enthusiastic, supportive, perfect gentleman. But in those rehearsals?

He seemed to me two different people—publicly confident and upbeat, but privately, when narrowing his gaze on an inexperienced actress striving earnestly to do what he asked, truly vicious. It was an approach to direction utterly foreign to me. No one in the company knew how to react to this; Rosemary turned a blind eye to it, and the others took their cue from her. Ellis eventually attended one run-through of *Herakles* with me by his side, and he dictated no fewer than seven pages of notes. There was much about the production that he not only disagreed with, but violently so. And, true to form, and I confess this with more than a bit of relish, I managed to get those notes transcribed on typewritten pages and into his hands in record speed, eager to see what the fallout would be. He accepted the pages in silence from me, and sat, chewing on a pencil and reading them over. Then he ripped them up and threw them into the wastebasket. "El!" I protested, looking down at the pieces. "Why on earth did you do that?" "Because," he answered, "if I honestly felt that way, I shouldn't have asked him to direct the play in the first place. I should have done it myself. But I didn't, and these notes might be *my* notes, but they sure as hell are not his. They won't help anything." Reluctantly, I understood the wisdom of what he was saying. It was a painful and revealing experience for Ellis. He knew that without a certain amount of the right kind of expansion, the company could not be expected to grow properly; but in the case of directors, he was far less courageous than with actors, and the occasional intuitive choice he sometimes made—Philip Minor, for example—backfired. Philip charmed him in San Diego when he and Ellis were socially thrown together at Craig Noel's pool. He liked Philip. Philip was obviously efficient. So why shouldn't Philip have a production? But the result, a lackluster production of Eliot's *The Cocktail Party* that came later at the Lyceum in the 1969 season, even with a stellar cast that consisted of Patricia Conolly, Sydney Walker, Ralph Williams, Frances Stern-hagen, and Brian Bedford, as well as the off-the-wall casting of the comedienne Nancy Walker as Julia Shuttlethwaite, was inert, and Philip's debut effort became just a creative crossover, never to be repeated. Alan never returned, either. He remained a good friend to Ellis and the company afterward, but Ellis never invited him back. It just wasn't a good mix.

So the axis of direction ran essentially between Ellis and Stephen Porter, and as direct opposites in philosophy and approach, they complemented each other. Stephen, whose scholarship was impeccable and who usually cast beautifully, had no real skill as a conceptualist nor with the art of stage magic. Given a solid text and good actors, he came up with balanced, intelligent work, which left the pyrotechnics securely in Ellis's court, where Ellis preferred them. Stephen was stable; you knew basically what you were getting. But with Ellis, it was anyone's guess. And so to the next lesson:

Do we ever really see the major events of life looming at us, like the freight trains they become? In retrospect, we like to flatter ourselves that we do, but we know better. On the first day of rehearsal in Ann Arbor, Ellis stood amid tables and chairs on a floor crisscrossed with colored tape representing where solid doors, stairs, and walls were to be. He held the French's acting edition of *You Can't Take It with You* in his hand. The greenish cover, like others of various hues, is familiar to actors the world over, wherein every gesture, every move, every prop, every ground plan has been meticulously recorded from the original script of the production stage manager, so that even amateur groups might have a blueprint of how the play originally worked to follow when restaging it. Talent might be questionable, but the road map was there to get one from lights-up to curtain. Many companies, and most professionals, using these editions prepare them by first blacking out every adjective, every indication of what has been done previously, in an attempt to stay as innocent as possible while absorbing material that can otherwise seem like a rote exercise. Now Ellis raised that same script, saying: "Do you see this? Do you all know what it is? Yes, it's the French's acting edition, and yes, you've pretty much managed to ignore these directions—to your credit—for the greater part of your professional lives." A chuckle like gravel ran through the company. "Well, this time we're not going to ignore them. Because this also happens to be the actual, and, so far as

I can understand, only record of what George S. Kaufman did creating this production in the first place. It is like a time capsule, when you come right down to it!" Several of the company looked down at the script in their hands; a few others thoughtfully opened theirs. "So here's what we're going to do: We're going to follow these moves. To the letter! We're going to replicate every single move in this script, we're going to subscribe to the placement of every chair, dust off every bit of business he asks for as meticulously as we can. Because if this play is as great as I believe it to be, these instructions hold the clue to everything that made it great, that made it decent and made it real. We are going to treat this with the respect it deserves, as if it were the actual Stanislavsky production of *The Seagull*, handed down generation after generation in the keeping of the Moscow Art Theatre, and we're going to give it the same respect our Russian colleagues give to their work. Because to me, this piece is as valid, as great as Chekhov's and Stanislavsky's, and it represents who we once were. It's our responsibility to cherish it and bring it back to life as best we can."

I was dumbstruck. I couldn't imagine any director worth his stripes following a French's acting text. Wasn't it the whole point for a director to put his individual "stamp" on whatever he touched, to strip away artifice and convention, to bring a contemporary spin to stale, out-of-date material? Wasn't that what I was waiting to see? Stephen Porter had usually stepped aside, disappearing into his work; and Alan Schneider had showed to me my very first example of what is known as a climate of crisis, stunning his cast into obedience with fear that only riveting concentration could relieve. And here was the most imaginative director I'd yet known, suspending his ego to serve a dead director's work. It was the last thing I would have expected.

And so he went at it, examining, then reconstructing every move and intention and even, as far as one could tell, the tone written into the script. It was not unlike opening some forgotten chest in an attic; and by not questioning any of it, we watched Kaufman's work begin to emerge, as if from the bottom of a developing pan.

The company was cast to surprising strength, with Dee Victor as Penny, Sydney Walker as her effusive husband, Joe Bird dancing attendance as Mr. DePinna, Donald Moffat, decades too young for the grandfatherly patriarch, Richard Woods the perfect foil for Betty Miller's rigid Mrs. Kirby, and Keene Curtis as Kolenkov, in for the banished Paul Sparer. The jury was still out so far as I was concerned with the casting of Rosemary as Alice and Clayton Corzatte as Tony. I was loyal, no question, but actors nearing forty in a play of American realism? Come on! Facing the first day of rehearsal, I had no idea what was in store for any of us, but after having attended that production through hundreds of subsequent performances, having been allowed to cut my teeth as an aspiring director by putting actor after actor into role after role, including Helen Hayes as the Grand Duchess, I can close my eyes and see every move, hear every line and inflection all these years later without so much as opening a script:

The house dims to half as we hear the period-perfect strains of a thirties recording. The orchestra strikes up a positively giddy intro to "The Sunny Side of the Street," and Gertrude Lawrence is the singer. She sings the song once through as the lights go to black. The curtain lifts on Act One, set in the Sycamore living room, and the music crossfades to an old Emerson radio tucked away on the set, a corny rendition of "I'll See You Again." At her typewriter sits Dee Victor in a crisp cotton dress, slowly typing on her L. C. Smith. She rips a page out of the carriage and, lifting a kitty who is sipping milk to her right, plops down the page, using the kitty as a paperweight. She lifts from behind her typewriter a human skull, her fingers probing its open crown. Extracting a peppermint for inspiration, she attacks a fresh page with alacrity as Jennifer Harmon waddles through the kitchen door wearing toe shoes and a tutu. She's carrying a small plate and says, "My, that kitchen's hot!" "What, Essie?" answers her mother, still typing. "I say that kitchen's awful hot. That new candy I just made will never get cool." "Do you have to make candy today, Essie?" says Penny, turning her full attention to her daughter. "It's such a hot day." "Well, we've got these new orders . . . Ed went out and got a bunch of new orders." "My," replies Penny. "If it keeps up like this you'll be opening up a store." "That's what Ed was saying last night, but I said no, I want to be a dancer." She has now relevéed *en pointe* as best she can, near the dining room table. "The only thing is, dancing takes so long," her mother continues. "You've been at it such a long time." Essie is struggling, pulling a dining room chair out from under the table. "Only . . . eight . . . years!" she says, painfully pulling up and thumping her leg down on its arm. "After all, you've been writing plays for eight years, Mother, don't you remember? We started about the same time." Penny turns back to her work. "Yes, but you can't count my first two years, because I was learning to type!"

We are, what? literally moments into this play, and already the audience has exploded in solid laughter at least four times. No one is pushing, no one is being funny, no one is doing anything but executing the blocking of George S. Kaufman, with the additional benefit of thirty or so years of patina, offered by a company of actors so in tune with each other that they seem merely to be living. They might as well be in *The Seagull*. Which, of course, was the point.

And so it goes: Donald Moffat wanders in from graduation exercises at Columbia, just around the corner; Nat Simmons, doing as honest and unapologetic a black comic character as is yet permissible in the sixties, has entered, "bringing flies (for Grandpa's snakes) with him," as Paulette Waters, the sweet, no-nonsense Rheba has promised, but it isn't until Rosemary Harris enters from her working day that the subtle miracle occurs. Because what Rosemary was bringing to the table, beautifully augmented by her swain, Clayton Corzatte as Tony, was what I couldn't have imagined: a loving take on the romantic heroine and hero of the thirties that only experienced actors with true perspective could offer. I was unfamiliar with someone like the film actress Kay Francis, who had a slight *r* problem, until Rosemary, in rehearsal, sweetly and perfectly mocked her style with a coy, self-conscious cross of the room, ending in a period-perfect pose. Having followed the template with precision, Ellis, in partnership with his muse, Rosemary, could work magic no one had expected. When the production opened in Ann Arbor, there was a discussion between the heirs to the Kaufman/Hart estate, Kitty Carlisle Hart, the widow of Moss, and Anne Kaufman Schneider, daughter of George S., whether it was worth it for either of them to fly out to Ann Arbor to take a look. After all, the play had languished in recent years, getting an occasional dusting off but surely nothing that warranted special attention. Revivals, in those days, were just that—fodder hoisted into view usually because nothing more interesting was available. So Anne, with her late husband Irving, had reluctantly made the flight, not because they wanted to but because they thought they should. After seeing the results, Anne added a crucial piece to the puzzle that was already beginning to glow on the stage of the Lydia Mendelssohn. Whenever the love scenes involving Alice and Tony had taken place in the original production, Kaufman simply went up the aisle and out of the theater for a smoke, avoiding, as often as possible, any contamination with the sentimentality those scenes offered. He knew that they needed to exist, Moss Hart's essential contribution, but personally, he couldn't bear them. So there they had lain, inert, for the better part of thirty years, filler for the subplot of the young man and young woman that were links for Kaufman between the farce elements he knew so well.

Now, under Ellis's ministrations, and with Rosemary's Alice for inspiration, something unexpected was emerging. Audiences were allowed to look back on this play with simultaneous sets of values— one from the thirties and another from today. Rosemary floated down the staircase, her shoulders encased in a film of gauzy chiffon cascading down behind her, breathing, as she wafted to a stop, "Well . . . here I am . . . a vision in blue!" It could have been cocky, it could have been cynical, it might even have been embarrassing. What it was, was pure, tinged with enough edge to produce in the audience laughter and a round of applause for something so exquisite and yet real. Later, at the end of the scene between Alice and Tony, Clayton stood up at the dining room table, having just understood that Alice might stay in the city during the summer if Tony did. Clenching and unclenching his fists, and squaring to her with the kind of restraint a bird dog exhibits confronting a covey of quail, he got grimly serious: "You know what you're saying, don't you?" Rosemary rose, floating slightly away, and wafting her right hand up, replied, "What?" The audience were beside themselves. "That you'd rather be here with me in the summer than anywhere else," came the resolute answer. She lifted the stakes so high now that they nearly floated away above her head: "Was I?" Another roar. Clayton moved a tentative step toward her. "Well, if you felt that way about the summer . . . how would you feel about . . ."—he gathered all his determination into a lead ball and rolled it on—"the winter?"

Bliss. Sheer, unadulterated alchemy. We were not seeing something being made fun of; we were being transported thirty years back, to a time less compromised, far less sophisticated than the one in which sexual mores were having all their constraints dropped. We laughed and we wept, simultaneously.

The company hadn't had enough actors on salary to cover every part. We didn't have an elderly character actress on the roster for the final arrival of the Grand Duchess Olga Katrina, an expatriate friend of Kolenkov's who comes to dinner and ends up cooking blintzes for the ultraconservative Kirby family. But there on the faculty was my mentor, Claribel Baird, and Ellis had gone to her in desperation, asking if, as a favor to him, she would consent fill in just for this short engagement. Claribel, then in her seventies, did still act from time to time; in my graduate days I had had the enormous satisfaction of playing the Sewerman in *The Madwoman of Chaillot* to her biscuit-crisp Aurelia. Now, in black lace with accents of silver, she created a cameo turn so disarmingly simple that it was as if we had managed to go out and dig up the Grand Duchess herself. It was, as no less than Walter Kerr was later to observe in his rave review in the *Herald Tribune*, "the chopped egg on top of the caviar."

Ellis stood with me at the back of the theater during one matinee watching an Ann Arbor audience helpless with love, nostalgia, and jubilation. "Hmmm!" he intoned. I looked up at him standing next to me. There was no need to pack, no immediate threat of escape. We had a few more weeks of residency, and then . . . "What, El?" I whispered. "Hmmm!" he repeated, and edged out into the lobby. I followed him. "What did you just see?" I asked. He lit a cigarette and moved out into the autumn sunlight. "I've got to call T.," he said after a moment's thought, turning on his heel and heading suddenly back in toward the small office that had been assigned to us. "I want to take it in." "In? Where?" "Broadway," came the answer. "Maybe we're stopped, and maybe it's all over, but I think that New York should see this for just, I don't know, six weeks. We need to remind them who we are, and why we deserve to continue. It might take a year to get the funding together, and maybe we won't get it after all, but dammit, I want them to see this. Because it's that good." He opened the door to the little office, and not even flipping on the light, ground his cigarette into the overflowing ashtray on the desk, reaching for the phone. "Six weeks. That's what I want."

But that wasn't to be all. T. Edward Hambleton went with his

Rosemary Harris in *You Can't Take It with You*. As her character, Alice, remarks, "a vision in blue!" (Robert Alan Gold)

associate Norman Kean to the Shuberts and secured a temporary booking at the Lyceum on Forty-Fifth Street, east of Broadway, a glorious, antiquated theater built in the early part of the century by E. H. Frohman for his own repertory company. And on the night of November 23, 1965, *You Can't Take It with You* opened at the Lyceum, with Claribel Baird along for her brief ride, uncorking an astonishing rush of excitement that not only swept APA-Phoenix on to national prominence, but also triggered the entire reevaluation of American plays that has continued ever since.

There we all were, unexpectedly and suddenly the toast of New York—Sydney, Jennifer, Dee, Joe, Betty, Gordon Gould, Trish, Richard Woods, Paulette and Nat, Jimmy Greene, Chuck Daniels, Keene Curtis, Donald in his white starched collar, Claribel Baird on leave from the university, George Pentecost, and even Bob Moss, our production stage manager pressed into service as a G-man. And Clayton . . . and Rosie . . . and Ellis, of course . . .

. . . oh yes! And me!

Bang! goes the flipper. *Zip!* whizzes the pinball. TILT says the flashing board above. Game over? Not quite! Not yet.

PART THREE

TO EVERY ACTION THERE IS AN EQUAL AND OPPOSITE REACTION

16

When does the game take over? When do we stop analyzing what we're doing and, letting go of our grip on the side of the pool, simply swim? When, frankly, does it cease to be a game at all, the pinball no longer differentiated from the table upon which it is just a giddy blur, a happy event among other happy events, popping in and out of holes, ringing bells, lighting up lights, too fast for comprehension? The pace should pick up a little now: the stakes are becoming higher, whatever else. And with higher stakes, more risk. More challenges. More pleasure. Perhaps a little less control? APA-Phoenix is becoming successful.

You Can't Take It with You at the beautiful Lyceum Theatre in New York was certainly successful. No question. Not only did it easily eclipse its six-week run, it settled into a substantial hot-ticket Broadway engagement. What a miracle: after a hairsbreadth escape, we ended up in a hit! Whatever had preceded this production—and plenty had—this was a major breakout, that subtle difference between good and really good that can change everything. Rosemary was not merely on the radar, she was commercially viable, and if she'd played leads on Broadway before, with Jason Robards and George Grizzard in *The Disenchanted*, with Charlton Heston in *The Tumbler*, this was altogether different, and soon she was being invited to create the role of Eleanor of Aquitaine opposite Robert Preston in *The Lion in Winter*. Ellis, too, was being proclaimed a wizard who could put the touch of springtime into a very old chestnut. We were gathering momentum.

Revivals of American classics had been the bread and butter of

Welcome to the Lyceum Theatre! Ellis standing atop the marquee, with Rosemary, in her celebrated mod coat, at the window, 1967. (Robert Alan Gold)

resident theaters across the country, but until now they had not been considered seriously commercial. Timing is everything, and the timing seemed right to look back as well as forward, not only to reexamine our past, but to search it for overlooked values. This production had gained universal raves, allowing the company a full year's employment to sold-out audiences while Ellis and T. pursued the dream of expanding their enterprise. True to Guthrie's advice about repertory, the company was growing, flexing, gaining confidence. Given time and continuity, a group of talented professionals can begin to achieve that most elusive of all qualities, true ensemble acting, and APA-Phoenix was gaining on it, and gaining quickly.

This was part of what made it possible for T. and Ellis to strike a bargain with Huntington Hartford out in Los Angeles to inaugurate a summer engagement at his Vine Street theater, including the vast outdoor Greek Theatre in Griffith Park, adding one more leaf to the banquet table of theater Ellis wished to concoct on a national scale. Rosemary, obviously, would be absent for this first Los Angeles season. There was no question but that she would accept the offer of *The Lion in Winter*, although when Robert Preston was diplomatically approached as to whether he thought she might be too young to portray his wife and queen, he quipped, "Too young? She's too *old!*" This fork in the road would also bring into focus another important debut, that of a former Broadway gypsy cast in *Lion in Winter* in the choice role of Philip, King of France—a young, glamorous Christopher Walken, whom Rosemary nailed immediately as more than promising. With Rosie unavailable for this Los Angeles premiere season, Patricia Conolly would step into Lady Teazle as well as Natasha in *War and Peace*, so it was obvious that Ellis's desire to double-cast all the roles in the rep needed immediate attention across the board. It was also a condition of this invitation that we open with an expanded *War and Peace*, sizable enough to fill the enormous open-air Greek Theatre, which could transfer to Broadway in the next season, substantially different from the cocktail-napkin version we'd presented off-Broadway. Who might be recalled to swell the ranks? Who else might be ripe for such an invitation? Within the year, Richard Easton was summoned from his comfortable life in London, and Brian Bedford, teaching a few acting classes at Juilliard, was solicited by Houseman. Things were looking up.

Houseman, long a veteran of these repertory wars, began to step up on several fronts—as consultant and dramaturge, as well as possessing a new pair of eyes to augment Ellis's. He encouraged searching out other actors who might now be more receptive to join the company. Through his and Hambleton's efforts, both Melvyn Douglas and Helen Hayes were approached. Mr. Douglas consented to take on the role of Sir Peter Teazle in *Scandal*, and immediately submitted to the pro forma physical exam for the company's insurance policy. After having been given a clean bill of health, the elderly Douglas was entertaining a young intern on the morning he was waiting to be released. "What's that?" said the intern, glancing at the bottom of the bare foot extending from Douglas's hospital bed. "What?" asked the movie star. The young fan pointed to an ugly black wart on the sole of Douglas's left foot, and called in someone else for an opinion. It was judged to be a melanoma overlooked in the exam, which meant that Douglas had to tender his regrets, withdraw from the season, and look after his own health. He died a year or two later of complications from this melanoma, as it turned out. Ellis engaged in a series of interviews and luncheons with the likes of Kenneth Mars, recently such a success in the film of *The Producers*, and the veteran Hal Holbrook. While trying to persuade the latter to play Andrei Bolkonsky in the refurbished *War and Peace* and Grandpa Vanderhof in *You Can't Take It with You*, it became evident that Holbrook's burdensome alimony payments would make a rep actor's salary impossible for him to accept. And Kenny Mars was already being courted by more films. Ellis and Rosemary went together to visit Christopher Plummer in a hospital where he was laid up with a broken leg. I pouted a bit, left in the car at the curb and disinvited to the merry reunion in Chris's room, while they lounged on his bed singing their siren song with disappointing results. But others came on board: Rae Allen, whom Rosemary had admired in an off-Broadway O'Casey, joined to alternate as Essie in *You Can't Take It with You* and Gina in *The Wild Duck*. Ellis, determined to introduce younger members into the mix, found Marco St. John to play Andrei and Kazamir Garas for Pierre to spearhead a "younger" *War and Peace* cast. The former became a valuable addition to the company, while the latter disappeared swiftly from view. Houseman and I made a trip up to Providence for a look at Adrian Hall's Trinity Square Company, and we returned suitably impressed with its ingénue, Pamela Payton-Wright, and its leading lady, Katherine Helmond. Eventually both women joined the troupe, leaving Hall and Trinity's celebrated ensemble. There was neither rancor nor anger involving a move that would have provoked outrage in comparable sports teams. In the theater, a lateral move to another job is considered something of a betrayal, but everyone understands a move up, and now an invitation from APA-Phoenix constituted just that. In the interest of potential expansion, I had one unforgettable blocking rehearsal, prior to leaving for Los Angeles, with Elaine Stritch, who in her formative years had studied with the German theater impresario Erwin Piscator, and as a recent, enthusiastic pal of Ellis's, showed up one afternoon, toe shoes in hand, to rehearse Essie in *You Can't Take It with You*. She was also mentioned as another Gina in *The Wild Duck*, but she vanished that very afternoon from any further consideration. Brilliant as Elaine was, she wasn't too keen on sharing roles with anyone—that much seemed clear. Ellis had chosen that particular day to be absent, I recall.

But a remarkable pattern was beginning to emerge. The Broadway season was followed by a summer engagement in Los Angeles, and then came Ann Arbor and the the University of Michigan. Three consecutive engagements. Opportunities sometimes occur simultaneously or not at all, and suddenly the Mirvishes in Toronto, with their Canadian empire, were knocking at the door. T. and Ellis quickly cobbled together a split arrangement by which half the company could be accommodated at the Royal Alexandra Theatre in Toronto while the other half honored the Ann Arbor dates. Only a year earlier we had seen ourselves plummeting out of sight, denied a grant that would secure a Broadway booking, with but a slender hold on our future. Now this same company was looking at a solid year of employment playing in repertory in Los Angeles, Ann Arbor, and Toronto, ending up in New York on Broadway. Not only was this the first time a company had played actual repertory in New York since Le Gallienne's Civic Rep days, but it was the only time any company had ever linked itself across the continent on an international schedule while offering its players a full year's employment.

Something new was happening within the company. We began to

relax—an unusual posture for theater folk. Although we knew better than to believe our future was assured, there was no cause for alarm, no need to privately scan the trades for other casting opportunities. Members of the company began to depend on one another socially rather than seek outside interests. The core group of gay men, who tend to activate a company's social calendar—Keene Curtis, Dick Woods, Nicky Martin, George Pentecost, and I among them—set a brisk pace of entertainment, dinners, plans, parties. I was more and more a frequent weekend visitor out at the Housemans' baronial home on South Mountain Road in New City. Houseman, lofty and imperial, genuinely loved having people around him, sitting Jove-like at the head of the table, gazing benignly just over his guests' heads and holding forth with his wicked sense of humor. And in Joan he had a perfect complement. Whether or not Joan loved the social swim, the planning of dinners, the providing of hospitality, she remained beyond gifted at all of it. Over decades of endlessly alternating residences on both coasts she worked her transforming magic. I saw her revive small, underlit rooms on Gramercy Park with pale blue silk moiré walls, watched her carve generous, gouache-vivid living spaces out on Gretna Green in Santa Monica, the very opposite end of the cultural spectrum, with equal ease. She was happiest in an aerie teetering precariously on stilts over the ocean at the far edge of the Malibu Colony, or finally, in a rambling series of rooms on Central Park West, not two blocks from my own apartment, where she eventually died. She owned stacks of canvases, eccentric artifacts, and curiosities culled from her imaginative past with which she could transform the most indifferent space and make it glow. She insisted one was meant to change the paintings on one's walls every six months or "you forget to look at them," and she usually managed to accomplish it.

Out in New City, as we referred to their home, she had it down to a science. The ground plan was massive if simple, a product of Houseman's spartan influence blended with the rough, masculine architecture of the New City artist in residence, Henry Varner Poor. It did not seem, with its thick cement and stone walls, altogether compatible with Joan's French accents, rising fortresslike above the wooded road below, where the homes of Burgess Meredith, Henry Varner Poor himself, and his daughter Annie, an artist, were scattered along with that of Lotte Lenya and Bertolt Brecht. The softening of New

City, however, had altogether to do with Joan. The living room on the ground floor was large, with plump, inviting armchairs and sofas, white bookcases containing volumes in both French and English, and wide windows opening onto a breathtaking view of Rockland County—miles and miles stretching into the afternoon sunlight. The living room abutted the kitchen, which has influenced me everywhere I've lived as an adult. It was not so much a kitchen as a kind of cozy command central, where every aspect of work or entertainment could happen simultaneously. It had at the near end a stone fireplace with a small grill area and grate affixed in which she could grill things like kidneys, if she wished, and before which sat a lumpy overstuffed easy chair and an elegant petit point footstool. In retrospect, they might have stood as the personification of the gracious owners. Beyond the fireplace was a generous island for preparing and serving food, with a small vegetable sink secreted at the far end, a place for a willing guest with a glass of wine and an urge to help to be safely parked. Opposite was the long plank dining table facing a window running the length of the kitchen without a single pane to interrupt it, at which ten or more guests could easily be accommodated. And at the far end of the kitchen, beyond the stove, ovens, and refrigerator, was a small door opening into Joan's personal retreat, a pristine, cell-like bedroom with everything in immaculate white. Over her bed she had the saved remnants of a cross made from stiff Easter palm leaves, as well as a tiny religious Russian shadow box of silver and ivory, all Byzantine ornamentation. Joan was born Catholic, though she no longer practiced and rarely made her spiritual feelings known. She once gave me a needlepoint pillow that proclaimed "I believe in angels." That's as far as it ever went.

She had a curious affection for inanimate objects, like the clumsy blackened dresser that stood sentinel at the top of the staircase to the second floor, a gift, or rather on permanent loan, from the actress Nina Foch (featured in one of Houseman's best films, *Executive Suite*), which Joan referred to always as "Nina," caring for it as she might an eccentric relative, or the actress herself.

We enjoyed simple suppers out on South Mountain Road, drank considerable amounts of very good wines, were privileged to participate in shards of gossip while trying to piece together various famous identities from unexplained first names only. "Lilianne" or "Renata" or "Nick-Ray" (as one word), clues flying by without benefit of so much as a footnote. "Catch up!" the table seemed to demand. We were given culinary secrets, such as how to save a piece of stale cake by pouring white wine over it, or the need to split garlic gloves and remove the bitter green core (a technique applied to the ribs of Romaine lettuce), or the French tradition of enlivening a banal green salad with a dollop of gorgeous runny cheese. We laughed ourselves sick when, being allowed to draw from the inexhaustible collection of china and crystal she owned, we selected huge cut-crystal goblets for our Bloody Marys, only to hear Joan growl, "I cannot abide such heaviness against my lips!" We had the phrase emblazoned on T-shirts and wore them as a group the next time we visited.

In the country, Houseman suspended his intimidating, icy posture, which was nothing more than his patented armor. I eventually understood that like his younger son, Sebastian, he had stuttered badly in his early years. The only time I ever noticed this was during his impromptu acceptance speech for the supporting-actor Oscar awarded him for *The Paper Chase*, which once more pitched his career into another realm. He was so stunned to receive an Oscar— something his former collaborator Orson Welles never had—that he was undone. As we spent more time together, John realized that he could more easily read Ellis's moods by asking me first, and in this way, without discussing it, we grew closer. And here, of course, for me, was another unlooked-for experience—my own forever-distant father, who had abandoned me far too soon, had been recast in the guise of an equally witty, powerful man who seemed actually to like me.

The phone rings. It's just past seven in the morning, and wan light seeps through the third-floor window of my small apartment on West Sixteenth Street in Chelsea, where the shade doesn't quite meet the sill. Blindly, I reach for the receiver. A very strong, fairly refined voice speaks: "Jack? This is . . ." and now, an interminable passage of time elapses, something so characteristic of the speaker that anyone familiar with him has only to take a similar pause to reduce his audience to paroxysms of laughter.

". . . T." goes the remainder of the text, finally completed. I have propped the pillow up by this time to wait for the rest of the sentence. The voice tries again: "I was wondering if you . . ."

Another inexplicable pause. What is he doing? Is he ill? Has he lost the power of speech, or is this simply how he communicates? No, I know the answer: it is indeed how he communicates. ". . . might spare me a minute or two of your valuable . . ."

The unspoken "time" hangs between us, but both of us know where we're headed, so I'm less confused than I might have been. T. Edward Hambleton, who, along with the now retired Norris Houghton, first founded the Phoenix Theatre off-Broadway, is on the phone to me, his omnipresent pipe clamped in the corner of his mouth. A figure of patrician and fatherly mien, he is universally loved in the theater community for his charm, his reassuring presence, and his loyalty. Within the spacious, elegant pauses of this telephone conversation it becomes clear that for some reason of which I had been uninformed, Ellis has suddenly stalked out once again. I say "once again," as it was a favorite last resort of his whenever he had failed to get his own way, and an act that someone—T. Edward himself, Rosemary more often than not, and even occasionally I—could usually cancel . . . eventually. Truth to tell, the fits were somewhat understandable, so far as Ellis's logic was concerned, and to be honest, they were sort of fun! You just never knew.

But this particular walkout occurs in late spring 1966 while we are in rehearsal for the upcoming revamped and enlarged version of *War and Peace*. Casting has been completed, an expanded company now includes a category of journeymen, young actors who are not yet ripe for the roster of Equity contracts but who are helping fill the need for ubiquitous spears while learning more of their craft by occupying the trenches with veterans used to speaking verse, and juggling more than one part while doing it. It is a category that has fallen off the charts in later years and that I, for one, am sad to see abandoned. In our case, Kermit Brown, Alan Fudge, James Whittle, and Chuck Daniel were eventually absorbed into playing larger roles in the rep, though many others were not.

On this particular morning, Ellis had been scheduled to stage a battle of Borodino suitable for the immense Greek Theatre with added soldiers and brilliant red banners. I doubt that anyone else in this period handled large crowds with the panache and style of Ellis. His work was just a step away from seeming choreographed. And whatever the nature of the disappointment or disagreement with management, this was the perfect moment for him to make his point: virtually no one was ready to step into his shoes—not Houseman, not Stephen Porter, no one.

This was not T. Edward's opinion, obviously. He wondered, with the kind of grim, tenacious hold his ancestors must have used in creating the Baltimore and Ohio Railroad, if I might not simply step in and somehow finish the job?

Damned if I did, and damned if I didn't, but after a consultation with Trish and Rosemary, it was believed that the best thing I could do for Ellis was to "keep the ball in the air" until things cooled down. The company was stoic and supportive as I did my best "in the manner of" directing. Ellis liked swooping moves, clashes of bodies, and tableau vivant compositions, and that was what I set out to do. I completed a stab at the sequence just before we moved out to Los Angeles. Ellis, as usual, returned to his duties and his company in a matter of days, but schedules being structured as they were, and the availability of actors always a matter of compromise, *War and Peace* was shelved by the time he returned. So it was a hot day, and under very different circumstances, when we found ourselves out on the West Coast finishing *War and Peace*. I sat with Ellis far back in the endless rows of the Greek Theatre. We all wore straw hats, with damp kerchiefs around our necks, except for Ellis, who defied the sun by donning his preferred uniform of sleeveless shirt open to the waist, cut-off jeans, and sandals. He couldn't get enough sun, and his ability to ripen to mahogany in a matter of hours was one more difference between us. He squinted thoughtfully at the stage, his eyes protected by gigantic sunglasses, knotting his long legs over the seat in front of him. I sat with my notepad, my Irish skin covered as much as was practical, a veritable haystack of cotton.

We'd been going through basic rough blocking of familiar scenes cue to cue prior to lighting techs in the evenings when I realized with a start that next up was something Ellis had never seen before: my version of the battle of Borodino. The cue was given, and eight or ten young men, howling with Russian indignation, charged from the wings and crashed together in the middle of the stage.

"What's that?" Ellis said, sitting up and suddenly unfolding his legs. "It's the battle of Borodino," I said as quietly as I could, writing something furiously on my legal pad. "No it isn't!" he said, half rising. And then he trumpeted to the stage, "Stop, everyone, just stop where you are! Hold everything . . . please just stop!" I scrambled to my feet next to him, dropping the pad. "I'm sorry . . . I can fix it," I began, struggling to get into the aisle before he did. I felt a hand on my shoulder. It was Trish, who had been sitting behind us, a floppy straw hat on her head. Ellis moved swiftly down the aisle while she continued to hold on to me. "Let him!" she whispered. "Just let him do it! It's what he loves best!"

I stood red-faced and useless as the eyes of the journeymen swiveled anxiously in my direction. Trish relaxed her grasp, and nodding "I will!" to her, I scrambled after him. He mounted the stage in a single step while I remained respectfully below. "Stop right here," he began, moving the boys efficiently. "Don't cross there, move over here . . ." and he simplified the moves, not taking everything back to the wood but clarifying it with larger, more powerful arcs. "Hold that banner in your other hand: here, look how it moves!" And what had seemed earnest chaos was different, more direct, simpler! No; better. Period. It was as if a couturier with scissors were slashing at material on a dress form—within a matter of minutes he had made something out of what I had done. Something that might well have originally been there, but I couldn't see it.

After the rehearsal, we never spoke of it again. I realized that he assumed I would indeed come up with "something" and that that "something" would have merit; it never occurred to him that it wouldn't. And later the boys were sympathetic about having watched my work ripped apart. But Trish had prepared me, and it was a lesson very few young directors ever get the opportunity to experience. Like a professional correcting a student's work, Ellis allowed me to see what I had done correctly and what I hadn't. Cellini and the gold leaf! Although in my case, I had been working in tinfoil.

17

It was active, it was fun, and I was making swift inroads, not as a lyricist, of course, and not on every front, either. My ability to negotiate a personal relationship lagged far behind my professional acumen. Identifying myself as gay in my mind didn't mean I was able to do much about it. But to be fair, a child of the fifties, a product of the Eisenhower years and all that entailed, I had hardly any positive images, as a young gay man, to identify with. Who did we have? Liberace? My grandmother was actually fond of this entertainer, but it was, even at her advanced age, a wink-wink approval. Pursed lips and a giggle were immediately countered by the condescending remark that "whatever you say, he is good to his mother." Wasn't he ever!

But a confident risk taker I never was. I sought approval, I needed to belong, to be accepted, and proclaiming myself gay was hardly in synch with being the "good boy" that my breeding and my comfort zone demanded. Then, too, in my early twenties, I began losing my hair; and by the time I was twenty-three or twenty-four, the handwriting was distinctly on my forehead, if nowhere else. It was truly devastating, particularly with the Beatles coming in, to see my hairline going out. I could imagine myself as entertaining, even fun, but not particularly "hot," except in the more repressed areas of my dreamworld.

After I had staggered through a colorless series of inconsequential sexual exercises, my eye eventually was caught at a theater one night by a dark-haired, dark-eyed young designer named Hal, whom I found attractive and who was interested enough in me to obtain an introduction. He was, in age, confidence, and experience, my superior, and although our affair began enthusiastically, I found myself tagging along rather than feeling like a peer. But as we slipped alongside Ellis into a booth at a restaurant one evening, my mentor remarked with his most charming smile that it was deeply satisfying to finally be able to identify and greet someone I found appealing. He approved. I was later to discover just how much.

My new swain turned out to be quite a drinker, and my dismay began to interfere with my ardor the night he, in his cups, decided to serenade me in bed playing the guitar and singing, at the top of his voice, a country song called "My Dog Blue," in what must be described as a paint-scraping countertenor. Considering the other attention-grabbing devices he was capable of employing, the fact that he might also burst into raptures of country music at the drop of a pick began to give me pause. We were not destined to survive all that long as an item, although my first real love was a heartbeat away, and in any case Hal didn't exactly disappear.

It was at this point that Rosemary and Ellis began to understand how much the loss of my hair might be eroding my sense of self-confidence, and for my twenty-fifth birthday, they decided to give me a gift designed to keep on giving—a hairpiece. Stanley Hall was the industry's reigning wigmaker, having ascended to prominence in London, where Rosemary, always a stickler about her own hair and wig needs, first encountered him. Ellis and Rosie were determined I should have nothing but the best, and the best was Stanley Hall. But I would have to find some way to get to London first.

If Rosemary's professional stock was on the rise, so was Ellis's. One evening I sat with him in a brightly lit restaurant called the Lobster next door to the Lyceum while he was being wooed by Larry Kelly, the head of both the Kansas City and Dallas civic opera companies, and his musical director, Maestro Nicola Rescigno, the close friend and collaborator of Maria Callas. Ellis had already directed a production of *Dido and Aeneas* for these gentlemen, and now they were back to ask him to create an English language version of Offenbach's *Orphée aux Enfers* to be performed first in Dallas, and then Kansas City, designed by the British artist Peter Hall and featuring Jacques d'Amboise and Melissa Hayden of the New York City Ballet. I sat in rapt attention while these three men burbled and chortled their seductive way through plans for this production over dinner. Larry Kelly, much balder than I, had just recently endured hair transplants, which at that time meant small, evenly spaced little plugs of hair taken from the nape of the neck and, I supposed, painfully hammered into place. I couldn't take my eyes off his scalp, try as I might, thinking all the while how much more beautiful my Stanley Hall toupee would be than something that looked to me like a seeded lawn. Ellis pushed his plate away and, glancing in my direction, inquired, "So, if this is to be sung in English, who is doing the translation?" They hadn't thought much about it, and mentioned one or two possibilities until Ellis interrupted them: "Well, here sits one of the most brilliant lyricists I know! Why don't you have Jack do it?"

And so began my brief career as translator of opera. With the security of having Joan Houseman near my elbow, I believed my experience with lyrics and my superficial understanding of French might just see me through. Best of all, of course, was that I would be finally doing what I always believed I was destined to do—write lyrics. Not with live Bob James, granted, but dead Jacques Offenbach. I immediately began rehearsing my speech to Bob persuading him what a good deal this was for us! What it all meant, beyond a new kind of working relationship between Ellis and me (less mentor/ student and more creative peers, I imagined), was that I was invited to join Nicola and Ellis in Europe for a few weeks during the exact period my mother and stepfather were touring on their honeymoon. My mother had finally decided to marry again after eight years of widowhood, a friend of our family and the widower of one of her own cronies. For their honeymoon that spring, Harry Martens wanted to take Mother to Europe for her very first time. They were to visit London, Paris, Switzerland, and finally Italy, and here was the unlooked-for opportunity for me to accompany them from London to Paris, serving as their French-speaking aide after first having had my fittings at Stanley Hall's in London, and subsequently joining Ellis at Rignano Flaminio, Maestro Rescigno's converted abbey residence outside Rome, to do some work on the Offenbach. What could be more opportune?

In the late spring, a draft of *Orpheus in the Underworld* freshly completed, I presented myself at Stanley Hall's shop near the West

End for my first appointment. They were expecting me, but I was told Stanley Hall, himself, regrettably had to be absent—he was working on a film in Paris, I believe. Into the waiting room where I had been placed came a young man only a few years older than I, who introduced himself as Paul Huntley. He was not at the time yet a ranking member of the industry, and he asked me politely what I had in mind. "Well, basically just this, but a little more, do you know what I mean?" I answered. "I just hate it when you can obviously tell that someone is wearing a piece. I would like to look like me, but . . . I don't know . . . just a little bit more!" He couldn't believe what I was saying, and spun out hilarious anecdotes about men wanting curls, or hair down below the collar, hair they could "shake," as a matter of fact, all scenarios he had feared I would request. He seemed as pleased with me as I was with him, and we came to a swift understanding. A few snips of my own hair left behind to match color and texture, and I was out the door, with the assumption that I would return briefly for another fitting on my way back to the States, and the little miracle could follow me out to Los Angeles. What I couldn't know at the time was that this same young artist would one day create the outlandish wigs and sensational hairstyles for the musical *Hairspray*, and that beyond this initial encounter, we were destined to become friends and collaborators in a century and a career yet to happen.

18

Music is a Proustian madeleine, an often cruel zinger that can cata-
pult one backward into memory with enough power to snap the
neck. "Wouldn't it be nice to live together / In the kind of world where
we belong . . ." sang the Beach Boys all through the summer of 1967.
In the Hollywood Hills, three of us had taken refuge in the boxy,
rather tacky residence that had been rumored to formerly belong to
George Chakiris, but then practically every shack in Hollywood used
to belong to someone in the business, so why not? I have no idea how
it fell to George Pentecost, Nicholas Martin, and me, but it did, and
since this was our second season in Los Angeles and we were very
much feeling our oats, I even rented a white convertible for us to
share, roaring down from the Hollywood Hills to the theater top
down, the Beach Boys urging us on, or alternately, the Cyrkle, accurately forecasting "the morning sun is shining like a red rubber ball!"

The event of this second residency in Los Angeles was going to be
the debut of Helen Hayes. Ellis had chosen one of APA's old chest-
nuts, Pirandello's *Right You Are (If You Think You Are)*, effectively
staged by Stephen Porter, as the perfect vehicle for the First Lady of
the American Theatre, an epithet usually delivered with withering
sarcasm by none other than Eva Le Gallienne, who was on hand to
direct Richard Easton in Ionesco's *Exit the King*. LeG might have privately claimed the title Dowager Empress of the American Theatre,
but it didn't have quite the same ring. Truth to tell, the difference was
that LeG was formidable, Miss Hayes beloved. She had sat backstage
at one point, when she was rehearsing Mrs. Candour in *The School for
Scandal*, swinging her tiny brocaded slippers and contemplating the

forthcoming rehearsals of a rather obscure collection of Whitman's poetry, put into the barest semblance of a play, *We, Comrades Three*, the legacy of the deceased Richard Baldridge and something Ellis had felt compelled to trot out as a kind of memorial gesture to his fallen comrade in arms. Miss Hayes, cast simply as "the Mother," along with Sydney Walker, Trish Conolly, and young Marco St. John, was at one point asked to wrap herself in a cannon-shredded American flag representing Lady Liberty during the Civil War, something Donald Moffat acidly observed she had had the good sense to refuse to do for every elementary school in Nyack, New York. *We, Comrades Three* was an utter failure, so much so that on its closing performance in New York, Ellis had the property master craft four purple hearts as awards for his actors when the play came shuddering out of the repertory. But prior to that, Miss Hayes was thoughtfully musing backstage, dressed as the garrulous Mrs. Candour: "You know what? At the height of my career, I played just three roles for over twelve years! Imagine that . . . Just three! *Dulcie* for two years on Broadway and two years on the road, then *What Every Woman Knows* for another two on Broadway and two more on the road, and finally *Victoria Regina* . . . same thing. Three roles in twelve years! And here I am, now, rehearsing three parts all at the same time! Boy, you just never know, do you?" And about this time, since Rae Allen had recently been let go as an unhappy match for the ensemble, Miss Hayes, who was struggling valiantly with the scatterbrained nonsense of Mrs. Candour's lines in *Scandal*, sat ruefully among the other actors waiting to go onstage. "They should fire me as well," she said grimly. "I can't learn these stupid lines!" Then, after a silent moment, she finished brightly, "But they really couldn't, could they? It would be like spitting on the American flag!"

We loved her. She was game, she was gritty, and she was good. If she had the same horrible problem with the role of Mrs. Candour as every other actress since Sheridan first created it, she doggedly conquered both her fear and her text and was ultimately hilarious, stumping across the stage on her tiny heels, chin down, ribbons bouncing. She had an odd little facial tic, wincing in a spasm of a swift, grotesque grin. She would sit, looking vaguely in your direction, and suddenly this little grimace took over, her eyes crinkling shut, her teeth gritted,

her lips parted wide. One couldn't be certain that she might not actually *be* grinning, so, naturally, one grinned back, maybe with a little
wave, until it was discovered it was just the tic. Oops!

The opening night of *Right You Are* was bound to be something
special, a revered early Oscar winner for *The Sin of Madelon Claudet*
now returning decades later to Hollywood in an actual repertory
company, something her peers in the movie business could not even
conceive of attempting, and the premiere performance happened to
coincide with the arrival of a brown paper package at the stage door,
postmarked London, which I immediately recognized and tucked
under my arm, rushing back to our bachelor pad.

Neither Nicky Martin nor George Pentecost was involved in the
evening's performance, so we were preparing a bite to get us through
the show and on to the party afterward that was to be held in the ballroom of the Beverly Hills Hotel. Nicky and George were in the kitchen
prepping salad and hamburgers, and I ducked up to my bedroom with
my package, wildly excited. I unwrapped the paper and lifted the lid:
there it lay, my hair, my youth, my one shot at glamour, matching my
own hair but looking healthier. I held it up. The toupee had been attached, as we had discussed, to a kind of yarmulke cap, designed with
four clips that were to be fastened into my own hair and then eventually secured with toupee tape when all else was lost. I rushed into the
bathroom to put it on and, to my horror, discovered that only one clip
had been sewn in—at the very back of the hairpiece. The other three
were missing! Damn! I couldn't possibly wear it to the opening . . . or
could I? Carefully, I snapped the single clip into place, did a little combing, and stood back to survey the effect. I was astounded. Although
hairpieces and wigs, most particularly for me, are always so obvious as
to be laughable, this was something different. You could not see where
my hair left off and Paul Huntley's masterpiece began. I was beside
myself, and wondered what my friends might think. I realized, of
course, that insecure as it was, I couldn't actually wear it out in public,
but I longed to see if, at the very least, I might "pass"!

I ran downstairs, skidding to a stop just outside the kitchen. I
could hear Nicky and George bickering hilariously as they sliced tomatoes and patted ground beef into shape. I strolled in, as conspicuously as possible. "Is there anything I can do?" I inquired loudly. No

one looked up. "You might put the ketchup and mustard on the table, if that's not too much trouble," Nicky sniped. I passed by, leaning elaborately over in front of him to pick up the condiments. He didn't bat an eye. Finally, fit to be tied, I stood up and said, "Notice anything?" "You're considerably fatter than you were ten minutes ago," George snorted, trying to edge past me into the dining room with plates of food. "No, look!" I insisted. Finally they stopped, staring blankly. I semaphored wildly at my head.

"Oh . . . my . . . God!" they said as the penny dropped, both of them having been eager as I to see what Stanley Hall's artists might deliver. We gabbled in a kind of delirium until Nicky saw the time. We were due at the theater for the half-hour ceremony of good wishes in less than an hour, and no one was dressed. "Are you going to wear it?" George inquired, clearing the dishes and dumping them without rinsing into the sink. I looked them both in the eye in silence. Was I?

Within an hour I was sitting in the convertible, wearing my Jacques Esterel blazer and sporting a new Pierre Cardin necktie. The top of the convertible was buttoned up tight, and on my head sat the new hairpiece, not buttoned remotely as tight. In fact, it was being held in place by its one stable clip, augmented by my stiff-necked posture. But I had to be at my best, and my best was definitely in order for the Hollywood debut of Helen Hayes in *Right You Are*. Rigid, as if my neck were in a brace, I took my aisle seat in the Huntington Hartford Theatre for the first act. And how was it? I have no recollection. Well, it's a charming chestnut, and right up Hayes's alley, which is not in any way to be dismissed, even if she was later to far eclipse it with her unforgettable Ma Fisher in *The Show-Off*. Whatever else, the evening seemed to me to be far more about my hair than her performance.

At the intermission, I walked up to the mezzanine to purchase a plastic glass of white wine and saw, coming toward me, Nancy Potts, our no-nonsense costumer. "Enjoying it?" she asked, looking vaguely around at the crowd. "Very much," I replied. Then she looked at me closer, her eyes narrowing. I held my breath. "Is that a new tie?" she asked. "Yes. Cardin," I managed. "Beautiful," was her judgment, and then, looking me over before she moved off, she said "I thought there was something . . ." God! If a costume designer who really knew me well couldn't perceive that I was wearing a toupee, it must be even better than I dreamed! Sailing back to my seat with much more confidence than I had left it, I really managed to enjoy both the second act and the enormous reception Hollywood gave the company and the triumphant Miss Hayes at the curtain call.

Trish Conolly rode out with me to the Beverly Hills Hotel and the party that was to follow, and after we surrendered the car to the valet service, we found ourselves descending a staircase to the ballroom just as the orchestra began "The Way You Look Tonight," and with only three or four couples already on the dance floor, we sailed, as if in a film, onto the floor to join them, dancing lightly and happily around the floor. *Tout* Old Hollywood seemed to be on hand to salute Miss Hayes—the likes of Jennifer Jones, Danny Kaye, Norma Shearer, Rosalind Russell—everywhere you looked you saw one famous person after another, relaxed, secure, and utterly approachable in the way only uncontested success effortlessly allows. "Any friend of Helen's . . ."

It all went by in a blur, and eventually the core group were invited back to Ellis's poolside bungalow at the famous Chateau Marmont to share what Ellis's new assistant, the eccentric Camilla Clay, liked to call "some nightcaps." The bungalow was generous, with a couple of bedrooms and baths upstairs and a sunken living room that opened out onto a sunporch that unfolded directly in turn onto a private patio adjacent to the enormous swimming pool. It was here, about one o'clock or so, that I found myself sitting at a round table with T. Edward Hambleton, his wife, Merrill, Richard Woods, who had been in the performance, and Miss Hayes, attended as usual by her duenna/companion, Vera, a slight, birdlike woman about Miss Hayes's age with the blinking demeanor of a nun *manquée*, which, indeed, she well might have been, Miss Hayes being such a faithful Catholic.

Most of the journeymen had also been invited back, ostensibly for a swim, and as the evening drew to a close, most of them could resist the lure of the famous pool no longer. So, having brought along their swimming suits, they trooped out to the water, walking through the midst of our cozy group as they did. Up to this point, of course, not only did no one seem to notice or mention anything that might blow my cover, but I myself had begun to forget what I was wearing, helped in no small degree by a series of vodka stingers I was nursing. Plowing through our little cocktail group with hulking displays of masculinity, the boys called out for me to join them, and, with just a tinge of condescension, I demurred. On went the relaxed conversations, and down went a few more cocktails. The night was balmy, the splashing beyond the hedge in the pool nicely muted, and I stretched out my legs luxuriously, contented with the event and proud to be in the company of the First Lady of the American Theatre at the conclusion of her triumphant evening. Perhaps fifteen or twenty minutes later, back came the journeymen—still high on exercise and partying, laughing, spraying water, and clumping through our midst as they made their way upstairs to dry off and change. A cheeky lad named Michael at the procession's end tossed off an affectionate "Hey, there, Jack, whatcha say?" as he passed, placing his hand on the top of my head and giving my hair an affectionate ruffle.

Well, "ruffle" doesn't exactly cover it: what he managed to do was flip the toupee off the back of my head like the deft handiwork of an Arapaho. The boys continued on their way, not looking back, but across from me four pairs of eyes—the Hambletons', Vera's, and the intrepid First Lady's—popped from their sockets, and as one, four jaws dropped in unison. "Jesus, Mary, and Joseph!" I heard Miss Hayes breathe involuntarily. There was a beat of perhaps three or four seconds when no one at the table could speak. My mind raced as I stared at Vera and Miss Hayes, staring back at me as if captured in still photography. I could practically read their minds: "What else can he do? Unscrew a hand? Pop out a glass eye?" I reached back with my right hand and as casually as possible flipped the hairpiece back up, but in the attempt I overshot and landed it off to one side. It looked now like a beret made from a beaver pelt. Still no one spoke. I rose, muttered "Excuse me," and walked swiftly into the room beyond, mounting to the bathroom above. Once there, I slammed the door shut and stared at my image in the mirror. The piece was indeed off center, and nearer my left eyebrow than it should be, and in spite of the humiliation I had to laugh. It was priceless. I unclipped the poor thing and, not knowing what else to do, tucked it into the lapel pocket of the blazer. Then I strolled back to the table, where my friends were still whispering, and sitting down, said, "Well, that's a relief! Is the bar closed?"

And that was it, pretty much. Because of this incident, the tale of which was endlessly repeated, I could never take the damn thing seriously again. I wore it for a while longer, encouraging everyone to refer to it as Harriet Piece, since it seemed to me subtler and easier for intimates to inquire, "Is Harriet with us tonight?" offering me a swell opportunity to peer around the room so they could get a better look while I replied, "I'm not sure, I think I saw her somewhere earlier." But over careless afternoons in the open convertible she began to turn, as Oscar Wilde might put it, "quite gold with grief," and eventually she was retired to a little wooden box I kept in a closet, from which she emerged less and less frequently. Vanity, in my case, was not going to be an enduring option.

By this time I had fallen in love with one of the journeymen, a lithe young actor named Jim Whittle, sweet, agreeable, and popular, a relationship that managed to sustain itself over the next seven years until my rising career and his fading one pulled us apart. Many of the younger gays in the company were in relationships patterned for the most part on the only models we'd observed all our lives. Like our parents, we engaged in rounds of dinner parties, birthday celebrations, side trips, and cultural excursions, all while skillfully ignoring the signs that we might not in truth be doing anything more than blindly replicating our parents' routine marriages, but it still made touring life fairly pleasant. I don't like dismissing those seven years, even though the last few relationships I have enjoyed, challenging and complex as they might have been, seem more real to me than that one did. I was doing too much of the heavy lifting—cooking, cleaning, the basic financial support—willingly, mind you, and I felt I was getting as good as I gave, but that, too, was an illusion. As willing a partner as Jimmy was, we were not that well matched. The APA-Phoenix, of course, was the good ship that made all things possible, so to be part of a couple, working together, rehearsing together, on the same schedule, and interested in many of the same things . . . well, it was pretty seductive.

Hal, my emotional "trial balloon," as it were, didn't vanish, as I've already mentioned. It wasn't long before he found his own way to Ellis, and I never really knew which of them initiated it. The fact that I now had someone very significant in my life made it far less sensitive for me than it might have been, but still, the news managed to shock

my immediate circle that Ellis, of all people, would . . . well, what was
the proper phrase—poach? I, of course, knew better from my select
vantage point. Ellis was, as he endlessly reminded us, "Southern,"
and for him, that covered a multitude of what others might easily
consider sins. One of his signature songs was "Falling in Love Again,"
the Marlene Dietrich classic on which he insisted I accompany him
on the piano. He couldn't really sing very well, but how he relished
the heady bliss of performing! And I, ever eager to please, ever the
Delt House jukebox, could alter any mood by sitting down and playing the first few bars of the little "act" I had cobbled together for him
to entertain his friends—"Falling in Love Again," "Real Live Girl"
from *Little Me*, "Stouthearted Men," which blended into "Just One
of Those Things" . . . He was, as ever, hilarious, a cigarette swinging
from one hand, finessing the lyrics with gusto, and for the most part
staying pretty much on key. But in the Dietrich song, his eyes closed,
crooning the excuse "I was made that way!" it seemed to him and the
rest of us like the mantra of his brand of charm, and he expected everyone to understand, to forgive, to move on. For years and years, we
did so. This is what we now know as "enabling"; but to us, at the
time, it was just the way of our world, and worth it.

Rosemary, as schedules decreed, was absent from L.A.—always a
difficult situation for Ellis, because when she was there, she was the
focus of his concentration. She was major, she was his muse, she was
"center stage" no matter what, but when she was elsewhere—in this
case, still in *The Lion in Winter* on Broadway—and when he, too, was
elsewhere, he needed the assurance that he was the very center of
someone's concern, as they were of his. He was not by nature given to
quietude or self-reflection, not amused by being alone. He depended
upon, was drawn to, became high on activity, and if activity included
someone both attractive and available, he took it in his stride as inevitable. "I was made that way" pretty much covered it. How many
times, in the twelve or more years of our most intense friendship, was
I to be awakened on any particular morning to that crooning, mellif-
luous voice murmuring the phrase I could practically lip-synch as he
spoke it—"I've never felt anything like this before!" Even he knew it
was funny. And yet, not.

Ellis welcoming Hal into his intimate circle might appear to be questionable; but then, why not? Hal was a talented designer who also had a career as a director. Craig Noel had hired him in San Diego to direct and design a *Tempest* with Will Geer as Prospero, and none other than Jon Voight as a most arresting Ariel, and it was on the pretext of paying a visit to Craig and Will that Ellis came up against that production, which he pronounced "stunning," which seemed to refer to Hal as well. It was not long before Ellis had hired him into the company, all under the guise of a second pair of eyes on the upcoming production of *We, Comrades Three*, as well as possibly leading to other projects. I avoided direct contact with Hal and bore myself with slightly wounded dignity. It wasn't until I learned that Hal had been hired at the top salary in the company that I saw red.

I knew better than to confront Ellis directly about this, so I went, supposedly over his head, to management. I wrote a modest and controlled letter to T. himself, then asked the general manager, Norman Kean, to have lunch with me while we were in Ann Arbor. As the company's only associate director I had to work with stage management, attending all rehearsals, giving notes as required, and seeing that the respective productions were thoroughly maintained. Bob Moss as production stage manager commanded a staff of first-rate professionals— Bruce Alan Hoover, Sean Gillespie, Dan Bly—but from the outset there was something odd about my standing with one foot in Ellis's camp and another in management's. It mirrored my first directive—to serve Ellis and serve Rosemary and even serve "Rosemary and Ellis" without dropping a pin, a plate, or an innuendo. Having somehow managed that early on, my people-pleasing skills on high display, I had learned to keep my own counsel by neither carrying tales nor playing politics, and as a result, I had been able to keep my head above fast water, no matter who was in favor or who out. For this I was paid the minimum wage in the company—$125 a week. And now here was my former . . . well, I would have to draw the line at the label "lover" out of, okay . . . honesty!—but still, here comes this new "person" Ellis whimsically hires at the *top* salary without so much as an active assignment, while I have yet to have received a single raise during the entire two-plus years of my employment! At lunch at the Michigan Union that day, I told Norman Kean that without some additional compensation, I would tender my resignation. I knew full well that the schedule being what it was, there was no way that APA-Phoenix could replace me on short notice, or in fact at all: I had sat through the creation of all the current productions and had the ear of each director—no one, not even stage management, had the perspective I enjoyed.

Norman Kean was no fool; you couldn't be involved in something as both complicated and personal as APA-Phoenix was and not know how baroque were the highways and byways by which the plays got rehearsed, produced, and maintained. T. Edward might be able to turn an avuncular eye to what was happening in the trenches, but someone as savvy as general manager Norman Kean could hardly afford to work alongside an individual as passionate, as combustible, as brilliant as Ellis without knowing that he had to be placated and accommodated while remaining within the purview of responsible business. If Ellis needed this new person on staff, there had to be some way to make it happen. And, yet, if Jack was to defect?

But Jack wasn't going to defect. And everyone knew it; but still it necessitated my taking Norman Kean to lunch at one of my alma mater's conservative dining rooms and, typical of me, paying for it as well in order to underscore the seriousness of the matter. My compensation was increased, not the three tiers I had suggested, but enough for me to save face. And there was so much going on, so much to look forward to now, that making any more out of this would prove just a distraction, and essentially narcissistic.

Helen Hayes had made the transition from revered icon to rep actress with grace and enthusiasm, and now we would be returning in the fall to the Lyceum in New York with a refurbished, Broadway-buffed version of *The School for Scandal*, polished during the Ann Arbor residence with her as Mrs. Candour, Ellis as Joseph, Sydney Walker substituting for the absent Melvyn Douglas, and best of all, Rosemary Harris as Lady Teazle, returning after winning the Tony Award for *The Lion in Winter*. Leaving Eleanor of Aquitaine behind, she had taken a few weeks to visit her sisters in England and to enjoy a much-deserved rest from all theatrical activity.

When I say I had kept my own counsel in terms of the choppy

waters that existed between friendship and my official capacity, I could never divorce myself from my affection and loyalty to Rosie any more than to Ellis, although my role with each was necessarily different. For years I had honed my performance as "the perfect third," an effective way to become intimate, with couples especially, without affecting the balance. I was almost too good at it. My relationship with Bob and Judy James was a major case in point to which I constantly referred. I had one relationship with Judy, based on our mutual attraction, our performing history, and that early bonding that can seal the bargain for a lifetime. Then, equally significant, there was my creative relationship with Bob. We wrote songs and scores together; we played golf; we confided in each other. I had one friendship with Bob, another with Judy, and in truth a third in which I was a kind of buffer between them. It was an ideal arrangement for someone uncomfortable about embracing his own homosexuality, and for years prior to my committing to Jimmy Whittle and subsequent lovers, it afforded me the vicarious feeling that I was needed and involved. And here I was again applying my skill, but on a far more challenging level. I clearly had to be complicit in confidences that excluded Rosemary, but I was never comfortable about it, because Ellis had instilled in me as well the respect and affection that she was to be accorded, and over time, she became comfortable with me; I was clearly no emotional threat, and eager to be of help—to both of them. He had constructed the tightwire he needed and plopped me on top of it, and if I teetered, somehow I managed to stick. This attribute was going to come in handy, since Rosemary was due to return to Ann Arbor to brush up her Lady Teazle prior to Broadway. Although she and Ellis had been separated physically, they were maintaining some kind of contact, so she was aware of things professional and private that were within her provenance. Ellis was the public persona; Rosemary kept to herself, with the exception of a few intimates—basically her two sisters and Trish—the arbiter of her own story, her own truth. Whatever she knew of Ellis's whereabouts and activities, she had the ability to shut out whatever she chose to obliterate—probably a key to her great skills as an actress. When she had left the company after *Judith*, the specter of John Allan had been ebbing nearby. So now who might have entered the arena in the interim? She could demonstrate a practically military dignity when confronted by any social situation not to her liking, and only once, in all the years I was present, did I ever see that remarkable guard give way.

Strange as it might seem, it was almost exactly a year earlier that I had witnessed one unlikely scene, in the incongruous setting of a noisy Ann Arbor bowling alley on a wet night when Rosie and Trish, with Dee Victor and Jennifer Harmon, had adjourned for impromptu drinks during one of Ellis's many absences. The rehearsals for the MacLeish *Herakles*, under the icy gaze of Alan Schneider, had stressed and exhausted everyone. Emotions were strained, and Rosemary, already Alan's "favorite," found herself very much in the middle of an unhappy company whose true leader was missing in action. With me as the lone attending male that evening, we were endeavoring to make the best of a fairly grim situation. Crowded together in a banquette away from the clatter of the bowling alleys, we all nervously downed a few too many sweet drinks while trying to steer the conversation toward happier and less bleak subjects. Rosemary was having none of it. She was painfully aware how alone she was—the incipient leading lady of the company rehearsing a difficult, obscure play and not cut out to both do the work and supply the emotional support to everyone else that an absent artistic director would be expected to give. Everything going out, nothing coming in. Fueled by the whiskey sours, she let her frustrations get the better of her. She burst into tears within the tiny banquette of stunned observers and suddenly blurted out: "My body needs to open up, to give birth! I'm not a woman if I can't do this." Her head went back, and out of her open mouth came: "I want to have a baby!" Aside from the fact that none of the other women present were exactly ripe candidates for either marriage or motherhood, the pain was as heartbreaking as it was sincere. Her unexpected vulnerability caught us all off guard. What could we say? I especially had nothing to offer that might mitigate the unexpected nakedness of our most private member in her most public outburst.

Now, over the intervening year of 1966, she had achieved a new pinnacle of personal success with her Broadway appearance, and after the show had closed she had gone off to London over the summer, where she fell in with two old friends, Rex Harrison and his second wife, Rachel Roberts. They began to see a great deal of each other, especially Rosie and Rachel, who would in subsequent years descend into depression resulting in suicide. But at this point she was still very much in charge. The world was mod, and mod unquestionably became Rachel, as did the prospect of an eager acolyte unaccustomed to the world of high fashion and an even higher public profile. Rachel swept Rosie along in her wake, and the very next thing to happen was the arrival of a transformed Rosemary Harris in Ann Arbor, dressed and encouraged by Rachel as well as by Sybil Burton. "My idea of heaven on earth," Mrs. Harrison had reportedly trumpeted, "is to be able to put my hands down anywhere in my bathroom upon a pair of false eyelashes!" The woman who descended from the train in Ann Arbor that autumn was wearing false eyelashes, but that was only part of it. She was dressed in a smart gray and pumpkin plaid wool coat with gray fake fur at the cuffs and collar, snug around her svelte body, in black heels, her hair secured chicly at the nape with a black velvet bow. Very Carnaby Street! Very Liberty of London! From her ears dangled large orange balls on gold chains that bobbled and swung to the right and left as she laughed. She was breathtaking.

Ellis was dazzled. The morose Niobe of the previous year was gone, and in her place stood a giggling, enchanting creature filled with confidence and looking like the proverbial million dollars. We must celebrate! We crowded around, Trish, Ellis, myself. Hal was, need I add, absent. We would devote a few days to getting Rosemary up in Lady Teazle, and then, once the performance was secure, treat ourselves to a celebration! Two nights and a day away from every-thing. Ellis had it all planned out!

Did he? Trish and I eyed each other in disbelief. Could the pendu-lum swing quite this swiftly in the opposite direction? And what, in fact, were his plans for us? For we found ourselves included and in-vited along in this rush of exuberant planning. The tight little quartet of friends was meant to pick up very much where it left off—if some-where in the dim past—but I, even more than Trish, knew to what degree he had been absent and isolated with the newest object of his interest.

Real estate agents were called, deposits were offered, plans were made, and on Saturday night after the performance, we all piled into a rented car and drove an hour or so north of Ann Arbor to a small cabin on a lake, where we flung our overnight bags in various corners, built a fire, opened champagne, and finally looked at each other seriously for the first time since Rosemary had arrived.

It all began innocently enough—a natural subject of conversation among four good friends settling down together in front of a fireplace—nothing more complicated than a précis of the evening's performance, during which Rosemary had received a warm round of welcoming applause on her entrance as Lady Teazle, and Ellis, as Joseph Surface, had not. This wasn't the only occasion of that kind, but there was something in the air, attributable perhaps to the eagerly anticipated return of the leading lady, that may well have affected the audience. Whatever the cause, as one bottle of champagne was replaced by a second, the discussion turned to whether one could control entrance applause at will. Rosemary, perhaps sensitive to the fact that she usually got her entrance round whereas Ellis rarely did, thought it could just be a matter of how one was blocked. Ellis took exception. Some people "had it" and others didn't, he asserted.

Inconsequential, actually. Pointless, really. After all, Ellis had directed his own entrance to an uninterrupted first line of dialogue and Rosemary had that rush of Scarlatti and package-bearing servants preceding hers. One would have to have been made of stone not to applaud. So the discussion had included, if only out of politeness, the odd contribution by Trish or me, but quickly the two of us were left in the dust as the principals rose to the occasion. And the occasion wasn't, in all honesty, about entrance applause at all, but rather about the undefinable difference Miss Harris could make in the quality of an evening of theater. Radiant with confidence and secure in a part she virtually owned, Rosemary might have played her hand a bit floridly at that performance, and Ellis was revealing, after his fourth or fifth glass of champagne, that he resented it. It was a given, if unexpressed, that when Rosie was in the company, the company played better. Her absence hadn't dimmed the luster of its reputation, but she had only to step onstage with her old confreres for them to give just that much extra. This wasn't the entire explanation, of course; it rarely is. Something else bubbled under the framework of a normal disagreement until Ellis stood up, filling his glass and slamming the bottle back onto the mantel without offering to anyone else. "Oh, bullshit!" he snapped. "Credit me with some brains, will you? You're a big fucking star, that's what this is all about, do you pretend it's something else?"

"Ellis, darling," Rosemary began, her brows contracting in the concerned way she had whenever sensing a storm ahead, "I don't know why you have to harp on this, it's nonsense!" Trish and I looked up at them from the floor, then at each other. It was suddenly going wrong, and we were about to find ourselves trapped within the demilitarized zone. Up to this moment, I can't remember seeing one of their disagreements that couldn't have been witnessed by anyone else. Passion is de rigueur in the theater, and the closest of collaborators, lovers, and friends take even violent exception when the occasion arises. I knew the difference. This wasn't one of those occasions. Once or twice I made an effort to deflect the rising energy, but no one was listening to me. Not even Trish. She had tucked herself against one of the wicker chairs and was chewing a tendril of her hair.

The next several minutes are a blur. And in retrospect, I have always wondered if this innocent evening didn't represent a turning point. Do other couples in crisis require an audience in the sense that a more dramatic couple might—an audience to witness the fact that an impasse was indeed being reached? Someone else to turn to if only to ask, "Did you hear that? Did you see that? Isn't that the worst?" Whatever was occurring in front of us couldn't be stopped. Perhaps *the* truth wasn't being aired, but some version of truth was. The voices rose and clashed; Ellis began to pace, running an impatient hand through his hair, while Rosemary tried to placate him, color rising to her face, the muted notes of her voice gaining edge as she felt pushed away. She stood her ground. "I beg your pardon!" she said finally, blocking his path. "Are you actually suggesting that this is deliberate? Are you actually saying I'm doing this, what? on purpose to spite you?" She spat out the words "on purpose" in her most powerful way, like mailed fists. "Well, thank you for the vote of confidence! You're drunk! And I'm going to bed!" She turned toward the bedroom.

Crash! He threw his glass across the room—if not at her, certainly in her direction. "Fuck! Fuck! Fuck!" he yelled. "Fuck the whole

fucking thing! I don't want any part of it." And with one defiant gesture, he swept up the car keys from the nearby table and was out the
door into the black Michigan night.

There was a minute of shock before Rosemary ran after him to
the door. "Ellis, come back here! Come back immediately, for God's
sake! This is idiotic!" but the sound of the car igniting and roaring its
furious answer obliterated her. Ellis whirled the car around, the tires
kicking up gravel, and we three stood at the screen door, watching
two red lights disappearing down the road.

"Where is he going?" Trish wondered. "You know bloody well
where he's going!" Rosemary answered, fury swelling into her throat.
"Anywhere so long as it's away from me! It doesn't seem to matter who
it is, so long as it isn't me!" She pushed by us and ran into the bedroom, where she began to cry. Trish looked at me. "Oh, God! Where
is Hal? Is he in town?"

"Are you nuts?" was my answer. "I'm the last person in the state
of Michigan who would know." "But now we don't even have a car,"
she whispered pitifully, looking over her shoulder at the closed bedroom door. "What are we supposed to do?"

I looked at the clock on the stove. It said 12:50 a.m. Trish crossed
back to the bedroom and disappeared just inside. "Rosie? Rosie?" I
heard her calling quietly. "May I come in?" The weeping mounted
into a wail. I looked out through the screen door where the car had
been parked. I could see nothing. Nor feel it, either.

I lay huddled under an army blanket on the dank porch, trying
not to hear. In the distance, across the darkened living room and
around a corner, the sound droned on, a percussive figure, low, re-
petitive. She was crying. Or not exactly crying, she was sort of revving, dry-heaving, like someone stuck in a snowbank who resolutely
grinds the gears in the futile hope that something might finally
engage.

I became aware of Trish standing next to me in the darkness in
her white cotton nightdress, looping her lank brown hair over an ear
and peering down. "Are you sleeping?" she said by way of apology.

"No, Jesus, how can I? Aren't you exhausted? Isn't she?" It must
have been past three in the morning now, and the sobbing had sustained itself over the last hour. "She can't help it. I can't get her to

stop." Trish sat down on the edge of the cot. I was certain she was right; I had been aware of the low obbligato of Trish's soothing voice, sustained under the irritating pattern of grief like an accompanist. "What do you want me to do about it?" I moved over a bit.

"I don't know." She crossed her legs and picked absently at a toe-nail. I felt a rush of sympathy for her. Her position was as impossible as my own. Whenever Rosie was in the company, Trish was still a principal actress, if not its leading lady, surely a valued friend. When Rosie was absent, Trish found herself in the unenviable position of disappointing expectant audiences while repeatedly having to prove her own worth in some of Rosemary's signature parts. Rising to the occasion as Lady Teazle in the recent Los Angeles season, she had shaken like an aspen leaf through at least her first two or three per-formances before finding more secure footing. But tonight she was not here as a company member. She was, as I was, an emotional buf-fer, one of two public witnesses to a private war meant to indemnify just how bad it was becoming.

"I don't know," Trish repeated. "I'm at my wit's end." She stood up and then said impatiently, "She isn't really crying, you know. That isn't crying, what she's doing. I don't know what it is—hysteria, I sup-pose, but whatever it is, she obviously can't stop."

We padded in silence across the pine floor just outside the bed-room. We'd both been originally destined for our comic cots on the porch, but with Ellis having disappeared into the night, it seemed only right for Trish to stay with Rosie, somehow to comfort her.

"Rosie?" I tentatively queried. "Rosie?" Nothing. Trish disap-peared into the darkened room and I heard her murmuring some-thing I couldn't make out. And suddenly, without so much as a dropped measure in the little passacaglia of sobbing, Rosie was standing in front of me, her hair in utter disarray, her face splotchy with red, and her mouth wide open, staring unseeing into my face, that "sob-sob-sob-shudder" now so on automatic pilot, she couldn't even hear what I was saying. She was in her bare feet, standing like an unhappy school-girl, her arms crossed over her celebrated breasts. "The big-brrrreasted Harris girls," Olivier had deliciously named her and her sisters, Pam and Patsy. I took her shoulders. "Rosie, stop it! You've got to stop it." She tried to pull away from me, but I held tight. "Rosie! Rosie! Listen to me! Dammit, listen to me!"

Did I really strike Rosemary Harris? Did I actually physically hit her? Since puberty, I cannot remember raising my hand either in defense or aggression to nearly anyone or anything. If there's a chance to duck it, I will streak in the opposite direction, and as a result have never felt completely comfortable with my own anger. It flares up, but it has never resulted in anything physical, which is probably why I depend on words so entirely. And now as I sit down to recall one of the most painful moments in what seems to be my own *Coming of Age in Samoa of the American Theater*—save for the surreal event of years ahead that would one day separate Ellis and me for good—I cannot help but feel inadequate. Moments, events, even conversations during this part of my life I recall confidently with near academic precision; details such as what someone was wearing, or the words they used, seem as vivid as when they happened. Yet what transpired in a little cottage by an inland lake north of Ann Arbor one Saturday night in the wet autumn of 1967 is like a tape being fast-forwarded randomly, or as if one were listening to a radio signal fading in and out, sometimes crystal clear, sometimes just white noise. This was no ordinary evening, that is true. If any single moment represents a fulcrum separating what was past and what was to be, I believe this event defined it, although none of the four of us who were playing out our seriocomic parts were aware of it.

It's about 3:35, the blackest slice of night, and I am standing in the little hallway, my hands gripping Rosemary's shoulders. She is still trying to pull away from me, turning back toward the bedroom where Trish stands in the door, one hand blocking the room beyond. "Rosie, stop it!" I hear myself saying, as in a bad script. "You've got to stop." I tug her back to face me. "Rosie! Rosie! Listen to me! Dammit, listen to me!" The noise bleats on without interruption while she sways back and forth in a mindless attempt to pull away from me.

I release her shoulder with my right hand, and without a thought, I pull it back and slap her directly across the face. The earth stands still. So does she. All sound stops, and we three are frozen, not breathing. She looks at me, and her eyes widen. What will she do? Attack me? Scream?

She threw herself into my arms, hard against my chest, and what came from her then was a genuine wail of sadness and grief. Her body heaving, she wept, truly wept this time, and I held her awkwardly, rubbing her shoulders and back and trying my best to shush her. "It's all right," I said stupidly. "It'll be all right."

It was past four in the morning when we all finally lay down to get whatever sleep we could. Rosemary had had tea by this time; she'd washed her face and was calmer. Trish and I had tried to keep up a roundelay of idiotic conversation until it seemed as if we had earned the right to stop for a bit. There was to be a matinee of *The School for Scandal* at two o'clock that afternoon. We had no one to call, nor a way to get back to Ann Arbor, and with both Trish and Rosemary in the room, there was no other Lady Teazle in Ann Arbor who could step in; but that was a problem we had yet to face.

What did we do before cell phones? It's so difficult to realize how cut off everyone was prior to being able to shop for groceries while carrying on one's psychotherapy session at the same time. We had an ordinary dial telephone and no number to call; the methodology for just getting back to Ann Arbor was mystifying to say the least. In Rosemary's purse we found a scrap of paper with the telephone number of someone who lived near Ann Arbor, Zeke Jabbour, a friend who had come to the company's rescue on more than one occasion, supplying, at one point, raw lumber to provide elements of the set when the university's budget wouldn't sustain it and who had, like many fans, fallen into a perpetual state of adoration for Rosemary. I called him. It seemed there was no need to explain. With the discretion of someone who had always somehow intuited the truth without ever having been told it, Zeke came out to fetch us sometime past noon, and we four made the hour's drive back to the city in complete silence.

He left us without comment outside the stage door of the Lydia Mendelssohn Theatre, where the company was performing, and Rosemary, a paper cup of soup in her hand, looking haggard, worn, and defeated, wearily climbed the steps backstage to her dressing room. Trish and I stood together at the bottom.

"What are you going to do?" she asked. "I'm going to sleep," I said resolutely. "I don't give a shit whether there's a matinee today or not, I haven't closed my eyes for more than forty minutes all night, and if I don't get some sleep I'll faint."

"Me, too," said Trish. "Do we dare leave?" "Yes!" I said. "Tell you what: I'll meet you back here after the matinee, okay? Let's both

Ellis Rabb as Joseph and Rosemary Harris as Lady Teazle in *The School for Scandal.* (Robert Alan Gold)

at least get some sleep; we can pick up the pieces later. There isn't anything more we can do now—Rosemary obviously intends to play. God knows where Ellis is, but I can't do anything about that."

We turned away from each other and I walked back to the Michigan Union, where I had a small room. I fell, completely clothed, onto the bed and was instantly unconscious.

At ten before five in the afternoon, after having had a couple of hours' sleep and a shower, I showed up at the bottom of those same steps. Trish was already there, looking as bad as I did, our showers notwithstanding. Her hair was plastered to her head, and she had no color at all in her face. "Did you sleep?" I asked.

"Sort of. How do you think it went?" she said with a nod above to the backstage area. I shook my head, having no idea of the carnage that must have taken place onstage, but clearly some kind of performance had been given, and evidently both Rosemary and Ellis must have given it. I bent over from the waist and put my forehead on the iron railing. It felt cold and uncomfortable, like the night we'd passed. From the corridor above we could hear the low sound of Ellis's voice. "Here we go!" I said, straightening up.

On the landing above, two people emerged from the dressing area. Ellis, dressed smartly, and Rosemary, her hair coifed carefully with some of the afternoon's makeup still on her face, emerged arm in arm, laughing. They were talking over each other as they descended the stairs to where Trish and I stood waiting, but we couldn't make sense of a word they said until they finally saw us. They barely broke stride.

"'Bye, darlings," Rosie cooed. "We're off to dinner. See you both later?"

"Bye-bye," Ellis tossed back as he held the door for her. "We might still have a drink after the show tonight, if you both feel up to it." And they were gone, the door slamming behind them, reducing their stream of conversation so that all we could basically identify, as our eyes found each other, was the diminuendo of Rosemary's laugh.

"Jesus wept!" was all I could say. Trish nodded. "Jesus wept!"

19

And so the axis perceptibly shifted; with a kind of click, just that simply, as befits a company and a family. I have no recollection of the leave-taking, nor the arrangements that attended it. After about ten years of marriage, Rosemary and Ellis were to separate, and for all the previous fireworks, I remember nothing particularly dramatic about the parting. Thinking back on it all, I now begin to marvel that any couple so involved, so deeply and even creatively intertwined, could manage a separation with such poise and mutual respect. Hal was finally no threat, and shortly after the swift demise of the ill-advised *We, Comrades Three*, he, too, vanished. The consequences had nothing to do with him. It was just time—for the company to shrug and adjust and expand, and for Rosemary to get on with her life, which, after a few amusing social encounters, she did. There was one rather bizarre dating period involving a gentleman so horrified of germs that he needed to bring sterilized handkerchiefs with him everywhere he went, simply for opening doorknobs. Rosie demonstrated equal measures of fascination and sympathy, never mocking him. None of the rest of us knew exactly what to do with that information, nor the images it conjured up, but before long, the solid, secure, immensely satisfying silhouette of the Southern author John Ehle appeared, and Rosemary's continuing story was to have all the happy resolution she had longed for and deserved, including that cherished daughter, Jennifer, destined to rise before long to complement as well as challenge her mother's vast reputation and succeed as an award-winning actress in her own right. Grandchildren, *Spider-Man* movie celebrity, and more acting triumphs to come, Rosie appears to float effortlessly above her own narrative, the smiling, secure keeper of her own flame as well as her own secrets.

Ellis threw himself into his work, as was his patented response, conceiving a production of Ionesco's *Exit the King* for Richard Easton, with a stunning brass score by Conrad Susa, augmenting the cutting-edge physical design of Rouben Ter-Arutunian, a glamorous recruit from Houseman's side of the artistic ledger and the world of ballet. Rouben had been a personal friend of the Housemans, and had created for Joan a gift of the most exquisite dragonfly pin, made of bits of painted glass, that clipped to the shoulder of whatever Chanel suit she might choose to wear. For the Ionesco, he had invented a three-sided box of clear plastic, with three modern sculptural thrones on a severely raked stage, which, when finally covered over by a fourth "curtain" in the front and lit by instruments from the balcony rail at the conclusion, afforded the illusion of Easton literally disappearing before one's eyes in a shattered blaze of light. The production was initially meant to be directed by Le Gallienne in L.A., with Will Geer as the attendant soldier, Patricia Conolly as the young Queen Marie, Richard Woods as the Doctor, and originally Louise Latham as the older queen, Marguerite. Rehearsals had begun the summer before with the company gathered in the living room of Ellis's Chateau Marmont cottage, where LeG talked casually about death, the subject of the play. There was something incongruous about a discussion of the end of life taking place adjacent to the swimming pool ordinarily occupied by Dustin Hoffman floating about while waiting to film *The Graduate*. LeG leaned in from her straight-backed chair toward the company, all sharing seedless grapes, lying about on the carpet before her. "The thing about death, of course, is the dread of whatever form it might ultimately take, not necessarily the event itself. What one longs for, you know, is just to make a good end. That's all. Wouldn't you say so, Will?" She looked across the room at the only other senior member in the room, Will Geer, sitting in the shadows against the wall. "That's it, Eva," he growled with encouragement. "A good end! That's about it!" Such candor, such direct honesty felt somehow shocking to a roomful of observers fully thirty or more years younger, almost as if we were silently observing an exchange not intended for us to overhear.

When the production eventually reached the Lyceum in New York, changes in casting that repertory naturally affords had occurred. Ellis persuaded LeG that she must return to the New York stage in a role clearly too old for Louise Latham, although Richard Easton, ever a resourceful and commanding presence and more Louise's contemporary than LeG's, didn't read too young as Berenger. Will Geer was replaced first by Clayton Corzatte on the production's way east, and then Nicholas Martin, while Pamela Payton-Wright remained as the housemaid, as did Conolly as the younger queen. When LeG took the lead, Ellis stepped in as director, at her insistence, not his. She intuited that she was no rival for his theatrical fireworks, but in the case of this absurdist tract, even Ellis couldn't lift the production in any significant way. Although Richard Easton enjoyed considerable success, it never registered as more interesting than it was beautiful.

However, in one of the more bizarre turns of repertory planning, an alternate branch of the company seemed about to be opening up independently within the ranks. Miss Hayes also needed a vehicle for the coming New York season, and George Kelly's masterpiece *The Show-Off* was chosen for her, a production that would eventually break off from the season and tour successfully across the country. What made this even more remarkable was the fact that two legendary figures of twentieth-century New York theater, two near polar opposites, existed side by side in the same company at the same time, performing diametrically different roles in utterly different styles of acting, a proximity they would have both gone to any extreme to avoid in the commercial world; and try as I may, I cannot remember a single instance of both of them ever appearing at the theater, or even in the same room, at the same time. True, LeG became Queen Marguerite long after the triumph Miss Hayes enjoyed as Ma Fisher, but these classic rivals certainly had to have confronted each other at some time, and yet there is not one single moment I recall when that happened. It must have taken considerable thought and negotiation, to say nothing of animal instinct. Years later, when Miss Hayes had had a Broadway theater named after her, Le Gallienne was heard sniffing as she entered, "I will always prefer to think of this place as the Fulton!" But a delicious American intramural version of Fotheringay, with LeG as Elizabeth and Miss Hayes as Mary, Queen of Scots, was not in the cards, at least now, backstage at the Lyceum.

If the cool, cerebral, silverpoint technique of Le Gallienne guided with intelligence the deterioration of Easton's Berenger in *Exit the King*, Miss Hayes uncorked under Stephen Porter's direction one of her last and perhaps greatest stage creations, a tiny, resolute, sympathetic, yet hilarious biddy of a woman who was the querulous, irritated head of a household deeply infected with the shenanigans of a shallow ne'er-do-well son-in-law, Aubrey Piper, played to irritating perfection by Clayton Corzatte. Miss Hayes was amazing, direct, and utterly free of artifice as Ma Fisher. "You can't catch her acting!" remarked Donald Moffat, who was always respectful but never over-generous in his praise of fellow actors. And indeed you could not. She had, no question, a bag of tricks honed to perfection by a lifetime on American stages in American roles—Queen Victoria excepted—and this plainspoken character fitted her as if made to order. "Here, Gypsy!" she cooed in a super-soprano voice to a completely imaginary dog located in an imaginary basement. Then, dropping her voice to a tough baritone, she'd remind her son, Joe, not to let the dog into the kitchen, barking commands like a drill instructor. Then, "Back, Gypsy, back, you bad, bad dog!" she'd squeal, up at least three octaves without taking a breath. My own grandmother had died long before the time of this performance, but I cannot think of Helen Hayes without seeing my mother's mother, breathing, cursing, admonishing, dimensional and real. One often has a misconceived, decorated, even quaint idea of the great actors of our past; it is, as it was in this case, something of a revelation to realize that great acting is always shockingly direct and simple, in the sense that love is. I imagine it holds true of Ellen Terry, of Maud Adams, and of Mrs. Siddons as well.

The company now was solid and unmistakably confident. The members of the ensemble were growing because of continuity as much as the frequency of their assignments. Dee Victor, a sweet character actress who had transitioned from early lush and blowsy roles into ones more motherly, was at her best as Penny in *You Can't Take It with You*, never quite hitting that mark in anything else, nor was she expected to. Ellis was fond of murmuring encouragement to various players after hours while cradling his glass of white wine, cooing in that beguiling Southern manner that juicier parts glimmered just ahead and inevitably employing the phrase "in terms of your development," which too often came to nothing at all. I doubt that he had much interest in Dee past the role of Penny Sycamore, but she had scored so solidly in that part that she hung on for several more seasons, acting less and drinking a bit more as a consequence. Sydney Walker, a company stalwart trained at Jasper Deeter's Hedgerow Theatre in the forties, with his sour face and his curious nineteenth-century stance, as if he were eternally leaning into a wind, was far more successful in a range of parts that could stretch from the benign, goofy Paul Sycamore in the Kaufman/Hart to the terrifying Old Prince Bolkonsky in *War and Peace*, and even an extravagant Boris Pishchik in *The Cherry Orchard*. He once privately suggested having a button created and given out to other members of the ensemble with "APA Will Break Your Heart" emblazoned upon it, as proof of his own evenings of Ellis spinning his dreams. Donald Moffat could also stretch, in the rep sense of the word, from being nearly unrecognizable as Grandpa Vanderhof in the Kaufman/Hart farce, Prince Andrei in *War and Peace*, or Lopakhin in *The Cherry Orchard*. Jennifer Harmon, who began just out of university in a series of walk-on parts, grew to play Maria in *Scandal* and Essie in *You Can't Take It with You*. Another with that range was Trish, who created one of the company's truly singular female performances, Rachel Silberschatz in *Pantagleize*, something Rosemary would have been hard-pressed to breathe life into, yet someone like Marco St. John never found a niche quite as individual. It seemed as if there were often two different categories of actor involved—the useful rep talent, like Richard Woods, Joe Bird, or Gordon Gould, who were always in contention for supporting parts, and the inner circle of Ellis's social friends. Betty Miller and her husband, James Greene, came in as a stopgap measure when Nancy Marchand and Paul Sparer were ousted but never managed to socially conquer Ellis. At the same time, he could be nearly reckless if charmed by someone far from appropriate as a company member. His attempt to hire Elaine Stritch was surely socially motivated, as was his falling under the spell of a cabaret chanteuse named Anne Francine, nearly six feet tall with a bellowing voice and a ribald sense of humor, who was anything but classical. Ellis determinedly shoe-horned her into parts like Lady Sneerwell for a while, where she floundered around flummoxing the language and mixing up the words. Rosemary and her fellow actors bent over, stifling their laughter, when a line like Lady Sneerwell's "her bulk is her misfortune" came out as "her fat is her cross to bear." Ralph Williams, another of Ellis's pals, had achieved a reputation in various successful New York productions, but when transplanted to APA-Phoenix, was never able to find the right showcase for his originality.

The result was a growing company comprised of column A and column B—and the common denominator came down to either someone who was useful to the rep, practically speaking, or someone whose company Ellis wanted to enjoy. An example of the latter category was Nicholas Martin, a close friend from Carnegie Tech onward, who became a successful director later in his life but was present every bit as much for his ebullient social spirit as for his skill as an actor. After all, companies, like royal courts, need jesters and diplomats as much as they need soldiers and advisers, and there was more than one occasion when Nicky, sailing into some fraught social scene, was able to lift the entire evening with an airy wave of his hand. Actual theatrical talent can exist on more platforms than just a stage. True, in roles like that of Sir Benjamin Backbite in *Scandal*, Nicky's arch, high-camp attack was the perfect note to strike, and although he performed effectively as the Poet in *Pantagleize*, whenever Ellis needed to reach out for "comfort casting"—gathering around him the kind of personal support that might buoy up his own confidence in something risky—Nicky might find himself out of his depth, but he never let the event, the opportunity, or Ellis down.

Clayton Corzatte, Ellis's early young leading man, who had been Constantin in the Folksbeine *Seagull*, was controversial in another way: with his intense regional Texas rhythms, he tended to sound contemporary no matter what the text. But he was attractive, with the confidence and the attack that allowed him not only to succeed as Tony in *You Can't Take It with You*, but to stand up against Miss Hayes as costar in *The Show-Off*. Keene Curtis, who began his career as a stage manager for Noël Coward and Martha Graham, and whose enrollment in the company as an actor was almost an accidental inclusion from the early workshops, played major roles in *War and Peace, You Can't Take It with You, Scandal,* and *Pantagleize* and went on to play major roles on Broadway in *Annie* and *La Cage aux Folles,* among other vehicles, after APA-Phoenix disbanded.

With Rosemary about to leave the company, Ellis and Houseman found it necessary to spread the net of the company's acting roster more aggressively. They were going to need additional flash at the top of the bill. Ellis, as the company's leader, was never going to be considered the star Rosemary was, or even Richard Easton, who brought with him the edge required to hold the stage opposite Uta Hagen in *Who's Afraid of Virginia Woolf?* in the West End. Houseman was determined to woo Brian Bedford, newly relocated to the States from England, into the company. Brian had made a dazzling debut in Peter Shaffer's *Five Finger Exercise* in London and had recently begun to secure a toehold in films such as *Grand Prix.* He had made himself available to do some coaching for Houseman in the latter's new role as head of the Drama Division at Juilliard, and Houseman and Ellis invited him into the company, offering the lead in T. S. Eliot's *The Cocktail Party* as well as a plum comedy turn as Acaste in *The Misanthrope,* which was being prepared for Easton. For the obscure and complicated Eliot play, Frances Sternhagen rejoined the company after having been absent since the early Princeton season when she was Gwendolyn to Rosemary's Cecily. Franny, over the intervening years, had raised something like six children, all born very close to each other, so the fact that she was a working mother as well as nearly always pregnant made her impossible to consider for earlier seasons. Along with Bedford and Sternhagen, Ellis managed to pull off one of his most original casting coups. He had been friends over the years with the great comic satirist Nancy Walker, for whom entire musicals had been created during the forties and fifties but who in her later years became more famous for portraying Rosie, the "Quicker Picker-Upper," in paper towel commercials. Nancy was a woman of intelligence and wit, capable of far more than ads on television. Ellis first cast her incorrectly as the aristocratic Julia Shuttlethwaite in *The Cocktail Party,* and then brilliantly as Charlotta Ivanovna in *The Cherry Orchard,* where her sly comic sensibilities could shine. And finally, with Le Gallienne on hand to re-create her celebrated Civic Rep production of *The Cherry Orchard*, done originally for her lover, the great Nazimova, Houseman and Ellis approached Uta Hagen, absent from the Broadway stage since *Virginia Woolf*, to play Lyubov Ranevskaya in their revival of the Chekhov. Early in her career, Hagen debuted as Juliet for LeG, and more recently had been with Easton in the West End, so what what might have appeared a long shot was transformed into star power for the coming season. Looking back now on a roster that included Uta Hagen, Richard Easton, Brian Bedford, Helen Hayes, Eva Le Gallienne, Frances Sternhagen, and Nancy Walker, as well as the existing ensemble, one can understand how Clive Barnes was to write in *The New York Times*, "a theatre company is either growing or it is not, and APA/Phoenix is growing and growing impressively."

One more event was to take place around this time, early in 1967, born out of a kind of necessity and with consequences we couldn't have imagined at the time. John Houseman was, in addition to his role as educator, writer, and impresario, that rarest of all creatures in the theater—a true producer. It would be years before he would be tapped as a last-minute replacement for James Mason by director James Bridges, another of his string of acolytes, to play the part of Professor Kingsfield in the film *The Paper Chase*, earning him that Oscar for best performance by a supporting actor and kicking him into yet another realm of fame and fortune. Houseman possessed the alchemic quality of not only seeing what was available, but knowing how to market it. Born in Romania and educated in England, he was an admirer of the Belgian playwright Michel de Ghelderode, a talent virtually unknown in America other than in academic circles, whose grotesque yet gorgeous works included *Woman at the Tomb*, *Escurial*, and *Barabbas*. De Ghelderode had only recently died, in 1962, and among his works was Houseman's particular favorite, *Pantagleize*, a black farce about an innocent who inadvertently triggers a revolution in an unnamed European country by uttering a simple phrase—"What a lovely day!"—which is the secret signal for revolt. Houseman had always longed to see it produced, and now had found the perfect opportunity; he suggested it as a vehicle for Ellis as actor and director as well.

Ellis was feeling the pressure of increased expectations with the departure of his leading lady following the dissolution of their marriage. This new project was exotic and risky, and as it was unknown, Ellis had no defenses against it. It wasn't a play he had ever read, or in fact that anyone seemed to know, and there must have been some relief in having as strong an advocate as Houseman pushing it toward him, as opposed to his having to come up with something from his own experience. Why not, then? Everyone went immediately into action—possibly too immediately. On his part, Houseman immersed himself in the translation. Because he was fluent in French, as was Joan, this was pure pleasure for him, whereas Ellis, as might have been predicted, reached immediately for his circle of intimates for support in casting. He wanted Sydney Walker as the waiter Innocenti, Nicholas Martin as the Poet, Keene Curtis as the Anarchist, and in the key role of the Policeman, Creep, first Richard Easton, who, burdened with leads in both *Exit the King* and *The Misanthrope*, had to be replaced by Stephan Gierasch. The lone woman's part, the firebrand Rachel Silbershatz, went to Trish Conolly, her first chance to create something original within the rep rather than inheriting or, worse, having to share another of Rosemary's roles. With Rosemary absent, Trish became Ellis's instant substitute, whether as a confidant, a dinner guest, or the solution to a casting problem; and yet just as swiftly he could withdraw his support, as if challenging her loyalty. She, more than any of us, sustained his continual mood swings and rejections, and this pattern continued long after the company ceased to function. "APA Will Break Your Heart," said Sydney Walker's imaginary button. Trish endlessly earned hers. As the alternate Rachel, Christina Pickles was chosen, to whom had also fallen the unfortunate assignment of Célimène in *The Misanthrope* opposite Easton. I say "unfortunate" because this role would be considered the undisputed province of Miss Harris in conception, but now, without her, it would be virtual open season for the critics, whoever might play it, and Christina was no exception. COME HOME, COME HOME, ROSEMARY HARRIS, WHEREVER YOU ARE, ran the cruel headline in one review for *The Misanthrope*, but Christina bore both that insult as well as her assignment as the alternate Rachel with panache and class, and she turned out to be extremely effective in both.

Conolly, it must be said, was a revelation. With her petite, sexy body, her prodigious energy, and her comic timing, dressed in butch military garb and high boots, her fists shaking in the air over her head as she barked orders, she was something to behold. Opposite romantic, languid Ellis in the title role, they had remarkable chemistry onstage, a major reason for the production's success. Eventually, that is . . . for although both Houseman and Ellis began with enthusiasm, things soon began to cool. Sitting in the makeshift rehearsal space provided for APA-Phoenix, Ellis slumped low, his sunglasses on, smoking incessantly and squinting at the lit space before him while repeatedly refusing to rehearse. Whenever Pantagleize was needed, he indicated with a vague wave of his hand that I should execute the moves, a natural convenience left over from my early assignment for *The Tavern*. With me, as opposed to an official understudy, no one needed to be concerned; in other words, he wasn't *not* rehearsing, he wasn't abandoning his responsibility, Jack was merely going through the paces in his stead so he might study the work as a whole, but Houseman suspected that Ellis was trying to distance himself further and further from the role.

Houseman and I, on the other hand, were getting on like the proverbial house on fire. John was anything but a cozy pal and kept himself pretty much at icy reserve from everyone but Ellis, Richard Easton, and T., but I was quick to realize that this was a matter of defense, not indifference. And I was spending more and more time with Joan as a charming respite from the parallel rigors of life with John and Ellis. It pleased her, and her happiness was always a major concern of John's, although he seldom seemed to demonstrate the fact. "The perfect third," having learned the act from Bob and Judy through Ellis and Rosemary, found this niche with the Housemans infinitely less stressful and far more civilized, and as Ellis's amanuensis, I was in the best position to offer information, a kind of emotional tea-leaf reader. John and my father had been very different men, but there was something similar, a coolness about both of them, with which I felt comfortable. Perhaps the fact that Dad and John would be near contemporaries, had my father survived, put me at ease. I would sit with Houseman, or behind him and Ellis, listening and observing, and would step in instantly to supply whatever was needed, a continuation of my first assignment as Ellis's assistant. I knew then what I knew best, that my survival depended upon making myself indispensable, and I continued to go about it with a driving passion. John was to discover that whenever Ellis seemed indifferent to his suggestions, there might be another way to get around him. He loved existing high above the fray and yet having unrestrained access to it. And so came his suggestion that I should work to prepare Ellis privately, just us two, so that as an actor, Ellis would not be allowed to fall too far behind. After all, technical rehearsals were looming.

"Park"—I paused for a fraction, then pointed insistently— "there!" Ellis and I had been driving around Hollywood for a good fifteen minutes looking for a parking place. We were presumably headed to the abandoned ABC television studio on Vine that had been secured for the company's rehearsal space, two blocks equidistant between the Huntington Hartford Theatre, as the Doolittle was then known, and the tacky Villa Elaine Hotel across the street from the Hollywood Ranch Market, where most of the company had been bivouacked during the first year of our residency. I glanced over to my left. Ellis was not nailing down a parking place at the moment, nor was it his intention to abandon the security of the car.

"Right there!" I pointed again, and he brought the car to a halt. He was wearing two sets of eyeglasses now, his normal glasses covered by an enormous black plastic buglike affair that fitted completely over the first pair, making him look like something out of science fiction. He was stressed, and stress triggered the hovering threat of a detached retina—all the excuse he needed for a lack of activity. It was a coolish, gray day, uncharacteristic in the Los Angeles basin except in those presummer weeks when the offshore marine layer oppressively intrudes. The unvaried light did nothing for our spirits, and although it was not cold, Ellis was wrapped in a corduroy jacket, its wide collar turned up to obscure all but his celebrated profile. He held a cigarette in one hand, which shook slightly as he put the car into reverse and peered through the double lenses into the rearview mirror for confirmation. Round and round we'd driven—down Vine to the corner, left up Sunset Boulevard past the garish Cinerama to the next corner, left again down to Vine and around once more. We hadn't seen any parking places here in one of the denser midtown areas except for this one. In Ellis's case, the appearance of this one was surely going to be a mixed blessing.

Yesterday had not gone well. Scenes not involving the character of Pantagleize got some refining, but whenever it came to one of his scenes, Ellis turned to me with a curt "You do this, will you?" and looked away from meeting either Houseman's eyes or mine. About four in the afternoon, fed up with this, Houseman had risen and stamped out, muttering. Ellis ended the day's work shortly thereafter, and one could feel the company peering anxiously around, not daring to express their concerns. I received a call from Houseman that same evening. "Haut-Brion," he began, never calling me Jack but preferring the witty adaptation he liked to make of my last name, "take the sonofabitch in hand, will you? Get him to rehearse tomorrow, whatever you do. There's a matinee, so no one else will be around. I've had more than enough of this shit." "John!" I began in protest, but he cut me off: "Just go about it, dear boy" was all he said, and he hung up.

Ellis sighed, his hands still trembling, took another puff, and stuck the cigarette into the ashtray. He backed the car into the curb, turned off the ignition, and sighed again. His face was splotchy with patches of angry skin which spoke of the stress he was under, and he pursed his lips in sour resignation. He looked awful.

"What is it?" I said finally. He stared out the car window lost in thought, pushing the black glasses up on his brow. Over the years, we'd performed this exchange to amuse our friends as emblematic of our working relationship. "What's wrong?" I'd go. "What's wrong, El?" Silence. I'd pause for effect. Then I'd mimic his answer, a heartsearing sigh of ennui and boredom, as if it were articulate speech. "I'll pack!" I'd say, jumping up. Everyone would laugh at this comic routine, no one more than Ellis. There was, of course, some truth in it.

But not today. No laughs. Just silence. I stared out my window at the dirty ABC studio before which we sat on Vine Street, deserted on this Sunday morning. "Come on, El," I said, opening the passenger side of the car door. "Let's get it over with." He sighed again and picked up his pack of cigarettes, and we walked together in silence toward the blanked-out windows of the building. The door was open, probably because maintenance workers took Sunday mornings to do a little cleaning, but it seemed completely empty. The studio that had been arranged for us was grim and ghostly, a low-ceilinged affair with black boxes scattered around. Down at one end lay a piece of mocked-up scenery representing a judge's desk that, when stood up on end, doubled as the wall against which the final executions would take place. Other than a rickety card table pretending to be a café, and a few folding chairs strewn about, there was nothing else to suggest a theatrical endeavor of any kind.

Ellis slumped down in one of the folding chairs, putting his feet up on the card table and glaring at me. "This is nonsense," he said sullenly. "Why are you putting yourself through all this?" I couldn't help but notice this was suddenly about me, not him. Not a good sign.

"Because we have to, that's why. And because, dammit, you're going to be wonderful in this part, and you know it!"

"Because John probably made you," he contradicted me, "that's why we're here, and I know no such thing." He put his feet down heavily and, leaning forward, stared between his knees at the dirty cement floor. I started to protest further, but he put a hand up to silence me. "No, you don't understand. You really don't." He looked up at me. There was no posing this time. He was in genuine pain. "I can't. I just can't anymore. I know it's important to John, and I think everyone thinks its important to me, but honest to God, I don't think I care. Maybe I'm just tired. Maybe I'm finally burned out. But I don't give a shit." He looked off to one side, removing the buglike plastic glasses and carefully, deliberately pulling at the lash of his left eye. I could see in the soft light of the studio the pale blue color of his eyes, and, what was more bizarre, the fact that the iris itself seemed to jiggle whenever he worried it, as if it were made of Jell-O. How many operations had he undergone by this time for his detached retina? Two? Three?

"But what are we going to do?" I was not negotiating any longer. I knew the signs, I'd been here before. Rock bottom. No excuses . . . no games. "You have to rehearse this sometime! You honestly don't know the lines, El, and you've got to learn them! We go into techs next week!" Uh-oh. Bad choice: "You have to . . ." Never the best words to employ when confronting Ellis. I could hear my Midwestern voice rising in a distinct whine. I felt futile.

He rose and looked down at me, and something snapped. He

picked up the black plastic sunglasses and slammed them onto his face, his mouth twisting into a sneer. "Well, here's my solution. How about this? You do it if it's so goddamn important," he said, turning on me. "See, you know the blocking, and you sure as hell know the fucking lines by this time. I've just tried to tell you something, but you and everyone else keep insisting it's all so fucking important. So you play the part. Because know what? I'm leaving!"

He grabbed the cigarettes and the lighter from the little table, fished in his coat pocket for the car keys, and tossed them up in the air. Catching them, he strode back out the way we came, leaving me alone. What would I tell Houseman? Whom could I call for a ride? I hadn't even gotten him to take his jacket off!

Unfortunately for me, I did know "the fucking lines." And as a result, I found myself days later standing atop the rehearsal "wall" in the third scene of the play. Out in front of me I could just make out, from my precarious vantage point, Ellis sitting to the right of Houseman in the dimness of the rehearsal hall, glaring at the run-through before him. Houseman was still furious because Ellis was, once more, watching, not acting.

"The Great Parade," I say, rotating in some approximation of the way I had seen Ellis swivel on the few occasions he had gone through the scene. My upstage foot is forward, on the narrow surface of the wall, my downstage foot is back. I have Ellis's white umbrella in my upstage hand, and this way I can look upstage and then turn downstage to report what I'm seeing.

This particular scene was a demonstration of Ellis at the top of his conceptual game. It calls for scores of flags somehow visible to the audience, a phalanx of flags, all red, representing a May Day demonstration going on upstage at the same time as a total eclipse of the sun occurs, but none of it is realistic. The character of Pantagleize can see everything, having clambered up on the wall for a better view, and it is he who explains what can only be suggested. The cast is already extensive if one counts only the named roles, but in addition there is meant to be a vast army of other players, one of the many reasons this play is rarely produced: in the present economic climate, no management can afford numbers that exceed those required for a musical, especially for an obscure Belgian text. Ellis has devised a simple but brilliant solution. Each of our individual journeymen is pushing a small triangular cart mounted on universal wheels, and extending up from these pieces of movable wood are three to five poles, upon which are fixed red flags. At the beginning of the scene, the boys, hunkered down out of the sight lines, roll these carts back and forth in formation while Pantagleize describes the scene from the wall. But as the carts drift toward the wings, each gets replaced by an identical cart with ever-darkening red flags, and finally, the last set is made up entirely of black flags, while the lights have been dimming slowly to an impenetrable gloom. The Grand Parade has morphed into the Great Eclipse, and it's as simple as it is theatrical.

"The Great Parade!" I continue to narrate as the journeymen double their responsibilities by hurling rude epithets at me while exchanging red flags for darker ones. Pantagleize, trying to cheer them up, dances for them, waving his absurd umbrella as an accompaniment. The scene, a bit flattened by my workmanlike performance, is still pretty exciting. I leap down from the wall.

Trish Conolly bolts onstage as Rachel Silbershatz, the pint-sized revolutionary, her feet resolutely planted, the embodiment of fiery determination. She grabs me by the elbow, pumps one tiny fist into the air above her head, barks "Magnificent!" at the top of her lungs, kisses me, and bolts off. Pantagleize is astounded. He is not the only one.

In the darkened rehearsal space I can hear the deep chortle of Ellis's laugh. He's not laughing at me, I know very well that he's laughing at Trish. This is one of those perfect moments when actress and role intersect, and Ellis is as vulnerable as any audience. At this point in the production, Sydney Walker has been stamping around effectively as Innocenti; Nicholas Martin has been converted into a walking bush, a massive wig and a veritable hedge of facial hair added for additional grit and gravitas; and Keene Curtis, clad in leather, is the only one at present resembling what will finally reach the Lyceum stage in New York, his bald head a shiny bullet. Even with me tentatively holding center stage, the company is rising to the challenge, and as Trish disappears, even Houseman grunts a kind of laugh. Ellis stands up.

"Hold on a minute, will you?" he says, thoughtfully studying the

Patricia Conolly as the minuscule firebrand Rachel Silbershatz and Ellis Rabb as
the eponymous Pantagleize, his finest and final acting achievement. (Van Williams)

ashtray before him as he stabs out the cigarette. "I think . . . yes . . . hmmm! . . . I think we'll try that once more, shall we?" The company, already prepared to move on, look around in surprise. "Jack," he says, dropping his glasses at Houseman's elbow and moving away, "take John's notes, will you? I think I'll try it."

20

There was a semblance of a performance in Los Angeles—history bears witness; it went off as scheduled, amazingly enough, and if the reception wasn't ecstatic, it was probably a great deal better than we deserved. The director's approach seemed clear and logical, there were occasional glints of something edgy and original at work, and at the very least, Ellis managed to get a version of the production onstage at the Huntington Hartford. What it lacked, in Los Angeles, was him. The "him" element that would make the difference between something effective and the feeling that occurs when one is in the presence of an original creative mind. He played the part, and, because it was beautifully suited to him—an apolitical aesthete, forty years old, simplistic, romantic, and in some aspects, almost childlike—his natural authority carried the day. Dressed in a cream-colored suit, a blue bachelor-button boutonniere in his lapel, white canvas shoes on his feet, very much like the kind of look he regularly chose for himself, he had merely to saunter in and out of the scenes to evoke the actual character de Ghelderode had written on the page, and a few of the effects called for—the suitcase with treasure in it made entirely of tiny sparkling electrical lights, the riveting execution on top of a wall, based as it was on Brando's harrowing death in *Viva Zapata!* in which, according to Ellis, you could see every individual bullet entering the actor's body—these were certainly sketched, if not yet inhabited. The glum spirit of Los Angeles, mirrored by its gray, inclement weather, gave way, and Ellis's depression began to lift. We moved on to Ann Arbor, where his engine began to turn over.

And much of it was indeed great fun. Even in the depths of a low period, Ellis was extremely generous as a host. He entertained with flair, cooking, serving quantities of wine, and, with his close friends around him, laughing as much as possible. It was a reminder to me of how a leader seriously affects the spirit of those around him, and abetted by the Housemans, it all made a lasting impression on me.

He was always accessible, always looking for diversions, and it wasn't long before he, too, fell under the spell of my best friends, Bob and Judy James. Judy, in particular, delighted him. Quick-witted, funny, and indefatigable, Judy never found herself, to my recollection, in a social occasion she couldn't conquer. She took risks. If Judy had an anecdote to offer, she'd bound recklessly out on a limb with nary a net in sight and work the material, no matter how pedestrian, until she had everyone howling with laughter. Bob, on the other hand, trolled the quiet shallows behind her, secure and wise, a successful recording artist who had found his path early and never swerved from it. He never felt the urge to compete, nor, in truth, could he. Caught between Judy and me, Ellis found himself in Gemini heaven. For our part—every one of us—we simply wished to please him. He inspired that kind of loyalty, and he demanded it.

Ellis admired most those with skills he didn't possess, so Bob, a composer of proven excellence, was immediately his answer for anything that required original music rather than something he could habitually pull from his own collection of records. *Pantagleize* fit the bill. At this point, Bob and I had been pursuing the dream that we would still succeed as a writing team for Broadway. After all, our efforts had attracted the music publisher Edwin H. Morris & Co., particularly Sylvia Herscher, who worked for them. Sylvia brought us to a writer named Stu Hample, who was working on an adaptation of Joe McGinniss's *The Selling of the President*, and what started as a request for a few political jingles soon expanded into a full Broadway score. Since the script of *Pantagleize* also called for several songs, Bob was soon persuaded to create that score as well. The first of the needed songs was a silly little lullaby, sung by Pantagleize, which went: "Sleep my stupid baby / Destiny's mistake. You don't remember your mother / But then, neither do I." It didn't rhyme and it didn't make much sense, but it hit the exact note of ludicrousness and naïve sweetness and, crafted to Ellis's narrow range, pleased him as well as Houseman. The

Bob and Judy James: Lake Tahoe, 1972. (Collection of the author)

second, a much larger and more violent number, was meant to be both military and racy, and we toiled over it for some time. As the company arrived in Ann Arbor, we were still trying to come up with the right version, and Michigan was nostalgia revisited—the evocative beauty of a golden Midwestern autumn, the scene of the crime, as it were. With Bob rejoining us for this leg of the journey, everyone's spirits were on the rise. Ellis and I dropped our baggage and hurried over to the Mendelssohn Theatre to see how the load-in was progressing.

"Christ!" Ellis says, stopping in his tracks. "What are we supposed to do about *that?*"

"That," it would appear, is the cyclorama of the Mendelssohn Theatre, a perfectly shaped, slightly curved plaster wall that doubles as the back of the stage house itself. It has been the pride of the university for ages, and as a reflecting surface for lighting effects, it is nigh perfect. What it isn't, however, is as deep a space as we've just left behind us in L.A. How we are to cram into this tiny theater all we've brought with us?

Standing next to Ellis at the edge of the stage was James Tilton, the mild-mannered and modest scenic designer of APA-Phoenix, who had been pretty much marking time during these past weeks like a sous-chef waiting for instructions. Jimmy, who designed practically all the scenery and lights for every previous production and had Ellis's complete trust, had given the production a functional simplicity. What he had not been able to do was cloak it in a cohesive whole that lifted us into visual excitement. We got from scene to scene smoothly, but something Tilton, Houseman, and the audiences all needed was missing, something we all knew should be Ellis's exclusive touch. In other words, it was all just "fine," and a duller word cannot be applied to stagecraft. Tilton showed the strain of these past weeks, because he'd been struggling just to catch up, not to step out.

"Sorry! I'm stumped, El," Jimmy was saying. "We just don't have the depth here we had at the Huntington, but don't worry, it's only temporary; we'll get it all back again at the Royal Alex. We just have to make it work here somehow."

Ellis steps back, folding his arms and framing his brow with his hand to protect his eyes from the work light. "Can't you hang a black in front of it?" He jumps easily up onto the stage, squinting and peering up into the flies. "Nope," Jimmy responds. "See? That's the last pipe right there. I've already cut two sets of drapes, and the panel profile for the parade. I need everything else for lights."

Ellis turns and looks down where I am standing near the first row of seats. "We're practically in the audience's laps as it is!" He thinks a bit. "Shit!" Then, without another word, he leaps easily off the stage and strides up the aisle, moving too fast for me. "Cover it up," he said, walking to the back of the house.

"With what?" Tilton says to his disappearing back. Silence. Then louder, "With what, El?" In the distance the theater door to the auditorium briefly lights up as Ellis opens it, exiting. "Whatever you've got!" says the silhouette, and he's gone.

Some time later, Ellis and I were having supper in the Women's League dining room, at the opposite end of the building from the Mendelssohn. He was toying with some overcooked green beans with a few slivered almonds on them, gnawing absently at a pork chop, and sitting forward in his chair with his legs wound around each other, his favorite posture.

"Tech tonight," I said unnecessarily, about the five-hour call ahead of us that would extend through the rest of the night. "Mmm," came the response. "Stephan is concerned about lifting you, did he mention it?" I went on. "That *Coriolanus* exit nearly killed him." "He exaggerates," Ellis replied, staring off across the room. Laurence Olivier had contrived a famous death for himself in the title role when he threw himself off a tremendously high parapet and was caught by two attendants by his ankles and left dangling upside down. Ellis had always thought it a sensational idea and was having the actor playing Creep pick him up, unconscious, by the ankles and haul him offstage like a hod of bricks. Richard Easton had had difficulty with the awkward move in Los Angeles, and now Stephan Gierasch was demanding a back brace. Ellis's mind was not on the move, the meal, or my gossip. He stood up abruptly. "Let's go," he said, putting down his napkin.

We walked down the corridor toward the theater. Bob and I had done one more draft of the soldiers' song before the last scene, concluding with the refrain "She's a soldier's daughter and a soldier's girl, and she knows a rifle from a gun!"—our oblique gesture to Bob's six months' military service, where "rifle" means one thing and "gun" another. I was scrambling to fill Ellis's silences. "We did a quick rehearsal of the new song this afternoon," I offered. "It's funny. Anyway, I think it's funny." And with that, I gave up trying. Ellis's mind was somewhere else. We walked into the auditorium. I was looking for the right aisle seat when I heard Ellis speak to Jimmy Tilton, who was up on a ladder against the cyc.

"Newspaper? You're covering the entire thing?" I looked up to see that Tilton had made his way three-quarters across the space since the dinner break, pasting newsprint directly onto its surface. He turned on the ladder, his hands wet with paste. "Yeah. I think so. I keep thinking about the rest of the play, and maybe it all hangs together, you know, with your newspaper?" He was referring to the prop newspaper Pantagleize reads sitting on the wall in the eclipse scene. Ellis was standing at the edge of the stage.

"Hmmm!" came the familiar response. How many times had I stood in one theater or another, at one rehearsal or another, and watched him do this? He would stop abruptly, shield his eyes from the glare of stage light, and muse, suddenly seeing something where there had been nothing before. I'd immediately look in the same direction. Nothing. I knew there was some gear shifting going on, but I could never see it myself.

It seemed I would never amount to much as a director.

Ellis dropped his hand. "It's gorgeous!" he said. "Gorgeous!" "You think?" Tilton said, backing away from the ladder, seeing what he had done for the first time. Ellis's face lit up. "It's genius!"

It was beautiful, interestingly enough. The blank back wall of the theater house was now a background of pure black-and-white paper, pasted together, which, given the randomness of newsprint, had a mottled, abstract quality. Tilton was making his way off the stage to us, looking at the effect he'd created with his head cocked to one side, backing up as he came. "Yeah . . . I think we just might get away with it, don't you?" he said.

"No," Ellis said, "don't you see? This is what we've got to do with the rest of it. All of it." "Cover everything in newsprint?" Jimmy said dubiously. "Well, it's cheap, anyway." But Ellis pushed past him now and walked up on the stage, studying the effect. "No, it's perfect! It makes complete sense. We have to do the whole production this way. We have to redo the entire thing! No color! No color at all, don't you see?" Tilton wrinkled his brow. "Maybe . . ." he began, but Ellis was off and running. "Black and white," he enthused, lighting up. "Costumes, too. We've got to take another look at everything!" He had gone from first to fifth gear in a heartbeat, without even appearing to shift. He moved with lightning speed to organize a production meeting before the evening session, sending for Houseman, for Nancy Potts, for anyone who might be creatively involved. Tilton's improvised solution to the cyc might well have been the Rosetta stone.

I wondered how Houseman would react, having held the reins patiently up to this point. Ellis had played almost passive second fiddle to him as codirector until now, and suddenly he was everywhere, sweeping away everything that didn't fit into his new idea.

At just past eleven o'clock that night, with the company dispersing, I plunked down in a seat next to Houseman, who had been attentive but silent throughout most of the evening. "So, John," I said, curious to know whether he might have felt the wind being taken out of his own sails, "is this nuts, or what?" Houseman loftily peered at me from his aisle seat. "What do you mean?" he said, looking at me as if he barely recognized me. "Well, God!" I went on. "Is this going to work? He's pretty much ripped up most of what we've been doing, hasn't he?" Houseman hauled his considerable bulk out of the narrow seat with some difficulty and, straightening up, actually smiled for the first time all night. "Genius," was all he said. "Genius. I've only seen it once before in my life. Orson. He could be a prick, exactly like Ellis, but you just had to hold your temper as well as your your breath because, you see . . . when they're geniuses, it's worth it!" For a moment, it seemed suddenly possible that the entire enterprise had been nothing but a scenario of Houseman's authorship—Ellis vacillating, the weeks of pain, the grim, resolute endurance of the company, all leading up to the mad rush of creativity that was unfolding before us. Ellis was waving his hands at John from the stage, yelling, "Puppets, John, you know? The jury can wear those white plastic masks, and be suspended from one of these pipes up here by elastic bands, and bounce onto the stage like dolls . . ." John moved a step or two toward the stage, but Ellis had turned to Tilton and Nancy Potts, continuing his train of thought. Houseman looked back at me, smiling. "See? Well, there you have it!" And as he moved toward the stage he added over his shoulder, "Oh, Haut-Brion?" he said, changing the subject. "That soldiers' song? It's all right. But you can do better than that, can't you?"

There was to be one more "Hmmm" moment, however, before the end. The beautiful Lyceum Theatre in New York, east of Broadway on Forty-Fifth Street (the location of which, curiously enough, is the reason none of the APA-Phoenix productions were ever eligible for Tony Awards, since, in the sixties, any theater east of Broadway was not considered a "legitimate" Broadway house) is a rabbit warren of curiosities and aberrations unlike what other theaters, even of that period, might offer. In addition to an elegant living apartment on the top floor with a small peephole through which the manager could spy on whatever happened to be going on onstage at the moment—the current repository for the Shubert archives—there is even a paint frame on the fourth floor in the rear of the building with a slot cut into the floor on every successive level down to the stage, through which painted drops could be carefully lowered before being hung.

Although the capacity of the theater is under a thousand seats and most of those seats are in the mezzanine and second balcony, making it less desirable for managers with properties that need high ticket availability in orchestra seating, it was ideal for APA-Phoenix. The building ran all the way through the block between Forty-Fifth and Forty-Sixth Streets, with a passageway from the center of the upstage area out to Forty-Sixth Street, above which the dressing rooms rose. The rear dressing room on the second floor, above Forty-Sixth Street and the stage door, had a small anteroom attached, making it perfect for Ellis, as actor-manager, to accommodate his dressing table and still have plenty of space for production meetings or entertaining guests in the adjacent sitting room. The short corridor accommodated three other dressing rooms, the closest occupied by Sydney Walker, the next closest by Keene Curtis. You could read volumes in the assignments alone. In addition, right and left of the proscenium itself, twin staircases ascended to two other "star" dressing rooms, the first originally assigned to Rosemary, the one on the left given as a gesture of esteem to Richard Easton. But Ellis also allowed someone like Brian Bedford to be his "roommate" in his suite, especially since he and Brian never appeared in the same production.

We had arrived back in New York, and I had unpacked Ellis's personal items and was following him downstairs and out onto the stage on our way to lunch at the restaurant next door, the Lobster. We walked through the passageway between the corridor and the stage itself, then down right, to the pass door connecting the stage to the orchestra. Our scenery hadn't been loaded in yet, and the ghost light was in its place onstage, casting shadows left and right to the bundled blacks, roped into dusky columns so that the stage itself might be mopped. It was silent and beautiful, this space conceived to harbor imagination with no imaginings yet in place. We walked silently through the pass door, up the house left aisle into the narrow wood-paneled passageway behind the seats. As we reached the house left aisle, Ellis stopped so suddenly that I nearly bumped into him. I stood back and saw him, squinting at the stage. "Hmmm!" he said once more, and once more I turned to see what he was looking at. There was nothing there. Virtually nothing. And that, I was to learn, was the point.

21

The audience enters the theater, and before them is, in fact, nothing: the raw, unadorned space of the Lyceum. The black curtains that ordinarily line the sides of the stage—"tormenters," they are traditionally called—are not only pulled together and bound, but doubled up from the floor. One can make out the sides of the stage left and right, nothing more. Up center is a small corridor disappearing into darkness, bisecting the stage. Onstage is nothing but a large wooden box with a tattered gray blanket thrown over it; just that, and, stage right, up on the proscenium itself, a gigantic calendar with the inky date April 30 stamped on its white leaf. The stage itself is unlit. It seems that what light exists, raking the wooden planks of the stage floor, is nothing more than visual dust. No movement. No music. Silence.

The audience settle in their seats, quietly for the most part, as often happens when a show begins with the curtain up. They seem to chat less, perhaps both expectant and wary, the suggestion being that something already might have begun. Little by little it becomes apparent that a pair of naked feet is protruding over the edge of the wooden crate, the rest of the form obliterated by the dirty blanket. The house lights dim and go out. By an unseen hand, the page of the huge calendar that reads April 30 falls and flutters to the stage. The date now reads May 1. Then, from up center, a trapdoor in the floor bangs open. A blinding column of light pierces the dark, hitting unlit instruments above. Up a ladder climbs a gaunt, lithe black actor, naked to the waist, a band of colored fabric knotted around his forehead. This is Nat Simmons. He is playing Bamboola. He has appeared only once before in the rep, as Donald, the sweet, stereotypical black boyfriend of Rheba in *You Can't Take It with You,* but there is little of that cartoon skill in evidence now. He squats, dances, makes grotesque balletic moves as he chants. The figure under the blanket stirs, awakens, sits boldly up, stares out: pale blue eyes, startlingly direct, "the master of the middle-distance stare," as Walter Kerr was to write of this performance. Ellis is stepping up at last.

It's hard to perceive what might be different this time. Ellis was, at the very least, interesting and effective. If he lacked the incisive attack of Brian Bedford or the effortless magnetism of Richard Easton, he had beautiful speech and an imperious driving energy; more than anything else, he clearly loved to act. The salient point was that here he had managed to back into a character with an emotional arc virtually parallel to his own. As someone accustomed to choosing the perfect role for others, he hadn't always done as well for himself. Now, once he began to settle in and relinquish his "director's hat," effort melted away, and there stood a character none of us had quite recognized before—sweet, funny, wistful, and appealing. We weren't thinking about this—neither Houseman nor I, neither the company nor Ellis—but it was becoming increasingly difficult to see where the actor left off and the character began. Both were in distress and in danger. And both were original. He was headed toward that rarest of theatrical events—a personal triumph.

A few scenes later, a gray wall stretches across the proscenium, stippled with rough plaster. Ellis, as Pantagleize, sits before it on the very lip of the stage, his canvas deck shoes dangling into the orchestra pit, dressed in his white suit and reading a newspaper, an umbrella folded at his side. He is a bit goofy, altogether Hulot-like. The headlines of the newspaper read THE GREAT PARADE and THE TOTAL ECLIPSE, and he peers over the paper while delivering one of the many wistfully philosophic soliloquies of the play. As he stands and jumps up on the wall to describe the parade behind him, and as the red and black flags begin to swirl in the semidarkness, one is aware of the power of the Lyceum proscenium itself, towering high enough over the action to generously accommodate two balconies rising in the darkness. This is odd chemistry indeed . . . a bitter, extravagant charade of a Belgian play, completely theatrical, which yet never denies that it exists in a theater. Fantasy and reality vie for our attention.

Against the starkness, against the vast abstract size of the theater it-self, Ellis's artless narration, his enthusiasm as he dances left and right, teetering on the wall—it's otherworldly.

He jumps down and Trish charges in, compelling him into the next scene; and in the blackout that ensues, their swift, blunt ex-changes—"Here!" "Where?" "This way!" "Oh!" "Watch out!" "For what?" (Crash!) "For that . . . !"—read as a familiar vaudevillian rou-tine. Instantly the stage is lit with the light of a single bulb hanging down on an exposed wire. The wall and the flags are gone. An ugly overstuffed chair represents the room of Rachel Silbershatz, where Conolly grills the innocent Pantagleize, hurling herself forward with messianic madness while managing to misinterpret everything he says. She is inflamed. He is in love.

We revisit this same reductive scene in the second act, but now Rachel Silbershatz is slumped, legs askew, head back against the ratty cushions, dead. The overhead lightbulb is unlit. From somewhere upstage, bleaching moonlight streams down on the stage in such a way as to obliterate her face. Pantagleize runs on, clutching his large black valise and his umbrella. He is running from his pursuers, para-noid, manic. He puts down the valise and babbles to her, although he is the only one talking. He believes her to be sleeping. He kneels in front of the chair and opens the valise. We see his face over its lid, and slumped behind him, her indistinct and immobile shape in the chair. As Pantagleize opens the suitcase, Bob James's music begins, magically underscoring the speech that follows. Within the case is the treasure that has inadvertently fallen into Pantagleize's hands, a glittery jumble of tiny lights, as if diamonds and jewels are giving off their own illumination. Pantagleize proclaims his love while showing her the treasure, then rises, pulling her body out of her supposed sleep in an embrace. He crushes her to his chest, rocking her back and forth while her lifeless limbs hang, swinging at her sides. Slowly, he begins to understand. He lets her body sink back into the chair and, closing the valise, extinguishing the magic, he runs out.

And finally, lit by only the narrow band of light, military men en-ter, dressed in uniform and carrying rifles, marching in strict rhythm to a percussive tattoo. They are singing a catchy tune as they line up across the front. It is the song Houseman insisted we improve:

My girl is a looker . . . She's an army hooker . . .
She's got somethin' goin' . . . That she isn't showin' . . .

More drumbeats before the chorus:

She's . . . got a Blue Tattoo, she's got a Blue Tattoo, right on
    her
You-know-who!
When she gets through with you, you'll have a
Blue Tattoo there, too!

"Ready! Aim! Fire!" come the commands: a deafening sound, and the soldiers and the smoke clear to reveal the four conspirators sprawled against the wall, covered in blood, shot dead. They look like broken dolls propped against the gray surface of the wall. Pantagleize enters carrying his furled umbrella, inquires "Is this the way out?" and speaks briefly to the dead collaborators. When he asks for the exit, the officer silently points to the wall. Pantagleize heaves his body up so that he can look in the direction the officer has suggested. The officer calls back the firing squad. They return, a solid black silhouette. Pantagleize doesn't see them enter. The officer announces, "Ready, aim . . ." and Pantagleize turns, with the single inquiry, "Where?" The command "Fire!" is given. Twelve rifles explode, and Pantagleize takes twelve volleys of ammunition, registering each one in a grotesque dance, as the umbrella unfurls to reveal blasted holes apparently made by the shells. The soldiers are dismissed and Pantagleize drops, puppetlike, to the floor among the dead conspirators, his body twitching, his hands held out before him. "What . . . a . . . lovely . . . day!" he manages. Slowly, the curtain falls in silence.

Pantagleize was a hit, popular and critical, and probably the most original of all the APA-Phoenix successes. The cyclorama in Ann Arbor was the catalyst to push Ellis and the production over the top. The result was edgy, and it gave Ellis the major acting success of his life. He, Houseman, and everyone else involved with the production were covered in praise. Over the years, everyone from Stephen Sondheim to various contemporary directors have singled out this production as a revelation to them. Bob James and I were featured in an

article for the Sunday *New York Times* for "Blue Tattoo," which suggested more doors might open because of it. In the Lyceum, which
virtually made love to the production, it seemed like a blend of
Broadway know-how and European eclecticism. And then, of course,
there was the curtain call. Ellis, more than any other director of my
experience, perfected and cherished curtain calls. They were elaborate, varied, an extension of the evening itself, and there was a time
we all longed for an entire evening comprised of nothing but Ellis's
curtain calls. Some had flags; some were stark; some were done with
individual spotlights on static actors' faces; some were danced; and
some were giddy, as when the cast of *You Can't Take It with You* two-
stepped in pairs for their individual bows to a cheery recording of
"For All We Know We May Never Meet Again" and then sang "Good-
night, Sweetheart" directly to the audience—outrageous kitsch! Ellis
handled each occasion with such honor to the company, the play, and
its audience that they have had a singular lasting influence on me and
my own work. For *Pantagleize*, Ellis had asked Bob to compose a
march, thinking a military tone the most appropriate way to rouse
the audience after a somber conclusion. "How long do you want it,
El?" Bob asked. Ellis blocked the call, put a stopwatch on the final
tableau, and said simply, "Forty-five seconds," and within a matter of
moments, Bob presented him with a spirited, jocular piece he named
"The Forty-Five-Second March." The curtain came down in silence
on the tableau of dead bodies against the wall and went immediately
back up to the sound of the snappy march. The principal actors were
found in a line on top of the wall, the supporting players and soldiers
below, standing at ease, their hands behind their backs, expression-
less. In the time it took the curtain to come down and up again, the
soldiers disappeared, then the supporting players, and with each
bounce of the curtain, more actors until it was just Trish, Sydney,
and Ellis, and finally Ellis alone. As the last curtain fell, the only gesture anyone had made during the entire call was Ellis bowing his
head as the curtain wiped him out. House lights up. A cheer from the
crowd. I know I've done a few good ones of my own over the years, as
have others. But I seriously doubt any of us could touch Ellis at his
best.

22

To every action there is an equal and opposite reaction. Toughie, that one. The first two laws of physics make a kind of encouraging sense, but the third? I recall, at some moment during our Ann Arbor residence, Rosemary referring to a book entitled *Enemies of Promise*. I never read it, and, quite honestly, never wished to. The title alone staggered me. Was that possible? Something was out there, waiting for the opportunity to destroy something as golden as "promise"? (That it was the autobiography of Cyril Connolly never came up, and only recently, still haunted by that odd title, did I unearth that fact.) The seasons remind us that something always awaits us; winter follows summer, spring replaces that. The I Ching counsels that at the very moment of greatest fortune one must be alert to incipient danger, and the classic Wheel of Fortune is all over Chaucer, Dante, and the Carmina Burana; we can't say we haven't been warned.

The seeds of disintegration were already present as Ellis was lowering his gaze in the *Pantagleize* curtain call to our loudest applause. After all, how long could he or anyone be expected to sustain the amount of energy, inspiration, and output that a year-round theater enterprise took? How long could it be expected to survive?

About a season more, is the answer. The effort to deliver *Pantagleize*, for all the help others provided, took its toll on Ellis; and, having suffered a major depression the year before, coming to grips with the failure of his marriage and all it represented—it was a lot to absorb. The recent successes, ironically, were also beginning to split the resources of the company. Tours were launched. Miss Hayes, by definition a trouper, wanted to take *The Show-Off* on the road, and

Richard Easton agreed to go out in *Exit the King* and *The Misanthrope* in an attempt to replenish coffers drained by the Lyceum season. These secondary activities indicate that Ellis was relaxing his grip on the center of the company and its destiny—art was one thing, but bills had to be paid.

And what of the pinball? After so much activity, excitement, and intense proximity, I wasn't feeling much like a whirling pinball anymore, but more like an ordinary ball bearing, stuck near the corner. Oh, the game was still going on, bells were ringing, lights were flashing, and Ellis and I were tight as wax, as always. We dined together, we laughed, and I continued to function for him, but my personal goals felt less and less clear. True of him, too, interestingly enough. Reaching for fresh material and inspiration, Ellis once again turned to San Diego and his friend Craig Noel, as he had so often in the past. In his apartment Ellis kept a framed pen-and-ink cartoon of himself directing *A Midsummer Night's Dream* clipped from a San Diego publication of the sixties that portrayed him leaning forward, legs crossed, a cigarette in his hand and a hat on his head, and beneath it the inscription YOU WILL ALWAYS BE MY *"DREAM"* DIRECTOR . . . LOVE, CRAIG.

Nourishment is as essential in art as in life, and the symbiotic relationship between Ellis and San Diego was enduring and significant. It had begun with Ellis's and Bill Ball's own mentor from Carnegie Tech, Alan Fletcher, who had been hired in the late fifties by Craig to direct in the summer festivals and who brought along with him his prize students, Bill and subsequently Ellis, to act. Clever, ambitious Ball rose quickly from leading roles like Hamlet to directing for Craig, creating a landmark production one summer in Balboa Park of *Henry V* in which he managed to play the title role and actually crown himself in his own coronation scene. His appetite soon led him to an overreaching encounter with the Globe's board of directors, attempting to replace the benign, self-effacing Noel. But Craig's gentleness belied a steely core, and he faced down the threat of insurrection with a show of temperament that resulted in Ball's being basically banished from the Globe until a moving reconciliation in the late eighties.

Ellis had no designs of this sort on the Globe, and he quickly became Craig's "dream director" whenever the project proved to be of interest. Craig and Ellis were both social charmers, and when they were together they created a truly irresistible ambience. They remained best friends for life, and whenever Ellis was in residence he stayed with Craig, cooking up a storm for everyone, the center of activity and attention.

So with the relinquishing of Rosemary's influence and the continual drain on his own resources, Ellis began to look to the Globe as a possible bush league training experience. He conceived of a situation in which he might contemplate enriching Craig's artistic coffers with his own intermittent support, all the while exploring properties that might prove effective for an APA-Phoenix season. In 1968, the Globe was ready for *Hamlet* again, and Craig turned to Ellis for a production. For the title role, Ellis was eager to explore the potential of Marco St. John, who had not yet attempted anything as major for us and who began reserving for himself the early summer weeks for a San Diego *Hamlet* with an eye to the future.

Bob Moss, our original production stage manager, had already left APA-Phoenix by this time, turning over the responsibility for maintaining our productions to lay the foundation for his own directing career. It led to his creating one of New York's most valuable theatrical institutions—Playwrights Horizons, which Moss guided for years until he was replaced by André Bishop. And so the roundelay of theatrical careers, intrinsic to American classical talent, was to cross once more, when Moss arrived in San Diego to direct *As You Like It* for the Shakespeare festival. He had hired, for the role of Feste, a young actor named Barry Bostwick, just out of college. Ellis, crossing through San Diego with me as his inevitable Sherpa, saw the production and was instantly taken with Barry.

Over the years I lamented that Ellis inevitably cast his recycled favorites. If there wasn't an ideal role for Rosemary, then it had to be played by Nancy Marchand, or another one of his usual suspects, despite considerations of being age-appropriate. But he was also vulnerable to much younger players, sometimes because their talent arrested him, and often simply because *they* arrested him. When Craig offered him the production of *Hamlet* with Marco in the title role, Ellis decided that Barry Bostwick had to play the Ghost. The amusing wrinkle in this case was that Barry would "act" the part to a recording of Ellis himself. Pygmalion was once more on the prowl.

And as a guest on his way through Carnegie Tech, he was struck by the audition of a young graduating senior, Amy Levitt, performing a speech from *Twelfth Night* while he stood unseen in the back of the auditorium. Utterly captivated, he decided on the spot that she was his Ophelia. He was off and running.

But before any of this could happen, there was still the final production in the spring of 1968 to be produced. Le Gallienne was directing *The Cherry Orchard*. Uta Hagen was making her return to Broadway—her first since *Who's Afraid of Virginia Woolf?* T. Edward and Houseman had been coauthors of this idea, but the entire company was meant be on display, Ellis included. And looming beyond this was another entire season to be cast, budgeted, and announced. There was no rest for the weary with so much at stake. But Ellis was smacking his lips over *Hamlet*—somewhat inconveniently, as he was needed at home. A *Hamlet* in San Diego would prove a serious distraction. Ordinarily, with all this activity around me—a furor of designing, casting, and preparation for *The Cherry Orchard*, *The Misanthrope* being brought back into the rep, and Eliot's *The Cocktail Party* taking shape, I would have been at Ellis's elbow while he turned all his attention to this, his crucial role as artistic adviser; but instead, he was now brimming with ideas for *Hamlet*, as if looking into the distance and just over the heads of his immediate staff.

And San Diego and the Old Globe were about to supply additional impetus for *The Cocktail Party*, as it turned out. Houseman had decided that Eliot's dense poetic work was the ideal vehicle to introduce the incisive, witty edge of Brian Bedford into the company. The play, long missing from New York exposure, seemed like a fascinating choice, especially with the new company members like Frances Sternhagen and Nancy Walker added into the mix.

In 1967, when Ellis was visiting the Globe, he had witnessed, in the same season as Bob Moss's *As You Like It*, a production of the rarely produced *Henry VIII* which was directed by Philip Minor, a neighbor of Donald Moffat, Nicholas Martin, and Christina Pickles near Princeton. Ellis felt the *Henry* was both clear and direct, no mean feat given this famously difficult play, and after the two men had shared an extended social evening of drinks and swimming around Craig's pool, Philip found himself with the unexpected offer to direct

Nicholas Martin and Conrad Susa in Craig Noel's famous pool. Ellis reading at the right. If that pool could talk, it would, at the very least, have a well-followed Twitter account. (Collection of the author)

the Eliot. I found Philip as witty and antic a social treat as Ellis did, but what I witnessed that evening—that invitation to direct on Broadway—took me by surprise. I cannot suggest that I in any way considered myself an expert on the dramatic work of T. S. Eliot, or felt ready to throw my hat, if not in the ring, certainly somewhere near Ellis's feet as a possible choice to direct. And yet how long was I to be passed over, if in fact I was being groomed for anything? And with so much activity bubbling everywhere around me, and so little attention coming my way, either as a lyric writer or as a director, I felt as if I were standing silent and unmoving in the middle of a rushing stream, wondering in which direction I was supposed to go—farther on, or back to the safety of the former solid ground?

Philip, clearly overwhelmed with this unexpected prize of being invited into APA with a plum directing assignment, to say nothing of steady employment as a character actor, snapped up the offer and immediately experienced that fleeting, too-frequent feeling of becoming "Ellis's Latest Best New Friend." And so, with Bedford, Sternhagen, and Nancy Walker cast, the remaining roles fell swiftly to Sydney Walker, Trish, Keene Curtis, and Ralph Williams, and Ellis was able to turn back to *Hamlet* with a sense of relief. There were further possibilities for the organization opening up—a short residency scheduled for Stanford, up in Palo Alto, which would bring APA-Phoenix into close proximity with Bill Ball's ACT in San Francisco, as well as funding for other new productions. Precarious as the balance inevitably seemed, Ellis felt secure.

However, here I was once more, the resident watchdog, this time assigned to Philip Minor while Ellis pursued his extracurricular Shakespeare. As Minor was unused to me and nervous about being observed, I tried to remain very much in the background; I wasn't even asked to take his notes. His behavior reflected a pattern I began to recognize over the intervening years wherein directors feel violated if their "process" comes under the scrutiny of anyone but their actors. I don't know if this is a matter of insecurity, or simply the suspicion that some "mojo" might be neutralized and trade secrets exposed. Ellis felt differently. The generation of directors that preceded him, the Clurmans and the Kazans, had, he felt, kept themselves apart, showing neither encouragement to nor interest in younger directors. He said repeatedly that no one on that level had reached out to him, to Bill Ball, or to anyone of their generation, and probably as a consequence he remained responsibly and generously open to me. He was encouraging to others as well, eager with guidance, information, even creative insight when asked. I'm not certain Le Gallienne, Houseman, Porter, or Schneider would have been so forthcoming on their own; but because this was the way Ellis treated me, the others dutifully followed his example. You don't accept such gifts as a matter of course; they are life-changing.

But Ellis, Stephen, LeG, and Houseman were another category altogether from a Philip Minor, and he would have been the first to admit it. If he was daunted by the obscurity of the text, he never gave any indication of it. But neither do I have any specific memories of insights, of his conceptual approach, or of anything that challenged or helped his actors. There was one day during initial blocking when he tried to coax a specific move from Nancy Walker, already uncomfortable enough in the complicated role of Julia Shuttlethwaite, caught between poetic inference and psychological game playing. He wanted her to skip around the sofa and alight mischievously on its arm—insouciant and elfin. Those are two adjectives that would not be found anywhere in Nancy Walker's lexicon. She simply could not give him what he wanted, and the more he tried to clarify it— demonstrating it himself by perching on the arm and coyly crossing his legs—the less she was able to accomplish it. We all stood around stoically, not knowing where to look, pretending this was normal. But some line had been crossed, some confidence had been violated, and from then on actors began to withdraw, falling back into their com-fort zones and relying on their usual habits. Sydney Walker calcified into a clenched figure of authority; Keene Curtis brayed mirthlessly in the role of Alexander Gibbs, while Franny Sternhagen as Lavinia and Brian Bedford as Edward, their sights on a far, far shore, rowed steadily ahead for all they were worth. Ralph Williams, ordinarily charming and real onstage, got very little help from his old friend Philip, and as Peter Quilpe he remained muted and mystified. Only Trish Conolly managed to find within the suffering and martyrdom of Celia Coplestone something of herself, giving an affecting and mov-ing performance. Critically, the show was quietly passed over, but no one ever understood exactly why Ellis cast Nancy Walker so much against type, unable as she was to show any of the edge or the dry sa-tiric wit for which she was famous. Nancy, as she wryly reminded us, remained equally clueless.

So on we went into *The Cherry Orchard*, storm warnings to the right of us, storm warnings to the left, but the promise of LeG re-creating one of her most celebrated successes, as she had done for Nazimova, and now the vehicle that Uta Hagen would use for her re-turn to Broadway, blinded us to anything but assured success. On the morning of January 14, 1968, practically the entire company charged up the narrow staircase across from the Lyceum stage door on Forty-Sixth Street for the first reading.

I'm no longer certain how the shows were actually cast. Origi-nally, of course, Ellis made all the decisions, chose the plays, exercis-ing protection for his favorites as he warmly employed his familiar refrain—"in terms of your development"—to justify getting his own way. But with the inclusion of Houseman, and under the influence of someone like Le Gallienne, the choices began to blur. Ellis was distracted with the imminent *Hamlet*, and all too happy to give over responsibility. Favorites were favorites, naturally, and some of the choices for *The Cherry Orchard* were obvious and natural: Sydney Walker to play Simeonov-Pishchik, or Pamela Payton-Wright as the dreamy Anya. But if the peripheral characters seemed on target for this great ensemble work, the proverbial elephant in the room, the unforeseen complication, had to be a staggering piece of miscasting—the actress for whom the production was being conceived: Uta Hagen. At perhaps the height of her popularity, a result of her towering performance in *Who's Afraid of Virginia Woolf?*, Miss Hagen had not stepped back on a Broadway stage since that achievement, so there was a genuine frisson of excitement that she was at last about to return. Still, what of Martha's energy, passion, and bitter, sardonic wit exists within the aristocratic fragility of Lyubov Andreevna? As brilliant an actress as Miss Hagen was, she was anything but lyric, anything but helpless. Le Gallienne herself had an intriguing reference for categorizing actresses: she said there were two kinds, "white wine" actresses or "red wine." If that is true, Hagen was Châteauneuf-du-Pape. The voice was deep, explosive, and rich, but refined? No. Somewhere, in spite of all the admiration one had for this gifted artist, was the possibility that she was fully capable of taking up the nearest ax and felling the orchard herself.

Elsewhere, the casting ran the gamut of familiar to off base or even peculiar, with the inevitable surprises that a company of solid working actors can provide . . . Donald Moffat, a Scot by birth and nature, elegantly handsome, stiffly refined as Andrei Bolkonsky in *War and Peace*, might not have been an obvious choice for the peasant Lopakhin, but at his core he knew the man's rage, knew what drove him, and step-by-step he built up to a brilliant performance. Betty Miller never represented herself as a classical actress, but the coiled spring that simulated her passion, as well as her beauty, survived not only the role of Varya but Le Gallienne's constant harping. Clayton Corzatte finally proved a very moving Firs; and in the case of both Walkers—Sydney and Nancy—the choices were remarkable. Whatever Nancy Walker could not find of herself in *The Cocktail Party*, she doubled and redoubled in flinty, throwaway bemusement as Charlotta Ivanovna, the governess. Finally, the role of Gayev, the brother of Ranevskaya, fell to Richard Woods, a spiky, capable comedic actor for a fairly narrow range of parts. LeG had loved him as her Pastor Manders for the Ann Arbor *Ghosts* in the first Michigan season, but Miss Hagen and he were from opposite ends of the spectrum, and it seemed impossible to conceive of any family with such disparate siblings.

The first of a series of unusual revelations occurred at the very top of that staircase on the first day as everyone, cups of coffee in hand, settled around the clustered card tables to begin the read-through. Le Gallienne announced without any explanation that she intended to read the play to the company herself, straight through. This was certainly a surprise. Especially with Hagen, a glowing figure dressed in vibrant green, settling in among a company essentially composed of actors who were strangers to her. If she was disappointed not to be able to establish her credentials immediately, if she even knew of LeG's plan, she gave no indication. The rest of the company exchanged glances and murmurs. LeG had originally intended to play Charlotta Ivanova herself, but such a small part would hardly suffice to demonstrate the precise attack she needed to illustrate to the group at large. The translation was, after all, her own, and her familiarity with the names, the places, the intricate Russian syllables, would be imperative for them to hear and understand. She would simply lay out the tracks as from the horse's mouth, as it were, the correct tone of the entire work. No flubbing around, a swift, uncluttered sketch, nothing more.

Politics play heavily at the beginning of any production; everyone wants the reputation of being a team player, so it is nearly impossible to assess how this registered, not so much on the younger members of the company, nor the classical neophytes, as it might be, the Nancy Walkers, the Betty Millers, who were bound to be awed to some degree by the very presence of Le Gallienne, to say nothing of Miss Hagen, but on the more experienced actors. One can only recall that it was in fact Le Gallienne herself we were facing, and if this was her intention, there must be a good reason for it. So we hunkered close to the table and alternated between burying our heads in the printed version and stealing sidelong glances at whoever's role was being etched by the director herself, trying to gauge whether or not they were pleased, mystified, relieved, or just plain intimidated by the adroit swiftness with which LeG rendered everything in her modulated and refined tone.

Looking back through the decades, one might have perceived hovering over the collection of card tables a flashing yellow light. This was not just a director demonstrating to the uninitiated the correct pronunciations of strange names, this was a road map of what she wanted them to replicate. Le Gallienne herself might not have confessed as much; surely she was contemplating the most inclusive of creative days ahead. But she had waited a very long time with her memories stacked like bound reference volumes in her mind, so there was only one right way to do this. Hers.

And on to the Riviera rehearsal studios, the abandoned space above the old theater on the corner of Ninety-Sixth and Broadway. Since the Lyceum had no actual rehearsal space—a concession to the ownership of the original landlord, who never had to worry about paying union fees for changeovers after a performance—this forgotten world above a desiccated theater was secured for us. It couldn't have been more Chekhovian if it tried. Vast, dark, and kitschy, it was a relic of another time, not only for the Upper West Side but down on trashy Forty-Second Street as well, before the renovations that would lure the likes of Disney to that forgotten, drug-infested territory.

In this mysterious space the company began exploring one of the world's most celebrated ensemble vehicles, goaded into mild submission by the insistent probings of a woman sixty-nine years of age who was getting one more moment in the sun. Miss Hagen was, after all, her preferred choice, having made her professional debut as Ophelia opposite LeG in the role of Hamlet in 1937. There was considerable history involved. It was LeG's habit, while working, to take her actors on a stroll around the perimeter of the rehearsal space, an arm around the actor or actress, murmuring things no one else could hear. Secrets, as it were, were being breathed, and many, like Trish Conolly and Hagen herself, seemed to take both comfort and reassurance from these coachings. Others, like Betty Miller, felt tortured by LeG's insistence on a specific line reading—"No, Varya, darling," LeG would

say, an edge coming into her voice, "hit the word 'bee,' you see? 'You
have a new brooch, like a *bee!*'"—and for emphasis, she'd jab at Betty's collarbone until a small red mark appeared. Or Donald Moffat,
who imperceptibly seemed to be able to move just beyond the en-
croaching embrace, either holding back a step or two or moving, as if
electrically wired, half a step ahead. Try as one might, one couldn't
hear what was being said.

And I tried, believe me, I tried! Because here I was, once more,
the assistant director. But once more, the familiar feeling . . . For how
many assignments past had I supplied this professional party trick?
How many more lay ahead of me? Even after the obvious disappointment of Philip Minor I trusted that my moment would come, and I
waited. My willingness, my growing confidence so actively present
day after day . . . he couldn't ignore it much longer, could he? And
how could I possibly continue to be expected to stay as riveted, fo-
cused as I had been initially?

I decided to set down literally everything that was said and done,
everything that happened within the rehearsal process itself. I'm not
sure why I thought this valuable, or how I hit upon it, but I kept meticulous notes for nearly the entire six weeks of rehearsal; not every
single day, but as much as I could. I felt that if I wasn't alert in every
single moment of each rehearsal, not only would my mind wander,
but I would literally die of boredom. The result was faithfully transcribed by me each day from handwritten pages and typed onto onionskin to be tucked away among my other papers, where it surfaced
not long ago. Twenty-five single-spaced pages of observation, down to
what people wore and what they said, presented with my youthfully
respectful if gimletlike observations intact. I wonder if anyone else
has ever has done anything similar—a historical eyewitness account
of a private rehearsal process involving major actors, with a legendary figure directing? For the record, I've included these pages as an
appendix, surely far more detail than anyone but graduate students
might require. And yet . . .

As one might imagine, it's "warts and all," and perhaps that is
what is most revealing; because the sweetness and light with which it
all began ultimately wore away as practicality inevitably replaced po-
litesse. All creative processes have their ups and downs, to be sure,

but one must remember that this production opened to mostly positive reviews. In spite of everything, I have the testimony of professional colleagues who assure me that APA-Phoenix's *The Cherry Orchard* was one of the major theater experiences of their lives. It is also true that a mysterious connection exists between good actors and Chekhov. Left to their own devices and given enough time, the actor and the role tend to organically unite. The legendary soprano Kiri Te Kanawa, whom I once directed as Pamina in *The Magic Flute* in San Francisco, told me that the damage a steady diet of Strauss can do to the voice can be miraculously reversed by singing Mozart. The purity of the music and the natural affinity of the voice for that music is restorative. So, too, Chekhov. He transcends any concept, no matter how perverse, and once the actor is immersed in the role, it all somehow manages to come right. As Tom Stoppard so charmingly sums it up in his glorious *Shakespeare in Love*: "It's a mystery." So it was to be with Le Gallienne's *Cherry Orchard* . . . but not before a certain amount of blood was spilled.

First was the issue of casting. On the occasion of the first blocking rehearsal, Nancy Walker, dressed smartly, her hair close to her head, teetered at the periphery of the activity, introduced briefly as possibly relieving LeG as Charlotta at some point. Hagen seemed to know Nancy, at least socially, but as the day proceeded, Walker slipped away, neither assimilated nor confirmed. Nancy was not only present because of her role in *The Cocktail Party* but also contracted to cover Helen Hayes in *The Show-Off*, so if LeG was out, Nancy would be the natural choice. The fly in the ointment from the beginning was Ellis himself. He could hardly refuse to play Trofimov, especially as a gesture to his beloved Le Gallienne, and yet over and over again he was late or missing, distracted and ill-prepared. When he did come, it would be without apology, and everyone, including LeG, tried to overlook this chronic tardiness in the interest of just getting on with it. Trofimov was probably not ideal casting for him, and despite the seductive lure of being submerged in Chekhov, he must have sensed it. The idealism, the blunt earnestness of the part was foreign to him, and there was virtually no chemistry between him and Pamela Payton-Wright as Anya. Whenever his natural instincts failed him as an actor, Ellis would lapse into generalized sentimentality, which was more and more the case here, so when on the morning of February 23 he was once again absent and rumored to be "indisposed," something obviously had to be done. The company nervously worked through the first three acts of the play with me holding a script and executing the moves that Ellis's alternate, Marco St. John, was yet to observe.

Then, as the fourth act of the Chekhov was being set up, Richard Easton walked into the room, confirming with his silent embrace of LeG and Hagen that he had consented to take over as Trofimov. The real action, in this case, had been offstage—there must have been a scene, a telephone call between Ellis and LeG, some kind of brisk confrontation, but we were never told. Easton, a no-nonsense, thorough professional, shouldered the responsibility without a backward glance, and his positive energy was a shot of adrenaline for the entire company. It seemed, briefly, that everything might now fall easily into place.

But as the days narrowed into techs and the opening loomed, LeG found it less and less possible to be flexible. Maybe it was a kind of insecurity or even panic, because things weren't going as she had imagined. Her choices inevitably reflected what she'd done years ago at the Civic, including the famous harp-string sound for the end of the play so many decades ago. Uncomfortable with anything electronic or even abstract, she longed for and finally insisted on the sound of the musical saw she'd employed decades ago. And no matter how many recordings we played for her of the chopping of wood, it was never right. In deep frustration I finally took an ax and went down under the stage. There were huge wooden pillars holding up the stage floor, and determined to give her what she wanted, I was whaling away on one of them, shouting up through the traps, "Is that any better? Can you hear *that*, LeG?" when the head carpenter came down to explain that should I persist with this as my solution, the stage would collapse. Like the other directors in the company, she was simply going to have to settle for a goddamn sound cue!

Performances that were already on track were building beautifully, but LeG could never let Donald Moffat alone; she fussed at him, as she did at poor Betty Miller. They became twin symbols of stubborn ineptitude for LeG—Betty ultimately unable to mimic the performance LeG must have given opposite Nazimova in the Civic production, and Donald never able to shake whatever habits of his she found impossible to reconcile with her concept of Lopahin. Her barrage of notes were never helpful, and, enraged and angered beyond endurance, he finally stood up, red-faced and humiliated before everyone, shouting at the top of his lungs, as I recall, "Stop it, stop it, stop it, will you, Eva? Either leave me alone . . . or play it yourself, you fucking cunt!"

There was an audible gasp, and LeG staggered a bit and sat down, her face covered with her fragile, badly scarred hands. "Break!" someone called, and during the next five or ten minutes, LeG was dramatically helped from the auditorium by the stage management, shattered and pale, which everyone present seemed to agree constituted one of the better performances given by anyone during the entire rehearsal period. But soon the news came back to us that whatever we thought, LeG had suffered "a mild heart attack," and she did not appear thereafter. The work had essentially been finished, the performances were finding their footing, and all that was left was for the cues to be routined; so the company, heads down, marched quietly toward opening night.

It had all begun so gloriously and with such promise, and now, to me, it was blighted. I stood backstage during one of the previews to see Uta standing in the wings, swinging her skirts malevolently in the direction of an unseen audience she felt unresponsive and indifferent, and, just before her entrance, sticking her tongue out at them. She was restless, nearly violent, and took enormous pleasure in making faces at the audience unseen but by her fellow actors. The production opened to lukewarm reviews, Walter Kerr of *The New York Times* praising particularly "the two Walkers, Sydney and Nancy," and seemingly respectful of Le Gallienne, Hagen, and the others. No further mention was ever made of the contretemps between LeG and Donald, and soon afterward I stopped going altogether, stopped taking notes, and actually left the city for a few weeks to visit friends and clear my head of it all. When I came back to sit in the audience, three weeks later, I was astonished at what had transpired: the performance had settled, the beats were clear and honest, the performances beautifully calibrated, in total synch with one another. The production was quite wonderful. Uta herself, in spite of all the problems and the wrongheadedness of the casting, was committed, and she conveyed, whatever else, the desperation of a woman emotionally out of control and hopelessly in love. In Chekhov's third act she had a terrific exchange with Easton as Trofimov in the ballroom when out of her reticule, fell the crumpled telegram she had secreted in a handkerchief. It was from her lover in Paris, and caught, exposed before the idealistic Trofimov, she stood behind a red upholstered chair and, hammering her fists down on its back, breathed out the phrase "I *love* him!" with such naked passion that it was painful to witness. Whatever her weaknesses might be, emotional honesty was her stock in trade, and when unleashed, in Albee or in Chekhov, it was something to behold.

23

Like those of a schoolboy released from class for the summer, Ellis's spirits lifted almost immediately as he plunged headlong into the creation of his San Diego *Hamlet*, buoyed by the assurance of directing a script he knew intimately and surrounded by youth—Marco, Amy, Barry—all hanging on his every word and desperate to rise to the occasion. That kind of feverish approval can pull some of the best work out of any director: one senses oneself in a kind of surreal spotlight, the scrutiny intensifying word choices, selection of insights . . . it's heady stuff. We never discussed it much, but Ellis's approach to great classical scripts was almost against the grain; he followed very much his own instincts—emotionally, intuitively, passionately, carnally— because, of course, the word "period" has finally and fundamentally to do with the kind of clothing being worn and how that affects behavior, social conventions, physical movement. It has virtually nothing at all to do with emotional truth, which has probably been the same since the Greeks first donned their masks. So as best he could, he put figures onstage that were familiar to audiences, behaving naturally and not "acting" at all. That they happened to speak Shakespeare's lines or Sheridan's was, for him, beside the point. That they reacted to each other as anyone does was paramount. He demanded and expected a high degree of technique: his own vocal training at Carnegie Tech, under the ruthless attention of Edith Skinner, the standard-bearer of so much of classical theatrical speech in the United States, had been exemplary, as was that of his contemporaries. Their voices and their speech were a proud part of the arsenal they had assembled that led them to explore plays John Houseman was forever to refer to as "elevated text." It is a tradition that has fallen somewhat into disuse, although many graduate programs still try to adhere to this methodology; but perhaps few subsequent generations of acting students have taken it as seriously as Ellis's did.

He was able to work almost directly from his subconscious, confident that if the beats felt real and actable, he could easily shape them to fit any period. Now, with the acrid aftertaste of the Chekhov behind him, he rushed to immerse himself in situations, scenarios, possibilities that would again illuminate this great text. He adored Amy, and if there was a kind of blunt, naïve openness about her acting, it was coming from a very honest impulse. Marco was trickier; but then, although Ellis had never played the role himself, his actor's instincts were aroused by proximity with the part, as, in all probability, Le Gallienne's had been by the Chekhov. Why couldn't Marco simply play the beats as Ellis would? He was patient with Marco, but I was aware of an echo that paralleled LeG's relationship with Betty Miller.

I found Ellis on Craig's long couch late one morning, low windows opening on the seductive swimming pool beyond. He had been sitting silently with the text of *Hamlet* open on his lap for some time as he smoked. "Hmmm!" came the familiar sound. I was busy sorting through mail at the nearby dining table, and the noise stopped me in midactivity. I confess to an involuntary shiver of discomfort as well, though I couldn't say why. Perhaps because things had been too calm for too long. I turned to see him slightly worrying the lid of his right eye, as he habitually did, pulling away at the lash. "What?" I said. "Hmmm!" he intoned again, pursing his lips. I moved over to the couch. "What are you *hmmm*-ing about now?"

He rose, tossing the script onto the window seat, and pushed past me on his way to the kitchen. He opened the refrigerator and took out the omnipresent half gallon of Almaden Chablis. Although it was only about 11:30 in the morning, he selected a fresh glass from the stack in the drying rack and filled it. "Oh, it's just this part . . . It's nothing . . . it's just . . ." He looked quizzically over at me. "It's a rather good part for me, wouldn't you say?"

A few weeks later, I was again in New City with the Housemans, standing next to Joan preparing food for our lunch while John sat like an emperor at the end of the long table opposite, leaning back,

John and Joan Houseman at their home on South Mountain Road in New City in the early 1970s, lunching with Ellis Rabb. (J. Erik Hendriks)

his eyes narrowed, keeping up a steady flow of opinions. Joan was peeling fresh garlic. "Look here, Haut-Brion, dear boy," John intoned, "for Christ's sake, be sensible. Ellis isn't going to give you a play, and I don't think he even knows it. He wants everything to stay as it is, and not consider you, or anyone else for that matter, moving on, or moving at all! No, I'm thinking about Ann Arbor, the next Ann Arbor season. We're going to need something up our sleeve. Something perhaps . . . um . . . you know . . . that might prove 'useful.' Do you know O'Casey? *Cock-a-Doodle Dandy?*" He got up with some effort and breezed past the two of us standing with our heads together over the cutting block. "I'm sure I have a copy of it here somewhere . . ." and he disappeared into the next room. I moved to follow, but Joan shoved the garlic press into my hands and turned instead to a large white bowl filled with lima beans, scallions, corn, and chopped peppers into which she was spooning olive oil. "Now do something about those," she said dismissively, waving at the pared garlic cloves, "I need all of it." John returned and tossed a worn volume of O'Casey onto the island near where we were working. "There!"

he said, returning to the table. He swept up some white plates from the sideboard, and dealt them out around to our place settings like chips at a baccarat table. "See if you find it funny. I find it funny. Nobody does O'Casey, at least not this one, and we could cast it easily." He turned his back and opened a drawer, and I heard the sound of bunched silver. John was enthusiastic when food was involved.

I was, frankly, stunned. I'd said nothing to Houseman about my mounting frustration, and here he was, talking about "us" as if I were one of the conspirators in *Julius Caesar*. The rest of the afternoon was a blur, with me sitting alone down in the garden while the other guests lingered over coffee and fresh fruit. I sat on a warm slate step where, to my right, the corroded Emmy statuette Houseman had received for the television series *The Seven Lively Arts* had been wittily buried up to its waist long ago near a clump of irises. I read the play rapidly, hardly digesting what it was about, or even grasping the complicated collision of passion, sex, and the iron fist of Catholicism that O'Casey was skewering. All I knew was that I was being given more than lunch, given more than the training of a sous-chef. A door was opening, and I was being pushed through it.

The season ahead was to feature *The Misanthrope*, prior to its tour, and *The Cocktail Party* should it survive its tryout in the new Stamford residence. It was anyone's guess how it would do in the fall lineup, but everyone felt hopeful. Still, three productions were required for a New York roster, meaning *The Misanthrope*, *The Cocktail Party*, and something else, perhaps a Shakespeare yet to be selected. There were no plans to extend *The Cherry Orchard*, as Uta Hagen had a limited amount of time available to us. Ellis, Houseman, and Hambleton were hard-pressed to come up with a shape for a season that was commercially viable and fiscally modest, and although the Molière was classy, the Eliot was never considered a blockbuster. Inspiration was at a premium.

Hamlet in San Diego, however, was successful; it usually is. As one of the world's most nearly perfect works, it traditionally sells well, no matter how indifferent the cast. Marco was appealing in the lead, and Ellis was able to pull off a more than creditable production. He cut almost all the political themes, but then he never minded editing out things that didn't interest him personally. He loved to quote Gielgud at such moments, speaking of his own editing process and saying slyly of the Bard, "He wouldn't mind!" A success in Balboa Park was decidedly one thing, but did it necessarily cry out for further investment? Amy Levitt was raw and over the top in her mad scene, urged on by Ellis, and Barry Bostwick, his ragged leggings streaming carbon dioxide and leaving trails of ghostly smoke wherever he walked, mimed Ellis's recorded speeches as the Ghost as best he could while doubling as Osric. Over the years, Ellis inevitably imposed on his long friendship with Edith Skinner to have her give intermittent notes to whatever company he was directing, especially APA. She appeared in San Diego for the *Hamlet* as well, going over and over the rich and complicated text. It was a source of continual hilarity that one would sit in on these notes sessions only to hear Edith, wielding her pencil like a dagger, smacking her lips over the same note: "Dear Ghost, if you would, please, extend the third medial vowel in the word . . ." She repeatedly corrected Ellis's recorded performance, never grasping that Barry wasn't the culprit.

Meanwhile, to my utter astonishment, Houseman managed to secure an Ann Arbor berth for *Cock-a-Doodle Dandy* to complete that season. This was it . . . not the mantle I had dreamed of having placed affectionately around my shoulders by my true mentor, but a gift from an Olympian "god" nevertheless, and my entire being was occupied with the preparation, the casting, the designing, the thrill of finally getting my own show. The response from the company was immediate and heartwarming, as if they might have been silently cheering me on all along. I offered Donald Moffat the key role of Sailor Mahan. His enthusiasm for O'Casey and for the play seemed even to exceed my own, and it was his suggestion that we should enlist his old Princeton neighbor Philip Minor to act opposite him in the role of Michael. Philip was still officially part of the company, so not only available but eager to contribute, especially after the overlooked *Cocktail Party*. I agreed that his manic quality was a perfect foil for cool Donald, pepper to his salt. I offered Amy Levitt the young temptress, Loreleen, not only because I thought she could do it, but to ensure Ellis's sanction of the entire event. I cast the savvy Katherine Helmond as Maid Marian, since she was already appearing as

Arsinoe in *The Misanthrope*, which was about to go out on tour in repertory with *Exit the King*. For the rest, I filled from basically the lower tier of the company's resources so as to be loyal without having to compete dangerously with Ellis or his eventual next New York production: Nicholas Martin was the eccentric One-Eyed Larry; young, handsome Peter Coffield was the Messenger, with a lovely Irish song to sing; and for the solid, womanly Lorna, I had to tap into the university community to find an experienced graduate actress, Gwen Arner, sexy and appealing, recommended by Claribel Baird, Gwen's adviser and ever my champion. The chemistry between Gwen and the recently divorced Donald Moffat ignited almost immediately, and within the year they were married. Gwen eventually went on to become a very successful television director in Los Angeles. Barry Bostwick, absorbed immediately with Amy from Ellis's Globe company, rounded out my cast as the Cock, a larger-than-life phantom rooster, the Dionysian spirit of unbridled sex pitted against the stern discipline of the Catholic Church in the guise of Richard Woods's Father Domineer. Barry, leaping spectacularly over the garden wall throughout the play, was given a brilliant costume by Nancy Potts and was probably the most exciting thing onstage. It is safe to say that the subject of Barry's Cock occupied considerable speculation onstage and off, much to the merriment of the gossips, Ellis's discomfort, and Barry's utter confusion.

Once again, I reached for musical support to Bob James, my closest collaborator. We were already working on a score for a Broadway show, and once again he stepped up to the mark, producing a delicious faux-Irish score of wit and beauty, one of the highlights of a production that went off charmingly, supplying a variety of magic effects, such as horns suddenly appearing on Miss Helmond's head to the consternation of the two old boyos, Moffat and Minor.

I couldn't have asked for more—back in Ann Arbor, my comfort zone, with the benign encouragement of Houseman himself, Ellis distracted with his own new theatrical plaything, and a cast of actors I had literally grown up around. The designers, Jim Tilton and Nancy Potts, put their complete trust in my conceptual choices, such as they were. In truth, I struggled to come up with something "interesting," at least something that spoke to and made use of all the experiences I

had witnessed and absorbed over the years. And yet I couldn't shake
the suspicion that something seemed off-kilter. The actors, for the
most part close personal friends like Katherine Helmond, Nicholas
Martin, and Peter Coffield, seemed to be pulling ever so slightly away
from me, and I sensed a rift occurring that I couldn't identify. There
was an evening I rode past the apartment Katherine occupied, virtually brimming with my friends and compatriots, all of whom were in
the play, all guests at a marvelous party to which I had not been invited. Had I stepped beyond some acceptable line of demarcation
now, as a director, that would begin to distance me from my chums? I
comforted myself with that thought, as if it were a rite of passage. But
was that it? And was that all? I attacked my rehearsals as if I hadn't
noticed, didn't care. But something wasn't thrumming within the
production, and I couldn't identify it.

Houseman proved an encouraging champion of the production
as I piloted my small craft into Ann Arbor. And with a nose for the
gathering clouds ahead, he quietly positioned the production as a
possible backup for New York. Money was tight, *The Misanthrope*
and *The Cocktail Party* were up and running, but the former had already been reviewed, and the latter had turned out to be a mixed effort. This is the moment an artistic director inevitably faces: the
best-laid plans, and so forth, and the job entails the final responsibility of pulling a creative rabbit out of a hat. Ellis was once more on the
spot, and he responded by announcing his intention to mount a
"bare-bones" Shakespeare. The play would be done on a bare stage
with as few props as possible, and with no costumes that couldn't be
contributed from local sources for no money. It all sounded most responsible, but for many of us, having experienced Ellis's "bare-bones"
approaches before, we knew they often ended up being the most expensive productions of all. *War and Peace* and *Pantagleize* were both
minimalist productions—conceived in the first case against a black
surround in which set pieces like a chandelier, or Napoleon's robes,
stood out dramatically, and in the second case, powerful use of the
stage space itself, much in the same manner Peter Brook would employ in his Bouffes du Nord experiments in Paris. But Napoleon's
coronation robe was costly, and exposing the back wall and side areas
of the theater meant stripping the space of everything needed for

other productions. No, when Ellis said "bare-bones," those responsible for finances inevitably felt their own bones quaking.

It was with considerable relief that we learned Ellis intended to mount *A Midsummer Night's Dream*. Well, why not? It's one of the most commercially popular of all plays, he knew it well, he had done it with enormous success more than once, and, despite a cast the median age of which was edging dangerously into the forties, he had sensational actors on hand. The company were excited, the designers decidedly up for the challenge, and with Richard Easton as Oberon, Brian Bedford as Lysander, Ralph Williams as Puck, Nicholas Martin as Flute, Sydney Walker as Peter Quince, and on and on, we could barely contain our excitement at the creative playtime ahead. Nancy Potts hosted an afternoon of fittings when Franny Sternhagen, as Helena, Trish Conolly, as Hermia, and Christina Pickles, as Titania, all descended on a local bridal showroom where a series of wedding dresses were being promoted for the final scene. They returned giddy with laughter and eager to dive in.

But it was never to happen. Ten years of Ellis's life had swiftly passed, ten years of creativity, of dreaming, of the day-to-day drain of continual production. Ten years in which his marriage dissolved, his confidence rose and fell and rose again, with wine-fueled highs and lows piled one upon another that were beginning to reveal him as bipolar. I have no knowledge that Ellis recognized to what degree he needed to stop, but there was suddenly an about-face in which the entire production of *Dream* was jettisoned and it was announced that the fall production was to be *Hamlet*.

There was little time for me to absorb the consequences. *Cock-a-Doodle Dandy* was, as Houseman originally deduced, our single ace in the hole, in spite of the slightly baffled responses of the Ann Arbor audiences, and if it was going to be offered on Broadway, it was going to require serious buffing up, including a full court press of recasting. My merry band from Ann Arbor, it was assumed, would not do for New York, much to my personal discomfort, other than Donald Moffat, who was unquestionably the anchor of the piece. Everyone else had to be bumped up.

I felt a curious flash of disloyalty mixed with starry excitement. In spite of friends discarded, it seemed the sky was the limit for O'Casey and me. Richard Easton, with his burnished tenor voice, went in for Peter Coffield, Ralph Williams for Nicholas Martin, Sydney Walker for Philip Minor, and in the small, wildly eccentric role of Old Shanaar, even Ellis was being pressed into service. I was dizzy with conflicting feelings about it all. "Be careful what you wish for" floated somewhere just above my consciousness.

The women were more complicated to replace: to have Christina Pickles playing the part that a university graduate, Gwen Arner, had played was obvious; and although Katherine Helmond was wonderful as Marian, the role in seniority should really go to Trish Conolly, amounting to an even exchange. The sexy catalyst of the dilemma, Loreleen, played in Ann Arbor by Amy Levitt, was a casting puzzle. Moffat liked Amy well enough, but he didn't think she was ready to stand up on Broadway opposite him and Sydney Walker. I was out of my league. Goggle-eyed with excitement mixed with dread at finally having to face the company's leading players, I was at a loss to grasp fully what was so wrong with my Ann Arbor company, and anyway, who did we have in the company sexy enough to turn Irish heads and hearts?

"What about Franny?" Donald suggested. "Sternhagen?" I replied, in a tone that implied, perhaps, that Claribel Baird, in her late seventies, might just as easily come to mind. Franny was spirited and incisive, an indisputable leading lady, but not my image of a hot young Irish lass, especially with Amy, still in her early twenties, having recently sashayed through the play. "Ever see Franny let down that hair?" added Donald. "Ever take a good look at those legs?" His gaze narrowed as he scrutinized just how wide my range of heterosexual appreciation might be. I believed I gulped before quickly registering enthusiasm. Franny it was going to be. And how right he was! She struck a defiant silhouette in the garden of that Irish cottage, her beautiful legs flashing provocatively, brushing and brushing hair that, to my knowledge, I'd only seen before wound tightly around her head. The freshness, the clarity, the wicked exuberance she brought to her scenes were delightful.

Rehearsals proved somewhat tense. If on some level I had not really ever connected with my initial cast, facing the more experienced and leading actors of the company would take skills I was yet to acquire: patience, and trust that experienced actors will find their way without blatant interference—a sin I've come to describe as "finger-printing the performance." Beginning directors inevitably "demon-strate" in spite of their own instincts. "You should do it this way!" is the implicit fallback position. With true professionals, one gently lays out a path they must discover as if it were their own and not the director's. I was still ready to rush down the aisle and jump up on the stage to show everyone, as Trish had so wisely advised me against do-ing back at the Greek Theatre during *War and Peace*. I was caught be-tween a dull feeling of inadequacy and the burning need to be respected. The company, to its credit, never seemed to confront me about this. Ellis, with only a few scenes on his plate, managed to re-hearse as infrequently as possible, assuming, as did everyone else, that his patented "old age" characterization could be plugged in with just the addition of an Irish accent. I don't remember directing him at all: I stood by, grinning appreciatively as he slapped a performance he had so hilariously employed in an early Molière farce onto the pro-duction like a decal, his confreres howling their enthusiasm from the sidelines. I began to find I had issues with my beloved Trish. Feeling threatened, I was too rigid to listen to her and understand how differ-ent her quicksilver quality was from the foursquare, ribald attack of Miss Helmond. Red-faced and steaming, we had a confrontation in the wings that I blush to remember . . . how dare she question my authority! I felt betrayed, but then, so did she. But on we went, and on it went as well, and the ultimate revelation, and my first experi-ence with this phenomenon, was the astonishment that these easily more accomplished actors made so little difference to the final re-sults. How could that be? Why didn't the play bloom and erupt with all that additional wattage? Could it be that the initial discoveries made at the outset determine the theatrical DNA of all that is to fol-low? The surgeon's initial cut, the slash of paint on a blank canvas, is indelible and never can be replicated. So when supposedly "better" actors carved their way through the prescribed paths of the O'Casey under my cautious but green tutelage, only Sydney Walker man-aged to up the ante. The production was . . . fine. Just fine. It wasn't Franny's fault, or Donald or Sydney's, or perhaps mine, either. This play of O'Casey's, as wild and extravagant as any he wrote, is above everything decidedly anti-Catholic. And the major critic writing for *The New York Times* at that period was Walter Kerr, a Catholic and an enthusiastic believer. The *Times*, ever powerful and too often the sole arbiter of what succeeds and what fails on Broadway, was, as now, the defining voice, and Kerr came down like a mailed fist on O'Casey and his play while giving the rest of us but a sidelong glance. Whatever the charm of the actors in this dark, Dionysian, randy romp, he wasn't having any part of it.

Thanks to Houseman, I had been delivered, at twenty-nine, of my Broadway debut in a company that had borne me, nurtured me, encouraged me, and in this instance, finally served me honorably.

24

APA-Phoenix needed a hit. And to ease the financial strain that an extensive repertory demands, it needed to be a big hit. We had to uncork another *You Can't Take It with You,* or at the very least, a *Show-Off.* What we had was *Hamlet,* a production Nicholas Martin was famously to dub *Danes at Sea.*

Ellis's original concept was shrewd, at least in terms of suggesting something bold and original for the company. He began by returning to his idea of various actors sharing a role. It would be Marco, of course, and because it was appropriate, Brian Bedford, as well. And yes, he would be the third actor to share the role, although he had no vast plans for the other roles to be split up into threes.

Everyone was silent, wary, watching. His initial vision was already different from San Diego, disturbingly so. He intended to open the play with the final tableau, the bodies scattered everywhere—Claudius, Gertrude, Laertes, and Hamlet, all dead—and then return to the beginning, as if the entire play were a flashback. And as quickly as this became clear, what became even clearer was the fact that he didn't intend to share the role with anyone. He wanted to play it himself. Easton stoically accepted Claudius, and some of the subsequent casting bore witness to the Globe investment of the past summer—Amy Levitt as Ophelia, and Barry Bostwick again miming Ellis's recorded words as the Ghost. But Sydney Walker was conspicuously absent from the casting, Richard Woods taking the plum role of Polonius, and stalwarts like Keene Curtis and Christina Pickles were relegated to be the Player King and Player Queen, lovely roles, but with Philip Minor as the Gravedigger rather than Sydney, something was going awry.

The most support, interestingly enough, came from Brian Bedford, who, rather than being resentful at losing the opportunity to play Hamlet on Broadway, went to Ellis and asked if he might not serve as director, helping his friend, to whatever extent he could, to be as good as he possibly could be. Ellis acquiesced, and slowly, solemnly, the production began to take shape. Betty Miller was Gertrude, and Donald Moffat consented to play Horatio. There was something of a chill in the air, with no contrary position from Houseman or Hambleton to challenge Ellis's demands and concepts.

I sat, one afternoon, in the orchestra of the Lyceum Theatre with Joan Houseman wrapped in her red fox fur coat to my right. I held a clipboard in my lap, with very few notes written on it. We were fitfully half watching, half listening to the drone of voices onstage, the occasional staccato command of Brian urging this or that insight. I was wearing a new self-winding watch that inexplicably seemed to have died. "My watch has stopped," I said quietly to no one in particular. Joan looked over at me. "Well, wind it, for God's sake," she said shortly. "I don't need to. It's self-winding. You don't have to, you just have to move your arm back and forth . . . see?" I raised my hand and wiggled it a bit. "Well, shake your wrist more," she offered. "I have, that's the point! I've had it on this entire time, and have been moving around like mad—look!" I demonstrated. "And nothing . . . you see?" Joan contemplated the watch for a minute, and then she gave one of her patented opinions: "Perhaps it's had a mood!" She turned back to the distant action on the stage. I loved this observation—pure Joan. I could easily imagine a watch of hers communicating the lazy, oblique attitude of its mistress: "Oh, Joan! I really can't, today . . . I'm sorry, I simply can't!"

But what a shocking difference! What was happening in the orchestra seats for the first time was that I was more intrigued by Joan, by my watch, than by watching a production of *Hamlet* evolving on a Broadway stage before me. No heat was being given off, no fire. Everyone was quietly going about their business most professionally because, to be honest, Ellis was owed this much and more. None of the actors, none of the staff really admitted to themselves that continuing obediently and blindly on this course was not only wrong-headed, but probably suicidal; it was unquestionably what we were to do, because Ellis clearly needed to do it. That was Bedford's attitude, and we fell silently in behind him.

I remember only two moments of the entire piece. In one, Ellis staggered myopically onto the stage, his arms filled with books, and, dropping them with a clatter to the floor, he fell to his knees, speaking the all-too-familiar words "To be . . . or not to be . . ." He had to find some way to more or less trick himself into attempting to speak this dangerously familiar speech, and collapsing on the edge of the stage among a pile of books was what he found. The other image is from the opening night. Betty Miller got a hair from her wig caught in her eyelash. She was not only distracted but unable to understand what was happening. Amid the fury of the exchange between Hamlet and Gertrude, Ellis reached down and tenderly removed the hair, whereupon she gratefully burst into tears, and so did he. It was of personal significance to him, surely, but not, alas, to Hamlet, nor to the audience. The production concluded, the actors took their bows to polite applause, and if there was a party to attend, no one felt much relish for it. Still, we went.

The final blow of that opening night, both awful and comical, involved Ellis's car and a young black employee of his named Fred. Some months earlier, Ellis's mother, Mary Carolyn, always obsessed about her son's welfare, bemoaning his lack of proper diet and fretting that he never took proper care of himself, arranged for this young man, a relative of her housekeeper, Louise, to come to New York and serve as what can only be described as Ellis's valet. Fred couldn't have been kinder, less politically liberated, nor more determined to take good care of Ellis, as his elder relative had attended to Mrs. Rabb for nearly a lifetime. This was the tail end of the sixties, and civil rights were only beginning to work actively on the Northern consciousness; in Memphis, things for the Rabbs and their friends seemed to continue pretty much as they always had. The idea of Fred helping Ellis made perfect sense to Mary Carolyn, and to Ellis as well. We all pretty much looked the other way and refused to comment, even among ourselves.

There had already been a few other incidents involving Ellis and Fred, like the New Year's Eve party Nicholas Martin and George

Pentecost and I hosted the previous winter in a West End apartment during one of the winter's worst blizzards. Ellis had arrived, driven to the party in his convertible by Fred, and dressed in a kilt. It was a tailored and beautiful kilt, but still, it was a kilt, and at this time you wouldn't even find a Scot on the streets of Manhattan in one of them. By the time the party eventually broke up, the streets were buried in snow, and the convertible was useless. So, at two-thirty in the morning, Ellis and Fred were seen sitting side by side on a subway, going grimly home while the open-mouthed partygoers of Manhattan stared, trying to make sense of a polite young black man accompanying a gentleman in a skirt. Only in New York.

Now, as the company milled backstage before heading out for the quiet celebration that was to mark the company's final opening, Ellis and Fred came back through the stage door together. "What's wrong?" I said, assuming they had gone on ahead. "My car has been stolen," Ellis said flatly. "Can you believe this shit? That performance—my debut as Hamlet on Broadway to the worst audience in theater history, and as if that's not bad enough, someone's stolen my fucking car!"

"Not with a bang," goes the poem, and it is remarkable how quietly it all fell to earth. *Hamlet* played just forty-five performances before the bruised and truncated season closed on April 26. And that was that. No protestations, no articles in *The New York Times* lamenting either the season past nor a plan for the future. T. had done all he could; so had Houseman. But John was now the head of the new Drama Division at the Juilliard School, T. had family in Baltimore to attend to, and Ellis was tired.

Was a champagne toast offered on that last night? Did confetti fall from the second balcony? Was I even present? As one who remembered the very earrings of the company's leading lady as she stepped from an airplane in Detroit . . . as one who believed the entire production of *The School for Scandal* had been designed around that same actress's hair color . . . as someone who had held his breath lying up in the flies of Trueblood Auditorium while the star backed perilously across an entire stage . . . wouldn't you think I would recall this last moment of an American theater company's life?

And did we think it was in fact the end? Ellis had begun my initial

Left to right: me, Christina Pickles, and Jim Whittle, Princeton, New Jersey, **1969.** (Victor Lobl)

employment with the announcement that he was firing everyone to do something "really significant" instead; surely he could rise from these ashes as well! And he did. It was not long before he joined forces with Jules Irving at Lincoln Center to create a series of remarkable productions such as Gorky's *Enemies, A Streetcar Named Desire,* and others, leading up to his Tony for directing *The Royal Family* on Broadway with LeG, Rosie, Sam Levene, George Grizzard, Nicky Martin—the entire Old Guard, practically—in a revival as brilliant and individual as *You Can't Take It with You* had been, and declaiming during his acceptance speech that he was seizing that moment to "relaunch" APA, to wild applause. But that's another story altogether.

And what of me? I still had my lover, Jimmy Whittle; I had my apartment downstairs from Christina Pickles and Victor Lobl on Riverside Drive; I had completed, unknown to me at the time, possibly the single greatest postgraduate course in directing of anyone of my generation; and I still had Bob James, already a dawning jazz great, writing songs alongside me. And with *The Selling of the President*, we finally had an honest-to-God Broadway musical in our future.

I was going to be fine. With a last swipe of the flippers, the ball bearing goes careening completely off the table, escaping the game and rolling off into the world. No longer a pinball at all . . . But then what, exactly?

PART FOUR

DON'T WEAR WHITE
AFTER LABOR DAY

25

There are rules, and then one day there are no rules. Or you learn to make up your own. I recall walking into a graduate course at Michigan years ago. The self-consciously hip professor, after having chalked his syllabus across the board behind him, sat cross-legged on the desk in sandals staring at us. Ten minutes spent listening to him, and I realized how I could ace the course. And that was the day I knew it was time to leave. Because education is ultimately about teaching yourself how to learn. One day you are a student. And then one day you aren't.

How long does it take to become a director? Martha Graham once said it took ten years to make a dancer. Ten years! So how long for a director? More than a teacher or a dentist? Less than a constitutional lawyer or a rocket scientist? And how does one go about it? Which pretty much brings us right back to where we began—Cellini and the gold leaf. Obviously, there are plenty of people—actors, usually—who, with enough experience under their belt, believe they can stand behind a camera or out in a darkened auditorium and have a shot at it—and why shouldn't they? I confess to moments of frustration when I am convinced I could act better than whoever is lurching about in the rehearsal before me. But those incidents are not the stuff careers are made of, and the directing actor may ultimately decide he might be safer back onstage than having to answer to a phalanx of producers, which is what you face on Broadway these days.

APA-Phoenix had run its extraordinary course, although none of us seemed to fully accept the fact, and armed with Ellis's friendship, as well as Houseman's and the rest, I began to look around at where the road might take me. That I was standing on a road of any kind wasn't immediately apparent. After all, APA-Phoenix hadn't gone up in a puff of smoke with the last performance of Ellis's *Hamlet*. There were tours to be scheduled—of *The Show-Off*, and *Harvey*, both with Miss Hayes, directed by Stephen Porter, as well as his *Private Lives* with Brian Bedford and Tammy Grimes moving successfully on; and there was to be another summer at the Globe as well as existing contracts at the University of Michigan to fulfill.

For the previous six or seven years, under the umbrella of APA-Phoenix, I'd had little else to do but hold on with both hands, listen, watch, and absorb as much as I could. But with the dissolution of that parent organization, I was now in open water, whether I knew it or not, and I was becoming . . . well, something other than an acolyte. A new chapter was opening, but for years I would still be influenced by the process I'd been privy to, unable to do more than ape the techniques of the men and women I'd been observing. How many times had I sat beside Ellis in a lighting session, hearing him ask for what he referred to as "high side clears"—lights that cut through color from midstage, giving crisp edge to actors in space. I found myself replicating his same palette, using his very words, because his results were familiar and proven to work. I had watched LeG, as well, walk an actor away from the fray for words not meant to be shared with others, an effective way to make an actor feel special, but even more important, to communicate something possibly too painful to be uttered in public. I couldn't avoid incorporating that approach with my own actors, and I still do. Alan Schneider was not interested in being "liked" or popular; he was relentless, a quality that did not come naturally to me, particularly when it registered as willfulness. The real quality he was after was to be uncompromising. At the time, I perceived Alan as being a bully. What I was yet to learn was that to be liked may be a desired social amenity, but when it comes to directing, to speak the truth is crucial. Trust trumps comfort, which is a tough thing for a born enabler to hear, and so it took me the longest time to acknowledge what was possibly Alan's most valuable lesson to me.

But more than any other of these priceless lessons, the most valuable of all came down to note sessions. That technique—because it is a technique!—is what, to some degree, may possibly distance me somewhat from my peers—at least as actor friends remind me. Ellis's note sessions were mesmerizing. They represented to me a territory forbidden to the uninitiated, a circle marking a director's own sphere of enchantment, if you will, like nothing I'd experienced before. Or since. If I learned anything over those five or six years, it was that the hour or so after a day's rehearsal is the crucial moment in which to imprint passion and a common sense of purpose into a company, without which all is lost. If you bore an exhausted cast with perfunctory stage business that neither inspires nor stimulates them—be it on your head! In years that followed, I would find myself an echo, a pale imprint of the vibrant and generous men and women who had allowed me to observe them firsthand. How their influences blended into whatever I have become since belongs to another story; this one, however, might finally be best summed up with examples of three specific productions that run the gamut: one surprise, one disaster, and one accident of fate that finally delivered me. And so, in order . . .

One would suppose that my Broadway debut of *Cock-a-Doodle Dandy* should occupy a more prominent position in my memory bank than it in fact does. The Major Events in one's career, as identified, often do not end up being major at all; it is the unexpected ones that are, if one is lucky enough to experience them, the ones beyond our control—like lightning. If I think back on the O'Casey at all, it is some innocent version of the Ann Arbor production that I recall. Polished and enriched for Broadway, it barely registers now. The excitement, the innocence, that originally bound the "second tier" and me together had at least the spark of a first love affair, if perhaps a bit unrequited from their point of view. But it was the very next time I went up to bat that bore evidence of what I might have to offer. Eventually.

If it was Houseman who helped me slip past Ellis's paternal guard to a Broadway debut, it was my second spiritual father, Craig Noel, who brought me face-to-face with Shakespeare. Ellis, on the rebound from his *Hamlet*, had committed to return to San Diego the following summer. His plan was to create a *Macbeth* for Richard Easton and to cast opposite him one of their dearest friends from the Stratford days, Sada Thompson. On paper, this was Ellis at his best. The production would begin in San Diego, then move on at the end of Craig's season to Ann Arbor, where it could open with confidence and polish. Expenses could be shared by both organizations. Craig, long the sole creative mainstay of the Globe, had to direct as many as ten non-Equity productions a year before hiring professionals for the trio of Shakespeare plays that comprised the summer festival. With all that creative work on his shoulders, he welcomed any contribution from Ellis. Craig was also pleased when Ellis suggested that Easton could direct a production of *Julius Caesar* as well as play the role of Brutus. With *Macbeth* and *Julius Caesar*, they had only to add a comedy into the lineup. It was time for *The Comedy of Errors* to come around once again. Ellis, in a burst of generosity, recommended that I might have a go at it. The heft of the other two tragedies at the box office was secure, so how bad could my *Comedy* be? Craig offered no resistance; we'd known each other since I appeared as Ellis' Sherpa, and I felt nothing but support from him.

As for the casting of *Macbeth*, Sada Thompson was an actress Ellis had courted without success for APA-Phoenix. She was closely associated with Bill Ball, having received her first Tony Award for her performance as Dorine in his *Tartuffe* for the inaugural Lincoln Center season down in Washington Square, which also included the Elia Kazan premiere of Arthur Miller's *After the Fall* and José Quintero's *Marco Millions*. Sada, witty and sympathetic as she was, was no one's image of the grim, bloodthirsty Lady Macbeth, so it was as arresting a concept for Ellis as it was for her. Sada indicated that she might be induced to come if a season was offered to her best friend, Priscilla Morrill, who lived in Los Angeles. The promise of a summer with Pam, as she was known, was enough of a lure for Sada to leave her family in Jackson Heights for the lengthy engagements in San Diego and Ann Arbor. The catch here was that I would have to accept Pam as one of my two principal leads in *Comedy*. Then in their early forties, neither Pam nor Sada would read as ingénues, so I was brought out to California for a meeting. Craig wanted to be sure I was going to be comfortable with the casting. I had no specific image in mind for the play at that point, so I committed to Pam as Adriana, with Sada agreeing to supply a cameo appearance in the small role of the Courtesan. The other major prize of the summer was Christopher Walken, whom

Rosemary had spotted in *The Lion in Winter* and who was eager to come along. Rosemary had always demonstrated a gimlet eye for talent, and on the spot, Chris was offered Mark Antony and Macduff, as well as to play my Antipholus of Syracuse.

Richard and Ellis . . . Sada and Pam . . . it was shaping up to be a summer based on friendship, and true to form, Chris's best friend, Lawrence Guittard, was offered the other Antipholus for me, Banquo in *Macbeth*, and Cassius in *Julius Caesar*. I proposed my lover, Jimmy Whittle, who had done solid work in the APA-Phoenix seasons, to play Dromio opposite Chris, and with two more pals, James Tripp and his partner, Peter Coffield, we were off and running. Sada's daughter, Liza, turned out to be free for much of the summer, as was Chris's wife, Georgeanne Thon (later to become a celebrated casting director for projects including *The Sopranos*), and that completed the circle of friends for the summer of 1969, when man would finally walk on the moon, I would grow my only beard, and possibly somewhat more significantly, I would face my first Shakespeare.

The attention was on the *Macbeth* and the *Julius Caesar*, and I was left pretty much to myself with a very funny script and marvelous actors. I took the title *The Comedy of Errors* at face value, and before long the actors were romping around in every contrasting period of costuming possible to the giddy, seductive music of Bob James, who also offered his music to Ellis and to Richard, while Judy joined us, supplying a steady stream of hilarious banter. God! Summer rehearsals in San Diego—Black's Beach, enchiladas in Old Town, margaritas by Craig's pool with all of those young, beautiful friends . . . it's enough to scar one for life. "It must always be like this" was the mantra unspoken. If only . . .

With my concept of actors watching actors act, and the improvisatory spirit of the enterprise at risk to go merrily overboard, Craig took me into his office one afternoon after witnessing a run-through, and in the kindest and most positive tones pretty much raked me over the coals. "Why are there so many people everywhere on the goddamn stage?" he thundered. "I never know where to look!" "Edit! edit! edit!" went his dictum, and truly grateful for the stern drubbing, I pared and simplified. We were rehearsing opposite the *Julius Caesar* when Jimmy Whittle fell on his knee in a tech rehearsal, seriously bruising it. Rather than make a fuss, he soldiered on with his knee swelling and growing more and more inflamed each day. The two shows opened back to back in alternating repertory (the Macbeth was meant to join the rotation after its more concentrated rehearsal period four or five weeks later), and Jim managed to get through the opening performances of both Julius Caesar and the Comedy on sheer willpower and adrenaline alone. Although the Caesar proved strong and intelligent, it was the winner-take-all astonishment of my Comedy that raised the roof of the Globe in Balboa Park. It was irreverent, it was vulgar, it was hilarious, and it was, in fact, a big fat honest-to-God hit!

The resulting success, with some finger-wagging by amused critics (Christopher Walken, at the top of his blond, Adonis-like youth, was taken to task for "posing for his own baby pictures," which gives an indication of how much discipline I exercised), was short-lived. Jimmy Whittle had to be rushed to the hospital directly from his Comedy opening night curtain call. There was nothing to be done but to operate on the enlarged bursa, a consequence that promised to keep him in the hospital for several days and off his feet for at least ten days more. Like other summer festivals, the Globe could barely cover the principal casting; a responsible understudy plan was out of the question. The Comedy of Errors was scheduled to play the very next night. Whatever were we to do for a Dromio?

The very next morning I faced an ashen stage manager who might have been many things to many people, but a first-rate comic actor was not among them. Who could conceivably be expected to learn the lines and blocking for any role on the second day of performance?

Well, there was one person who certainly knew them. In the first years of directing, there wasn't a role, male or female, that I didn't know cold by the time the show opened. It didn't matter that Jim Whittle, a lithe, loopy puppy dog of a comedian, was at the opposite end of the casting universe from me, the show had to go on, and I was going to go on with it. What is more, I was going on opposite Christopher Walken.

At precisely eight p.m. the next evening, I walked out to face the audience. "Good evening," I began. "I am Jack O'Brien, the director of tonight's production . . ."—I raised my hand to stifle a smattering of applause—". . . and I have some bad news, and some . . . well, some . . . um . . . just news for you. The actor playing the crucial role of Dromio of Syracuse just had surgery on his knee this morning and will be unable to play the role tonight. So . . . um . . . I'm afraid you are stuck with me!" Of course, there was an immediate cheer and round of applause: Hirohito might have garnered a standing ovation from the San Diego Naval Base with a lesser announcement. And so we took our places and began. Before every entrance, I stood behind one portal or another, feverishly whispering my lines over and over, and then, my face beet red, I dashed out onstage to alter whatever business I had given Jimmy into something that would possibly work for me and not either upstage or confuse Chris. Chris, of course, was solid as a rock, and beyond generous. And when we came downstage together for the final curtain call, the house rose and roared their approval. I was in no way better than Jimmy had been—I was just different, certainly self-conscious, but I was probably funny enough. I didn't know Shakespeare all that well, but I had an oblique grasp on "funny," and I gave as best I could.

In the ten performances until Jimmy returned, the routine was the same: I went out, gave my "apology" to the audience, and performed like a trained seal from the San Diego Zoo next door. And in spite of the fact that I got more comfortable with each performance, I could never conquer the terror in the wings before every entrance. I was, in the time-honored "Jack" way, showing off. I cannot pretend that it was acting. But in the second half of the play comes the moment when Dromio confides in his master about his encounter with the fat kitchen wench. Since she can function as an offstage presence if so conceived, the character is free to play outrageous jokes at her expense, and even at this early stage in his career Shakespeare was able to uncork a few beauties that have lasted well four hundred years: "I warrant her rags and the tallow in them will burn a Poland winter: if she lives till doomsday, she'll burn a week longer than the whole world." It's good stuff, and Chris Walken was the most generous of straight men, serving up cue after cue in that scene like puffballs. There is a trick that can happen with comedy—if one delivers a funny line and gets the laugh, and then can shift the thought another way without speaking, one can often get a second laugh. And if you bounce that tacit thought a *third* way—unspoken to an understanding audience—one can even earn a round of applause. Each night I made the jumps—getting the first laugh, and as it was dying, thinking "What have I just said?" thus getting the second one, and finally the third thought: "Yup! That's right!" and landing the round. As I was holding for the round one night, I had the realization that such a moment is what any comic actor lives for—having the audience so in the palm of one's hand that you can virtually twist them with a thought; and it was not making me happy in the least. I was, in truth, miserable. I loved discovering that route—no question; I adored encouraging an actor to find it. But for me? It did nothing. Whatever I was, or was going to be, it would not be an actor.

I had also created a prologue to the play in which actors wandered onstage from the aisles, chatting as they arrived for rehearsal as if from a day of playing in San Diego, while from overhead, the sound of jet planes could be heard—a curse of the theater in Balboa Park in those days—recorded double and redoubled again so the audience would think, privately: Oh, God! . . . it's another of *those* nights! . . . and then presto! . . . the sound effects cut suddenly off, and music and the magic of the play began. The actors, sitting around the stage, listened to the argument of the story recited by the character Egeon before choosing which costume they would wear for the evening. I had blocked Dromio to sit on the inner above, with his legs hanging over the edge for this recitation, while Sada Thompson, in modern street clothes, was blocked by the staircase. One night, during the second week, I could sense her sidling over to me until I felt her knee in my back, and the clenched teeth whisper of her voice just behind me: "Don't you think it's time to quit apologizing to the audience? The rest of us up here are starting to look pretty silly!"

It was done with the kindest of intentions, but the point was clear: I couldn't continue to pretend to the audience that I wasn't an actor and then earn a triple round of laughter at every performance. No wonder they were standing up each night! I took it in good faith and stopped apologizing, and as soon as Jimmy was well enough, also stopped acting entirely. It would be more than twenty-five years before I made another attempt.

One other moment stands out above all the others in that summer

of 1969, and it wasn't Neil Armstrong stepping onto the moon's surface. It was Ellis, stepping out into the blinding light of a San Diego
afternoon three weeks later after a run-through of his *Macbeth*. I happened to be waiting on the green for him to conclude his rehearsal,
but the moment I saw him, I knew something was very wrong. He
stood against the building, lighting a cigarette, his face nearly obliterated by the giant black sunglasses he affected. "How is it going, El?" I
said as I moved over to him. His hands were shaking, and he was
ghostly pale, his mouth drawn tight. "Look!" he said, holding out his
shaking clipboard to me. "Not a single note. I've been in there for
two and a half hours, and I haven't taken a single note!" "Why not?"
I asked. "I don't know," he responded. "I'm panicked! I'm just terri-
fied! What's wrong with me? What's happening? What am I going
to do?"

It was inevitable, of course. And to some degree, I had seen it
coming. He had arrived in San Diego later than the rest of us, because of the *Julius Caesar* and the *Comedy* leading off, but when he finally joined us he looked awful, his face splotched with red, gaunt,
clearly drinking too much and smoking incessantly. His early out-
pouring of ideas for *Macbeth* had dwindled to a trickle. After the
early images had been dispersed, very little else followed. The climate
was tense, watchful. Ellis was coming apart, crashing, useless.

With alacrity I took over—because it was also clear that he was
deeply embarrassed and begging me to. I called his mother in Memphis, had a flight booked, drove him to pick up his things from
Craig's, where he had been staying, and had him on a flight home that
afternoon with no resistance whatsoever. After consulting with
Craig, since the show was basically blocked and teched, I felt confident I could finish the work myself. The only scene left was the encounter between Peter Coffield as Malcolm and Chris Walken as
Macduff, and I dispatched it the next morning. Sada was mostly distracted with negotiating the two enormous Renaissance gowns Nancy
Potts had designed for her: the white one she called "the White House"
and the gray velvet second dress was "the Public Library," and she
fumed and fussed while hiking up voluminous skirts to climb narrow steps to the inner above, which she then had to stagger right back
down again. But she and Richard were stunning together, and Walken

rose to the occasion: I can still see him blindly lurching from Duncan's room and the sound of his howling of "Horror . . . horror . . . horror!" He was to play the Scot himself years later in a singular and vivid performance for Lincoln Center.

Macbeth opened the Ann Arbor season, and I don't believe Ellis was there. I'm not at all certain he ever saw it again. There in Balboa Park, not on Broadway, was the excitement of my first genuine directing success. And with this unexpected success, the axis of my world began to shift, subtly at first, and then more obviously: Ellis, who was my gold standard, my polestar, was no longer my employer, but still my friend. Responsible for my introduction to both Craig Noel and Bill Ball, he nudged me out of the nest without instituting the kind of direct interference preferred by Houseman, and gradually we found ourselves less mentor/student than emerging colleagues. He was proud of me, there is no doubt in my mind, and that pride included subsequent productions in San Diego in which I directed him as Benedick and Prospero; he even lived for a while in my apartment on Riverside Drive, and continued his enthusiasm for working with Bob James and me, which took us all in another unexpected direction, but like occupants of separate ice floes, we began to move imperceptibly apart until the final devastating consequences, still to be revealed.

But so far as the disaster in our list is concerned, you'd have to go far to top *The Selling of the President*. It was indisputably a Broadway bomb, lasting only five performances, the poster for which remained secured to the famous Joe Allen "disaster" wall in the Manhattan theatrical watering hole long after anyone in memory could remember there had ever been such a musical. And although I believe that one never learns from success, only from failure, that was one failure so deeply immersed in wrong decisions that the Gordian knot is child's play by comparison. I will not go into "waves of self-pity," as Noël Coward so charmingly puts it, but to avoid it is equally wrong, because it was and remains a monumental wreck of an example of the road not taken. From childhood on, my determination to contribute somehow to the writing of musical theater—music, lyrics, libretto, anything—was the driving force in my life, brought to a shuddering stop after the closing Saturday night performance of March 25, 1972.

A significant parallel track had, of course, been running all this while. Even while working alongside Ellis, I had been commissioned first to translate Offenbach's *Orpheus in the Underworld* for the Kansas City Opera, and later Rimsky-Korsakov's *Le Coq d'Or* for the Panamanian director José Quintero in Dallas. From the mint-fresh success of *Land Ho!* in 1961 on, music and lyrics had always been principal in the mix for me. Those university experiences had brought Bob and me to the attention of Sylvia Herscher over at Edwin H. Morris's publishing house ("My Yiddische Mama," as I affectionately referred to her), and with the happy accident of "The Blue Tattoo" in *Pantagleize* we were finally delivered to a viable musical property. The novel *Love Story* came out in 1970, and on its dedication page author Erich Segal placed Sylvia's name alongside that of the producer John Flaxman, who was working with Hal Prince in the Prince/Abbott enclave in Rockefeller Center. Flaxman and Herscher didn't know each other at the time, but the serendipitous fact of their juxtaposition in print on that dedication page was enough for them to negotiate a friendly lunch. During the meal, Flaxman explained his intention to turn Joe McGinniss's recent book about the Nixon campaign into a play with music. Sylvia was thus able to employ the time-honored Jewish mother's refrain—"Have I got a team for you!"—and Bob and I were off to the races.

Well, "races" may be a bit extravagant. We had been commissioned to supply just a few "campaign songs" for the play, adapted by the children's book writer and lyricist Stu Hample. And so we did. But in our enthusiasm, we continued to write and write, urged on privately by Ellis, who liked nothing better than spending evenings with Bob and Judy and me involving hilarious improvs built around how fast Bob and I could make up songs to his wildest suggestions. If Sylvia Herscher "had a team" for John Flaxman, Ellis went her one better—he had a theater available to him. He contacted Bill Ball in San Francisco, and before we knew it, we were going out to ACT to do what amounted to an out-of-town tryout: Ellis directing, Stu Hample doing the book, Bob and me supplying, now, a full-scale score for what was no longer simply a play with a few songs, but a pre-Broadway musical.

Fade out, fade in: opening night at ACT in San Francisco in the spring of 1972. All is not well: Ellis had become so frustrated with

Stu Hample that he first barred the writer from rehearsals, then got him fired. Consistent with his practice of editing any text he didn't particularly like—as he had with *Hamlet*—he cut the book down to a running time of ninety minutes without intermission, which essentially reduced it to the score plus a few snatches of dialogue. Bill Ball had given Ellis carte blanche along with his best actors—Peter Donat and Michael Learned among them—and the show, lacking any semblance of a book, certainly looked stylish, designed by his APA standby collaborators, Tilton and Potts.

I cannot go any further without reporting one of the most hilarious scenes of my life, involving no one other than the irrepressible Judy James. She arrived just in time for opening night, having left Bob and me on our own in San Francisco during rehearsals, but as the wife of the composer, she had every intention of making a splash at the premiere. She and I had gone shopping in San Francisco and found an upscale outfit evoking at once the recent "Summer of Love" and Old California—long skirt with tiers of pioneer ruffles plus tall boots, both popular and truly horrendous. High on our discovery, she happened to spot a table of synthetic wigs in "pop art" shades, one in the very purple of her new ensemble. Now, Judy never had hair with much body to it, and as a petite woman she was always looking for more volume to balance her ample and much-admired breasts. No matter that the wig was too big for her head, coming down low on her brow. "I know exactly how to handle that," she said, whipping it into her shopping bag. "You just stuff a lot of toilet paper underneath it, rolled up and bobby-pinned, and it poofs it up just swell!" I was extremely impressed with her resourcefulness and supported this full-scale attack on the premiere audience.

The Selling of the President was playing without intermission at this point, and, hell-bent on being seen as much as possible in her Coal Miner's Daughter getup, Judy waltzed up and down the right aisle of the Geary Theater, waving up at the balcony to unseen friends. In truth, she had no friends in the balcony, but any self-respecting composer's wife, especially being a ringer for Loretta Lynn, would have to know somebody up there, and so . . .

And so we settled into the middle of the orchestra three-quarters back for the premiere performance. Judy and Bob were seated in the row directly ahead of me, and to my left, a very pregnant theatergoer arrived to squeeze by and plunk down behind Judy. This woman was wearing a velvet tunic festooned with brocaded frogs across the front, an effective disguise for a woman well into her third term. But with that baby pressing against her mother's bladder, a long one-act musical was going to prove a bit too much for her to endure. During the quietest part of the second half of the show, the woman got up, pushed against Judy's seat with some effort, and crossed out to find the relief of a bathroom. Judy, mildly irritated as the woman passed, leaned forward with a hand at the nape of her neck to secure her wig, then settled back into rapt concentration on the stage. When, however, the woman returned, Judy was still rapt. The woman hiked herself past me, and, reaching her own seat, sank like a stone into its recesses. But in the process, she managed to hook one of her frogs to the back of the Dolly Parton–sized Purple Rose of Texas hairdo, and it snapped off Judy's head, disappearing into the pregnant woman's ample lap. Like something out of a Disney movie, rolls of blinding white toilet paper shot up and out in all directions, great looping arcs of silent fireworks, each with a mind of its own, while in its still center Judy sat, pincurls clamped to her tiny head, stunned. Realizing what had just happened, she reached behind her into the playgoer's lap, tugging feverishly until she dislodged the mass like a giant merkin from the offending crotch. If this didn't qualify as an intermission, it came remarkably close!

We probably should have called it quits right then. But we didn't. Determined to salvage something from this less-than-auspicious beginning, and not to be outdone by Ellis Rabb's firing of Stu Hample, John Flaxman then fired Ellis, replacing him with a director celebrated for a recent off-Broadway success. There was, however, no longer a book writer in place, so when it came to the script, it was decided the simplest thing to do was for me basically to record what we played in San Francisco. Looking over the result, the producers liked what they read, and I found myself the new book writer. Of a political satire. Oh, never mind!

On we went, with Hal Prince's musical director, Hal Hastings, joining John Flaxman as coproducer along the way to Broadway. We cast the show and went off to Philadelphia, the very weekend that something that was to become known as Legionnaires' disease broke out in our own hotel. Miraculously, none of the collaborators contracted this affliction, but *The Selling of the President* itself didn't fare so well. The reviews were mixed to poor, and Talley Beatty, the gentle, talented black choreographer, a novice to the pressures and pace of a Broadway musical, was a resulting casualty, soon to be followed in quick succession by the director.

There was one weekend when the producers came to me privately. They had sent messages out to Hal Prince and Michael Bennett, both in Europe at the time, and were assured that one of them would be arriving the very next week to take over. Which one was unclear. But could I handle rehearsals for the weekend, until Our Savior arrived?

The company had been unhappy with their director for quite some time. Experienced hands including Pat Hingle, Barbara Barrie, and, in one really idiotic piece of insane miscasting, the great singer Karen Morrow, in a *non-singing* role—oh, never mind!—were all overwhelmed with relief that their lyricist/book writer was finally making sense of a libretto that had seemed inert. When neither Mr. Prince nor Mr. Bennett arrived the next week to take up the reins, they insisted that Jack be allowed to complete his work on the production rather than introduce someone new. As I recall, this was the same day the producers passed on to me the news that our lighting designer, Tom Skelton, was out with hepatitis, and did I think I could manage without him as well?

Claudius has a great line in *Hamlet* I'm fond of quoting at moments like these: "Ah, Gertrude," he breathes, "when troubles come, they come not single spies, but in battalions!" Well, the battalions were certainly on the march. At some time around here, Bob James withdrew from the fray with a bleeding ulcer. And on a Tuesday morning, I sat down with the company to read a rewritten scene I had finished just the night before, relieved when Pat Hingle and the rest of the cast agreed it seemed clearer and better. At that very moment, John Flaxman and Hal Hastings chose to interrupt me and ask me to step outside. The company took a break, and the men, both of them ashen, lowered the boom: there was simply no advance for our show, and although we were meant to have this week and the following one to continue to preview and refine . . . and the work, they assured me *was* getting much better . . . they couldn't survive even one more week with no box office. We were going to have to open this week. "When this week?" I managed. "Tomorrow night," they replied.

Jesus, Mary, and Joseph, in the immortal words of Helen Hayes! Tomorrow . . . Wednesday night? My first thought was—What of this new scene? Should we do it? We called the company together and explained the situation to the stone-faced actors. I rose and volunteered that ordinarily one would "freeze" the show for several performances before facing the critics; it was only fair that they be allowed to play the same script more than once, without changes, to secure their timing. Did they wish to perform this new, better scene, or simply play Tuesday evening and the Wednesday matinee with what they had? They reluctantly asked that the script be left alone—no changes. And I had no choice but to support them.

We thought that was as bad as it could get. But it wasn't. The next message that came down the pike was from *The New York Times*: Clive Barnes, the most powerful theater critic of the time, wasn't able to attend the Wednesday night performance. He asked to be allowed to review the next day's matinee!

I was sitting in the back row of the Shubert Theatre about 2:20 that afternoon. If there were 140 people scattered about the orchestra, I'm being generous. There was a wasteland of empty seats between me, in the back row, and the tiny matinee audience packed into the rows up front. I had blocked Karen Morrow as Irene, the public relations expert, to play her first scene and exit down the aisle as if she were leaving the building. The scene went fairly smoothly, I thought, no emotional letup. Karen stamped up the aisle with bristling purpose, and as she reached where I was sitting in the back row, I leaned forward. "Good!" I whispered with both my thumbs up. "Way to go!" She glared into my face: "The sonofabitch is asleep!" she hissed, and swept past me. The esteemed critic of New York's most powerful newspaper, who had requested to come to the matinee knowing full well how dreadful it was going to be for us, had not managed to stay awake for even the first ten minutes.

The next day he trod heavily all over the enterprise. There is an ironic truism in theater that one recalls nothing of good reviews, only the bad ones—those are etched in one's memory as solid as granite. And Barnes tossed us a beauty—Bob's and my music was in his opinion "a Sargasso Sea of mediocrity." I don't think it gets any worse than that.

We closed that Saturday night. Five performances, after a preview tryout of six. This was the promised land. This was what was "supposed" to happen to me: I "belonged on Broadway," everyone knew it. All my life, everyone had known it. Everyone, that is, but Clive Barnes.

Was there anything to be salvaged? Several individuals had been terrific, no question. In our business these days, it is not uncommon for a professional to be offered financial remuneration before consenting to go out of town to offer help to a struggling enterprise. But in the seventies it all seemed far more friendly, far less cut-and-dried, quite honestly. Friends went regularly out of town simply to help friends. Patsy Birch, who was predominantly responsible for the success of the off-Broadway hit laid at the feet of our deposed director, came to our rescue and staged a number for me, gratis. The late Ron Field came down to Philadelphia as well to stage another and hold my hand; and on the occasion of our first preview on Broadway, he insisted on treating me to dinner at the old Carnegie Tavern on Fifty-Sixth Street so he could walk me down Broadway to my first real Broadway performance in a real Broadway theater. "Don't be ridiculous," he said as we strolled arm in arm down to the Shubert. "This only happens to a director once in his lifetime: we're going to enjoy it!" How thoughtful, how kind, how utterly wonderful was that? He knew, of course, it was all going to turn to clay. Jonathan Tunick, who did the orchestrations, told Tammy Grimes that I was the "real deal," and she sweetly wrote me a note of condolence on pale blue paper shortly afterward, an act of kindness I can still close my eyes and see. Clive Barnes came often to San Diego and dined with me in the years that followed; he was no longer drinking, but even so, he remembered nothing of either the production or his review. And we laughed about it. How about that?

Bob James, thank God, had jazz. Without breaking his stride, he went on over the decades to record for Creed Taylor and then Warner Bros. an unbroken string of crossover and creative jazz albums, receiving Grammy nominations and awards for a distinguished career as one of our most celebrated and enduring musical artists. And even after this humiliating experience, he and I attempted to salvage our partnership. At Ellis's insistence, we threw ourselves at a nondenominational version of *Tarzan* disguised as *Jungleman*, never completed, but I swear the last several songs we wrote, unheard, unappreciated, were among our best. And ironically, many years later we were to learn that some of the "Sargasso Sea" mediocrities from our much-maligned Broadway show were used as audition material for *Les Miz*, so appropriate were they for the vocal demands of that score. So, take *that!*

But now what? The Big Dream shattered into smithereens, where was I to turn? While we had been out of town in Philadelphia, Craig Noel had called me: Would I come out for the summer of 1972 and direct *The Merry Wives of Windsor* for him? I was pleased that he wanted me back this time on my own, but was both polite and firm. "If the show is a hit, I'll have to stay in New York," I patiently explained. "And if it's a failure, I won't want to come." His answer was immediate: "If the show is a hit, you can afford to come; and if it's a failure, you'll need to!"

Hmmm. Some wisdom to that, no question. So there was my answer: I was not needed, scheduled, or sought as a lyricist, or God knows as a political satirist, for Broadway. But there might just be a market for my accumulated skills as a director! Who knew? Had I ever thought seriously about that? Not really. The APA-Phoenix experience with Ellis had been just that—the gift of proximity to my supposedly chosen field. And all the while I had held the belief that one day the mantle of Alan Jay Lerner would drop as lightly as cashmere onto my shoulders. How goes that priceless saying—"If you want to make God laugh, tell Him your plans?" I packed my bags and flew to Ocean Beach in San Diego, reporting for work without really having opened the play, failure roaring loudly in my ears. Sitting with the actors, I opened the script. Let's see . . . Act One, Scene One: the Garter Inn. Hmmm. So it's a bar . . . and I guess the table should be . . . over there! And, peering more closely at the text, now what happens . . . ?

26

The end is not in sight. A pinball, initially passive, then tempest-tossed, having leaped off the table entirely, having rolled beyond all respectable pinball limits, finds itself in a new decade, the 1970s, scarred, dented a bit, but capable of rolling with it. So not yet "the end."

Basically, directors don't retire; they are, when you come down to it, just passed over, or passed along. I keep reminding myself that the caravan travels over the dunes from left to right, while the camera pans left. One has the obligation to stay in the shot until, leaning precariously, one finally falls off the damned camel! When the phone stops ringing, when one's calendar is white as Joan Rivers's worst nightmare, when that caravan has traveled into the far distant dunes, taking the cameras and the excitement along with it, and night chills the sands, one stops. Or is stopped. At any event . . .

It can happen when least expected; for some, the "flavors of the month" barely out of university and popping like Chinese firecrackers off-off-Broadway to be proclaimed the next best thing, it can be disappointingly brief. For the great George Abbott, with whom I was eventually to share his last professional effort on earth with the Broadway revival of *Damn Yankees* in 1994, it was the longest of all possible roads. He was 105 years old when we met, and 107 when he finally died, vibrant, insistent, wise, and irascible to the bitter end.

The boost, the defining push came not from Ellis, but once again from Houseman. Beginning with our association with *Pantagleize*, my life was ever richer by association with John and Joan, my surrogate parents. Here, on the near edge of the seventies, it was John who reached out and dropped me once more within his circle of influence at the Juilliard School, where he headed the Drama Division, controlling the pieces on the board before me in such a way as to lead to the Moment That Made All the Difference.

I was first invited by Houseman to do some coaching for Group III at Juilliard and to direct a production for Group II, the class just behind the impressive achievements of Patti LuPone, Kevin Kline, Sam Tsoutsouvas, David Ogden Stiers, and the others who were beginning to become the Acting Company. It was the slightly blighted Group II, who everyone said "needed a hit," for whom I was asked to do Schnitzler's *La Ronde*, with a score supplied by Roland Gagnon, Beverly Sills's vocal coach, culled from the piano music of Schubert. I decided to represent the different sexual acts of the play as dances to these beautiful piano pieces, despite the fact that I didn't consider myself a choreographer. Group II had been something of a disappointment after that glittering first group so redolent of promise, and they'd never really had a resounding success of their own to perform before their peers. But I went ahead and threw myself into it, and the hoped-for "hit" was the happy result. The audience that afternoon comprised most of the Juilliard staff—Margot Harley, Michael Kahn, Elizabeth Smith, and Marian Seldes, who rewarded my effort by prostrating herself at my feet during the note session that followed. She was given to this kind of gesture, and later I recall accidentally stepping on her as she lay flat on the floor of Brian Bedford's dressing room after his "uncut" *Hamlet*. Others attending *La Ronde* included Peter Herman Adler, the guiding spark of the American Opera Center, who was so taken with my work that he began proposing me for everything he had available. Next up was a double bill of one-act operas, one of them perfect for me. Adler was offering me the bottom of that bill, *Il Cordovano*, a fragile sexual farce by the contemporary Italian composer Goffredo Pretrassi. Cast with Juilliard vocal students, it was to be conducted by John DeMain, formerly attached to the neighboring New York City Opera, who by this time had become the young musical director of the adventurous Houston Grand Opera. John and I met over lunch in the Juilliard cafeteria at Lincoln Center before diving into this atonal quasi-Molière bit of fluff. We weren't all that enthusiastic about the Pretrassi, but we liked each other instantly.

One night, supposedly alone with my lighting designer and stage crew, as I was trying to light our jerry-rigged set in such a way that it might not look like the mess it actually was, John DeMain stood unseen behind us in the top row of seats, watching. Unaware of his presence, I was simply luxuriating in the kind of happiness to which I aspired more than anything else: the joy of working among enthusiastic professionals giving the work at hand their best shot. APA had taught me that the best work arose from those moments in which we were "playing" in the truest sense of the word. Not grimly persevering or doggedly soldiering on, but with laughter and a light touch, ensuring that, whatever else, everyone in the room was having the same good time. I was characteristically making fun of myself and my pretensions to make "art," and by deflecting us from the paucity of material in front of us, we managed somehow, as John watched, to make a little corner of magic. John told me later that this was his first indication I might be destined for bigger things.

It was 1976 and the Houston Grand Opera was about to begin rehearsals for its Bicentennial production of Gershwin's *Porgy and Bess.* Amazingly, they had still not secured a director. They desperately wanted Hal Prince to do it, and he was more than eager, but his career as the highest-profile director in the business meant that he would be unavailable for months. They couldn't wait for Hal, because in a heartbeat, the Bicentennial would be over. John watched me transforming flats into a believable period room with the help of my colleagues, discovering that my previous six or seven years of servitude to some of the country's most experienced hands had paid off. I might be unknown, but I obviously knew what I was doing.

The next day, over coffee, he asked me who I thought would be the perfect director for *Porgy and Bess.* I didn't have much knowledge of the piece, since my experience had been restricted to seeing the Samuel Goldwyn film version with Sidney Poitier, Dorothy Dandridge, Pearl Bailey, and Sammy Davis, Jr. But impulsively I said, "A black woman!" "Why would you say that?" he asked. I said that I thought the most interesting character to a contemporary audience is Bess, a woman who obviously couldn't survive in the ghetto of Catfish Row, or even in Charleston in the twenties, without the protection of the strongest man available; she would have to become an emotional chameleon, able to make herself indispensable to whatever that man required. I thought an African American woman would understand those implications perfectly.

Where did my opinion come from? I have no idea. But perhaps for the first time in my life I was aware I might be tapping into something beyond instinct. (When all is said and done, I wonder if the ability to reach beyond the obvious, the given assignment, is what separates the wheat from the chaff in perhaps all professions, not just directing.) Only after I'd said it, after I had not only identified the idea but reflected on it, did I realize how valid it was, and yet I had pulled the intuition out of thin air: I didn't know this was going to be a viable or even a revisionist approach to this classic American work, but I just leaped for the truth of it, believing intuitively that one could fill in the blanks later.

"Do you know any black directors who are women?" John went on. Only one. Vinnette Carroll, a larger-than-life acquaintance of Ellis's who had gone in and out of APA-Phoenix at one point to create a production of Sartre's *The Flies* for Ann Arbor. Vinnette, a powerful proponent of experimental musical form who was later to uncork productions like *Black Nativity, Don't Bother Me, I Can't Cope*, and *Your Arms Too Short to Box with God*, emerging from her Urban Arts Workshop, wasn't a perfect fit with either APA-Phoenix or Sartre, but she was the first black woman to direct on Broadway, and true to his word, John DeMain and Houston's coproducer, Sherwin Goldman, met with her to see if she might be interested. "How long would I get to do this?" she was reported to have asked them. Three weeks was the answer. "Hell, honey," she trumpeted, "I couldn't do that damn thing in three months! You all crazy!" Vinnette passed.

And so, late one afternoon a week or so later, I stopped for a brief interview with John to meet Sherwin Goldman just after rehearsal on my way out of the building. It was all very tentative, it was extremely oblique, it was anything but an offer, but as a result of this interview, I found myself late for dinner with a former university mentor of mine, Marvin Feldheim, a witty educator with whom I had not studied, but who had become a good friend. We were scheduled to meet at seven o'clock at a nearby restaurant, the Red Baron, on Columbus, and I went streaking up the street at a dead run about 7:20 to find him sitting in a booth with his cocktail before him. We hardly said hello when I burst out with what I knew instinctively was about to happen: "Marvin! You won't believe it! I think I'm going to get to direct the Bicentennial revival of *Porgy and Bess!*"

Goldman and the Houston general director, David Gockley, had gone to Hal Prince with their ultimatum: Could Prince possibly do anything with or to his schedule that would allow him to take on the revival? With great reluctance, he explained it was impossible. Was there any other director they might want advice about? He knew virtually everyone in the business. "Well, there is one young man we like a lot," said Sherwin Goldman. "What's his name?" ask Hal. "I can't quite remember . . . it's Irish, though," said Sherwin. "I think it's Kelly!" Hal didn't recognize the name, although he certainly knew mine. As I had been a frequent visitor in and out of the Prince/Abbott office, he had been both warm and encouraging to me throughout the debacle that was *The Selling of the President*. "Look," he replied. "I don't know who this guy is, I've never heard of him, but sometimes you've just got to go with your gut. If you think he can do the job, you should just hire him."

And they did. What could be more unlikely? I was, I believe, the last person hired for the event, and a whiter candidate one could not find. All I really knew was that my response to this music was visceral; I didn't stop to consider just how difficult it would be or how it might affect my career. Just that the canvas of the piece, the characters, the community, felt instantly understandable to me.

The year is 1976, and APA and its world can only now be glimpsed in the rearview mirror. Ellis, by this time, has secured his only Tony, for the 1975 revival of *The Royal Family* in which he nestled enough alums of his familial past—Rosemary, George Grizzard, Le Gallienne, Nicky Martin—for his star to rise brilliantly one more time. But I'm no longer trailing behind; he and I are now on parallel courses. He's living at this point just down Riverside Drive from me, and the social good times continue to roll, our more infrequent contact making it more and more difficult for me to judge his state of mind, but I'm always grateful for his company and to be a guest at his table.

There is a week in New York in that year of 1976 when I find myself sitting beside John DeMain as he takes the company through musical rehearsals of Gershwin's glorious score. Clamma Dale, Donnie Ray Albert, Wilma Shakesnider, Betty Laws, Abraham Lind-Oquendo, Irene Oliver, rafter-rattling African American voices of depth and purity are pouring out the score, and John looks down at me smiling, wordlessly inquiring: Are you going to start doing something or not? Since I've only just been hired, I'm supposedly "catching up," music rehearsals and coaching have been going on for some time, which is a major difference between the world of plays and plays set to music. John is refining the score, the duets, the powerful ensembles, and even though most of that work has been prepared and polished, I have begged him to just let me listen a little longer, to watch, to look at these beautiful black singers, trying to figure out what I might possibly have to say to them. What of my protected, very white life in Saginaw, Michigan, is to be found in this room?

Finally we can wait no longer, and Helaine Head, the production stage manager I had brought from Bill Ball's ACT, announces we will begin with the funeral scene, "My Man's Gone Now," and the scene that follows. With the exception of Bess and Crown, the entire company is present, sitting, watching me warily. I stand up and face them for the first time.

Well, my parents are both dead. I know something about death. My first real relationship, with Jim Whittle, after seven years has crashed. I know something about love and loss. How different can it be? I begin. There is a woman, witnessed by a community. There is shock, disbelief; the curious feeling of being enlarged by grief. The body is . . . here, center stage. And over there she stands, Serena, held up by . . . one? . . . two women? Maybe we don't see her at first? Those thumping chords begin . . . *Whomp-pa-paaaah! Umpcha-umpcha-umpcha* . . . I suggest the mourners move away . . . revealing her. She looks down on Robbins's body and, extricating herself from the women supporting her, reaches for her dead husband . . . "My man's gone now! . . ."

Time goes by. We've gone well beyond the aria, through the funeral scene. The two white men have come. The two white men have gone. Break.

There is silence in the room and I look to John, but he's distracted with a question from the piano. I walk from the rehearsal room to the men's room and find a bank of urinals. Several of the cast are following me. We are standing silently at the urinals now, staring ahead, or down. Mute. Behind me, I hear the voice of one of the younger men of the ensemble.

"Jack, do you know what 'dreadful' means?" I don't. And I have the sense to say so. "Well," he goes on behind me, "we have this expression. 'Dreadful.' When anything is really, really good? We say it's 'dreadful'!" Pause. "You are one 'dreadful' director." There was something like the murmur of assent from the others assembled as they trooped out together, leaving me facing my reflection in the men's room mirror. I permitted myself a small, almost conspiratorial smile. "Dreadful?" I thought as I headed for the door. "Okay, well, it's a start!"

What I couldn't have known, of course, was the long, difficult struggle of those remarkable black singers waiting for me in the rehearsal hall. The path for African American opera singers has never been either smooth or easy in our country, and many exceptional singers have found a far more rewarding and encouraging climate abroad. There have been exceptions, of course—Paul Robeson, Marian Anderson, famously, and more recently Leontyne Price, Kathleen Battle, Jessye Norman, Simon Estes, and Willard White are all obvious success stories; but what of the men and women who are not destined for such great careers, but who still are professional singers of unquestioned professional caliber? For the most part during the middle of the last century, singers like these in the rehearsal hall were kept afloat by going basically from production to production, ensemble after ensemble, of *Porgy and Bess.* And if there were several revivals after the 1936 premiere, which had been severely edited and cut before it debuted—Gershwin never heard the completed score as he wrote it!—it was not until the 1950s that the director Bobby Breen famously put together an exceptional production, distinguished by the Bess of the young Leontyne Price, that found its way to Russia, attended by Truman Capote, who wrote vividly of the experience in *The Muses Are Heard*, and that became the new defining standard of what was obviously an emerging opera classic.

Few people realize that a director's work is often finished as of opening night, and then the director traditionally hands over the care of the production to the production stage manager, who has kept meticulous notes of movement, characterization, and technical elements and who is entrusted with the original stage business, which is meant to be faithfully maintained. In the case of Breen's production, the stage manager was a woman named Ella Gerber, and it so happened that in subsequent years, Ms. Gerber found her way into the wording of the rights to the opera, so that one was unable to produce *Porgy and Bess* without first employing her to direct it.

Although Ms. Gerber was still very active in the late seventies, and continued to work extensively as a director, teacher, and arts educator for years after, I never met the woman, but from the eagerly expressed opinions of our company, that was a principal saving grace. Whatever strengths Ms. Gerber had as a director did not endear her to the various ensembles she employed continually from the fifties onward. I was told she tended to condescend to them, was often short and dismissive, and yet demanded exact and precise adherence to her road map, devised by Breen. She had made no friends among the company I inherited, and yet for the better part of twenty years, hers was the directorial voice and the only voice that dictated how *Porgy* must be staged. If you worked in *Porgy and Bess*, you were working for Ella Gerber.

Interestingly enough, one of the surviving original members from the first company was alive at this time, if not as active as Ms. Gerber. That was Eva Jessye, whose own choir of black singers became the basis for the original chorus of the opera, and Miss Jessye's care, attention, and professionalism over the years that followed cannot be undervalued. She was its spiritual mother, its silent caretaker. If I never had occasion to meet Ella Gerber, I was privileged to enjoy one of the most extraordinary opportunities of my life during the Houston previews before we opened. Word went through the company before the curtain that Miss Jessye was present in the audience and would be invited back to join the members of the ensemble after the performance. By this time, the company had taken me intimately into their confidence, and the blessing of Miss Jessye would mean everything to them. They were determined that she and I should meet, and exhausted as

I was on that particular evening, I arrived at a hotel room where the company, for the most part, had assembled with plates of food, quantities of drink, and the great generosity of spirit that characterized them throughout the entire rehearsal period. I was plunked down on the floor at the feet of a fragile woman in her eighties, quiet, proud, and elegant, who, as I recall, never met my eyes once during the entire evening. She looked past me, just over my head at the others around her. Was it shyness? Distrust? I have no idea, but she had seen what I had done with the production, and having heard reports from her "chillun" of my methods of working, and the degree to which I had solicited their opinions and input as we proceeded, she was ready to give me, albeit obliquely, whatever she had. She dropped authentic bits of stage business into my lap as lightly as popped corn: "When the white man come to the funeral, you know, he always put somethin' in the saucer on the dead man's chest. No white man in the South would ever disrespect a funeral, no matter who they are!" Bleary with fatigue, I realized she was imparting to me the information that Ms. Gerber and probably no other white director had ever requested or been given.

And I folded that and every other instinct I had into the process both before and after the premiere in Houston. Larry Marshall, as Sportin' Life, was married at that time to the daughter of John W. Bubbles, one of the most famous Sportin' Life interpreters since Cab Calloway, and he and I quickly formed an alliance of shorthand insight and comic references that brought the Broadway jazz elements of the story into total relief. And I will never forget the thrill of finally feeling free from self-consciousness or any idea that the beautiful black singers and their provincial white Midwestern director were anything but joined at the hip. I stood behind Clamma Dale, our leading Bess, a glorious six-foot-tall panther of a soprano, while she stared across the stage at Donnie Ray Albert, her young, very agile, very sexual Porgy, kneeling in the braces we had devised to indicate his crippled status. Blocking their great duet for the first time, I whispered into her ear: "Slowly . . . slowly now, start sinking to your knees! Don't feel like you are coming down . . . see him, rather, rise up in your eyes until you are on the same level. Then, as you sing 'Porgy, I's your woman now,' just slowly begin to inch across the stage on your knees until you find yourself finally in his arms."

Wow! Where did that come from? Not Ellis, not LeG, not Houseman. Probably not from Saginaw, either. After years of trying, years of wanting to reach into a performer with something really helpful, I was finally free, finally unedited, just flying on my own.

Some time later, I encountered Hal and Judy Prince at a performance in Lincoln Center. He embraced me and said, "That is the greatest piece of musical direction I think I have ever seen." I said earlier that one remembers only the worst reviews. But a comment like that, coming once in one's life, and from one of one's genuine heroes, stays indelibly fresh, thank God!

John DeMain and I shared hotel rooms, meals, insights. He welcomed me to the process and held me up throughout it, and on the opening night in Houston, he personally came to the wings and dragged me center stage with him as the audience roared its approval. John, grinning, pumped his thumb down over my head, as if what they were applauding had been solely up to me, when a more collaborative effort would have been impossible to find. It all continued to unfold—from Houston to the unexpected move to Philadelphia, where Sherwin Goldman, the coproducer, put up his home as collateral to inch the production ever closer to New York. There in Philadelphia my directing twin, Dan Sullivan, who had grown up in Lincoln Center as I had in APA, took me aside as he and his first wife, Cecelia, passed through Philadelphia on their way to the West Coast, where he was about to make his home in Seattle, and told me in no uncertain terms just how major a piece of work we had before us. You don't always believe the press. Usually you cannot afford to. But when your peers think enough of your effort to insist you listen, you begin to accept it.

Encouraged by the company to continue to refine and give more as we headed toward a Broadway booking, I found myself in almost a continuing delirium of saying yes. I began to discover the kind of revelation that one only achieves after continual exposure to a great work—as I experienced once again at Radio City Music Hall in 1982, when I was able to add into the mix the brilliance of George Faison's choreography, which earned him a Tony nomination and furthered my determination to involve more authentic black talent in the production; and finally, ten years after our premiere, in 1986, when a fourteen-opera-company consortium toured the country in our best, most

Clamma Dale and Donnie Ray Albert in the Houston Grand Opera production of *Porgy and Bess.* (Jim Caldwell, courtesy of the Helen Armstead-Johnson Collection at the Schomburg Center of the New York Public Library)

complete version. I came to understand that the chorus of *Porgy and Bess* is, in many ways, its true leading character. All of the action, but for the section on Kittiwah Island, where Bess has her fatal reunion with Crown, takes place within the confines of Catfish Row, a series of rickety apartments, where the entire action is witnessed by the community. This is a drama of intense emotional conflict and danger of vivid personalities, but all of it—all of the drama—is played out in the front yard of the community itself. They see everything, and they're almost never offstage. So at the end of the opera, when Porgy calls for his goat to set out for New York to find his Bess, I told as the ensemble to rush ahead of him, as many of them as possible, to see if they could witness in his eyes the courage of the least physically able man in the ghetto leaving to pursue his own dream. I told them as characters that they had to see him for themselves so they could pass on to their own children and grandchildren that they had witnessed the first man to leave the ghetto. If Porgy could believe in a better life, why couldn't they? We built the production on the goodwill, the belief, and yes, the palpable relief of artists who in many cases had never before been invited to the party, tumbling over themselves to discover and identify and claim something of their own souls within Gershwin's world. Subsequent productions, many of them highly praised, have tended to curtail and limit the power of the chorus, perhaps the richest and most important in any contemporary opera. From Gershwin's point of view, they do so at their peril.

That final bit of direction wasn't in my first attempt, nor perhaps even the second. But as my experience with this great work deepened, so my passion for telling the story continued to evolve. I just never seemed to run dry. That was another of my lessons from Ellis, from LeG, from APA. When you truly tap into the work, it just keeps unfolding its secrets to you. Occasionally, probably for all of us, it's just a job; but when the lightning strikes, you find yourself in every sense truly blessed. And it isn't about you: it's about "it."

Porgy went on to win the Tony for Best Revival in 1977. I was to be awarded my first nomination. The impact of this production, an "overnight success," according to a headline in *The Village Voice*, allowed so much else to follow . . . Operas, television. An invitation from Craig Noel to join him at the Old Globe, where, as elsewhere across the country, the regional movement was about to unfold, involving the likes of me, Dan Sullivan, Des McAnuff, Mark Lamos, and others. I had found my direction at last. Or perhaps, more accurately, it had found me.

AFTERWORD

Like most of us in the theater, Ellis was an inveterate quoter. He had his patented phrases, culled from roles, plays, movies, and none was more appealing to him than one from the end of the film *That Hamilton Woman*, with Vivien Leigh and Laurence Olivier. In the closing moments, someone asks of Lady Hamilton, "What happened then? What happened after?" And as the camera closes in on that exquisite face comes Ellis's favorite line: "There was no 'then,' there was no 'after.'" That, along with *"Finita la commedia!"* could be counted on to "button," or nicely sum up, any of his chosen personal cadences.

So far as my own story was concerned, there would be both a then and an after. And whatever I was to become, it had little to do with Lady Hamilton. Between the demise of APA-Phoenix and the event that was *Porgy and Bess* were six or seven years of "seasoning," I suppose. I was basically on the road, going from regional job to regional job—Buffalo, St. Louis, San Francisco, with returns almost yearly to San Diego and Craig. A director directs, and to learn the craft, to refine the lessons into something of one's own, one needs to work, and for a while my sole professional goal was simply "to be asked back." No matter whether the show was a huge hit or not, I concentrated on the resident staff, my host, the community, determined to be supportive, grateful, helpful, and positive, hoping that the day might come when I was finally offered a job I couldn't accept because I was booked. There is no more wonderful feeling than to know one's dance card is full, no chillier one than to see the months stretch out ahead without a project.

I became attached for a while to Houseman's Acting Company as a kind of emotional sous-chef, traveling on the bus with them, counseling them, and directing several productions with the likes of LuPone, Kline, Rosato, and Tsoutsouvas. I begged Houseman to elevate me from "Associate Artistic Director" and just give me the company, only to hear him pronounce: "Not remotely possible, Haut-Brion. You're the best-kept secret in the theater, and I can't raise a dime on you. You must go out and earn your international reputation." The severity of that rejection was beautifully tempered by the implication that Houseman believed me *worthy* of an international reputation.

Ellis remained a major figure in my personal landscape for some time. Although I continued to see him, it was less frequently, and so I was never altogether certain how he was faring from one day to the next. There were continuing issues with his eyes; sometimes he would be wearing a patch, but eventually it seemed somehow to clear up, and he rarely commented on it. I was now no longer in his wake, so others intermittently became closer than I. We enjoyed a mutual summer engagement in San Diego in 1975, when I directed him as a brilliant Benedick opposite Marian Mercer as Beatrice. And when I became artistic director of the Old Globe Theatre in 1982, with Craig Noel present and active throughout my entire tenure, Ellis was the first person I called. He came out to play a wonderful Prospero in my inaugural *Tempest* and stayed on to play Lady Bracknell in drag for Tom Moore in *The Importance of Being Earnest*. He was funny, generous, and popular in that season, and despite the fact that he was drinking more and more, he behaved like a complete professional and a perfect guest.

A few years later it all went horribly wrong. After a period of activity at Lincoln Center in the seventies, he began to direct less and less. But in the early eighties his father died, and shortly thereafter he made a kind of pilgrimage west to see old friends, Craig and I among them. Brought face-to-face with mortality, he was as disciplined and pulled together as we had seen him for years, sober, involved, and generous. He made a charming and elaborate effort to take me out to dinner one night at his insistence and his own expense. He was his old self again. At the time we were planning a production of *Pygmalion*, which I was doing for another mutual friend from ACT days in San Francisco, Barbara Dirickson, who was to play Eliza. Ellis had recently spent time with Barbara and Ben Moore, her husband at the time, who was managing director for the Seattle Repertory. I had yet to cast the leading role of Higgins, and remembering vividly Ellis's Tanner in APA's early *Man and Superman*, I knew he had the energy, clarity, and pyrotechnics to be a first-rate Higgins. Once he had departed from San Diego, I called Ben and Barbara to suggest, since he seemed so much better, that he might be our Higgins. They confessed being seduced by him as well, and with great enthusiasm we planned the production. I was even able to secure his favorite "wingman," Sydney Walker, to play Pickering, assuring Ellis that he would be surrounded with people he loved and trusted, and we sealed our commitment for the following fall.

But over the summer, I began to hear disturbing rumors. He had visited friends at Williamstown, where his personal favorite, Carrie Nye, the wife of Dick Cavett, was in residence. The word came back: Ellis was drinking again, and drinking heavily. He seemed to be entering another manic phase. Still, I knew his love of Shaw, and his desire to play this role for me and for Barbara, and I believed he would rally. I chose to turn a deaf ear.

He arrived the weekend before we were to begin rehearsal. Ellis himself was the first director I knew who advised any actor in a Shaw play to come to the first day of work with the lines learned. It is dense, exacting material, and God knows there will be no rewrites, so one is wisest to get the script into one's head and mouth as quickly as possible. He walked into my home accompanied by Sydney and a few others, looked me straight in the eye, and said, "Where's the vodka?" I laughed, of course, thinking it was a joke, but he swept by me into the kitchen, found a bottle in a cupboard, and poured himself a drink, all the time watching me steadily, a willful and defiant posture I remembered only too well. I attempted to make conversation with him and the others, but when I suggested we all go out for dinner, he decided instead to stay home alone. Something had gone sour, and I couldn't for the life of me understand what it was.

Rehearsals were rocky. We would begin each day with Ellis, Barbara, Sydney, and the others eager to work; but when it was time for lunch, he would go next door with a few of the company to the restaurant in the sculptural garden of the museum, and come back an hour and a half and several glasses of white wine later. The first half of each day seemed to hold promise, but the second half was always a shambles. Whenever I tried to confront him, I was icily dismissed. This was uncharted territory: my role over the years had been to support and enable him, and now any effort on my part to discipline him was, in his opinion, pointless. That had never been my role, and he would not allow it. We were all walking on eggshells, and I needed somehow to keep moving ahead. There was no acceptable alternative. I quietly advised his understudy that it might be wise for him to learn the text as quickly as possible.

There was something else going on, some dark energy outside our relationship, which seemed to be spiraling downward. Sharing a condo with Sydney instead of staying with Craig, as he usually did, he announced one morning that he intended to retire to San Diego permanently, and on impulse he put an offer down on a small house several blocks from Craig's. Rather than working on his text, he spent most nights drinking, while endlessly sketching ideas of how he might redecorate the house. Craig, alarmed, could do nothing about it, and I was grimly determined just to press on and pray it might all somehow come together. One night, at about one a.m., when he walked over to the house he had not yet bought and climbed up on the roof, the neighbors spotted him and called the police. Craig and his partner got wind of this and reached the bungalow only seconds before the squad cars appeared, hastily bringing him down and spiriting him away before he could be questioned.

We opened in a kind of terror. Inevitably, he still had his moments of brilliance, such as when he chose to sit cross-legged on his desk in the play, like a spoiled, petulant brat, perfect for Higgins, as well as being a parallel reflection of Ellis's own state of mind.

The reviews were respectful, for the most part, but Barbara and Sydney revealed that he had never completely learned the part, instead getting through with his usual bravado and authority in full hue and cry, paraphrasing, cutting speeches, and giving a highly manic performance. I was emotionally exhausted and felt betrayed. I had got the show on, yes, but at the cost of my own self-respect. I felt utterly impotent. To clear my mind, I left San Diego with Tom Hall, my business partner, his wife, and a few others for three or four days of skiing up at Mammoth, in the eastern Sierra Nevada.

We had scheduled some student matinees at that time, so the first week of performance had no fewer than nine shows in a row. Ellis had missed at least two previews and one or two technical rehearsals, but after opening night, I had hoped that things might settle down. When we returned from skiing, it was reported that of the nine performances, Ellis had played only five. His understudy, sometimes with just an hour's notice, had played the rest. Worst of all was that Ellis had played the Saturday matinee, gone out to dine with Daniel Davis, a visiting actor friend, and, having enjoyed a bottle of wine at dinner, called in "sick," unable to make the evening curtain.

I got back to San Diego to find my leading lady in tears, not knowing who she would be facing when the curtain went up, and the company split into camps—those still wanting somehow to support Ellis, and the others disgusted by his lack of professionalism.

I had to deal with this once and for all, in spite of all the Oedipal signs flashing. I called him Monday morning and went over to his condo, where Sydney opened the door stoically and quickly disappeared. I asked Ellis to justify his behavior, and he lightly dismissed it all, saying he'd had a few bad days, but it wasn't all that significant. But a line had been crossed, and I could no longer pretend otherwise. I told him that as his friend, I was prepared to do whatever in my power I could to support him and make him happy, but as the artistic director of a theater we had both loved and served for so long, I simply couldn't sanction his behavior. He could do this to me personally, if he so chose. But he couldn't do it to the theater I was entrusted to run. I was replacing him. Period.

There was a moment in which I truly believed he thought I was kidding. But I wasn't. His eyes widening in disbelief, he finally said, "Are you telling me you are firing me?" "Yes, El, I am. Jim Winker will play Higgins tonight, and for the remainder of the run."

"What am I expected to do?" he said, his voice rising and his face red. "I'm sure I don't know," I replied. "As of this morning, that is no longer a concern of mine." And I left.

I was shaking, but I knew I was right. And it was the single most painful thing I had ever had to do, then or since. A flurry of letters arrived for me, cruel, angry, furious, even vicious. I would try to read them, but they so sickened me that I put them all in a bottom drawer of my desk and never read them again. Ellis left San Diego for Memphis and the comfort of his mother, and shortly thereafter staged his last Broadway effort, *The Loves of Anatol*, a Schnitzler adaption he had first done in the original Bermuda season in 1960 for Richard Easton. It was not a success, and he only occasionally directed after that.

There is no way to come back from this, nor can there be. He never forgave me. And, of course, on some level, how could he? For years I had had his back, supported him, emulated him, accompanied him in every way I could. How could he accept dismissal by me, of all people? After all, didn't he create me? I could see his point of view. But he could never see mine.

I would call over the years—on his birthday, on the occasion of the death of his best friend, Bill Ball . . . "El? It's Guck," I would say—using his short, affectionate nickname for me. "Howreyooo," came the cool, distant reply. It was perfunctory, polite, but I could never get through.

And then, in 1998, at the age of sixty-seven, he died of heart failure in Memphis. We never reconciled.

When I won my first Tony, for the musical *Hairspray*, I recall stating that everything I might be, everything I could do, was because I was standing on the shoulders of Ellis Rabb, of John Houseman, of Eva Le Gallienne, of the generation of mentors who influenced me, confided in me, took me in and shaped me. They all mattered. And much of what they taught me is every day in my mind and in my work. But no one more than Ellis.

Each generation gets, I suppose, the theater it not only deserves but works to create. So my "professional sibling," Dan Sullivan, emerging from the Actor's Workshop in San Francisco to tag along to Lincoln Center for Jules Irving's tenure there, directly parallels my own story before landing in Seattle and for years successfully running the Seattle Rep up there; and Des McAnuff, another iconic talent, comes down from Canada to revive the La Jolla Playhouse in La Jolla, virtually across the street from the Globe in San Diego; and Mark Lamos, who played my first Hamlet, finds his home at the Hartford Stage; and André Bishop, following our APA-Phoenix production stage manager Bob Moss's creation of Playwrights Horizons, picks

Left to right: Bob James, Judy James, and me, at a dinner party at Phyllis and Ira Wender's—in their bathtub, 1994. Taken nearly forty years after our first meeting, proof that we still prefer our own company. (Janet Beller)

that organization up before carrying his gifts to Lincoln Center, where, in partnership with Bernard Gersten, they significantly change the Broadway landscape from what Ellis and Jules Irving and Joe Papp had done before . . . None of us faced Guthrie's challenge directly, but we inherited it, and like Triple-A ball teams, raised our individual banners in regional markets everywhere across the country, ripe for development. We may not have been the innovators, but at the same time, we were not afraid to aim high and dream, and so a creative revolution began in the theatrical landscape from the eighties on.

What was clear—clearest, probably—was that like Sullivan, McAnuff, and Bishop, I was fatally infected with the bug. My means of expression, of creativity, of passion, remains the theater, and no matter how happy I've been creating, say, an *Il Trittico* for the Metropolitan Opera, or shooting any of the sequence of American Playhouse television shows I was privileged to direct for Lindsay Law, nothing but being alone in a room with actors, working on a script, or hearing music written for a specific character satisfies me. Nothing.

•

Just recently, in the basement of Imaginary Farms, my assistants un-earthed a single scarred red script of *The Selling of the President*. I've yet to open it and I am not sure why. The road not taken, I suppose. Bob and Judy James remain with me, vivid as ever. But as it turns out, Alan Jay Lerner had nothing to fear. The face I see in the mirror these days may no longer be quite so round and shiny. Yes, it's primarily the same pinball face, but I brush aside all comments about how well I look with my patented response: "When you start out looking sixty, it isn't hard to stay looking sixty!"

One of the seminal texts in our theatrical industry is a book by Peter Brook entitled *The Empty Space*, which has had immense influ-ence on directors the world over. I'm fortunate enough to arise each day thinking that there is an Empty Space for each of us. And as long as there is thought and there is imagination, nothing is to be done—something will wander out onto it.

APPENDIX

Between January and March 1968, in my capacity as associate director of the APA-Phoenix Repertory Company and once more assigned to the relatively silent duty of that position, this time assisting the legendary Eva Le Gallienne with her production of The Cherry Orchard, and desperate to direct something of my own, I decided that in order to focus my attention and not let it wander, nor to be in any way less than both completely professional and enthusiastic, I should literally record, by hand, as much of the rehearsal process as I could. That meant not only who was there and what they were wearing, for example, but what was said both within the rehearsal process and "in the wings," so to speak—comments overheard while actors were waiting on the sidelines.

It was, I thought, simply an exercise. I transcribed my handwritten notes to onionskin paper in something I entitled The Cherry Log, and some twenty-five single-spaced pages later, bound it all into a paper folder and promptly put it away. Only recently, I discovered it among my papers.

What follows is everything I recorded; and although it probably has no place in the book I have written, it exists, and it may well be the only such journal I have ever known or heard of. That it holds the behavior, the process, the lifeblood, the "sound" of an American company actually rehearsing a great Chekhovian play; that it follows the direction plan of one of the nation's most intriguing and famous auteurs; that it follows the creative process of the likes of Uta Hagen, Donald Moffat, Nancy Walker, Richard Easton, Ellis Rabb, and many others, is cause for curiosity, if not celebration: one actually gets to eavesdrop, not on the approximation of what it was, but on precisely what it was.

THE CHERRY LOG
a reportage of the rehearsals of the APA production of Chekhov's
The Cherry Orchard, directed by Eva Le Gallienne
January 14 to March 19, 1968
by Jack O'Brien

January 14, 1968: First reading

The rehearsal space chosen for the first reading of The Cherry Orchard is peculiar, secretive, a social club founded by the members of the APA Crew and sustained by them, across from the backstage door of the Lyceum on 46th Street up two or three flights of narrow, steep stairs. The room itself, then, is almost a surprise, brightly painted in a rosy beige, with a row of clean wide windows at one end, hung with bright rich red velour draperies. There are three bright blue card tables, two square and one round, huddled together in the center of the room to compose one enormous table area, and enough chairs around the table for the cast, but the rest of the company, invited out of courtesy, present out of curiosity, spill around the room on the floor or huddle in corners and back into the vestibule, where an electric coffee urn is bubbling, someone's idea of the proverbial samovar, perhaps.

Le Gallienne is prompt, in a navy blue dress, with printed silk knotted at the throat, the hair short and swept up away from her temples by fingers and apparently a ceaseless wind. Unquestionably the main attraction of the afternoon is Uta Hagen, present for the first time at an APA rehearsal and a stranger to most of the company. She is dressed in a bright blue woolen shift with beads around her neck, her face boldly ruddy with a high-keyed pancake base, giving her heightened theatricality, and the eyes are kind, forthright, alert. She laughs easily, seems relaxed and in total control, pushing her glasses into her bangs when she is not reading, and pulling down to begin.

LeG dislikes the forced and artificial quality of the first reading, and feels that she has nothing to say that digging into the play will not reveal more easily. She will read the play in its entirety to the company. The company, especially the visitors not reading, do not conceal their surprise and probably disappointment at this. Some are there out of politeness or politics, some, like Jennifer Harmon, out of a natural and insatiable curiosity which stretches in all directions, but all want to taste and sample the raw chemistry of the casting—a moment here, an exchange there, whose presence or absence suggests a revelation to the initiate, like cleverly revealed fingerprints which indicate a hit or a disaster. Such revelation will not come with Le Gallienne reading. But no one leaves, at least before the first act is completed, and Le Gallienne reads beautifully, easily, with consummate skill and a strong, brisk tempo, dropping off the names of the characters from the fabric of the drama as if she were shelling peas, done with such insight and lack of effort that one never realizes that she mentions the characters' names at all.

The humor is evident in the first act, and the company laugh and shake their incredulous heads with much appreciation. George Pentecost, who will play Yasha, sits in a white turtleneck sweater, stealing clandestine looks at whoever's part LeG happens to be reading at the moment—do they like their part? Did they get the significance of that line? He evaluates the reading as a croupier in a casino parcels out the chips—so many points to Anya, so many points to Pishchik.

At the end of the first act, Norman Kean, the General Manager, leaves, clearly indicating his initial interest, his political good will, and the indisputable fact that he is busy. T. Edward Hambleton sits benignly through the next act, and he, too, steals away. The first reading is complete, and LeG calls a break before discussion. Christine Pickles, who may or may not cover Le Gallienne as Charlotta, leaves now, as do most of the others. Coffee is exchanged, and the usual enthusiasms are voiced.

Trish Conolly, who will play Dunyasha, sidles up to Ellis Rabb: "It's such fun, Ellis, having you here with us just as an actor for a change." Rabb: "I'm a nervous wreck. I didn't sleep a wink last night. I don't know what's wrong with me." He is present under some pressure, secretly desiring to be rid of the role of Trofimov, but the withdrawal of Richard Easton from Epikhodov now makes his escape impossible. LeG and production stage manager George Darveris call the company back to order. The ranks have thinned, with only Jennifer Harmon and Louise Latham, who will cover Miss Hagen, still sitting to the side, with Ted Thompson, the administrative assistant, and two journeymen who will be extras—Jim Whittle, smoking laconically against the wall and moving his lips gently as he follows the script, and Gil Michaels, whose nearly manic enthusiasm causes him to topple from his chair at several key moments in the drama.

Le Gallienne opens the discussion of what she has just read by quoting directly the few and sparse notes from Chekhov himself: do it fast, not slow, it is a mistake to drag it all out. Chekhov claims that his acts should play in twelve minutes, but that Stanislavski makes them last at least forty. "Stanislavski has ruined my plays—bless him! The role of Varya is stupid, nun-like and tearful," and appropriate murmurs are made to Betty Miller who will play it, like a vocal applause, or a recognition of the worth of that particular actress. "Trofimov is clear." Huge laugh, Ellis Rabb's "round of recognition." "I'll write that down," Ellis says, leaning elaborately over his script and annotating. Again, LeG quotes Chekhov as saying, "I suggest you invite an actress in to play Lyubov." The company laughs delightedly in the direction of Miss Hagen, who is pleased. "Well, we've done that right," exhorts Keene Curtis.

Questions from the cast: Donald Moffat, assigned Lopakhin, asks about the misquoted lines from Shakespeare that Lopakhin taunts Varya with. "He doesn't know Shakespeare," answers LeG promptly. "He's never read it, you see." Miss Hagen offers the information that Varya seems to be adopted but that no reference is ever made specifically to that in the play, and Le Gallienne concurs. The company doesn't know this—Miss Hagen has a point in her favor.

Le Gallienne talks of various productions, the Moscow Art and the original casting, and the subsequent productions in Russia, those on the Continent, and even here, but certainly none mentioned more recently than twenty years ago, and the strange blend of foreign names, of French, of Russian, fall simply and easily from her tongue as if they were staples on a grocery list. The company is dazzled by her familiarity and her control, but she is too involved to notice or to care. As a direct result, there are no more questions, and the company begins to read. Act I, this time, each taking his own part. Le Gallienne: "I ask you only to read the lines, not like lines, let them come off the page. Find the words that carry the meaning of the line, and stress those, not each and every word you say. I always say to young actors, 'Take your line and write it out as if it were a telegram—as if you had to economize.' That way you learn what are the key words in each speech."

Moffat as Lopakhin and Miss Conolly as Dunyasha begin quietly, simply. Le Gallienne says she won't stop them, and then promptly stops them after the first three lines. "Don't rush. I think it's important to pick up our cues, but find the pauses within the lines. The spaces, the rests are as important as anything said. That's why Chekhov is so unlike anything else. You'll love doing it, there is just nothing like doing Chekhov for actors, because it's like music. And you have to find the music—the pauses are as important here as the rests are in music itself. Find these still moments within your lines, as well as between them. And darling," to Miss Conolly, "Dunyasha would never interrupt Lopakhin."

The reading picks up again. The company lean forward into their scripts with the listless concentration of a solitary breakfast. Le Gallienne stops Moffat again, with a point over the repeated "yeses" of Lopakhin. Keene Curtis attacks his role of Epikhodov with characteristic bluntness and directness, choosing the stammer that Le Gallienne has indicated in her reading. There are pauses by all to poke and ferret through the clumsy endless Russian names and syllables. Curtis goes on, admonished by Le Gallienne not to stammer all the time, but just on a certain sound or letter. "I once had a friend," she illustrates, "who stammered on the letter *l*. 'Miss L-l-l-le Gallienne. Or Vanil-l-l-la ice cream.' I used to wonder why he didn't switch to coffee." Keene continues, a bit shaken. Le Gallienne stops often, now, every few speeches.

Trish Conolly is straining hard, and somewhat off the mark in her first scene. She is physically against the stolid and bovine type of coarse peasant girl one pictures as Dunyasha, and she can't find her line. Miss Hagen reads her entrance unobtrusively, and the release of pressure comes with an enormous laugh by the company for the exchange between Le Gallienne as Charlotta and Sydney Walker as Pishchik. "My dog eats nuts, too." "Just imagine!"

Pamela Payton-Wright, APA's newest young actress, has a pleasant and honest feeling for Anya. She sits, wrapped in a raccoon coat, her light brown hair cascading around her face, soft, and clean, and very pretty. Betty Miller, who will be lovely as Varya, stumbles and stammers about, reading very badly, and Clayton Corzatte, in his most characterized role to date, that of the ancient servant Firs, indicates that his customary vocal attack, which makes him often hard to understand under the best of circumstances, promises to render him unintelligible now that he is muttering in the guise of an old man. Miss Hagen reads smoothly and extremely simply, in a low voice with a raspish hoarseness lacking in music, and giving her a sadly common feeling at this early stage. But she indicates great humor in her readings, and is obviously not trying to impress anyone unduly. The inimitable Sydney Walker lifts the reality of Pishchik straight from the page to the wonder and delight of the company, a clear example of dead-on casting which will alter very little between this first reading and the last time he ever performs the role. Richard Woods, cast in the plum and difficult role of Gayev, is strained and pinched, making an effort to do too little at this table, rather than too much.

Betty Miller stumbles over the Russian word "Mamotchka" and it is Uta Hagen who corrects her, not Le Gallienne. But Betty is helpless against all these florid Russian syllables—"Give her a week," laughs Ellis, and the company laughs approvingly—so that every time she comes to another Russian name she simply gestures perfunctorily to the center of the table. Her genuineness and lack of airs relaxes the company more, and we finish Act I. Le Gallienne promptly turns to Miss Hagen and asks,"Shall we go on?" The answer is bright and positive. "Yes!" Moffat exclaims in delight. "Twelve minutes! Can you believe that read in twelve minutes?!" "Was it? Was it really?" Ellis asks brightly. "No," says Moffat, and the company laugh easily over the joke.

Act II is begun with hardly a pause, and this time Keene Curtis gets laughs with stuttering on the *m*'s, especially from Le Gallienne, who confirms his choice. Miss Conolly finds a true and simple line now in her scene with Yasha, to her obvious delight. Miss Hagen is reading rapidly and naturally, copying Miss Le Gallienne's admonishment not to "act," and even on occasion copying a particular line reading that Le Gallienne had chosen earlier, her voice often sinking so low that it rasps softly without much sound. Ellis Rabb laughs genuinely at many of her readings. Moffat is warming both to the part and to the reading. Ellis himself reads Trofimov's big scene on the road extremely rapidly and nervously, but with an amazingly true instinct that indicates he has thought about the scene carefully—the rapidity betrays familiarity as well as his announced nerves.

The act finishes with a fine scene between Ellis and Miss Payton-Wright, and Le Gallienne stops the reading. There are a few small points left to be made. LeG discusses the harp-string sound. "In forty-four we didn't have tapes, of course, so the sound had to be made live. We had a gentleman who did it with a musical saw, I believe, but I was never awfully sure that it would occur at the right time. Perhaps Mr. Susa [the composer] can come up with something electronic, or what have you."

Miss Hagen has a misunderstanding about Gayev and Lyubov joking in the presence of Lopakhin: "Are they deliberately ignoring him and his news, or are they laughing because they aren't listening?" Le Gallienne asserts that in Act I, they are too happy to be united to be preoccupied with Lopakhin, and the reading is adjourned, the company filing off to dinners.

January 19: First time on blocking

The auditorium, stripped of all but three rows of seats, contains two upright pianos, a tall black ladder, hastily nailed tables and structures of scrap lumber. The walls, crusted and crumbling, are painted a robin's egg blue, and heavy dark mahogany chinoiserie abounds. The boxes are tattered pagodas, blackened and blistered as if from bombing. For this rehearsal, now that two days of straight reading and discussing have passed, the company has moved to a rehearsal hall in the Riviera Theatre at 96th Street and Broadway.

But although the Riviera is respectably showing *A Man for All Seasons* downstairs in the theater, upstairs an entirely different world exists. This is the old Japanese Gardens, a small reliquary of theater of an earlier day, once the prized possession of a man who, when he gave up his life, gave up the theater as well. Now all that is left is a blackened hole of an auditorium with three widely spaced rows of green leather seats pushed to the walls on either side, scrap pieces of lumber and hastily nailed scaffolding and mock-up tables. The crumbling proscenium shows evidence of gilt and chinoiserie, and high above the top arch, a stylized Fuji floats almost surreptitiously.

The stage walls are painted a somewhat bilious green halfway up only, but the stage is warmly illuminated. What lighting there is in the house comes from bald, staring spotlights hung under the balcony, each staring off in another direction, vacantly, aimlessly. The radiators hiss softly throughout the day, dimming the sounds of voices, softening the effect somewhat, as if the theater, the people, and the rehearsal were not quite taking place, but remembered in a dream. Le Gallienne strides about the stage, looking at chairs and indications of the set, dressed in a black sweater and a dark purple shift.

The company is about assembling, just before one o'clock, when Miss Hagen

charges in—"Am I late? Oh, God, it makes me so nervous. I'm usually twenty minutes early, so that when I am on time, I'm positive I'm late"—in a big black coat
which covers a gray plaid jumpsuit with a matching hat. She dumps her coat on a
chair and takes from her purse a pair of glasses with rims on the bottom only, heavy
dark plastic affairs that give her a charmingly cartoon touch.

Nancy Walker is present at the beginning of rehearsal, in a dark dress, her hair
smart and immaculately done, standing first to one side of the hall and then the
other, bobbing up and down a bit on her heels. Rumors are sweeping over the hall
that she is joining the company to play Charlotta and to cover Helen Hayes in *The
Show-Off*, but neither Ellis nor Norman nor any voice of authority is present to give
root to the rumors. LeG attempts to introduce Miss Hagen and Miss Walker, but
Hagen preempts her: "Nancy, what are you doing here?" She is told the rumor from
no less than the mouth of LeG herself, which gives the argument somewhat more
substance. Hagen trumpets, embracing Miss Walker, "We'll have a ball!" For the
next fifteen minutes, Miss Walker stands somewhat interestedly by, seemingly trying not to peer too intently at anyone peering back. The company is, by and large,
slightly in awe of her, and respectfully ignore her in the way everyone is ignored
until they have been introduced, or at least until the company knows why they are
there. A few members introduce themselves, but conversations die on the stalk, and
soon Miss Walker leaves.

Le Gallienne begins the rehearsal by working out the opening moves between
Dunyasha, played by Miss Conolly, and Lopakhin, played by Mr. Moffat. Hagen is
all charm and smiles, sitting on the side of the stage with Dick Woods, Keene Curtis, George Pentecost, and Clayton Corzatte, laughing and joking easily in whispers
while the rather difficult first moves are charted. Mingled with the soft coaxing
sounds of Le Gallienne and the replies and lines of her actors is the sibilance of
whispered jokes and that of the radiators, punctuated with the explosive aspirate
laughs of Curtis, who is most eagerly enjoying and encouraging the camaraderie
with Miss Hagen. On the other side of the stage, the understudies sit, checking the
blocking with more than usual interest. Alan Fudge, Joseph Bird, and Jimmy
Greene, and around the house several other actors stand in small groups, or apart.
Richard Easton, who was originally to play Epikhodov, is present on this occasion,
since Stephen Porter is double rehearsing *The Misanthrope* in a smaller room downstairs, and he, too, stays and looks on with interest.

At the outset, Le Gallienne has explained the set to the group, and now she begins to close in. She works very specifically—the moves, the business is part of the
same fabric to be realized in total from the very beginning. Speaking to Miss
Conolly, who plays the maid Dunyasha, she says, "Use the mirrors whenever you
can. Dunyasha's never tired of looking at herself." Curtis, as Epikhodov, enters.
LeG: "Let's find a reason why you drop the flowers. Have you thought of anything?"
Keene replies that he thought he could have been playing with them too far down
on their stems, which would make them unwieldy. He enters a beat before LeG is
ready and drops the flowers adroitly. Hagen laughs delightedly from the side, but
Keene must repeat it.

The downstage area is bristling with stage management. Two of the stage managers, Harley Hackett and Dan Bly, are busy making soft insistent sounds on their
scripts with pencil as they attempt to take down the moves. George Darveris, the

production stage manager, shoots strong reprimanding glances mingled with curiosity at Hagen and her pals, and moves busily about the hall. Keene, following both LeG and the script, omits a line, and LeG, who is without the script, supplies it and corrects him. He takes a cross onstage, saying "Squeak-squeak-squeak" to indicate the sound of his shoes. "Squeak-squeak-squeak," repeats Hagen, giggling from the side. She obviously likes him.

Le Gallienne is extraordinary. Her fast moves demonstrated to Conolly as Dunyasha are done with the rapidity and control of a woman half her age. The general entrance of the company is staged. Hagen enters on the build of the lines in a strong down-center position, and it is rerun for accuracy. Betty Miller, watching her script, misses her first line. Woods: "Are we wearing coats and mufflers on this entrance?" The corresponding exits are blocked. Moffat and Sydney Walker, in ebullient good spirits, bump stomachs in a mock embrace. Le Gallienne reblocks and reevaluates the blocking as soon as it is done. "Holy Christ," says stage manager Bly, erasing furiously.

The exit goes smoothly the second time. Conolly, backed into the down right corner, watches the family exit. Le Gallienne to her: "You'll be all right in the corner there, won't you?" Conolly: "I love it!" Betty Miller works smoothly in her scene with Pamela Payton-Wright, the first scene between the two sisters, taking long gasping inhalations, pulling up her shoulders and tapping her ankles together when she sits, but loosening up and filling her quiet charm in where she is comfortable. Le Gallienne is strict with her, trying to get her to simplify her moves physically.

On the repeat, Trish Conolly shows a splendid giggling relationship already when she laughs at Curtis/Epikhodov. George Pentecost, as Yasha, enters, and LeG indicates a mincing character, saying "I'd like you to find a rather 'swish' walk for Yasha." Conolly walks over to him, saying, "When you went away, I was that high!" Le Gallienne: "You must raise your hand only a few feet off the floor. Old ladies are always coming up to me and saying 'I was only that high when I saw you play Peter Pan,' and they're ten years older than I." She requests a saucer for Dunyasha to break which will scatter into many pieces. Clayton Corzatte enters, doing fussy little gestures around his wrists and reaching for a peculiar old man in First. LeG is warming to her task, and her inflections to the company—to Pamela: "Are you all right there, sweetie?" and "I think, darling Varya . . ."

She has not set this blocking and business before. Often as not the individual bits may have been cribbed from previous productions, but she proceeds quite organically, as is suggested by the situation. Blocking progresses, and when Anya exits closing the door, Sydney Walker burlesques as if the door had hit him in the nose. Moffat feels uncomfortable with a piece of business, and LeG allows a different timing. Now, while working, she tends to all the characters by their Russian diminutives—"Anychka, Varychka, etc."

Walker, as Pishchik, sings his song to Uta Hagen. LeG: "Darling Sydney," as she embraces him, "we mustn't let this seem to be a number. If it could come a little more out of the line." She looks so right on the stage. When she does a bit of business or assumes a position of another character, it has the authority of an engraving. The others are oblique and guarded, but LeG has lived intimately in this world. Her script is a heavy loose-leaf affair with pages of graph paper alternating the script upon which the moves are recorded in her neat, precise hand in terse sentences. She mentions the specific moves, often when a character rises or sits, but little else, and hardly any business at all. Onstage, she shows Sydney Walker the way in which Pishchik takes all of Lyubov's pills, executing it splendidly, and everyone laughs, so she does it again, even better. Sydney repeats the business with panache, making it indelibly his own, and equally funny. Then turning to Betty Miller, LeG reprimands her for moving and jerking so much. "There is an old Chinese saying—if you're standing, just stand, and if you're walking, just walk, but above all, don't wobble. I've always felt that's very good advice for actors."

Moffat's leave-taking as Lopahin is very formal and takes much time. He shakes hands with everyone onstage in silence, the idea of which delights him and the other actors. There is a break at 3:30 p.m. and this phase of rehearsal ends with a huge warm embrace of Miss Hagen by LeG. Relatively speaking, she is pleased with the progress so far, but makes a few sharp remarks pertinent to Ellis Rabb's absence. He is overworked and consequently tired, and she will permit it today, but won't allow him the weekend off to go out of town, since she wants him to rehearse on Sunday.

The company begin to rehearse again, and the stage is suddenly propped with cardboard cups of pale coffee. In explaining to Betty Miller why Varya is nervous about the noise waking up Anya, LeG calls Sydney's Pishchik a huge porpoise. Sydney erupts in luxurious laughter, and carried into his contagious spirit, LeG rushes to embrace him where he sits in the chair. When the actors have trouble with business at the windows, Le Gallienne says, "I've never done the play this way, with the windows there, so I especially wanted to ask your [Miss Hagen's] advice about it. I think, don't you, that Gayev and Lubov should use the downstage window, because of all this furniture in the way." Hagen concurs. As Miss Hagen prepares for her exit, LeG says to her, "Perhaps you have a reticule here on the table, which will fill the move to the door." Hagen whispers, "I've these two torn telegrams, and I thought I'd try to sneak them off with me." "Splendid!" crows LeG.

Hagen retracts somewhat to a speech with Gayev at the window, and prompts Woods on his next line. He points out that she has cut his cue, and Hagen does a little dance step and coyly chants, "Always whenever you correct another actor, it's your fault!" Le Gallienne has taken to applying the Russian diminutive names to Miss Hagen herself, calling her "Utka." In the scene between Lyubov and Trofimov, Miss Hagen stops on the line, "But, Petya, why have you grown so old and ugly." She says, "I know 'ugly' can be said so differently in Russian, but 'ugly'???" It is omitted, and Miss Hagen jots into her script, "Why have you grown so old and three dots." There is a general laugh, and the rehearsal goes on.

Offstage, Miss Hagen sips her coffee and tries line readings with silent shrugs of her shoulders as she jots notes in the margin of her script. At 4:50 the act is repeated once more. Miss Hagen watches the performances with more care than the others, especially Pamela Payton-Wright and the other women, with a look of familiar interest and the half-shadow of critique. Already this repetition has a quality which begins emerging. The relationships between the characters begin to take form, due in no small part to the fact that the majority of these actors have been playing together for years now, and the sensitivity of one actor to the other is extraordinary. Miss Hagen herself is strong and already interesting, moving easily and carefully, taking the moments as they come, rather than "acting" them.

January 23

For this rehearsal, the stage is cleared of extra chairs and of the stage management, who have moved their series of tables just off the edge of the stage and into the auditorium. Only LeG sits on the stage now, leaning on her elbows as she concentrates on the rehearsal before her. Miss Hagen, working through Act I, is off the book for the most part.

After the first scene, the general entrance occurs, and Nancy Walker enters and crosses out in a shocking pink shawl, which gets an enormous laugh of appreciation from the rest of the company. Corzatte, as Firs, is also off the book, but not without prompting. Nancy Walker proceeds to make her discoveries with the part of Charlotta, cautiously, simply, with so much honesty as to play completely away from her natural clown inclinations.

Betty Miller does not remember a move, and when she is called on it, expresses some confusion about why she moves at all. Crossly, LeG reprimands her, "Darling Varychka, you move because in that line you say you move. That's why you move." When blocking difficulties occur at the window, LeG complains that the windows are too narrow. The work is niggling, small, cramped, and the kind of rehearsal in which the total flow of the work suffers for the small problem areas to be worked out.

The company, for the most part, are either intensely involved with their own work or in a vague and somewhat playful frame of mind. Trish Conolly, who primarily loves to be working, and especially to be working well, has taken confidence and pleasure from her steady growth as the maid Dunyasha. She dramatizes her role to the other members of the company, blowing it out of proportion for comic effect. "What no one realizes is the tragedy of Dunyasha," she begins with a somewhat naughty gleam in her eye. "There she is alone, pregnant, and apparently no one has made any provision for her. I have a wonderful idea for the ending of the play, and once I've worked it out I intend to tell Miss Le Gallienne about it. You see, just after everyone has left and Firs lies down, Dunyasha reenters and finds Firs. She screams in terror." Trish backs away now, her eyes wide with fright and humiliation, clawing at her brow with her fingers, and dislodging a bit of her hair. "Then, suddenly, her labor pains begin, just subtly at first, but worse and worse, and she sinks, panting, to the floor. Curtain!" She is delighted with her game. "I told Ellis about it, and he thinks it should be a bit different. You see, she comes back and finds Firs, but she doesn't scream. He thinks that she backs away upstage with a maniacal gleam in her eye, then shouts, 'This house is mine!' Curtain. Don't you adore it?"

On stage, Miss Hagen is struggling with her lines, going through almost a physical agony of hammering the forgotten recently learned lines out of her head with the heels of her hands. At the end of the first act, Ellis Rabb enters for the first time, silent, stark, a marvelously dramatic figure dressed in tan slacks with a cocoa brown shirt and light high boots to match. He is staring curiously but intently at Hagen, and it is difficult to look at anyone but him for these first few moments.

Hagen herself is somewhat flamboyantly dressed this afternoon, in a deep green dress with turquoise chiffon knotted at her throat, and sporting a small Tyrolean-type fedora with a matching dark green band. One of the company in the house is heard to remark with genuine affection, "It's sort of a Pinocchio effect, don't you think?"

The rehearsals, heavily attended at first, have dwindled in spectatorship to a hardy few. Jennifer Harmon, who covers both Anya and Dunyasha at the moment, is present, as is Jimmy Greene, who sits occasionally reading *The New York Times* or quietly charting Clayton Corzatte's moves as Firs in the event that he will have to rehearse it. Keene Curtis, not needed onstage, either reads the *Times* intently or stretches his legs out between the wide aisles, and throwing his head back, naps easily.

The two journeymen, Kermit Brown, who has been awarded the plum of covering Ellis Rabb as Trofimov, and Jim Whittle, are still attending religiously, and the only new faces on this day are the designer, James Tilton, and his impeccably chic and rangy assistant, Paul Salimone. On stage, Dick Woods changes a move which is bothering him, and LeG is pleased with his choice. Gathering steam, he crosses to his exit, turns on his line, and can't find his place in the script. "Oh shit," he snaps irritatedly, stamping his foot in an involuntary complaint, then quickly recovering, he adds "Excuse me" to LeG, who guffaws at him encouragingly.

The scene between Varya and Anya follows, and Betty Miller's slow, painstaking assimilation begins to wear on LeG. "She's maddeningly slow," she mutters to her assistant, "but she needs patience, and God knows I've got plenty of patience." The rehearsal ends with a small enthusiastic word from Le Gallienne to all present. "It's been a marvelous week's work. Now, over the weekend, go over what we've been doing in your heads, and if anything doesn't sit right, make a note of it. We'll work through it slowly again, to make sure that you are comfortable with the moves and the business, but I think by and large we've done splendidly, and from now on, we start to work." She smiles, reaching for her omnipresent and minuscule Yorkshire terrier, and the company congeals into small conversational groups as they disperse.

January 26: Riviera Theatre

LeG is late, being detained, and the cast assembled wait aimlessly. For this rehearsal, long rehearsal skirts have been provided for the ladies, with the seeming exception of Nancy Walker, and the other women try them on while Miss Walker chats amiably with Ralph Williams, who understudies Yasha. Miss Hagen's skirt is slate gray, Miss Miller's a dark green, and Trish Conolly, who plays the maid Dunyasha, has a deep blue skirt with black velvet trim at the waist—"I'm the heroine of this play, you know," she crows. Pamela Payton-Wright is in dark purple with a small name tag pinned about mid-thigh which she ignores.

LeG arrives, grinning, a black knit stocking cap on her head, and surveys a bevy of new props on the Act I set, including a large candelabrum, which takes her into a complicated digression on cleaning candelabra. She puts an arm around Miss Conolly: "Trish, I've been thinking about Dunyasha . . ." and they drift away from the others, LeG nearly conducting her own comments with her expressive hands, and Conolly echoing the insistent little "yes-yes-yeses" she inevitably utters when she is listening, like an errant faucet.

Onstage, oblivious to the others, Clayton Corzatte works out a piece of business for himself as the aged Firs involving a small stool which he is to place under Miss Hagen's feet. Concentrating, Corzatte thinks carefully how an old man would move, and then proceeds to move slowly and deliberately, leaning weight on his hands when he bends down. Sydney Walker, moving buoyantly around the stage, announces his two new puns for the day: French for a "feeling-ful young girl—is fillet of sole." And German "for a shroud—tote bag!!"

On one side of the stage, Nancy Walker has finally found a spare rehearsal skirt and tries to get into it, but it proves too long and she rejects it for another, camping inconspicuously. On stage, Miss Hagen asks of LeG, "Can I smoke here at the table?" LeG: "Yes, you can smoke, Firs can bring on your cigarettes with the coffee." Le Gallienne turns to the stage management and the cast, who are now standing and waiting for instructions. "I thought today we'd take sections and re-work them—try to get some exactitude." Hagen nods enthusiastically. "I daresay before we get to the general entrance we'll redo this first bit." Miss Hagen inter-rupts, "Then we won't stand by until you tell us to." The stage clears, except for Donald Moffat and Trish Conolly. LeG walks over to Donald, saying, "I think we might as well clean up this first scene now." "I'd rather not clean it up yet," requests Moffat. "I don't want to start setting . . ." LeG interrupts him, "Not as it will be in performance, of course, but there are certain values I want to get out." Moffat be-grudgingly nods, feeling the underside of his new ginger beard which he is growing for Lopakhin. He turns suddenly in the doorway: "It's not even 'woolly' yet." Miss Le Gallienne, misconstruing him, answers, "Yes, it's farther along than that." Mof-fat grins grimly and goes to his place, tapping his chest. LeG calls after him, "Take this first line to yourself, not to Dunyasha. Then turn and ask her the time."

Moffat begins, very specifically indeed, in spite of his caution, and most effec-tive, pausing, visualizing, taking his time with the quiet, oblique authority that makes him nearly always interesting to watch. There is a stop, to clear up Dunya-sha's intricate business, and they begin again. LeG smokes absently, watching Conolly and Moffat.

The rest of the company is very still today, lost in their individual scripts but for the most part watching the scene with a concentrated involvement. Much of the gay camaraderie of the first rehearsals has faded now, and the company are as inter-ested in the progression of the others as themselves. In the first row of seats in the auditorium sits premier danseur Jacques d'Amboise of the New York City Ballet. Mr. d'Amboise is observing the rehearsals, and is dressed in a heavy-knit red sweater. His presence bespeaks the quiet kind of mystery which surrounds these rehearsals. More perhaps than at any previous APA production, and with first Uta Hagen and then Nancy Walker arriving, Mr. d'Amboise's attendance is taken for granted by the company, where in an earlier productions, he might have caused a sensation.

Onstage, Keene Curtis as Epikhodov makes his entrance carrying awful plastic flowers and drops them phonily at Conolly's feet. LeG demonstrates that he is pushing the move, rather than merely opening his hand. As the actors prepare to go back, Le Gallienne admonishes Trish, "Pick up your lines in this first scene, especially when Donald must take his time. I don't want the play to start like a funeral, because people always expect Chekhov to be like a funeral. Do you want to do it again?" They do. "That's what we're here for." Trish Conolly hangs back, a studied puzzled look on her face. LeG: "What's worrying you?" Conolly giggles, about to begin fussing over a piece of business and aware that Miss Le Gallienne is onto her game. Laughing, Le Gallienne interrupts her before she can speak: "Stop worrying! Get on with it!" and she slaps Trish on the bottom. The next time through, Keene enters and does the flower-dropping correctly, but Conolly muffs it. "Don't take so long a pause in the line," Le Gallienne reprimands. "I'm having trouble seeing myself in the glass," fusses Trish. LeG laughs shortly. "Yes, but you won't!"

Trish Conolly's giggles as Dunyasha are superbly infecting. She is getting the blend of harshness and delicious spirit which will work so well for her and for the production. Le Gallienne indicates the difference between the giggling in the first scene and the mock sophistication which will come later in the play, and she helps Conolly discover that Dunyasha is perhaps more the little girl in this scene than Conolly has been playing. Trish gets a new, more ingenuous line on the scene. Meanwhile, Moffat is illustrating to Keene Curtis an artificial movement of the arms, which might be right for Epikhodov, strident and exaggerated. Conolly listens intently to LeG, asking another of her "silly questions" with her head tilted on one side, running a nervous hand over her determinedly knit brow.

"Once more," says LeG to the stage at large, "and we go on." She turns to Moffat. "Donald, don't rush your first lines. Establish the entrance more clearly, don't feel you have to dash on." The actors are in place, waiting for her, and she turns downstage at her chair, saying, "The curtain goes up . . . there is a little moment . . . now!" Moffat enters, just right this time. The scene is run swiftly, and Curtis, preparing to make his comic exit, falls as he should, but in doing so, pushes the chair off its marks, and LeG stops the scene, indicating that should that happen in performance, it would be natural for Conolly as the maid to replace it. Conolly does so, and it works so effectively that they both agree to incorporate the business whether Keene literally moves the chair or not.

The company make their general entrances. No one carries a script now except Sydney Walker, and his is folded under his arm. On the first time there is great naturalness, warmth, and flow. Hagen takes a minutely delayed entrance, and sees the nursery. Her reaction is very moving. Nancy Walker gently plays in and around Charlotta, not spoofing nor extending, but working every bit as organically as anyone in the hall. Pamela Payton-Wright is working for more variety, and new colors begin to come through for her now, as offstage, Hagen studies her intently. Betty Miller enters as Varya, and promptly goes up in her line, so LeG uses the break to clear up some business.

Pamela Payton-Wright betrays a nervous quality in the first scene, touching her lips with her fingers and giggling, and some of this is identifiably usable for her exhaustion and her apprehension at returning home after so long. Le Gallienne corrects her emphasis on "I felt so sorry for *Maman*, too," to "I felt so *sorry* for Maman, too!" Pamela makes a wry face, indicating that it doesn't feel right yet, but LeG comforts her. Moffat does his "moo" offstage, and Miss Hagen breaks into loud, appreciative laughter.

Le Gallienne goes back in the scene once again, simplifying the nervous physical characteristics of Betty Miller. "I may devil you to simplify it," she says kindly, "but it will make it better." Betty has trouble with timing the seeing of Pamela's "bee-brooch" and LeG discusses its significance. "In that period, so much was sad and tragic in their lives that the slightest detail can change the focus, a hat, even a brooch. And don't break up the line into two parts, do it all together, or the gas runs out of it: 'You've got a new brooch, like a bee!'" The scene continues, with Betty struggling consistently for her lines, and LeG prompts softly under her.

Miss Hagen reenters, crossing into the room, and LeG interrupts the scene. "Utka, do you think it is necessary to go so far into the room?" It isn't. "Firs, darling, the steps must be fast, but the distance you cover is tiny, as if he were a little lame in one leg, perhaps, with terrible rheumatism." She demonstrates for Corzatte, who immediately practices. Le Gallienne discusses the problem of fatigue for the characters, telling how difficult and exhausting traveling was at this time, and exactly what a journey from Paris to Russia would entail, and the company is amazed to think of such distress over simple travel. LeG encourages Pamela to collapse in any chair she gets near. The day is one of adjustment. Bits of business and moves are changed as the progressing life of the production dictates. At one point, Miss Hagen lights the wrong end of a Russian cigarette, and it flares and sputters. From the corner of the set, Dick Woods baits her: "I'ver heard of scene-stealing before . . ." There is general laughter at Miss Hagen's misfortune. "That's what happens when I don't wear my glasses," she laughs back at them. She works on a thoroughly organic basis, getting her ideas with great precision and clarity from what she and the audience both hear, what she is told.

The day has great spaces, and Le Gallienne takes individual actors, Conolly, Miller, or Rabb, on small rather cozy strolls around the stage, murmuring to them things that are not meant for the others to hear. Ellis himself, as Trofimov, enters and the rather complicated beats of his greeting Lyubov for the first time are haltingly worked out. Miss Hagen is very touching as she breaks down to him and a small thoroughly realized moment has erupted. The cast begins to show enormous consistency in their style of playing, having to do with the individual stage of rehearsal as well. Three actors play somewhat outside this style at this point: Corzatte, who patently overdoes his "old man" characterization to find and experiment the difficult part of Firs, and Sydney Walker, whose enormous energy pushes him above the level of the others, both through the stimulation of the role and the fact that having played the play before, and being intimate with it, he may be more ready to let out steam than the others. Betty Miller, who is troubled by the lines at this point, is betrayed into jerky, nervous movements, and small faces she puts on, which tend to take her to another level than the strong, forthright note which has been key-set by Miss Hagen. But the common denominator of performance is already evident.

In the last scene of the first act, LeG's comments are sprayed at random to encompass a whole spectrum of problems and actors. (To Betty Miller) "That's awfully clumsy, darling, the way you do that. Perhaps I can help you." (To Pamela Payton-Wright) "Anychka, darling, don't come farther than the door, then when you move, make it a sharp one." (Back to Miller) "The move on 'Anychka's in the doorway' is all in one. Smooth it out, and don't go at such an angle." (To Pamela) "Your rehearsal skirt should not be that long, no longer than your ankles, since you're too young for a full-length skirt." (To Miller) "And if yours were that long, which it should be—you have too much work to do around the house to have a skirt that long dragging after you—you must never touch your skirt. Never! Never! You look as though you are aware you have on a long skirt. You live in them, you know." Pamela asks, "What are the bells that Anya is talking about?" LeG answers, "The trains. All night long, the bells ring for the various stops. 'En voiture, mesdames et messieurs!'" she proclaims loudly, laughing at her own accuracy.

A break is taken, and the stage management announces that in five minutes the first act will be repeated. There is a short, murmured conference between LeG and Hagen, and LeG turns to the house and announces, "Miss Hagen would rather do Act II." "That sounds just terrible," crows Miss Hagen. While the requests are being voiced, Mr. Rabb indicates that on the days he is to play *Pantagleize* in the evening, he would rather not rehearse until six o'clock, which doesn't give him sufficient time to rest up for the evening. Perhaps some of the rehearsals could be held from twelve to five, instead of one to six.

The set is cleared for Act II. Action is delayed somewhat for a discussion of a small purse and coins which Miss Hagen must carry with her. Amid the fussing with the coins, and the working out of how they are to be spilled on the ground, LeG says, "Do you know when I played in San Francisco in stock at the old Alcazar, I was paid in gold?!" Murmurs of disbelieving from the astonished listeners. "$168.00 a week in gold and silver. You really felt that you were being paid."

Miss Hagen volunteers, "I once played for gamblers in Florida, and they paid me in stacks of ones and fives with rubber bands around them. I so distrusted them that I made them count them out." She takes a belligerent stance, and waving a finger as at a naughty child, she admonishes, "There! Count them out, every one!" She is having problems getting the coins to drop from the purse in the right places, so that they roll nearest Woods, sitting on a bench. She repeats the action a few times, kicking them around when they refuse to roll in the right direction, relaxed and comfortable.

Moffat as Lopakhin has his fit of anger, and is persuaded to sit by Lyubov. Miss Hagen stops briefly to assert that she feels the need to work out more specific and spacious beats to accomplish the progression from soothing Lopakhin into the long and difficult speech which is coming up. The moment is repeated to accommodate her, and she launches into the big speech about her sins, her pale blue-rimmed glasses jerked first down to the end of her nose as she darts looks about the stage, then back into place as she quietly, energetically explores the text of which she is not yet completely in control. Her gestures in this rehearsal process are broad, as if she is deliberately banging against the retaining sides of the part to see exactly where the structures lie.

The values are unclouded, and yet she worries about taking too much time. "Goody," she remarks when LeG permits her a choice she requests. "Can I fluberty-bub through it again?" And once more the warm, direct eyes peer over the rims of the glasses, searching for the truth somewhere on the floor before her, then, finding it, going on. Nothing is set, it's all very natural and yet fluid. Still, the specific transitions, and the moments which depend on others, or upon which the others depend, are already solidly in place. Her own interior beats are still being allowed to "happen." She misses a cue for Moffat and baits him with it, joking, but he, perhaps sensing her power, does not laugh back.

Corzatte enters, muttering like an old man but striding youthfully, and LeG stops him to reprimand him for his oversight. Ellis Rabb gets physically con-fused as he probes his long and difficult narrative on the pride of man. "Where am I going over here?" he questions, an unmistakable note of confusion in his voice. Le Gallienne stares intently at the floor, searching as she walks in a small circle. "You might make a pattern over here to follow. One is quite apt to do that sort of thing while thinking heavily." It has a marvelous accuracy about it, and Ellis accepts it as justification enough for the move.

"There goes Epikhodov," sighs Miss Hagen. "There goes Epikhodov," echoes Pamela Payton-Wright. A slight pause, then Ellis answers, "Yes." Woods, staring off right, offers, "Ladies and gentlemen, the sun has set," and in these few lines the unmistakable voice of Chekhov speaks to everyone in the auditorium. The haunt-ing effect of the harp string breaking occurs for the first time, is discussed, and the mood sustains, pliant and thin, until the entrance of the tramp, when it is vulgarly broken. Kermit Brown, the understudy, repeats the scene, purposely grotesque, and better the second time. Then LeG takes Betty Miller aside for strong criticism which ends in laughter and an embrace, and Miller gallantly laughs back, looking around a bit nervously, as if she hears her own voice laughing and doesn't really believe it.

January 28: Act I is set up, but the second scene, which is literally Act II of the Chekhov script

The rehearsal begins on a small, almost intimate level, since only a few people are called at the beginning, and the seeming masses of the company are to arrive gradu-ally throughout the day. Now Trish Conolly and Keene Curtis, joined today by Ralph Williams, who will rehearse Yasha to give George Pentecost a badly needed day off, are met onstage by Nancy Walker and LeG, while the details of the road set are discussed and measurements and the raking are all noted. Curtis quietly picks on the guitar he carries, somewhat hesitantly, plaintively asserting to whoever will listen, "I get my first lesson tomorrow," but with his intuitive musical sense, he finds notes and even an occasional chord which seem right.

The rehearsal begins, and LeG sits downstage alone. Next to her, in a roomy handbag, her tiny Yorkshire terrier Nana sits, unattended for a change, with only a small, alert furry head showing above the zippered corner. LeG begins by setting the places in the scene where Yasha and Dunyasha should be kissing. "One place where Yasha and Dunyasha have a kiss, I think, is where Epikhodov says 'I should like to talk to you, Dunyasha,' then, there is one of those near throws to the floor by them," then, standing near Keene, and not even taking a breath, she notices, "Is that a six- or a seven-string guitar?"

She directs Nancy Walker to begin her lines to Yasha and Dunyasha, and then, getting no response, to turn out in isolation. Miss Walker queries, "I shouldn't look to see if they are involved, should I?" LeG: "I'd take it for granted." She then digresses for a moment about when she was ten years old and she would be taken to the park by her governess, who was always going off into the bushes with her lover. Le Gallienne knew nothing of what was going on, and was somewhat pleased to be left alone. She would find a place where four different paths converged, and there she would put on a whole show for whoever was in the neighborhood. She sang songs in German, French, and English, and afterward she would pass the hat, often collecting as much as five francs. The company enjoy these small diversions, and she pulls herself back into the work by indicating that traditionally Charlotta carries a gun and eats a cucumber. Nancy Walker decides to accept both. LeG answers that if she had played Charlotta, she wasn't going to use the cucumber, since she has too many bridges in her mouth—and opening to show the actors she adds quickly, "not that any of them come out . . ."

Miss Walker begins, honest and interesting, while Trish Conolly and Williams flirt arbitrarily upstage. A moment is reached where both are to laugh and divert Charlotta, and the laugh they offer is not strong enough, so the scene is begun again. LeG urges Keene to find a series of minor yet pleasing chords to play on his guitar, but not anything that would prove distracting. The second time through, the mood works well, and Miss Walker is smooth and strong. Continuing, LeG indicates which [part] of the song that Curtis will sing is truly sung, and which is merely hummed. She sings for him, in a sweet and charming voice, and showing Miss Conolly where to enter into the singing, she indicates a sweet ornamentation to be added. The company try what she has suggested, and the improvisation is charming and right. Curtis wonders how astringent to be on his line, "to a man mad with love . . ." and LeG answers him, "For Epikhodov, we must not have a comic trying to be funny, but a man who is funny in spite of himself."

In this rehearsal, as in those past, LeG seizes on a casual chance gesture or move to solidify the relationships that the actors are finding with each other which strengthens the mood and atmosphere. Miss Walker exits. Like Miss Hagen, she takes her time and works for an extraordinary sense of truth and logic. LeG comments, "It's beginning to get some human values, in spite of Trish's dissatisfactions." All laugh, since the complaints and pickings of Miss Conolly are a constant and not necessarily irritating diversion for all. Continuing, LeG asks without even looking at Trish, "What is it?" Trish giggles self-consciously but asserts herself. "I don't know, I'll tell you later." LeG notices the blouse and rehearsal skirt that Miss Conolly is wearing. "What are you wearing in this scene? A blouse? Because Yasha could have unbuttoned a few buttons, it would give him a good business there."

Williams, continuing, fumbles for the slightly coy line "You're a peach!" "You're a peach," giggles Miss Walker on the side of the stage. She is playing with a traveling rug with which she is to perform tricks in the next act. A break is taken, and Trish Conolly presses LeG for more information about her own world and the ambiguous status of Dunyasha. Le Gallienne is marvelous in this respect, too, a font of miscellaneous information about the living details, and Conolly is an actress who seems to need constant reassurance about what might appear meaningless and unusable to another actor, or even a spectator. The scene between Yasha and Dunyasha is run again, and at its conclusion, LeG confirms that the work has a true basis now, which will make it easy to get faster and to assimilate into the personalities of the actors.

Miss Hagen has arrived. She has brought with her today six or seven impressionistic postcards, reproductions of Renoir, Monet, and even van Gogh, and she passes them around, describing them as if they were authentic documentation of the lives of the characters which Chekhov never put onstage—Anya and her on the grass, Lopakhin passing with a hat on, a van Gogh tree in blossom which must be out of the orchard. She shows the postcards first to her colleagues and then to LeG herself, with obvious delight, like a prize student doing extra work. There is nothing self-conscious in her delight or belief, it is all quite charming.

She makes her entrance with Woods and Moffat, not carrying her script this time, and has the same difficulty dropping the coins. The scene is halting and hesitant. LeG offers from the edge of the stage, "Shall we go back and try it again? One always gets off on the wrong foot. How often in performance I've wished I could just go back and try it a second time." Everyone laughs that affirmative laugh of recognition and they begin again. Moffat confesses that he feels uncomfortable about his entrance, and LeG helps him with his business, listening intently and confirming his opinions. Hagen tries her business with the purse and coins again, and this time everything falls out, including the telegram she will need later. "I just must work with what I get when I get it to justify why I drop it, and what I drop." She spits the explanation out rapidly, not really thinking what she is saying. Le Gallienne suggests that she drop a few coins accidentally and then literally throw the bag down. "There, you see!" says Miss Hagen, trying it, and flinging the purse at her feet. It has just the right note of petulant truth about it, and the rehearsal can continue.

Miss Hagen pursues the long speech she was sketching with the script yesterday. Today it is infinitely more touching, right and fluid. When LeG makes a suggestion, she pleads that she is often likely to settle too soon on a choice, and she is trying to keep free and open and to make the emotional seem real. Then LeG turns to Moffat, explaining Lopakhin's discomfort in his relationship with Varya. "He shies away, like a . . . wild stallion!" She gives out with a long, strong laugh, peering at him, obviously enjoying her own analogy. It does not strike quite so responsive a chord in Moffat. Corzatte totters on as Firs, and when he speaks his line LeG stops him, saying "It was better the other day, make it more matter-of-fact." He does so.

There is another discussion of the broken harp string, and LeG repeats the story she told at the first reading of her previous use of a musical saw. "I don't know what sound Mr. Susa will come up with," she says, bemused. Miss Hagen interrupts: "The soundman's name is Susa?" LeG: "The composer . . . yes . . ." Hagen: "Oh, how divine!"

Later, in the scene, Anya and Trofimov have the concluding moments, and LeG works patiently with Rabb and Pamela Payton-Wright. "Anya," she says, addressing Pamela, "there is a thought track connected with her youthful disappointment in Trofimov, wishing perhaps he weren't quite so much 'above love.' That will help you sit right at this moment." Then, later, "You need more variety here, it's so much better throughout, but we must stay right on it." She puts an arm around Pamela, then sinks to her side, talking softly, conspiratorially of how at Anya's age girls were still more children than young women. Pamela reacts to LeG's promise of what will happen to her in the role by smiling up at LeG: "That's comforting." The reading of her own line is pure Anya.

Ellis, working with his script, says, "Think of it, Varya . . ." "Anya!" Pamela corrects him, giggling, and he sinks to her side on the stump. Le Gallienne turns to the stage management. "Is it possible to sit two on that stump at a time?" Ellis smiles at her: "I have a very small ass." LeG, waiting for the stage managers to produce the sizes of the properties, says pensively, "Yes, very small . . . enviably small . . . beauti-fully small, I should say!" Everyone laughs delightedly, and it is decided that they will sit together.

Through this scene, Miss Hagen and Miss Walker whisper energetically off-stage. Rabb sentimentalizes a line and shoots a remark to LeG: "I'm sorry, I didn't mean that." She laughs approvingly. A break is taken, and Ellis walks over to Le Gallienne. "I'm so sorry I don't know it, but this past week has been hectic . . ." "Oh, for heaven's sake," she interrupts, "don't be ridiculous." "It's so frustrating with this play," Ellis says, moving offstage with her, "not knowing it, the words and all." LeG places a hand on the small of his back. "Yes, it's frustrating to oneself . . ."

The scene is rerun, and Le Gallienne leaves the stage and sits in the auditorium, cradling the Yorkshire in one hand and watching in a detached manner. She takes no notes at this point. Leaning to her assistant, she confides, "The structure is pretty much there already, and it will work quite well, I think. This is the point when the director must be terribly patient, while they are still fumbling for words. You can't hurry them up now, and you can't set rhythms and tempi until they are absolutely on top of every word." She sighs, stroking the tiny dog, "Yes, it's a time when you need incredible patience." A small, hard glint comes into her eyes, and she cocks her head at nobody in particular. "I've got lots of patience," she reasserts.

The third act is set up. Now, rather than talking idly on the sidelines, the actors are more inclined to do their homework during someone else's scene. Ellis Rabb sits in the down-right corner of the stage, legs crossed, leaning into his script as he wills the words into his mind. Far back in the murky rear of the auditorium, under the bald, bleak lights beneath the balcony, Donald Moffat paces, speaking silently, and gesturing wildly in his characteristic style, swinging an arm stiffly from the elbow, loping ahead, and running a hand through the shocks of dark blond hair. Miss Ha-gen, seated at a table in the upstage corner of the stage, stares expressively at the floor, her script opened and seemingly neglected on her lap, changing the looks in her eyes without moving her lips, as if her rehearsal homework is done deep, deep inside.

Well into Act III, Ellis hits a snag when Varya baits him about being suspended from the university, and he heatedly discusses the relative tension of the characters at this point in the drama. His impetus is to rise to Varya's teasing, as she does to his, but Le Gallienne asserts that it is Lyubov who gets under his skin, not Varya. Actually, he doesn't give a damn for Varya's baiting. Betty Miller, caught between Miss Hagen and Rabb, has trouble with her exit, and LeG works and reworks it for her. "Get your next line from Lyubov's eyes, darling," and Miss Miller tries, turn-ing first too late, then too soon. LeG gets a bit impatient with her. "Give yourself time to see her eyes!" "She did," defends Miss Hagen, "very clearly that time."

In midthought, LeG turns to Ellis, saying "Use the world 'banalities' more. It's a wonderful low-type word." She moves over to him, acting the moment in her own way, "I'm not interested in such . . . 'banalities'!" she says, spitting out the word as if it is foul. This sequence between Trofimov and Lyubov is worked slowly, pains-takingly. Miss Hagen is in and out of the mood, maddened like the others by her dependence on the script. She seeks a new choice for a line reading, but is unsure that she can communicate it. She wants the line "Don't say anything, Petya" to mean that he is not to talk to anyone about her revelation. "You know how you talk to young people," she says, then she demonstrates her point by improvising vigorously and desperately, " 'Christ! don't say anything about this,' and they run off and tell the first person they see." LeG muses, pleased, "One must be very careful of young people!" Miss Hagen is entreated by LeG not to hurry her values and to take time in working everything out. With an enormous sigh, she extols the virtues of this leisurely rehearsal period, and the luxury of time that can be taken. The difficult waltzing sequences are briefly sketched—Trofimov and Lyubov, then Trofimov, and Anya, then Pishchik and Lyubov, and Miss Hagen, smoking her French Gitanes, scatters the special pungent smoke after her, leaving, as she points out, almost an entirely different world behind her.

The act progresses in this way with LeG working very specifically and stopping often until Donald Moffat enters as Lopakhin for his big scene where he confesses having bought the cherry orchard. He has done his preparation carefully earlier in the back of the theater, and he comes on prepared to try the scene with all stops out. He stutters, stammers, but as the character, and not fumbling for his lines, alternately belligerent and grossly drunk, and he is enormously moving, as the rehearsal hall quiets down and concentrates on what he is doing. Le Gallienne moves back, allowing him to try it without stopping. On his exit, suddenly, and without seeming provocation, he executes a brief, grotesque dance, and doing so, falls against the tiny table upon which a vase or a glass will stand. Righting himself, he slaps the table and exits, saying almost bitterly, "I can pay for everything." Anya rushes into the room, followed by Trofimov, and still LeG doesn't stop them. Miss Payton-Wright takes Miss Hagen in her arms, speaking softly, gently of a new life and a new joy. Miss Hagen raises her head for the first time since Moffat confessed having bought the orchard, and tears are streaming down her face. Pamela cradles her, saying softly, ". . . and joy, pure joy will fill your heart." "Curtain," says the stage manager softly, and no one speaks. No one moves.

January 29: Rehearsal begins at the top of III

LeG calls "Cavaliers à genoux," and Sydney Walker echoes "à genoux!" For some inexplicable reason, Sydney is wearing red track shoes with white stripes on the sides. When LeG breaks to talk to Ellis Rabb about his reactions to Pishchik, Sydney, seated, pantomimes going up on his toes, making his point to the stage management—"the red shoes!" In turn, Nancy Walker has a small hand puppet which looks like one of the Campbell's Soup kids. "I hit it with a hammer," she says, doing a little time step while she waits for her entrance. The work is slow today, and largely a repetition of yesterday's problems and yesterday's mistakes, while all the actors flounder about for their lines, Ellis, about to waltz on with Miss Hagen, quips, "Will someone please give Marge and Gower their cue?" and everyone laughs appreciatively.

LeG is going very slowly today, especially in the difficult beats of Lopakhin and Gayev's entrance. Some tension is evident. Hagen and Woods communicate a point of blocking so silently, they seem to be speaking only with their eyes. "Let's do it, let's just do it," Moffat urges, who doesn't like stopping often once he begins working on a series of beats. LeG demonstrates Varya's flinging the keys at Lopakhin's feet. She is nearly ferocious as she sketches it out. "Like most saintly people, she can be quite a hellion." Moffat proceeds hot and cold with his big scene, and LeG calls him on the the the use of too many upward inflections, which she feels is habitual.

LeG, explaining the end of the act between Anya and Lyubov, takes Hagen's hands. "Your hands are so cold," says Hagen. Halfway back to her chair, LeG remembers, and says, "That's because . . ." and Hagen finishes with her . . . "your heart is so warm!" A laugh, and an embrace between them before the scene can continue. At the end of the act, LeG and Hagen take another "little walk" with Hagen embracing LeG's shoulder and LeG speaking soundlessly, barely moving her lips as they discuss Lyubov's scene with Lopakhin.

Act IV: Rabb plays his search for his galoshes, and Betty Miller flings a tattered pair of pink satin toe shoes onstage, the only available props. Rabb picks them up, muttering, "They aren't my galoshes anyway," and then adds, "they're my toe shoes!" The house breaks up. A curious thing has happened with the actors' clothes. In the opening rehearsals, one was quite conscious of what an individual actor was wearing, as if the individual actor was defining a personal statement and asserting himself at the outset, particularly true of Hagen, Rabb, Woods, Payton-Wright, and even on occasion LeG herself. But now the actors' clothes have gone inexplicably monochromatic, except for the mint green or shocking pinks of Nancy Walker, and an anonymous quality is evident, as if not the actors, but the characters themselves were waiting for ideas from the designer, and preferred no choice by the actor himself.

In analyzing the moves between Lopakhin and Trofimov, LeG recites the story of Etienne de Crux, whom she saw in Paris years ago in a play about Pasteur stand for twenty minutes with his hands in his pockets without moving, but always fascinating because of the variety and articulation of thought alone. LeG admonishes Pentecost to restrict his moves as he drinks all the champagne, for big moves make him more the peasant, whereas clean, neat gestures with the champagne glasses are subtler and hence funnier. Rabb and Hagen laugh energetically offstage, enjoying each other enormously.

Miss Hagen and Woods enter—she makes an idle, subconscious gesture with her necklace, and with a look of recognition, asks for a lavaliere watch. Sydney enters as Pishchik, and LeG interrupts him to remind him of being very happy in this scene. "Otherwise, you won't get your switch." The note rings a bell for Sydney. "Oh yes," he says pleasantly—"Right now, I'm just being exhausted." Around three o'clock, rehearsal gremlins begin to set in, it being a slow day. Nancy Walker rises and tap-dances softly by the proscenium, staring down at her feet and lost in thought. Trish Conolly wanders aimlessly onstage, making little faces and placing first the water pitcher, then a cup on her head. Donald Moffat does little half-dance steps, catching one eye, then another.

January 30: 4 o'clock

Yesterday's work is repeated. Everyone seems surer, especially Betty Miller, who is very moving in confrontation with Lopakhin. Somehow Keene Curtis is moving with a stiff leg. LeG watches Clayton Corzatte go to lie down, moving imperceptibly with him as she acts simultaneously with him.

LeG calls the company together. "Thanks for the wonderful way you've worked. Thursday, Utka will be absent, so we'll do bits and pieces, which won't involve Sydney, and we can do without Woods, if that must be his day off." Friday LeG will be absent, and her associate will run the rehearsal. "It's going to be a good show, and thank God we have time. No scripts, now, and Miss Walker, you must start using your dog." Nancy Walker cringes. LeG insists that she must make friends, and tells the story of a Manchester terrier and Wilfred Lawson as Wagner. The dog, "Chico," hated him, and he never troubled to make friends with it. In this case, LeG asserts how important the relationship between Charlotta and the dog is, since it's her only friend. Rehearsal is over, and Nancy Walker goes over to Pamela's dog, Grindl, but without much conviction.

February 1: LeG works small details, bits and pieces
February 2: LeG is absent
February 4: The first run-through

The company are nearly all on time, and the day begins with LeG explaining that today will not be a "bogey-performance," but just to see where we are. They may feel free to stop if they wish, although they shouldn't be encouraged to, and she won't stop them unless there is a disaster of some kind. The company sit in absolute silence to the sides of the stage, not reading, not studying, not drinking coffee, but concentrating on the opening moments between Moffat and Miss Conolly. Uta Hagen wears a fur coat over her rehearsal clothes, and laughs loyally at Miss Conolly's giggling. Except for the quiet, insistent rhythms of the first scene, the only sound is the percussive tattoo of Grindl, Miss Payton-Wright's dog, who plays Charlotta's pet in the play, as she dances nervously backstage, her toenails clattering about on the stage.

The general entrance is begun, and Grindl barks with excitement. Woods ad-libs offstage, "Even the dog is happy to be home," and the company enters. From the back of the house comes Ellis Rabb's laughter as he revels in Nancy Walker's entrance with the dog. For the most part, the work is extremely honest and clean. The company, unencumbered by scripts, begin achieving a true sense of ensemble, and the action flows smoothly. James Greene has replaced Corzatte as Firs for this rehearsal, and although he carries his script, he is very accurate about moves and business. However, the timing is missed when he places the footstool for Miss Hagen, and as she is always uncertain about this sequence, she fumbles a bit for the lines. In the first act, both Moffat and Woods also trip over rough spots that have plagued them through the past weeks. Moffat swings his arms a bit, and hops on one foot as he asks for his line, like an impatient athlete, and Woods stamps his foot with a mighty, ringing "Goddammit!" before he can continue. Darveris calls "Curtain." No sound offstage or on. LeG speaks silently, "I guess we'd better go on," and the stage management scurry to move the furniture.

LeG has low words with James Tilton, the designer, who points out differences between what the cast appears to be doing and what they actually can do on the set. LeG mutters that "the cast is gabbling. They've lost all the musical phrasing. But God, that's natural." The second act goes smoothly. Rabb had learned his lines, and even he has forsaken his script. In his long speech on the Pride of Man, he strains to remember, stopping his ambling pace across the stage to lean back in his tracks, his hand on his brow, as if by bending back he can recover a line he has merely passed by. He gets his cue and continues.

Act III: Nancy Walker is still skipping the early tricks as Charlotta, and as she maneuvers the traveling rug to make Anya and Varya appear, she swings it wide and knocks down a 1 x 2 post which indicates one of the arches. "I brought down the house," she mutters softly, turning around. "She brought down the house!" echoes Miss Hagen, laughing to Ellis.

Payton-Wright misses her entrance to tell Lyubov about the rumor of the cherry orchard being sold, and scrambling for the stage she whispers, "I'm sorry." She runs to Hagen, earnestly, with the line. Hagen inexplicably laughs in her face, which nearly breaks Pamela up and does cause Pentecost and Rabb to laugh a good deal. Moffat is wonderful in the big scene, and Pamela makes tears come to the eyes of a few standing around. The set is cleared, and Pamela and Hagen stand alone on the set, Hagen talking to Pamela softly and insistently about her last moment. Pamela smiles, pleased with what she has heard, and Hagen kisses her as they walk off.

Act IV: Just as a small orchestra truly playing the music for the first time forget the notes as they discover the line, the company grow progressively warmer and better. By Act IV, the breathing spaces begin to appear in the action. Scenes show an inclination of paying off, and when Moffat fails to propose to Betty Miller, the stage management involuntarily cluck to themselves, a concession of being touched. Dan Bly obliges with a soft high whistle, and Darveris calls curtain. LeG asks for ax sounds and the happy work song, and the run-through is completed by 3:30 p.m.

The Notes, by LeG: "Extremely useful for the first go at it. Useful and funnily enough, the last act was the one you seemed to settle down into. The other scenes seemed rushed. At the moment, it lacks orchestration and music—it is within your own—in a long speech for want of a better word—in your own speeches that those rhythms be better." (LeG, her back to the auditorium, gives the notes while wrapped in a light purple shawl with darker fringe.)

To Conolly: "Open the curtains earlier. Strip the giggles, so there aren't so many, and when they come, they are more effective."

To Moffat: "[You] put an extra 'yes' in earlier, and watch that habit."

To Curtis: "The dropping of the flowers looks phony, but the falling down was good. Also, as an actor, you should be bolder in the scene with Lopakhin. It's too pausey."

To Conolly: "'He loves me to distraction,' a phrase that is not Dunyasha's, is lost in the general flutteriness."

To Curtis: "I'm sure Epikhodov is a vain man . . . which is very funny, especially if we can get the wig and mustache that we want."

To Pamela: "Don't rush, particularly 'ahhhh what I've been through.' You went at it in a gallop." LeG laughs.

To Miller: "Slow down your crosses. You gallop in a beeline, as if you were terribly conscious that it is where you are supposed to go. The moves must come naturally out of your mood, out of your own consciousness. If any seem artificial to you, and I don't think they do, you must tell me, for it's very important that you feel natural, and we'll either change it or change the mood."

To Pamela: "You mustn't lose the truth you have, and I like it all immensely, everything you're doing is lovely, but you mustn't lose the truth, you must give it more kick. Don't worry if you can't feel it all right now. It's more important that it happen now rather than later, when you are playing it."

To Moffat: "I think it's much more important that the voice has more vitality, especially in the second scene. Their voices are all indolent and soft, but yours must have great directness. Sometimes your voice has it, but mostly it's vitality. He's a man of great vitality, he's driving toward a thing, and he gets it, and we must have more of that in your voice. Does that make sense to you?" "Yes, it does." "Because they are people whose lives are very shallow and spread in a kind of meaningless activity, but he has immense vitality."

Grindl is restless, and Pamela hooks her leash over the toe of her boot. Ellis watches her with a tiny smile at the corners of his mouth, and he leans to Hagen, soundlessly whispering something into her shoulder; a small conference results.

To Woods: "Today, darling Gayev, you dropped 'dear honored bookcase' for the first time. That's the most important line; what comes after can go under."

To Hagen (and the others): "And you are all most not to rush the first reference to the cherry orchard." Hagen interrupts, moaning, "Ohhh, yes, I did that so well last night all by myself, and then I rushed right through . . ." Rabb laughs appreciatively. LeG continues: "Because it's like a new theme in music, and it's terribly important that we get it all. Varychka, you too rushed terribly through that."

LeG continues, exhorting the cast to slow down here, clarifying that transition. Hagen wants a line and a piece of business switched. She demonstrates what she wants with Woods and makes her point. Delighted, she scrambles back to her chair, her knees drawn up together. "Thank you, Richard," she purrs smugly to Woods, and they exchange a wink.

To Conolly: "Darling Dunyasha, the song in II is 'her heart is aglow with love's flame,' not 'aflame with love's glow.'" There is general laughter.

To Curtis: "Epikhodov, hit the *b* on 'buckle,' and make a violent sound, too, on the guitar. The interesting thing about Epikhodov, especially as you begin to get it, is the contrast between his exterior and his interior. He acts ridiculous, and indeed, he is ridiculous, but inside he believes himself to be immensely romantic . . ." She laughs. "I notice Dunyasha got her 'rrrrrolling on the grass' in today. You got your 'rrrrrolling on the grass' in," she announces gaily to Miss Conolly, smiling. A beat. Then softly, "I'm not sure it works, of course." Huge laugh from the cast.

Miss Hagen discusses her long speech. "Now that I'm more in control of it, I thought I'd open it up more, maybe move over here more, or even there." LeG agrees. "Are there pockets, do you remember from the sketch?" LeG affirms definitely, "It's perfectly within the period—any of you women who want pockets, simply tell Miss Potts—the skirts are very full and the pockets are low down." "Goody," exclaims Miss Hagen, rising to demonstrate to the company how she wants to find her telegram in the pocket. "It's there the whole time, and she says 'forgive us our sins'"—big gesture from the "pocket"—"oops, there it is!"

LeG pleads with Ellis to set up the theme of yesterday's discussion of the Pride of Man. "The rest was excellent, but the beginning was frightfully rushed." She demonstrates how Ellis rattles on.

To Moffat: "Lopakhin, I'm awfully sorry, but you won't be able to climb the trees on 'Aurelia, get thee to a nunnery.' I wish you could, but you can't." Moffat:

"Well, while I can, I will." Sydney turns to the stage managers, repeating Donald's words with amazement: "While he can, he will!"

Ellis Rabb asks how aware Trofimov is of the failings of those present, when LeG asks for more passion in the lines. She counters by saying Trofimov is utterly in love with Anya, although nothing is directly said about it. Miss Hagen nods sagely. Trofimov, LeG continues, is showing off for the girl he loves. So he proclaims more attractively these great idealistic speeches. "If you have a beautiful voice, you sing. If you can recite poetry, you recite poetry . . ." she demonstrates his joy at being in Anya's presence. "Don't be self-conscious, Ellis, when you say 'We are above love.' Really mean it. He is in love with her, deeply, tenderly, but I felt a kind of self-consciousness on the line, which you wouldn't feel."

LeG finds a note for Moffat and walks over to him silently to show him her pad. He nods silently, and she touches his cheek, saying "Eh?" as she walks back. Then to Pamela, "Yes, Anya, more voice, please, without losing what you have here," circling her face. "But more voice." Another secret note for Moffat, and she takes the trouble to walk over to him and let him read it rather than have the company see it. She cautions Ellis not to get poetic in his scene with Lopakhin in Act IV, and recites several lines swiftly, naturally, and beautifully. Grindl, restless again, pops up on her hind legs to peer into Nancy Walker's face, and she acknowledges the friendly, almost intimate gesture with one of her own.

LeG corrects Nancy not to say "city," but "town." "'City' is very American." "The luggage is all much heavier than you make it seem. They've got quite a lot to take with them. Aside from the reading, and the read-backs, we've only had 10 rehearsals." "Really?" says Woods. "Yes, and we have a nice amount of time left to catch it and firm it. In spite of the fact, great acting always looks as if it is easy. People always say, 'Oh, I could get up there and do that,' and the better the performance, the more that's true, but although it must seem effortless, the architecture and shape must be specific. Chekhov was such a great artist that he can conceal his craft. You are all true and sincere actors, thank God, because that's what Chekhov needs, and if you can keep the structure and fill the truth, you will have something memorable."

Act I is repeated, and the rehearsal is over.

February 9 (Friday)

Trish Conolly has bought a new piano, and there is considerable excitement from her about it. Ellis Rabb is late, called to the doctor's, and the company stands around talking and laughing and drinking coffee. Finally, since the extras are present—Harmon, O'Malley, Durrell, Whittle, Fudge, Hackett, and Bly—the action is begun with Rabb's part read in. It is repeated twice. Miss Hagen enters late, and her line is "What can be keeping Leonid so long?" She says, "What can be keeping me so long?" LeG, in the house, answers, "You mean, what can be keeping Ellis so long?" In the middle of the repeat, he appears with an inflamed eyelid. "Mascara poisoning," someone proffers.

The dancing begins, with Ellis falling easily into place, and Nancy Walker is doing her tricks with Pishchik's money, with ropes, and the rug trick. Ellis Rabb, laughing at her, ad-libs "That's wonderful" as she does the rope trick. "I know," she coos back, crossing for the rugs.

LeG stops for an intense conversation with Rabb and Hagen about primarily his physical discomforts in the role. Nancy Potts, in the auditorium, arrives to check on progress. "We're approaching this show from an entirely different point than ever before. For one thing, no one regards his part as a small one, and then, too, I feel that Le Gallienne is an actor's director, you know? So we're all taking much more time with everything, discussing where they got the shoes and where they might have bought the jewelry."

The act is repeated from the top with all concerned. Miss Hagen, in her scene with Ellis, is to drop a telegram from her handkerchief. It fails to fall, and she snaps it harshly, burlesquing the move, and she and Ellis erupt in their argument. Miss Hagen moves center, gesturing to him, moving in abruptly to fling a word or a gesture. LeG stops her. "Utka, I still feel you shouldn't be so far away from him," sensing that the space is forcing her into broader moves. She answers by explaining that she is having problems with the shape of the scene. One thought is not yet leading smoothly into the next, so she starts and stops, "like hiccoughs." She and Ellis suddenly have extraordinary difficulties remembering lines. Ellis sinks disgustedly back on the chaise, cupping the sides of his sunglasses with his hands, like an anxious owl. "It's only taken me four weeks to get that line straight," he says. "I'm terribly sorry." He picks up the cue; then Miss Hagen catches the disease from him, moving and speaking in short jerks. Suddenly, in mid-line, she turns front, saying, "What am I doing?" She tries new blocking and a new turn, and then goes ahead.

These rehearsals are mostly devoid of the gentle, real discoveries of the past weeks. Now the work is slow, pedestrian, heavily sketched. The cued laughter offstage by the ensemble is forced, strident, and the performances, too, are heavy-handed, as if only by hitting hard can the actor hear himself and sustain his concentration. Moffat enters as Lopakhin, and Betty Miller actually hits him on the head with the stick that up until now she's only pretended to swing. Her moment of panic at the realization is completely real, and though she attempts to stop, Moffat grabs her by the shoulders, kissing her, saying "That's *per*-fect! Go on!" and they do. When they stop again, he goes to her saying, "That's perfect, what you did, and believe me, it doesn't hurt at all!" Sydney Walker gives her a smart rap on the head to prove it. "Ow!" is her answer; the business is repeated, and Betty, now aware of what she has to do, repeatedly misses Donald, sometimes taking two or three little hits with the stick, as if she has just hooked a marlin.

Backing up, LeG gets Curtis and Miller in a small huddle and exhorts them to speak their argument simultaneously, and they do with the right effect. LeG patiently works out the difficult beats the crowd must play to Lopakhin.

February 12: Act IV

Ellis Rabb is late again, detained by excessive consultation and concern over the budget, pressures for the current season and the season to come. When he does arrive, dressed like an elegant country squire in tan slacks, high brown boots, and a full printed scarf knotted about the neck, he climbs slowly to the stage followed by his enormous black Royal Standard poodle, Sam. "I'm terribly sorry," he intones to the up-right corner of the stage, where most of the company are gathered. "That's all right," Miss Hagen burlesques, "we're getting used to it!"

The act begins, and LeG sits before the apron of the stage, just into the auditorium, wrapped in her purple mohair shawl and cradling the Yorkshire, which peeps out comically between her thumb and fingers. Rabb is sleek, competent, correct in his scene with Lopakhin. LeG stops them and sits with Rabb on a steamer trunk, both of them facing front, like two weary people waiting for a train. LeG rubs her hands over her face as she quietly discusses the scene with Ellis. He sits, his long legs crossed, pinching the corners of his mouth together with his fingers, lost in thought. LeG exhorts him to probe deeper, to spread the scene out by breaking into more specific beats. He asks for different blocking, which will let his confrontation with Moffat look less contrived, and she concurs. The changes are incorporated and the scene is rerun, and this time Rabb gets more variety and strength into the scene. At its conclusion, they discuss the differences, and Ellis asserts that he understands and would like to run it again. The third time through he breaks into excitement as he refuses the money Lopakhin would offer him, and the company sitting around the stage lift their heads from their scripts and turn in the direction of the action, as if sniffing for a new presence.

The day is slow, deliberate, at times bloodless. In the dully lit damp of the darkened house, the two or three spectators huddle in their coats, seemingly separated by their thoughts from the stage. Miss Hagen, wearing the same long strand of variegated colored beads as she wore to the first reading, stops to ask LeG how she can communicate her belief that Firs has been taken care of without any lines. LeG strolls slowly onstage, staring down at her feet in silence as she considers, and discusses as a timing device the putting on of Lyubov's coat, which might emphasize the point.

In the house, Sydney Walker, now through with his scene in this act, speculates on the changes in Trofimov's character as he has been reading correlated material. "Originally Trofimov had a lot of political references in his lines about the conditions of the people at the time, but they were censored, you know. Yes, and all those references to his being expelled from the university, that was because of his political feelings. But when the politics were taken out, it made the part something of a mystery. You know, Act II originally started with Anya and Trofimov? Yes, she had been to the aunt in Yaroslavl, making the family pitch, and there were brief references to that, then they moved off. Charlotta's story of her life which now begins the act was given to Firs. Isn't that interesting?"

The rehearsal plods on with starts and stops. Midway through the umpteenth repeat of his scene, Ellis suddenly hugs Moffat and announces to the room, "I've discovered the key to this scene!—Louder and faster!" At 2:30, IV is concluded. LeG comes onstage and kisses Clayton, announces a break will be taken, and the act will be run again. Miss Hagen, who has tried her wig, removes it. "I have no opinions on clothes or wigs, because you . . . don't . . . know. You know how it feels, and that's all!"

At the end of the day, LeG sets up the basic schedule for the following week.

February 16

At the Riviera tempers are short, and the mood is foul. LeG and the stage management arrive to find the tape recorder has been stolen, and with it the only existing show tapes from the Arena Stage production, on loan to APA for reference. The company straggle in, fidgety, or ill, or both, and by 10 past Ellis has still not arrived. Nancy Walker, head in her hands, suspects she has the flu, and the inertia she projects is reflected by the remainder of the company. Woods, scheduled for his day off, is absent, and consequently only Act III will be worked.

When Ellis arrives, it is without fuss or fanfare. "Hello, Ellis," says Le Gallienne cooly. "Hello, love," he counters pleasantly, and she puts her arms around him, indicating a little stroll and talk are in order, but Ellis doesn't feel like walking far, and he sits promptly in the corner of the stage. She talks low to him, indicating that she intends to concentrate on his scenes today. Leaving him, she announces to the house, "Let's do the third act, ladies and gentlemen."

Sydney Walker leads the dance with a feigned alacrity which no one feels. LeG stops after the dance and exhorts Alan Fudge, one of the dinner guests, to clap strong and slow to accompany the dance. She indicates with four strong claps, and he echoes with four of his own. Nancy Walker leans heavily on a post representing one of the arches, and LeG asks to begin again. By this time the blood is flowing, and the ad-libbed enthusiasm is more sincere than before. Nancy Walker gets two chances to execute her parlor tricks, which she is beginning to perform with confidence, and the difficult scene between Lyubov and Trofimov begins. LeG stops often, changing a move here, questioning a value there. She concentrates on Ellis, who begins working with more concentration and reality than he has before, being more vulnerable and less facile. At one point LeG, after reworking a moment, goes to Ellis, embracing him and ruffling his hair. "How are you, darling, do you feel all right?" "Yes," he answers a bit perfunctorily, "fine." She doesn't believe him, but he reassures her, then makes a wry little face at Miss Hagen as she walks away, like a schoolboy caught chewing gum.

Hagen, whose difficulty with this scene tends to equal Rabb's, although she has trouble with the lines, reacts not unlike a caged cat in her frustration, pacing back and forth, with furious energy, gnawing on a knuckle, or stamping and giving a little gallop when she can't remember the line sequence, belaboring her short hair with her hands. For the most part, the day seems maddeningly slow and the work static. Rather than studying, the cast stand or sit around, talking amiably like people at a reception, smiling, relaxed, smoking, drinking coffee, and eating bits of this or that—polite and seemingly uninvolved. "I don't feel like being Dunyasha today," snaps Miss Conolly to no one in particular. "I feel like being someone else. I'm sick of her."

"Let's do Act III again," says LeG. She has been showing Betty Miller how to handle the keys at her waist. "When one wears keys, one is apt to keep a hand on them, like those men with daggers in Shakespeare." "May we have places for Act III again, ladies and gentlemen," George Darveris, the production stage manager, announces from somewhere in the house. Clayton is still eating his lunch at three. His wife packs a lunch for him, and he spreads it out through the afternoon, carefully peeling a banana, sorting through carrot and celery strips, or peering with deliberate interest into a thermos bottle of soup, like a little boy who has always been very good about eating his hot lunches.

Midway through the next run-through of III, Jacques d'Amboise arrives with a young woman and sits watching in the house. LeG, feeling perhaps a draft from the back of the hall, pulls her purple shawl over her head and sits just before the apron of the stage, peering like an alert and involved version of her own Yorkshire terrier.

February 19
Onstage—picture call.

February 20
At the Riverside Plaza: a string of mirrored ballrooms, low ornate ceilings, pale blue-backed chairs sitting sentinel around—soft turquoise walls, piano, and metal serving tables. Pickles, Easton, and Latham to observe. Act I twice, II and III once, and IV twice. Ellis has galoshes for the first time. Notes from this session are mine: obviously, I took the rehearsal.

February 23
Rehearsal begins with an announcement by LeG that Ellis is indisposed. It is not clear whether he is ill or simply doesn't want to play the part. If the latter is true, LeG wants Easton to play, but with no contact with Ellis, no one knows what to expect. Very little time is left, and technical problems promise to eat up most of that anyway. The climate is most peculiar. At this very crucial stage in rehearsal, confidence is utterly shaken. What's gone wrong? Will Ellis play, and if not, why not?

Act I is begun, and as Keene Curtis drops the flowers for Dunyasha, offstage, Miss Hagen and Woods laugh loyally, and yet on his exit, Keene misses the stool he is to trip over, and shrugs with resigned defeat before trying again. On the general entrance, it is Moffat who stirs excitement and some sense of reality into the company. The company appear to work harder now because of their concern. Nancy Walker exits with her handbag, then sits immediately in a chair, worrying over what she has just said. When the company are good—Hagen, Moffat, Walker—they are very good indeed!

I, II, and III are done, and the key role of Trofimov is passed between the alternate (Kermit Brown) and the assistant director. By the end of III, Richard Easton has arrived. Ellis is ill, and after a hurried and somewhat arbitrary conference with LeG, she announces that Easton will take on the role. There is a flurry of applause, and Hagen runs up to kiss him, her old confrere from *Virginia Woolf* in London. A break is taken, the company cluster around Easton. "How is Ellis?" "Is he really ill?" "It's a very good part for you, Richard." "Oh yes, splendid. I said I was longing to do it."

II is begun, with Easton carrying his script and looking front for fingers pointing to the next moves. LeG stops him to indicate that the moves can be arbitrary. She then wanders around showing what the moves are. Moffat leans in to Easton, saying, "You needn't stick to any of this." "No!" says Easton conspiratorially, and the men burst into laughter. LeG stops, having missed the point and somewhat astonished, but the men keep laughing. "Richard," calls Hagen, "Miss Le Gallienne is showing you something." But Easton moves away from Moffat, pursuing his own tack with vitality, and LeG moves casually away, not displeased.

This was the end of the reportage. For reasons of both pressure and perhaps chemistry, no more notes were taken in this style after the arrival of Richard Easton to replace Ellis Rabb.

ACKNOWLEDGMENTS

This book has been, as many similar ones must surely have been, ages in the making; and along the way, various people have been key, supportive, and helpful.

I begin with Phyllis Wender, my agent and my only agent for decades: a wise, warm "family" voice of incontestable belief and determination. The gift can never be repaid.

Richard Easton and Trish Conolly in particular have listened, advised, prodded, and cautioned me repeatedly over various drafts of what became the final draft, while I read . . . and read . . . and read . . .

Bob Gold, APA's original managing director, arrived at the last moment, as on a white horse, with photographs no one had ever seen, and without which I couldn't have delivered the final product. And our beloved production stage manager, George Darveris, logged in from afar with crucial clarity about APA-Phoenix production dates and records. Anne Kaufman Schneider kindly gave me permission to quote from her father's *You Can't Take It with You*.

Over at Farrar, Straus and Giroux, Jonathan Galassi reached out with warmth and enthusiasm; the unflappable Mitzi Angel hovered, always quietly and benignly, over my efforts; and Chantal Clarke did most of the heavy lifting and prodding, and supplied badly needed advice.

And speaking of lifting, Tim Kava, my assistant and protector of my "household gods," my Norwich terriers Trudge and Winston, was invaluable in traveling between Central Park West and the publisher.

And from afar, dear, dear friends have happily urged me on: Tom

Stoppard read several clumsy early attempts of mine to find the tone, and insisted I "keep writing." Stephen Sondheim was gracious enough to send me his own brilliant analyses of the field of lyricists that so distinguishes his own two great volumes, *Finishing the Hat* and *Look! I Made a Hat*, displaying to me the clarity of his own voice, which helped me to define mine. André Bishop, a longtime loyal friend, was an early enthusiast whose genuine excitement impelled me on. Amy Bloom, a truly gifted writer (as well as my "natal twin"), cheerled as well, and counseled me as to just how remarkable and even atypical this entire effort was. Bob Crowley and his lovely niece, Katy, demonstrated an interest they couldn't possibly have faked, and over in Ireland, too!

For any omissions or ellipses, and any possible offense I may have given while tearing through these decades and chasing these memories, I apologize. Those mentioned above have done everything possible to keep me on the straight and narrow. The remaining sins are mine and mine alone.

INDEX

A NOTE ABOUT THE AUTHOR

Jack O'Brien was born in 1939 and is an American director, producer, writer, and lyricist who served as the artistic director of the Old Globe Theatre in San Diego from 1982 to 2007. He has won three Tony Awards and been nominated for seven more, and he has won five Drama Desk Awards. He lives in New York City.